TAXATION IN CANADA

J. HARVEY PERRY

TAXATION IN CANADA

SPONSORED BY THE
CANADIAN TAX FOUNDATION

UNIVERSITY OF TORONTO PRESS

Copyright, Canada, 1951
by University of Toronto Press
Printed in Canada

First printed, 1951
Second edition, revised, 1953
Third edition, revised, 1961

Reprinted in 2018
ISBN 978-1-4875-8152-7 (paper)

TO MY WIFE

FOREWORD

THE CANADIAN TAX FOUNDATION asked Mr. Perry to write this book because a systematic account of the Canadian tax structure was needed and he possessed exceptional qualifications for the task. He is an officer of the Department of Finance in the Canadian government, and it was therefore understood that he would write in a personal capacity, treating the subject in his own way. The Foundation is indebted both to Mr. Perry for undertaking this work in such spare time as his duties during the past two years have allowed, and to his superior officers for the permission that enabled him to do so.

This book is an original study which is designed to meet three distinct needs. It furnishes the grounds of informed public opinion by making accessible to the layman necessary factual information concerning the sinews of central, provincial, and local government under Canada's federal constitution. It sets out a frame of reference for business men and tax practitioners in Canada and abroad. And it provides students of public finance with a comprehensive view of Canadian methods.

This review of the tax system describes it on a cross-section as it operates today. The Foundation originally suggested to the author that this treatment of the subject should be combined with an historical survey of its development, the present scheme of tax arrangements being the result of past experience and necessity. After the author had assembled the material for such a survey its intrinsic interest and value, as well as convenience of separate publication, dictated the decision that he should do full justice to both aspects of the subject by writing the history of Canadian taxation in a second book, which will follow.

Taxation in Canada appears as the first of a projected series of authoritative tax studies of comparable size which will be published under the Foundation's sponsorship. It is in all respects appropriate that the first of the series should be the work of an experienced civil servant whose knowledge reflects his service to the Parliament and people of Canada.

MONTEATH DOUGLAS
Executive Director
Canadian Tax Foundation

Toronto
July 19, 1951

PREFACE

IT WAS WITH some misgivings that the author accepted the assignment of writing this book for the Canadian Tax Foundation. The prospect of compressing a phenomenon as volatile as the whole of the Canadian tax structure between the covers of a single volume for general circulation gave promise of several obstacles. Not the least of these was that it had never been done before. Another was that the ideal person for the job would have been one trained in both law and accountancy. The present writer, while having suffered long exposure to exponents of both these professions, is himself a member of neither. By training he is an economist. As if that were not sufficient handicap he is a civil servant as well. Further, it was obvious from the outset that during the preparation of the manuscript some revisions would be required to take account of new legislation. But it was certainly not contemplated that between the commencement of the work in 1949 and its conclusion in 1951 the whole face of the federal tax structure would be altered by events in Korea. Korea, and the defence programme in general, has probably had more effect on taxes than on any other aspect of national life up to June, 1951. None of this, of course, was foreseen in 1949.

Despite these difficulties the job is now done. Throughout the author has been guided only by one purpose: to give in simple and understandable terms an up-to-date description of each of the principal federal, provincial, and municipal taxes. To meet this objective has required a continual process of sifting and selection. The transient has not been omitted, but it has been subordinated to the enduring and permanent. To turn out an understandable text has also required a constant resistance to the jargon of the tax expert and the exact but dull language of the statutes. Some circumspection has of course been dictated by the author's position as a servant of the Crown, and it need hardly be added that views expressed or explanations given in this work are those of the author only and have no official sanction.

A project of this magnitude of course bears the imprint of many hands. While original writing in taxation in Canada has been conspicuously limited, the author has drawn on all the material available in academic and general periodicals and on several unpublished theses prepared for doctorate degrees. The periodical tax services have provided a ready source of current and up-to-date information, of which the author makes due recognition. Assistance was given by scores of officials of the federal, provincial, and municipal services, all of whom with the greatest kindness and co-operation have answered correspondence, read sections of the manuscript, and in many other ways shown their unstinting goodwill. To name even a long list of these would mean drawing distinctions where the author would most wish to avoid them, and he trusts that his appreciation will not be regarded as any less sincere because it is extended to all his friends both in Ottawa and throughout the country who have helped him. If the author mentions his particular gratitude to Mr. Abbott and Dr. Clark, the Minister and Deputy Minister respectively of the federal Department of Finance, without whose permission he could not have undertaken the work at all, he is sure that his other friends will not regard it as detracting from the sincerity of his appreciation for their assistance.

Finally, there are those indispensable persons without whom no book would ever be published. I refer to Miss Eleanor Harman and Miss Francess Halpenny, of the University of Toronto Press, who saw the book through the editing and printing stages, to Miss Mabel James, of the Department of Finance Library, who prepared the index and supplied much of the bibliography, and lastly to my own secretary, Mrs. E. Farrell, who, in addition to her other heavy daily work, found time and patience to type not only the original manuscript but the several subsequent revisions of it. To all these the author wishes to express his personal gratitude.

One last word. This writing was done by the author over

PREFACE xi

the last two years largely in his spare time. This has meant that for many evenings and weekends his wife and three children have not only been without his company but to a considerable extent have found their freedom of movement restricted by the fact that there was a writer in the house. One's family is probably expected to live through such episodes unquestioningly, but it was a strain, nonetheless, and the author would be an ungrateful husband and father if he did not express his appreciation for their sympathy and understanding.

J. H. P.

PREFACE TO SECOND EDITION

It is a revealing sign of the times that the first edition of *Taxation in Canada* was sold out a little more than a year after publication and that large sections of it were outdated only two years after its appearance.

This second edition has been revised throughout, and subject always to the unpredictable vagaries of government, should present an up-to-date picture of Canadian taxation as of the end of 1953.

The author was encouraged to find that his departure from government service to the position of Director of Research at the Canadian Tax Foundation made no less spontaneous the ready assistance given by several former colleagues at all levels of government in making this revision. To all these persons, who by virtue of their official position must remain anonymous, the author expresses his deepest appreciation. To his fellow workers at the Foundation who have assisted in many ways—in particular Mr. Roger Carswell, Research Assistant, Mrs. Gwyneth McGregor, Editorial Assistant, Miss Audrey Dean, Librarian, and Miss Mary Mackey, his secretary, and to the editorial staff of the University of Toronto Press, the author expresses his warmest thanks.

A word of appreciation should also be said for the many readers of the first edition who made both useful and encouraging comments on it.

J. H. P.

PREFACE TO THIRD EDITION

Revision of a complete survey of the Canadian tax system after eight years is like bringing out a new edition of an encyclopaedia. Almost everything seems to have changed in greater or lesser degree over a period that long. As a result there are few pages of this third edition of *Taxation in Canada* that have not been altered in some way, and in the case of several whole chapters complete rewriting has been necessary.

In this very considerable undertaking the assistance of several of my former colleagues in government service and the Canadian Tax Foundation was indispensable. The former, anonymous by calling, gave help with data and information not otherwise readily available. The latter read and in some cases revised outdated material, and helped in other ways. I would mention particularly David McGurran, Eric Finnis, Gerald Hoy, Mary Gurney, and Marion Bryden. The Press staff also assisted in their usual obliging and efficient manner. Thanks are also due to my wife and to Mrs. Frank Hessin, my secretary at the Bankers' Association, for help in the final job of cleaning up odds and ends.

As nearly as is humanly possible the text is going to the printer with everything brought up to date to September 1, 1961. Unfortunately there are always some big impending developments in taxation which make it impossible ever to tie up all the ends neatly, and the present time is no exception. The future setting of federal-provincial tax arrangements seemed clear enough by mid-1961 after several conferences and much correspondence, but few of the provinces had yet taken steps to fit themselves into the picture. Undoubtedly this phase will all be cleared up within a few months of the appearance of this book—only to be replaced, however, by some other emerging issue.

This third edition of *Taxation in Canada* represents a landmark of sorts for the author. As some readers will know he recently has left tax work and is now immersed in another career. Most of the revising was done while he was Director of the Canadian Tax Foundation and still in full command, as it were, of his tax faculties. This is his last major contribution to a vital area of study, therefore, and if even a few readers find some permanent value in it he will be well pleased.

J. H. P.

August, 1961

ACKNOWLEDGMENTS

GRATEFUL acknowledgment is made to the following publishers and journals for permission to quote from copyright material: The University of Chicago Press, *Personal Income Taxation* (1938), by H. C. Simons; The Ronald Press Company, *Taxable Income* (1936), by Roswell Magill; *National Tax Journal* (March, 1950), "Evolution of the Special Legal Status of Capital Gains under the Income Tax," by L. H. Seltzer; *Land Economics* (February, 1948), "The Property Tax in Canada and the United States," by Harold M. Groves; Canada and Newfoundland Education Association, *Property Taxation and School Finance in Canada* (1945), by M. A. Cameron; O. Lobley, "Municipal Taxation," a lecture delivered at McGill University in March, 1948.

CONTENTS

1	Influences in the Evolution of the Canadian Tax Structure	3
2	Dominion Income Tax: Resident Individuals	37
3	Dominion Income Tax: Resident Corporations	62
4	Dominion Income Tax: Non-Residents and Foreign Income of Residents	88
5	Dominion Death Duties and Gift Tax	102
6	Dominion Commodity Taxes: The Customs Tariff, the General Sales Tax	116
7	Dominion Commodity Taxes: Excise Taxes, Excise Duties, and Miscellaneous Taxes	137
8	Constitutional Limitations on Provincial Taxation	146
9	Provincial Income and Corporation Taxes	164
10	Provincial Succession Duties	183
11	Provincial Consumption and Expenditure Taxes	197
12	Provincial Liquor and Motor Vehicle Revenues and Miscellaneous Taxes	211
13	Provincial Revenues from the Public Domain	227
14	Municipal Taxation in Canada	251
15	Enactment of the Tax Laws of the Dominion: The Budgetary System, the Estimates	278
16	Enactment of the Tax Laws of the Dominion: The Budget Speech	290
17	Enactment of the Provincial and Municipal Tax Laws	301
18	Dominion Tax Administration: Direct Taxes	312
19	Dominion Tax Administration: Indirect Taxes	323
	Appendix	341
	Bibliography	369
	Index	407

TAXATION IN CANADA

Chapter 1

INFLUENCES IN THE EVOLUTION OF THE CANADIAN TAX STRUCTURE

THE MAIN PURPOSE of this volume is to describe in some detail the salient features of the Canadian taxation system of today. This is done in the following chapters with only a minimum of attention to the historical aspects of the subject. The reader who wishes to explore in full the unfolding of the Canadian tax system over the past three centuries may do so by consulting a companion book by the same author (*Taxes, Tariffs, and Subsidies*) and other sources in Canadian literature.

Even in the present book, however, the author has felt that he would not be excused lightly if he were to ask the reader to plunge unceremoniously into the chill waters of the personal income tax. By way of introduction it is proposed, therefore, in the present chapter to review in a general way some of the influences that have helped to make the Canadian tax structure what it is today, and to point out also some of the landmarks in its history.

It is assumed at the outset that every reader will recognize that the primary purpose of any system of taxation is to provide revenues for the operation of government. It is also assumed, perhaps with less warrant, that the reader understands that the amount of revenue required, and the manner of its getting, are the expression of a whole complex of legal, economic, social, and historical forces, resolved for the moment in a particular concrete programme. It is to some of these larger forces that consideration will be given in the pages immediately following.

It is difficult to judge in such matters, but of all the influences that have affected the development of taxation in Canada the federal form of our governmental structure has probably been the strongest. Such a system has within itself a basic contradiction. It is the antithesis of the monolithic state. Any forced and unnatural uniformity or centralization is abhorrent to it, and its great virtue is its preservation of local loyalties and diversities. On the other hand it has utterly failed in its purpose if a large degree of national consciousness and concerted action is not also achieved. To establish a balance between these two conflicting objectives, particularly in financial matters, requires the most delicate of compromises, and to maintain it calls for the highest degree of statesmanship.

Reduced to practical terms, the essence of the federal form of state is that powers and responsibilities are shared among levels of government. Since financial resources are the real meat and sinews of the legal skeleton of such powers the allocation of taxing powers is of vital concern. From an historical viewpoint the manner in which such financial resources are allotted in the basic constitution also gives fairly good testimony of the bias of authority contemplated by the founders in the new structure of government.

In this respect the Canadian financial arrangements of 1867 are of particular interest. The new national government was given an untrammelled power to levy taxation in any form, while the provinces were to receive subsidies from the Dominion and were to be restricted to direct taxation. The granting of the broadest financial powers to the Dominion suggests that the Fathers of Confederation expected that it would be the major level of government. At the same time the limitation of the provinces to direct taxation, so unpopular in 1867 that the right was considered more of an embarrassment than a privilege, suggests that a relatively minor role was anticipated for the provinces.

Many of the subsequent problems of the Canadian federation arose from the fact that only to a limited extent did the actual development of government and of taxation follow the expectations of 1867. The provinces and municipalities for considerable periods of our history have been responsible for outlays as large as the Dominion's, and during the late twenties their requirements taken together were considerably in excess of those of the Dominion. At the same time their legal powers under the British North America Act have been interpreted to cover several large (and expensive) fields of activity, fields with which the Dominion is best equipped financially to deal.

The effect of this turn of events on the development of taxation in Canada was extremely important. The original financial arrangements of Confederation, of which the subsidies from the Dominion to the provinces were the central arch, worked reasonably well for only about three decades, and then only with a considerable amount of patching and mending. It was apparent by the opening of the twentieth century that the role of the provinces was to be much larger than originally planned, a result for which the motor car, electricity, better educational standards, increasing urbanization, and a broader concept of social responsibility were largely responsible. The provinces therefore found themselves increasingly hard pressed, and they were forced to begin the serious exploitation of their sole power of direct taxation. Prior to World War I they had levied succession duties, corporation taxes, and in some cases income taxes. This development was recognized and facilitated by the Dominion, which consistently refrained from imposing any but indirect taxes until the middle of World War I. During the twenties the provinces found the key, through Privy Council interpretations of the concept of "direct taxation," to the imposition of gasoline taxes, and in the thirties all the stops were fully out on every kind of direct taxation. The same legal interpretations that made possible the levying of gasoline taxes also pointed the way to the retail sales tax, which is becoming the favourite tax of the current era.

Paradoxically this intensive development of direct taxation by the provinces appears only to have given support to a growing belief that an engine as powerful as the income tax should be reserved for national use. The economic consequences of the uncoordinated and unrestricted use of a tax of this importance are now fully appreciated, and there has been a growing realization also that the maximum potentialities for effective administration lie in the national sphere. In short, the scope of provincial tax powers as originally defined now appears in many respects to fit the national boundaries more appropriately. This statement is not advanced as an argument for or against "centralization." It is simply stated as a truth borne out by practical experience with which no unbiased tax authority could disagree.

Underlying this paradox is a second basic fact of the Canadian federation, viz., that the value of the power to impose direct taxes varies considerably between one province and another in Canada. This, of course, is only another way of saying that all provinces in Canada are not of equal wealth. The implication of this fundamental truth for the Canadian Confederation was recognized in the leniency towards some provinces in the original subsidy plan of 1867 and in the hectic history of inter-governmental payments. It has been recognized frequently in the appointment of special commissions and inquiries to consider grants to one section of the country or another, culminating in the Rowell-Sirois Commission, to which was delegated the task of examining the whole problem anew. In connection with taxation the main consequence of this fact in recent years has been that rather than exploit their powers of direct taxation themselves, some provinces have been willing to rent their income taxes and succession duties to the Dominion for temporary periods in return for compensation.

In this context it is apparent that the tax agreements between the Dominion and the provinces have played a unique and significant role. Their effect has been to assure that over wide areas of Canada there is uniform weight and uniform administration of income taxes and succession duties. This has brought an end, at least for the duration of the agreements, to much of the vexing and destructive competitive taxation that dominated the depressed thirties. Furthermore, the rental payments to some of the less wealthy provinces for these taxes have been fixed at a level higher than the revenues they would have produced in provincial hands. Thereby the historical "must" of Dominion support for these provinces has also been served. These agreements will be described in greater detail later.

This complex of influences arising out of our federal form of government, it need hardly be repeated, has exerted a profound effect on the course of taxation in Canada. Perhaps its most unfortunate effect has been that at crucial periods in our economic history, such as the depression of the thirties, there has been a complete lack of co-ordination of taxation policy at the two main levels of government.

This lack of direction was perhaps inevitable and fortunately is less evident today. In one sense, however, it was out of keeping with our historic tradition, in which taxation as a means to economic ends has been deeply rooted. The close relationship between government financial policy and economic development in Canada goes back to our very beginnings, and was indeed apparent even before Confederation. Galt's tariff increases of 1859 for United Canada were required to a large extent to finance the rapid expansion of railway and canal facilities of the pre-Confederation period. Although carried on by private capitalists these ventures, representing the earliest major form of capital investment in Canada, were dependent to a large extent on government support. That the customs duties levied for this purpose provided some "incidental protection" for the embryonic Canadian manufacturing industry was accepted with equanimity by Galt and his colleagues. The close relationship in this programme between government financial policy and internal economic development, both directly through assistance to heavy capital expenditures and indirectly through the "incidental protection" given industry, is in a pattern that became in time the basic tenet of federal financial policy for half a century.

This policy appeared to be going into the discard as Confederation approached and the central province of United Canada (Upper and Lower Canada) lowered its tariff to make the proposed union more palatable to the Maritimes. But during the seventies new circumstances brought it to the fore with renewed vitality. The abrogation of the Reciprocity Treaty by the United States in 1866, after a decade of experience that had been very satisfactory for Canada, was one of the forces promoting the Canadian union in 1867. The renewal of the Treaty after

1867 at the same time became one of the major objectives of the new Government. Repeated petitions to Washington failed to meet success, and when a serious and world-wide depression descended following 1873 the Dominion turned increasingly to the possibilities of at least assuring the home market to Canadian manufacturers and producers if they were not to have access to the American market. The Liberal Government in power from 1873 to 1878 resisted the pressure, but in the latter year a Conservative Government was elected to power on a frankly high-tariff policy.

The year 1879 marks a significant milestone in our economic history. The new Government pledged itself to a "National Policy" that would be directed toward forcing internal industrial development by any means available to government at that time. As a first instalment a tariff revision was made in 1879 that increased rates all along the line, but was significant principally for the protection granted to the fledgling iron and textile industries. In the following years the level of protective rates was raised, and subsidies for domestic manufactures, particularly for the iron and steel industry, were granted where protection alone was not sufficient.

Meantime during the seventies and eighties vast sums of money had been devoted by the young government to the construction of the Intercolonial Railway, linking the Maritimes with central Canada, and the Canadian Pacific Railway, linking central Canada with the West and British Columbia. A large part of the funds for this expansion were borrowed, but the tariff was expected, as the main source of revenue, to provide for the servicing of this debt and the support of normal government functions.

The National Policy probably reached its peak as a political doctrine about the mid-nineties. The Conservatives had been continuously in power since 1878, and were being challenged increasingly by the Liberals, who had adopted a low-tariff platform. In defending the tariff against Liberal attacks in his 1894 Budget Speech the Minister of Finance, Hon. George E. Foster, made the following remarkable statement. When one recalls that the tariff was the major source of revenue of the day, indeed almost the only source, the ideological implications of these words are all the more significant:

I wish, at this early stage of my remarks upon this subject, to say that, so far as the revenue aspect is concerned, it is of infinitely less importance than the effect of the principle in the details of the tariff upon the trade and development of the country.... The principle of the tariff has nothing to do in this year 1893-94 with the amount of money which is required for the country's expenditure, and the fact that thirty-eight millions of dollars are raised under it is neither an argument for its support nor an argument for its condemnation ... the principal aspect in which the tariff is to be viewed is as to its effect upon the trade and development of the country.

It will be conceded that not even under the strong influence of Keynesian economics in recent years has any Minister of Finance paid such tribute to the economic aspects of taxation. Nor is one likely to do so in the future.

While 1894 must be regarded therefore as marking the apotheosis of this relationship between taxation and economics there are ample signs of its continued influence in later years. The British Preferential schedule, introduced in 1896 by the Liberals, was initially the product of political and sentimental motives but became later an effective instrument of commercial policy. Although the financial history of World War I reveals an almost complete absence of an appreciation of the role of fiscal policy in wartime, memories of the Canadian taxation programme in World War II and in post-war years are still sufficiently fresh that many of the fiscal measures having economic implications readily come to mind. Among the more obvious one would list the "Baby Budget" programme of December 1940, when a host of taxes were introduced on goods having a high American content to save hard currency, and the similar programme for the same purpose introduced in November 1947; the compulsory savings feature of the income tax during the war as part of the anti-inflationary programme and the high taxes on many commodities in short supply to conserve materials; the special depreciation rates given for capital investment during the war to encourage sales in the dollar area and after the war to encourage capital investment in general; and more generally the attempt made to adhere as far as possible to an anti-cyclical budgetary policy in the post-war period and an anti-inflationary policy during the conflict itself.

If any further evidence were needed that in Canada taxes have not been employed solely for financing the operation of government one could also cite the use of the taxing power in connection with "social security." The essential feature of such social security as now exists in Canada is the transference of income from one group in the community to another. Family allowances and the new contributory old age pensions are excellent examples. For these two programmes approximately $1,130 million of taxes must be levied annually. Such transfer payments are part of the change that has been gradually developing a new social fabric over half a century, of which the full pattern has probably not yet appeared. Whatever the final form of the "welfare" state it is certain that taxation will play in it as significant a role as it did in the "industrial" state launched with the National Policy of 1879.

A fourth influence in forming our taxes in the past was almost an inevitable one. This was the American influence. With few exceptions almost all our new ventures in taxation, particularly at the provincial and municipal levels, were based on American precedents. The taxation of personal property, prevalent in most municipalities at Confederation, was definitely American in origin, since it had been abandoned in England centuries before. The first successful provincial experiment with corporation taxes, the Quebec legislation of 1884, was based directly on American precedent, and the first provincial succession duties, the Ontario legislation of 1892, followed almost to the word the New York State act. The Dominion Income War Tax Act of 1917, the first national income tax, bore an unmistakable resemblance to similar American legislation, and the first Canadian province to impose a gasoline tax, Alberta, did so in 1922 only after nineteen American states had set an example in the previous three years. More recently, of course, the retail sales taxes imposed by provincial governments have followed similarly an American precedent. Finally, the Canadian system of taxing real property on capital value follows the American system rather than the British, which employs rental value as the tax base.

In the light of this strong American influence the instances in which Canada has not followed the example of the United States are the more notable. Perhaps the most conspicuous is the adherence to the "English" concept of income, which apart from anything else has meant that capital gains are not taxed. Another, less conspicuous difference is that the taxation of personal property has now been virtually abandoned in Canada, whereas it is still in wide vogue in American states and municipalities. It might also be mentioned that the provinces in Canada have never relied to the same extent as the American states on property taxes, and have now almost entirely given over this field to municipalities. Finally, Canada has definitely departed from the American federal tax pattern in imposing a general manufacturers' sales tax. This must be put down to a basic difference in bias between the two countries, which is curious, in view of the extent to which their general tax systems parallel one another. It would appear from the relatively greater emphasis on direct taxation of incomes in the United States and the complete absence of anything comparable to the general 11 per cent Canadian sales tax that the American public is more ready to accept direct taxation (or less ready to accept indirect) than is the Canadian.

Finally, and perhaps predominant over all else in our tax history, there has been the grim shadow of war. Two world conflicts have forced the Dominion for increasingly long intervals to dominate government finances in Canada, and to exploit its taxing powers, which are unlimited, to an extent far beyond any normal expectation. The heritage of debt and pensions left by each war has also forced the retention of taxes far higher than would otherwise be necessary. Happy the day when it can be said with assurance that war and the fear of war will no more be a factor in taxation!

To these five general influences one might add certain others of lesser weight. The vast distances of the country, for example, probably explain in part why the Dominion government has never imposed a land tax (although the Australian Commonwealth government imposed such a tax under almost equal handicaps). The fact that a sizable part of our population is composed of farmers has had its effect, most noticeably perhaps on tariff policy, since farmers are traditionally a low-tariff group. One must also reckon in the account the direct and usually effective influence of official inquiries and Royal Commissions, whose recommendations have often been carried directly into action by the government. Finally there is also the "political" factor, the influence of politics not particularly in the sense of opposing party labels (although the parties have traditional attitudes towards fiscal policy) but in the deeper and more realistic sense of politics as the art of the possible. It is not unknown in the affairs of government that measures which should or might be taken are postponed because in the view of the political heads of government the times are not appropriate. This sense of "fitness" is to the art of government what the gift of "salesmanship" is to the art of business. Occasionally matters of taxation are the subject of an exercise in this political art.

Out of all these forces there is resolved at each phase in a nation's history a tax system that is sometimes good, sometimes bad, and at best a compromise with "ideal" text-book standards. Undoubtedly also because so many forces are at play the shape of the whole tax structure shows a surprising degree of mobility and instability. One would reasonably assume that such a pedestrian matter as allocating sources of revenue between levels of government might be accomplished without too much fuss and disposed of for all time. To expect as much as this, however, is to ignore entirely the influences discussed above. It is to blind oneself to war, to social change, to economic development, to geographical limitations, to regional dislocations, to foreign precedents, to constitutional evolution, to political judgment, and finally to the simple fact that the rational and logical solution is sometimes in public affairs not the best solution. Or if it is, its adoption overnight is by no means certain, nor its permanent retention assured. In taxation, as in many other matters of social policy, the only certainty is the certainty of change.

THE CANADIAN TAX STRUCTURE 13

HISTORICAL REVIEW

A brief review of the actual major changes in the historical development of the Canadian tax system can hardly start as far back as 1650 when the first recorded tax was levied. This was an export tax of 50 per cent on beaver pelts and 10 per cent on moose pelts levied by the King on the citizens of New France. It is doubtful if the Dominion and provincial taxes on furs would in the aggregate amount to 50 per cent today and one might venture the conclusion that the present citizens of the same land are better off in the way of taxation than the original settlers of 300 years before. No such happy solution can honestly be presented to the reader. Since there was a considerable development of taxation prior to Confederation too extensive to review here, the year 1867 will be taken as the starting point.

1867-1914: Developments Prior to World War I

By the end of the year 1867, which saw the union of Ontario, Quebec, Nova Scotia, and New Brunswick as the Dominion of Canada, all the tariffs imposed by the former provinces had been repealed and superseded by a national tariff. At the same time the Dominion also took over the provincial excises on spirits and tobacco.

Since the tariff had been almost the sole source of revenue of the existing provinces, the excises being relatively unimportant, the revolutionary nature of the effects of union on provincial finances is self-evident. The provinces were left with the revenue from the sale of their lands, royalties from the exploitation of their mines and forests, fees from miscellaneous licences, of which those for the manufacture and sale of spirits ranked first, and subsidy payments from the Dominion.

At Confederation municipal development had reached a degree of maturity only in Ontario, and here the municipalities levied real and personal property taxes and income taxes. In the other provinces such municipalities as there were also relied mainly on property and income taxes, although in Quebec there has never been a personal property tax, and only during a few years prior to World War II have there been municipal income taxes.

No reliable statistics are available, but it is doubtful if at the Confederation period the total revenues of all governments in Canada exceeded $25 million, of which about half was collected by the Dominion. This is considerably less than 1 per cent of the total tax bill of Canada in 1960, the population in the meantime having increased from about 2½ millions to about 18 millions.

As indicated earlier, the most prominent feature of the early development of the Dominion tariff, which accounted for two-thirds of federal revenues, was the considerable increase in rates in 1879 on adoption of the National Policy. It is difficult to assess the real significance of this event from the perspective of nearly eight decades, but it involved a general upward revision in rates that served to provide both increased revenues to the government and increased protection to industry. Its immediate influence was somewhat obscured by the renewal, after a three-year interlude between 1880 and 1883, of a depression that had commenced in 1874. But some indication of its effect may be gathered from one of the measurements of over-all tariff rates commonly employed at the time. The average rate of tariff was calculated by expressing the customs revenue as a percentage of the value of goods imported in the same year, and the resulting percentage gave a crude indication of the burden of the duties. This rate had ranged between 10 and 15 per cent in most years before Confederation and in 1867 was about 12 per cent. By 1889, the peak year of all time in tariff history for this rate, it had reached 32 per cent, and for several years held a level close to 30 per cent. Only after the mid-nineties, when some significant tariff reductions were made, did this over-all measurement begin a gradual decline.

The other significant development in the federal tariff prior to World War I was the adoption of the British Preferential Tariff in 1897 by a newly elected Liberal Government. The high-tariff Conservative party had been in power since 1878, and the Liberals had been forced to espouse a low-tariff policy, laying at the door of protection the long depression that lasted until the mid-nineties. So deeply rooted was the protective tariff in the whole economic fabric of the country that its abandonment was virtually impossible, and no government would have seriously contemplated such an action at that time. As a means of meeting its election promises, and also to encourage trade with Britain, which had been suffering in the face of American competition in Canada, the Liberal Government hit on the plan of giving a tariff reduction only on goods from Empire countries. The first preference was a reduction of one-eighth from the ordinary rates, increased in 1898 to one-quarter and in 1900 to one-third. The full implications of this move were hardly realized at the time, and indeed did not bear full fruit until the Ottawa Agreements of 1932 made the principle of Imperial Preference a working doctrine of Empire trade.

While these were the major developments of the pre-war tariff there were also many minor changes of significance for revenue. The Dominion also gradually increased its excise duties on spirits and tobacco. At Confederation the excise duty on a gallon of liquor had been 60 cents, and just before World War I was $1.90 a gallon (the 1960 rate was $13.00 a gallon). During the same period the duty on malt used in beer increased from 1 cent per pound to $1\frac{1}{2}$ cents, and the tax on cigarettes from about 25 cents per thousand to $2.40 per thousand. There were also other miscellaneous taxes, none of them important revenue sources.

Dominion revenues crept upward only gradually from about $14 million in 1868 to about $40 million in 1898. Under the stimulus of a great period of prosperity that swept in with the settlement of the West between 1898 and 1914, revenues increased four times, exceeding $160 million in the latter year. All of the tax revenue came from indirect levies, i.e., the customs and excise duties.

In the provincial and municipal fields there were also landmarks in this period. In 1876 British Columbia levied the first provincial income, personal property, and land taxes, long anticipating most of the other provinces. In 1877 Prince Edward Island also imposed a provincial land tax; it was abandoned in 1882 but re-introduced in 1894. Quebec, having become deeply involved in railway financing, introduced the first valid act imposing corporation taxes (on paid-up capital, place of business, insurance premiums, railway track mileage, etc.) in 1884, after a first attempt had been thrown out by the Privy Council in 1878. The other provinces were rather slow to follow this precedent, and although many had taken the step in the 1890's it was not until 1912 that all the provinces were levying substantially similar taxes. When Ontario levied the first Canadian provincial succession duty in 1892, however, every province followed her example within two or three years. In 1894 Prince Edward Island joined British Columbia in imposing an income tax. These were to be the only two provinces in this field until 1923, when Manitoba levied its first personal income tax.

Prior to 1914 there was a considerable development of mining in Quebec, Ontario, and British Columbia. This was signalled by the enactment of the Mineral Output Tax in British Columbia in 1898 and the Mining Profits Tax in Ontario in 1907. In all but the Prairie Provinces, where the natural resources had been retained by the Dominion, revenues were realized in some form from mining or timber.

In the municipal field there was increasing evidence of dissatisfaction with the personal property tax. As wealth in the developing industrial society more and more took the form of intangibles, such as shares, bonds, bank deposits, etc., a tax on personal wealth (as distinct from real estate) was so often evaded that it fell into disrepute. Since the inventory of merchants could not be as easily concealed the bulk of the revenue came from a tax on such goods. The first major break with the system was made in Winnipeg in 1893, when this tax was repealed and a business tax based on rental value was substituted. In Ontario, after several official inquiries had roundly criticized the tax, it was abandoned as a municipal source of revenue in 1904. It was also replaced by a tax on business, in this case one based on the assessed value of the premises occupied by the business. This trend became fairly common except in the Maritimes, where some vestiges of the personal property tax remain today. In most other municipalities it had been replaced by 1914 by a tax on businesses, for which there were three or four competing bases of calculation, the principal being (*a*) gross revenue of the business; (*b*) the rental value, capital value, or floor space of the premises occupied, or (*c*) a flat rate charge.

Another development in municipal taxation in Canada just prior to World War I that attracted international attention was the so-called single tax movement in the western municipalities. This fascinating phase of local government in the boom years of the Prairie Provinces and British Columbia must regrettably be passed over in a brief review of this sort, although no movement in our whole tax history captured the popular imagination or raised such a pitch of evangelical zeal as has Henry George's doctrine. The whole episode is one of extreme interest, and not without its permanent effects on taxation at the municipal level.

Another significant aspect of local taxation during this period was the continued and fairly successful employment of the personal income tax in Ontario and New Brunswick municipalities. Nova Scotia also permitted the municipalities to levy such a tax, as did some of the western provinces, but these taxes were not prosecuted with much vigour. Nowhere, however, did more than a small fraction of total revenues come from personal income taxes. At this period, as today, the real property tax was the backbone of the municipal tax structure.

By 1914 the total revenue of governments in Canada was about ten times the revenue of 1867, or $275 to $300 million. A remarkable expansion had taken place in municipal revenues, which by 1914 exceeded $100 million, practically all derived from the property tax. The rapid growth of population during the "Wheat Boom" prior to World War I and the increasing urbanization of the population enlarged the scope of municipal activities enormously. Revenues rose with property development. Provincial government revenues, on the other hand, despite the new taxes imposed, were less than $50 million.

1914-1929: War and Boom

The years between 1914 and 1920 were dominated by the problem of financing the war and post-war requirements of the federal government. In the following decade the problem of financing the greatly expanded activities of the provincial and municipal governments took precedence, although the Dominion's burden of interest charges inherited from the war and another period of railway financing necessitated the retention of national taxation at a relatively high level.

One of the aspects of World War I that arouses surprise is that almost the whole cost of the war programme was borrowed. This was partly owing to the reluctance of the federal government, until late in the conflict, to impose any substantial direct taxation. It was also owing in part to the drain of other requirements on the federal treasury, particularly for loans and subsidies to and finally for the taking-over of the two additional transcontinental railway lines which were in construction in 1914 and which could not be abandoned. There were also several other explanations, of which the most significant undoubtedly was that the federal financial authorities of the day felt it fitting that the war, which they regarded as being fought mainly for posterity, should be financed by bonds repayable in the future.

The economic consequences of this approach to war financing can hardly be explored here. Its implications for federal taxation, however, were that the traditional reliance on customs and excises was adhered to as long as possible, and only abandoned with caution. The first tax changes in the special war budget of August 1914 were limited entirely to increases in the tariff on such staples as coffee, sugar, and spirits, and increases in the internal excise duties on alcoholic and tobacco products. In 1915 further substantial tariff increases were made, and the Special War Revenue Act was introduced imposing a long list of new charges, none of great significance for revenue, on such subjects as bank note circulation, fire and casualty insurance premiums, telegrams and cables, railway and steamship tickets, cheques, patent medicine and perfumes, wines, and other similar items.

In 1916 the Business Profits War Tax was imposed, to be effective from January 1, 1915. In general this was a tax of 25 per cent on the profits of an incorporated business to the extent that such profits exceeded 7 per cent of capital employed in the business. Unincorporated businesses were also taxed, but at a lower rate. First imposed until December 31, 1917, this tax was finally extended by annual revisions to the end of 1920. It was also increased in rate, until the final form of the law imposed a graduated tax, of which the highest rate was 60 per cent on profits that exceeded 30 per cent of the capital employed. In all some $200 million was collected under this tax.

The regular budget of 1917 provided only for an increase in the Business Profits War Tax. By midsummer of 1917, however, the government had decided to call up an additional 100,000 men for service overseas, and felt that its position would be indefensible without further conscription of wealth. In July 1917, in a surprise move, the Minister of Finance introduced a measure imposing a tax of 4 per cent on corporate profits (payable if greater than the Business Profits War Tax) and levying a national tax for the first time on personal incomes. In the following year the war profits tax was increased and the corporate rate raised to 6 per cent, the personal income tax was increased, higher excise duties were levied on tobacco products and increased customs duties on tobacco, tea, and coffee, and some further excise taxes (as the levies under the Special War Revenue Act came to be called) were introduced, including for the first time a 10 per cent tax on automobiles.

Unlike the conclusion of World War II, the end of the war in 1918 saw an upward trend in federal taxation. The following year the corporation income tax was raised from 6 per cent to 10 per cent, the personal income tax again went up, and the Business Profits War Tax was extended. Reductions in the tariff offset these changes in direct taxation to some extent, but on the whole the level of Dominion taxes was higher in 1919 than at any time during the war. But still further taxes were levied in the following year, and again in the year after. A long list of luxury and semi-luxury goods were taxed at high rates in 1920 and at the same time the general sales tax, the largest source of indirect tax revenue today, was introduced. In 1921 a sharp increase was made in the liquor tax and the sales tax, although the extensive luxury taxes of the previous year were repealed.

This spate of post-war increases had a marked effect on

federal revenue. From about $312 million in fiscal year 1919 revenues increased by fiscal year 1921 to $436 million, or over 40 per cent.

The over-all magnitude of the tax programme in relation to the war effort in World War I is best indicated by the fact that in the five fiscal years 1915 to 1920, inclusive, tax revenues only about covered the ordinary expenditures of government, amounting to $1,130 million. Non-tax revenues of over $330 million offset slightly more than half of the capital expenditures and investments, and the whole of the war expenditure, exceeding $1,670 million, along with the balance of the capital expenditures and investments, was borrowed. Altogether total borrowings exceeded $1,940 million.

Of the total of $1,120 million collected in taxation, about $936 million, or 85 per cent, came from the customs and excise duties. If the other taxes are counted in, indirect taxation of goods and services accounted for almost 90 per cent of tax revenues. Of the balance of tax revenues, representing direct taxation, almost all came from the Business Profits War Tax. Of total tax revenues during the five years in question less than 1 per cent came from the personal income tax.

Despite the reluctance of the Dominion to impose heavier taxes during the war the federal tax structure emerged as a well-rounded system lacking only an internal commodity tax of broad application. As mentioned above this feature was added in 1920 with the introduction of the general sales tax. Post-war economic collapse and heavy federal financial burdens, of which the increase in interest charges from about $16 million in 1915 to $140 million in 1921 is a token, required the maintenance of this tax structure intact for several years. Indeed, increases appeared even after 1921. The four rates of sales tax (then almost a turn-over tax) were raised in 1922 and 1923. From January 1, 1924, it assumed its present form, with one rate of 6 per cent. Existing excise taxes were increased and several new ones were levied. Some tariff reductions were made in 1923, however, and in the 1924 budget the sales tax, with easier business conditions, was reduced to 5 per cent. In 1925 no significant changes were made but in 1926, effective for 1925, a substantial overhauling and reduction of the personal income tax was made and the corporate rate was reduced to 9 per cent. This was the first break in the post-war income tax, and is in marked contrast to the experience following World War II, when reductions of greater or less extent were made almost annually for several years until the Korean war.

The rest of the twenties is for the Dominion a story of annual reductions in almost all taxes, until in 1930 the sales tax was down to 1 per cent and there were confident predictions in the business world that both it and the personal income tax would be repealed entirely in the near future. The economic collapse of the thirties was to disappoint all such hopes.

These tax reductions by the Dominion in the later twenties were indicative of a change in the relative status of the two main levels of government that had started prior to World War I and had resumed at an accelerated pace almost with the firing of the last gun. One of the remarkable phenomena of this period was the rapid growth of the expenditures of local (provincial and municipal) governments. Whereas their total expenditures had increased only by about $20 million in the first thirty years of Confederation (to 1896) in the next thirty-four years (1896 to 1930) they increased by $433 million. This astounding change took place as the result of a vast expansion in expenditures for roads, bridges, schools, and public welfare measures of an essentially regional and local character that was not anticipated by the Fathers of Confederation. The advent of the automobile and the increasing size and number of the municipalities in Canada contributed, along with other factors, to this revolution.

The earliest signs of this change, as mentioned before, had brought forth the provincial corporation taxes and succession duties prior to World War I. During the war large-scale provincial and municipal capital expenditures slackened off, and the provinces enacted special taxes for contributions to the Allied war effort through their Patriotic Funds or in other ways. Almost all of these taxes were imposed on property. They were levied on the municipal assessment and the municipal authorities were required to collect them for the province. Every provincial government but Quebec imposed some such tax. Most of these were dropped following the war, but in the Prairie Provinces they were retained for some years. The last, that of Saskatchewan, was repealed only in 1952. It was also principally during World War I that the provinces introduced the entertainment taxes.

There were far too many significant changes in provincial revenues during the twenties to detail here. The main new sources that bridged the gap between the new responsibilities of the provinces and their historically narrow revenue base were motor vehicle licences, gasoline taxes, and liquor profits. Motor licences had been introduced in most provinces before the war, but were only beginning to produce a substantial revenue in the twenties. The gasoline tax was borrowed from the American states, Alberta taking the lead in 1922 with a levy of 2 cents per gallon. Within three years all provinces but Saskatchewan (1928) had followed suit. The other major revenue development was the introduction of monopoly sale of liquor by the provincial governments, marking the end of the prohibition era of the late war years and the early twenties. Quebec and British Columbia both took this significant step in 1921, Manitoba followed in 1923, Alberta in 1924, Saskatchewan in 1925, Ontario and New Brunswick in 1927, and Nova Scotia in 1930. (Prince Edward Island only abandoned prohibition for state monopoly sale in 1948.)

Revenues from these three sources were substantial and contributed in great measure to the financing of the provincial capital expansion during the twenties. For fiscal years ended nearest to December 31, 1913, provincial revenues had been $45 million. By the same date in 1921 they were $90 million, or just double, and by 1930 they were $174 million, or nearly double again. Of this latter amount almost $75 million came from the three sources just discussed.

Almost as spectacular was the increase in municipal revenue between these dates. With the real property tax remaining throughout the main tax base, the municipal revenues increased from $110 million in 1913 to $230 million in 1921, or more than double, and to $317 million in 1930. It was symbolic of the changing relationship in the level of governments during the

THE CANADIAN TAX STRUCTURE 23

twenties that while provincial and municipal revenues together were about equal to Dominion revenues in 1913 and 1921, by 1930 municipal revenues alone exceeded those of the Dominion. In 1930 provincial and municipal revenues together exceeded those of the Dominion by over 50 per cent.

1930-1939: *Taxes for a Depression*

With the onslaught of the depression the revenues of all governments declined sharply as prices and incomes fell. Deficits were almost universal as relief expenditures became increasingly burdensome. The accepted fiscal doctrines of the period called for a balanced budget under every circumstance, and this goal all governments started out to achieve. The resulting scramble for revenues was chaotic.

The Dominion led the way in 1931 by increasing the sales tax from 1 per cent to 4 per cent and by restoring many of the less important excise taxes dropped in the late twenties. In the same year Quebec increased its gasoline tax, Ontario introduced a new paid-up capital tax and British Columbia levied a tax on low wages and increased several other taxes. These were only the more notable of provincial changes.

In 1932 the Dominion increased the sales tax to 6 per cent, increased the corporation and the personal income taxes, and raised several excise taxes. Practically all the provinces increased their gasoline taxes. Manitoba raised its profits tax (first levied in 1930) from 2 per cent to 5 per cent and British Columbia enacted a new schedule having a top rate of 10 per cent. Corporation profits taxes were also levied for the first time at rates ranging from 1 per cent to 4 per cent in Quebec, Ontario, Saskatchewan, and Alberta. Existing taxes on corporations were increased in most other provinces, along with general increases in succession duties and amusement taxes. Two provinces—Saskatchewan and Alberta—imposed taxes on 1932 personal incomes, bringing to five the number of provinces with such a tax.

The Dominion turned to new indirect taxes on sugar and many other commodities for revenue in 1933. A 5 per cent withholding tax on payments to non-residents was also introduced.

Apart from a round of increases in succession duties in Ontario, British Columbia, and Prince Edward Island the significant provincial change was the introduction of the so-called "wages" tax (which applied to all income) in Manitoba. Corporations were left alone for the most part.

For 1934 the Dominion imposed a special additional graduated tax on unearned personal income and increased its profits tax from $12\frac{1}{2}$ per cent to $13\frac{1}{2}$ per cent. Some minor personal income tax changes were made by the provinces, and Saskatchewan increased its corporation profits tax from 4 per cent to 5 per cent. Nova Scotia and New Brunswick both increased their gasoline taxes.

Following the comparative calm of the previous two years 1935 marked a renewal of the attack on several fronts. The Dominion increased its profits tax from $13\frac{1}{2}$ per cent to 15 per cent, Quebec raised its profits tax from $1\frac{1}{2}$ per cent to $2\frac{1}{2}$ per cent, Ontario raised its succession duties and Saskatchewan and Alberta increased their gasoline taxes. Perhaps the most interesting development, however, was the introduction in Ontario (by 1936 legislation) of a provincial tax on 1935 incomes, in place of the historic municipal income tax. There were less vigorous pin-pricks as well in most of the other provinces.

There were interesting new developments in 1936 in the field of commodity taxation. In Alberta the first provincial retail sales tax was levied at 2 per cent as the Ultimate Purchasers Tax. In Saskatchewan the Jacoby Commission also proposed a similar tax for that province. The Dominion in the same year increased its sales tax rate from 6 per cent to 8 per cent.

This was the last significant tax change made by the Dominion until the first war budget in the fall of 1939, but such was not the case with the provinces. Nearly every provincial government made further increases in the following years in gasoline taxes, corporation taxes, and succession duties. In 1937 Alberta repealed its retail sales tax enacted the year before, but in the same year Saskatchewan introduced a similar tax at a 2 per cent rate. In 1938 New Brunswick introduced a 1 per cent profits tax and a levy on paid-up capital, and in the same year Manitoba reduced its wage tax from 2 per cent to 1 per cent but replaced its flat 5 per cent profits rate with a graduated schedule having a top bracket of 10 per cent. Alberta followed this lead, adopting a graduated schedule with a top rate of 7 per cent. For 1939, Nova Scotia levied a 1 per cent profits tax for the first time, Ontario increased its rate from 1 per cent to 5 per cent (by 1940 legislation), and many other changes were made across the country. Even the outbreak of war brought no let-up. New Brunswick increased its profits taxes for 1940 from 1 per cent to $2\frac{1}{2}$ per cent and introduced a 10 per cent tobacco tax; Nova Scotia also increased its rate from 1 per cent to $2\frac{1}{2}$ per cent for 1941 (this increase was later suspended under the Wartime Tax Agreements); Quebec introduced its 2 per cent retail tax and 10 per cent tobacco tax in the same year, increased its profits tax from $2\frac{1}{2}$ per cent to 5 per cent, and introduced a personal income tax, effective for 1939; Ontario maintained its profits tax at 5 per cent and enacted a 25 per cent surtax on most other taxes. There were some further changes in 1941, principally to extend existing rates, although Prince Edward Island introduced a 10 per cent retail sales tax on liquor and tobacco.

The effects of the depression on municipal finance were almost catastrophic. There was little that could be done but increase property and business taxes, although one or two new developments appeared. The withdrawal of the municipal income tax in Ontario in 1936 has been mentioned already. In 1935 Montreal was authorized to levy such a tax on its residents, along with a new 2 per cent municipal sales tax. In 1939 Quebec City introduced a personal income tax, and in the following year a 2 per cent retail sales tax. Other new developments included an experiment in Winnipeg with special taxes on motor vehicles, liquor purchases, and domestic gas and electric light bills, and another in Montreal with taxes on radios, telephones, and motor vehicles.

While it is not possible to summarize adequately the effect of the depression increases the following were the main developments:

Corporation income taxes. (1) The Dominion corporation income tax rate was increased from 8 per cent on 1929 incomes to 15 per cent on 1939 incomes, or almost double. (2) Whereas only two provinces taxed corporation incomes in 1929 (Prince Edward Island and British Columbia), by 1939 all nine were in the field at rates from 1 per cent to 10 per cent. The central provinces of Ontario and Quebec by 1940 were both charging 5 per cent. Even excluding the wartime increase in the Dominion rate, a corporation in either of these provinces paid a total rate of 20 per cent by 1940, as compared with 8 per cent in 1929.

Individual income tax. (1) Between 1930 and 1939 the Dominion personal income tax was doubled for most taxpayers. (2) Whereas only three provinces (Prince Edward Island, Manitoba, and British Columbia) taxed personal incomes in 1930, seven provinces were levying such taxes by 1939. In some cases the provincial tax was almost as heavy as that levied by the Dominion. (3) In Quebec, both Montreal and Quebec City introduced personal income taxes during the thirties.

Commodity taxes. (1) Between 1930 and 1939 the rate of the Dominion sales tax was increased from 1 per cent to 8 per cent. (2) The general level of provincial gasoline taxes increased from 5 cents per gallon in 1930 to 10 cents per gallon in the Maritimes, 8 cents in Quebec and Ontario, and 7 cents west of Ontario. (3) Retail sales taxes of 2 per cent were introduced in Saskatchewan and Quebec, and in Montreal and Quebec City. (4) Taxes of 10 per cent were levied on the retail price of tobacco in Quebec, New Brunswick, and Prince Edward Island.

The exact increase in burden resulting from this tax revolution is difficult to assess. Between 1929 and 1933 it must have been extreme in real terms. The decline in current revenues of all governments between the peak and the trough was held to about 10 per cent (a drop from $780 million to $705 million in terms of the nearest comparable statistics). Concurrently, however, the national income had all but collapsed, the actual drop between 1929 and 1933 being almost 49 per cent. The net increase in the "burden" of government, therefore, must have been in the neighbourhood of 40 per cent, a ratio borne out by other *indicia*. The weight of the burden eased moderately as income and employment revived, although with a national income in 1939 still 9 per cent below that of 1929 total government revenues were 30 per cent higher than a decade before.

THE CANADIAN TAX STRUCTURE   27

The Rowell-Sirois Report and the Tax Agreements

In the recent history of Canadian taxation two factors have been predominant. The first of these is the sequence of events that started with the appointment of the Rowell-Sirois Commission and culminated in the Dominion-provincial taxation agreements. The other of course is World War II.

The Royal Commission on Dominion-Provincial Relations, to give it the official title, was appointed in 1937 by the Dominion government to find a solution for the serious maladjustments in the federal financial structure that had appeared in the depression. Several provinces had come to the verge of bankruptcy, and the tax structure had been reduced to chaos by the uncoordinated onslaught of all governments. The Commission's proposals were submitted to the Dominion government in a voluminous three-book report in 1940 after the outbreak of war. It recommended a substantial revision of the subsidy arrangements between the Dominion and the provinces, proposed that the Dominion assume the existing provincial debt and undertake full responsibility for relief in the future. At the same time it urged that the Dominion be given for all time the sole right to impose corporation taxes (on income or any other basis), personal income taxes, and succession duties.

These specific proposals of the Commission met an unhappy fate. A conference of provincial premiers called by the Dominion in Ottawa in January 1941 met for only two days and broke down in complete failure. Such was the urgency of the need for revenues to finance the war that in April 1941 the Minister of Finance, Rt. Hon. J. L. Ilsley, set out in his Budget Speech terms on which an agreement could be negotiated only for the period of the war to clear the way for increasing Dominion taxes. Compensation was offered on one of two bases at the province's option, and succession duties were excluded from the proposal.

In response to this last appeal all provinces negotiated arrangements which have since become known as the Wartime Tax Agreements. Their effect was to repeal the personal income tax and the income and other taxes on corporations from 1941 to 1946 inclusive, thus leaving the Dominion a free hand to pursue an energetic fiscal policy during the war years. They undoubtedly contributed much to the remarkably successful prosecution of the Canadian wartime financial programme.

In anticipation of the expiry of the Wartime Tax Agreements the Dominion called the provincial premiers together at Ottawa in August 1945 to consider plans for the future. The Dominion submitted proposals for an ambitious joint social security programme, and offered increased compensation for the continued release to it of the provincial right to impose the taxes involved in the wartime agreement, with the addition of succession duties. The Dominion's offer, revised from time to time, and alternative offers submitted by some of the provinces, were discussed at meetings held between August 1945 and May 1946. As in 1941, however, it turned out to be impossible to achieve unanimous agreement and the conference was finally adjourned in May 1946. In his Budget Speech of a month later the same Minister of Finance, Rt. Hon. J. L. Ilsley, offered terms for a five-year agreement covering taxation only, which any province could reject or accept at its option. There followed detailed negotiations with individual provinces, in the course of which the Dominion increased the compensation for the release of the provincial taxes in view of the fact that the social security programme had been dropped. On the basis of this last offer agreements were entered into for the years 1947 to 1951 with all provinces but Ontario and Quebec. On entering the union in 1949 Newfoundland also entered into a similar agreement for the years 1949 to 1951. Payments under these agreements for the eight provinces, including Newfoundland, were guaranteed at a minimum of $89 million. The upward adjustment for per capita gross national product and provincial population provided in the agreements had raised the aggregate payment to about $137 million for the year 1951, the last year of the agreements.

A conference to consider new tax agreements was held in Ottawa in December 1950. The Dominion offered to enter into new arrangements for the five years 1952 to 1956 on revised financial terms involving an increase of about 50 per cent in the guaranteed minimum payments. It undertook also to meet the full cost of an old age pension of $40 a month without means test for all persons over 70, and to share the cost of old age assistance to persons between 65 and 70.

In subsequent counter-proposals the provinces requested higher guaranteed minimum payments than were offered at the conference. The Dominion stated that it could not accede to these requests, but agreed to changes which would accelerate payments more rapidly in order to assist economic growth. On this basis new agreements were entered into in 1952 for a further five years with all provinces but Quebec. Annual payments under these arrangements were guaranteed at $231 million, but were very substantially higher in every year. The same taxes were suspended, and a 5 per cent provincial profits tax levied for the five years of the 1947-51 agreements was replaced by an increase in the federal rate, against which a credit was allowed for corporations paying a tax on profits to Quebec. A credit against the federal death duty for duties paid to Ontario and Quebec was continued, Ontario having elected under its agreement to retain such duties.

Agreements were again negotiated with the provinces in 1956 for the five-year period 1957 to 1961, some interesting variations being introduced in the new terms. The same three tax sources were involved, but the basis of compensation was radically altered. The essence of the 1957-61 agreements is that the provinces may either impose certain taxes themselves at "standard" rates, with an abatement being allowed by the federal government against its tax, or it may contract to rent the tax source to the federal government and receive as a payment the revenue the tax would have produced in the province if imposed at the "standard" rate. In addition, every province, whether or not it has so contracted, receives an "equalization" payment from the federal government sufficient to bring the per capita yield of the three taxes involved up to the level of the average per capita yield in the two highest provinces, which are now Ontario and Quebec.

The "standard" rates for the three taxes are: (1) corporation profits tax at 9 per cent; (2) personal income tax at 13 per cent of the federal rates, and (3) death taxes at 50 per cent of the federal rates.

The actual position under the arrangements for the years 1957-61 is that all provinces but Ontario and Quebec contracted to rent their tax sources to the federal government and have received compensation plus equalization payments; in these provinces the only taxes of this character are now those levied by the federal government.

Ontario chose to continue to impose its succession duties and in 1957 reimposed a corporation profits tax at a rate of 11 per cent, 2 per cent higher than the federal abatement. It elected to rent its personal income tax, and receives compensation therefor.

Quebec rented none of its taxes. It raised its corporation profits tax to 9 per cent (from 7 per cent) to take full advantage of the federal abatement. In 1954, at a time when the federal personal income tax abatement was 10 per cent, it levied a personal income tax at a level which exceeded the abatement. The abatement was increased in 1958 to 13 per cent, and for many taxpayers subsequent increases in the Quebec tax again brought it in excess of the federal relief. The position in Quebec for 1961 is that the province levies a corporation profits tax at 12 per cent, a personal income tax somewhat in excess of 13 per cent of federal rates, and its own succession duties.

A significant change in the sharing of related tax sources was made in 1957 when the federal government gave up its insurance premium tax of 2 per cent; all provinces adopted this tax.

The old age security plan for persons over 70 came into effect on January 1, 1952. Three taxes were levied to finance the scheme, under the Old Age Security Act: (1) 2 per cent on corporate profits from January 1, 1952; (2) 2 per cent on personal taxable income from July 1, 1952 (maximum $30 in 1952, $60 thereafter); and 2 per cent of the 10 per cent sales tax, from January 1, 1952. These rates were each increased in 1959 to 3 per cent, when the lower rates proved inadequate to finance the cost of the pensions, and are now at that level.

1940-1953: War and Post-War Taxes

It would be impossible to attempt a detailed examination of so vast and complex a phenomenon as the wartime taxation of the Dominion government within the brief compass of this review. No such attempt will be made here. Only a few highlights will be given, and in extenuation it is submitted that the whole episode is so painfully fresh to most taxpayers and infor-

THE CANADIAN TAX STRUCTURE 31

mation on it so readily available that for present purposes this will suffice. It will also be documented completely in the forthcoming volume mentioned earlier.

First of all, some indications of the over-all dimensions of the financial effort. One naturally thinks of World War I as a bench mark, but the magnitudes are so different as to be almost incomparable. Total federal expenditures during World War I exceeded $3 billion. Total federal expenditures during World War II exceeded $23½ billion. In each of the last four years of World War II expenditures would have needed to be only moderately higher to be double the whole of the expenditures of World War I. In addition vast quantities of money were made available to our allies by loan that do not appear in the figures just given.

Despite the gargantuan size of this outlay a considerably larger proportion was financed from current revenues than in World War I. In the first three years (fiscal years 1940 to 1942), the proportion was 70 to 80 per cent, but fell back closer to 50 per cent at the peak of the contest. Altogether about 57 per cent of total expenditures were met from revenues, as compared with only about 46 per cent in World War I.

Revenues of the Dominion government were increased in a remarkably short period of time from a pre-war level of about $500 million to a peak wartime level (in fiscal year 1944) of $2,920 million, including almost $200 million of refundable income and excess profits taxes. They declined to a post-war low of about $2.6 billion in fiscal year 1950, but renewed defence spending raised them sharply to $4.4 billion in fiscal year 1953.

Some individual increases in tax revenues during the war are of interest. Taxation of corporations, which rarely in pre-war years yielded more than $50 million, produced a combined total of corporation and excess profits tax revenue of $740 million in fiscal year 1944, excluding another $40 million of refundable tax. Taxation of individual incomes, which seldom provided a revenue of more than $30 to $35 million in pre-war years, produced the astonishing total of nearly $700 million in fiscal year 1944, not including $155 million of refundable taxes. Revenue from total indirect taxation rose from a level that seldom exceeded

$300 million before the war to a peak of over $900 million in 1944.

This brief chronicle has now almost approached the point where it joins the main chapters of this volume. A word first as to developments in the years since the end of the war. In the Dominion's area there have been substantial reductions in taxation. The excess profits tax was gradually reduced until it disappeared at the end of 1947. The corporation income tax was established at a flat 30 per cent (10 per cent less than the minimum rate payable during the war) for 1947, was changed to a two-bracket levy of 10 per cent on the first $10,000 and 33 per cent on the excess for 1949 and 1950 to August 30. Following that date, in a round of increases necessitated by rising defence expenditures, these rates were raised to 15 per cent and 38 per cent respectively, and in the budget of April 1951 the 38 per cent rate was raised to 45.6 per cent (by a 20 per cent defence surtax) effective from January 1, 1951. From January 1, 1952, the surtax was repealed and these rates became 22 per cent and 52 per cent, of which 2 per cent was an old age security levy and 5 per cent was, in effect, the profits tax formerly levied by the "agreeing" provinces. From January 1, 1953, however, these rates were reduced to 20 per cent and 49 per cent respectively (including 2 per cent old age security tax) and the "low rate" bracket was widened from $10,000 to $20,000. Subsequent changes in corporation profits tax have not been major. From 1955 to 1957 the general rate was reduced to 47 per cent (including 2 per cent old age security); in 1958 the low bracket was widened from $20,000 to $25,000, and in 1959, by an increase in the old age security tax to 3 per cent and a raise in the general rate to 47 per cent, the rates became 21 per cent on the first $25,000 and 50 per cent on the excess. For 1961 the bracket to which the lower rate applies has been increased to $35,000.

By 1949 the personal income tax had been reduced 60 per cent or more from wartime peak rates, exemptions being restored to pre-war levels. In 1949 also a 10 per cent tax credit against dividend income was introduced and a wholly revised Income Tax Act, replacing the Income War Tax Act of 1917, came into effect. The downward post-war trend was reversed in the 1951 budget when a defence surtax on existing rates of 10 per cent for 1951 and 20 per cent thereafter was announced. On July 1, 1952, a 2 per cent old age security tax came into effect (maximum $30 in 1952, $60 thereafter) and a new rate schedule replaced the defence surtax, with some reduction. However the 1953 budget restored the 1949 rates from July 1, 1953, and increased the dividend tax credit from 10 per cent to 20 per cent. Further reductions were made in 1955 and 1958. From July 1, 1955, the rate in all brackets was reduced by 2 per cent, and in 1958 (December, 1957) the rate in the lowest $1,000 bracket was reduced by 2 per cent and in the next by 1 per cent. However in 1959 the downward trend was reversed with an increase of 1 per cent in all brackets beyond $3,000 and for 1960 and thereafter an increase of 2 per cent for the same brackets. The old age security tax was also increased to 3 per cent from July 1, 1959.

Other features of post-war direct taxation included special depreciation allowances to encourage investment, a new general system of depreciation that carries with it a write-off for obsolescence, an extension to a longer period of the carry-over of losses for businesses, an intermediate appeal step to the new Tax Appeal Board, the adoption of revised methods of taxing co-operatives and annuity payments (each after study by a Royal Commission) and of measures for the avoidance of the extreme tax penalty falling on surpluses when distributed.

Substantial revisions have also been made in the indirect taxes. Under the general sales tax significant exemptions have been granted for building materials, producer's apparatus and equipment, and processed foods. A drastic streamlining of the remaining excise taxes was undertaken in 1949, when many wartime levies were discarded and most of those retained were brought to a common rate of 10 per cent. However, in September 1950, under the increases for financing the expanded defence programme already mentioned, the general 10 per cent rate was increased to 15 per cent, new articles were brought into the scope of this tax, soft drinks, candy, and chewing gum were taxed at 30 per cent, and the tax on liquor was raised from $11 to $12 per gallon. Even more drastic increases were provided for in the April 1951 budget. The general sales tax was raised from 8 per cent to 10 per cent, the 15 per cent excise tax was increased to 25 per cent, refrigerators, washing machines, and stoves were brought under tax at 15 per cent, and cigarettes and tobacco were both taxed more heavily. Taxes on candy and chewing gum, however, were reduced to 15 per cent.

From January 1, 1952, under the Old Age Security Act 2 per cent of the 10 per cent sales tax was earmarked for old age security, and the budget of March 1952 reduced the 25 per cent excise taxes to 15 per cent, cancelled the 15 per cent taxes on refrigerators, washing machines, and stoves, removed the 1951 increase in the cigarette tax, and reduced the tax on soft drinks to 15 per cent. The 1953 budget reduced the cigarette tax by 4 cents per package, removed the cheque and stock transfer taxes and the $2.50 radio licence, and exempted books, newsprint, and other minor items from sales tax. Subsequent changes have been mainly in the direction of simplifying the commodity tax structure with greater concentration on a few main items. The tax on automobiles was reduced from 15 per cent to 10 per cent (1955), then to $7\frac{1}{2}$ per cent (1957), and finally was repealed (1961). The rate on most other commodities was reduced to 10 per cent and many of the items were made exempt. Increases were concentrated on liquor, tobacco, and the general sales tax, the old age security portion of the latter being raised from 2 per cent to 3 per cent in 1959. By 1961 the bulk of the commodity tax revenue came from liquor, tobacco, and the general sales tax.

The post-war agreements with eight provinces meant that, except for the 5 per cent profits tax levied from 1947 to 1951, no corporation taxes, income tax on either individuals or corporations, or succession duties were levied in these provinces. The two "non-agreeing" provinces, Ontario and Quebec, revived their pre-war tax system almost intact in 1947 on expiry of the Wartime Tax Agreements, with the corporation profits tax at

THE CANADIAN TAX STRUCTURE 35

7 per cent instead of the pre-war 5 per cent, but without personal income taxes. With later increases by 1961 corporation profits tax rates had reached 12 per cent in Quebec and 11 per cent in Ontario, and Quebec had been levying a personal income tax since 1954. Gasoline taxes now range from 12 cents to 19 cents per gallon. The introduction of provincial retail sales taxes in British Columbia in 1948, in New Brunswick and Newfoundland in 1950, in Nova Scotia in 1959, in Prince Edward Island in 1960, and in Ontario in 1961 (Sept. 1) meant that by the latter year all provinces but Manitoba and Alberta levied such taxes. Revenue from several of these levies was earmarked in whole or in part for financing the province's share of the hospital insurance plan introduced in 1958 (on a joint federal-provincial basis) and in most provinces, in addition, hospital insurance premiums have been introduced for the same purpose. Other significant post-war developments in the provincial field include the repeal of the provincial property tax in Alberta in 1947, in Prince Edward Island in 1948, and in Saskatchewan as from the end of 1952.

Summary of Taxes at September 1961

Personal income tax. Dominion and Quebec taxes only; none imposed by any other province or municipality.

Corporation income tax. For 1961 Dominion tax of 21 per cent on first $35,000 with 50 per cent on excess, including 3 per cent old age security tax; in addition 12 per cent in Quebec and 11 per cent in Ontario, for which the federal tax is abated by 10 per cent in Quebec and 9 per cent in Ontario.

Corporation and business taxes. Taxes in Quebec and Ontario on paid-up capital, places of business, railway mileage, etc., in most cases in lieu of (but in some in addition to) the tax on profits; all similar taxes, except for a tax on insurance premiums, are suspended in the other provinces; municipal business taxes, mainly levied on business premises (capital value, rental value, floor space) or on gross receipts; taxes of 2 per cent on life insurance premiums in all provinces.

Death duties. Dominion levy in all provinces; provincial

duties also in Ontario and Quebec, for which an abatement is allowed against Dominion duty in the amount of one-half that duty.

Commodity taxes. Dominion manufacturers' sales tax of 11 per cent, including old age security tax of 3 per cent; additional Dominion taxes and duties on liquor, tobacco, radios, television sets, matches, playing cards, pipes and toilet articles, and of course the customs tariff; provincial retail sales tax in Newfoundland, New Brunswick, Nova Scotia, Prince Edward Island, Quebec, Ontario, Saskatchewan, and British Columbia at rates from 2 to 5 per cent; provincial gasoline taxes of from 12 to 19 cents per gallon in all provinces; retail sales taxes in Quebec municipalities.

Other sources of revenue. In the provinces, revenue from motor vehicles, liquor sales, and natural resources; in the municipalities, principally the tax on property.

The end of the tax agreements. Major changes were afoot in mid-1961 for the period 1962-6. Under new federal-provincial arrangements the tax agreements will be terminated and the provinces will virtually be required to impose a corporation profits tax of 9 per cent and a personal income tax equal to 16 per cent of the federal rates for 1962 and rising by 1 per cent each following year to reach 20 per cent of federal rates in 1966. Relief against corresponding federal taxes in these amounts has been guaranteed under the new arrangements. Few provinces had passed implementing legislation at press time, but this action will be required in late 1961 or early 1962.

Chapter 2

DOMINION INCOME TAX
RESIDENT INDIVIDUALS

THE DOMINION INCOME TAX was introduced first in 1917 under the Income War Tax Act which continued in effect until December 31, 1948; the legislation has been completely redrafted and the new act, known as the Income Tax Act, came into effect on January 1, 1949.

Broadly speaking the Dominion income tax is imposed, in the case of individuals and corporations resident in Canada, on their total world income, and in the case of non-residents, only on their Canadian income. The subject falls naturally, therefore, under three main headings (*a*) individuals resident in Canada; (*b*) corporations resident in Canada; and (*c*) non-residents, including, for convenience, both individuals and corporations. This chapter is devoted to the income tax as it applies to individuals resident in Canada, the following to resident corporations (and business income in general), and the next following to non-residents, foreign income, and related matters.

THE GENERAL CONCEPT OF INCOME

At the outset, since the subject is an "income" tax, it is not unnatural to inquire "What is income?" This question would, of course, seem highly irrelevant to salary or wage earners (the majority of the taxpayers) since there is seldom any cause for doubt as to whether or not their remuneration is to be classed as income. They would therefore be the more surprised to learn that "income" is one of the most disturbingly elusive concepts in the whole field of taxation. One would almost be safe in saying that "income" for tax purposes is not a concept at all; that there is no universal and unchanging principle by which an amount of money may be measured and tested to determine whether or not it is of the species.

In judging such matters one turns ordinarily to the terms of the statute, to see what meaning may have been given the subject of the tax by legislation. In the Canadian Income Tax Act, however, the legislators have not even pretended to define income, much less capital, a concept of equal significance. In this respect our law differs little from that of any other country. The statute is normally of little help.

Having thus given this foretaste of frustration, it is necessary to add at once that all is not lost. One cannot ignore the fact that some billions of dollars are collected annually throughout the world in "income" taxes, and this incredible phenomenon could hardly continue year after year without the emergence of a glimmering of a principle.

To begin with, let it be agreed that it is income as understood for practical purposes of taxation which we seek. This may be, and normally is, a conception differing in several ways from an idealized version of it. Consider, for example, the definition advanced by the late Henry C. Simons, of the University of Chicago, in his stimulating *Personal Income Taxation*. Here an able economist applies his talents to the formulation of what he regarded as an ideal definition of personal taxable income. His definition follows: "Personal income may be defined as the algebraic sum of (1) the market value of rights exercised in consumption and (2) the change in the value of the store of property rights between the beginning and end of the period in question. In other words, it is merely the result obtained by adding consumption during the period to 'wealth' at the end of the period and then subtracting 'wealth' at the beginning."[1] While Simons acknowledges his heavy indebtedness to the German economists, his definition is not without resemblance to the better-known concept advanced by Robert Murray Haig in 1920 to the effect that "income is the money value of the net accretion to economic power between two points of time."

[1] H. C. Simons, *Personal Income Taxation*, p. 50.

Without analysing fully the implications of Henry Simons's proposed definition, and of course recognizing that his is neither the only nor the last word to be said by economists in this regard, we can easily discover in it significant and revealing divergences from the concept of income actually employed for tax purposes in most countries. It differs from both the American and English concepts, for example, in that gifts and bequests received during the year, being "wealth" at the end of the period not owned at the beginning of the period, would be treated as income. They are not so treated today. Further, it differs from the English basis by treating as income all gains arising from an increment in the capital value of property. This increment is now taxed in the United States on its realization, but this is a fundamental point of departure from the Canadian and English point of view.

So much for the attempt of one economist to construct a rational basis for an income tax. On the whole one finds little clue to the actual basis of income taxation from a study of the writings of economists in general. The Supreme Court of the United States has indeed said: "In determining the definition of the word 'income' (thus arrived at), this court has consistently refused to enter into the refinements of lexicographers or economists. . . ."[2] Similar sentiments have been expressed by the Privy Council on other occasions regarding the gloomy profession, with particular reference to the question of "direct taxation." (It would be of interest to trace the origin of the low repute of economists among jurists, who appear on the whole to have infinite patience for the esoteric refinements of any other profession.)

While the lexicographers were reduced by the Supreme Court to the low estate of the economists they hardly deserved this fate, since some of their definitions are not very wide of the mark. Consider, for example, that given by *Webster's International Dictionary:* income is "that gain which proceeds from labor, business, property, or capital of any kind, as the produce of a farm, the rent of houses, the proceeds of professional business, the profits of commerce or of occupation, or the interest of money

[2]*Merchants' Loan and Trust Co.* v. *Smietanka,* 255 U.S. 509, 41 Sup. Ct. 386 (1921).

or stock in funds." Lacking anything more precise this could be accepted as fairly representative of the English concept, although it is found wanting on close analysis. It begs the whole question, for example, of the nature of capital, and more particularly gives no suggestion that under some circumstances the gain that proceeds from capital, business, and property is itself regarded as capital and not income under English law.

Having abandoned the legislators, the economists, and the lexicographers, we have left the judges. With them we must end the search, not because in their decisions is found any lasting declaration of principles but rather because in the aggregate their rulings, turning on the facts in a multitude of individual circumstances, form a rough pattern that comes as close as one can get to a general concept. It should be stressed that they provide no more than a pattern, and certainly not a principle. As Lord MacMillan, the eminent English jurist, has said: ". . . it is to the decided cases that one must go in search of light . . . [but] . . . each case is found to turn upon its own facts, and no infallible criterion emerges."

The decided tax cases in the courts of the United Kingdom and the United States are legion, and it is by no means proposed to review them here. However, an attempt will be made to give a bare outline, based both on statute and on judicial law, of whatever semblance of a basic concept of income has emerged in these two great English-speaking spheres of law and government.

While, as previously mentioned, the statute law in each country has spoken only in general terms, it has had some bearing on the matter because it has indicated a bias in one direction rather than another. This bias has inevitably exerted an influence on the development of the more precise delineation of income in the decisions of the courts.

The English Concept of Income

Under the English Income Tax Act tax is charged not on income in total but on segments of income which, taken in the aggregate, amount to total income. Schedule D of the Act charges a tax on "the annual profit or gain arising or accruing . . . from any kind of property whatever . . . and from any trade, profession, employment or vocation. . . ." This is the schedule with which we are principally concerned.

It will be readily understood that the English courts, in interpreting this wording, have occupied themselves not with general consideration of the nature of "income" but with the question of the nature of annual profit or gain from a trade or employment. As a result they have apparently adopted a more restricted view of income than might have been the case under a more general wording. The over-all result of their decisions was summarized in the report of the 1920 Royal Commission on the Income Tax, as follows: "Casual, non-recurring or occasional profits arising from transactions that do not form part of the ordinary business of the person who makes them are accordingly held not to be within the scope of the Income Tax, and consequently escape taxation."[3]

In the English approach, therefore, many forms of gain, particularly speculative and casual gains, are not subject to tax, since they are not part of the returns that are normally associated with a trade or employment. Such gains in common parlance are usually known as "capital" gains, to distinguish them from "income" gains. In truth, however, there is no such concept in English law as a "capital" gain and the only test that is material to the result is whether or not the gain is the return from a trade. It follows, therefore, that when the regular possibility of making a "capital" gain presents itself in carrying on such a trade as a stockbroker's business, for example, or where the making of capital gains is the main purpose of a venture, the gains may be taxed as income of a trade. What degree of regularity makes the difference between casual gains and income cannot be established in advance. About as near as the courts have come to a general rule is the statement in *Pickford* v. *Quirke:* "One transaction of buying and selling does not make a trader, but if it is repeated and becomes systematic, then he becomes a trader."[4] It might be added that while one transaction does not *necessarily* make a trader, there have been circumstances in which the courts have ruled that a single transaction did have this result. In isolating

[3]*Report of the Royal Commission on the Income Tax*, note 8, sec. 85.
[4]B.T.C. 251.

such cases one finds that the legal mind has reached its maximum propensity for making hairline distinctions. No general rule has emerged, and the individual cases alone give any guidance in particular circumstances.[5]

In speculative vein one might advance the view that the English courts have considered a "purpose," or an "intent," as the philosophical basis for income. The cases suggest very strongly that income, far from being the product of a purely objective mathematical calculation such as that proposed by Simons, is on the contrary in the English view a subjective and personal thing; that the purposeful and continuous pursuit of a trade or employment, if not the whole essence, may be a large part of it. One is tempted to surmise that the English legislators and jurists of a century ago, despite the apparent contempt of the latter for the breed, were somewhat under the influence of the classical economists, who regarded the economic process as a serious and plodding affair with little room for the easy killing. It has also been suggested that the idea of *regularity* in income may have had its origin in older countries in the nature of agricultural income, with its purposeful and regular pursuit of seeding the land and regularly harvesting its yield.[6]

One of the most illuminating attempts to reduce the gist of the English jurisprudence to a code of rules was that made by the Royal Commission on the Taxation of Profits and Income in its Final Report (June, 1955). The six criteria the Royal Commission set out as "badges of trade" were:

1. The subject matter which is dealt in: e.g. commodities, or manufactured articles, or property which is incapable of yielding an income are more likely to be the subject of a business deal than property which yields income.
2. The length of the period of ownership.
3. The frequency or number of similar transactions by the same person.

[5]See, for example, *Martin* v. *Lowry*, 11 T.C. 297; *Commissioners of Inland Revenue* v. *Livingstone et al.*, 11 T.C. 538; *Lyons* v. *Cowcher*, 10 T.C. 438; *Pearn* v. *Miller*, 11 T.C. 610; *Leeming* v. *Jones*, 15 T.C. 333; *Stonehaven Recreation Ground Trustees Case*, 15 T.C. 419; *Rutledge* v. *Commissioners of Inland Revenue*, 14 T.C. 490.

[6]L. H. Seltzer, "Evolution of the Special Legal Status of Capital Gains under the Income Tax," p. 18.

4. Supplementary work on or in connection with the property sold so as to market it advantageously.
5. The circumstances that were responsible for the sale.
6. The motive for which the transaction was done (par. 116).

The American Concept of Income

In contrast to the English, the American approach to a concept of income is significantly broader. The taxation of "capital" gains, for example, has been apparent in American law from the beginning of its experience with an income tax. The Revenue Act of 1862, which imposed the first American income tax under a general definition of income, was interpreted to apply to profits made on the sale of real estate. The charging section was broadened by the 1864 act specifically to include "all income or gains derived from the purchase and sale of stocks or other property, real or personal." In the act of 1867 this wide definition was dropped but was replaced by a narrower specific charge on profits made from real estate transactions. The general charging section of the 1867 act imposed a tax on "the gains, profits and income of every person, . . . whether derived from any kind of property, rents, interest, dividends, or salaries, or from any profession, trade, employment or vocation, . . . or from any other source whatever" and, in addition, it specifically included as income "profits realized within the year from sales of real estate purchased within the year, or within two years previous to the year for which income is estimated. . . ."[7]

While the original American law (which was first enacted in 1913 following the Sixteenth Amendment) made no specific mention of "capital" gains, there has been little doubt in the minds of the judges from the beginning that the statute was intended to include such gains within its ambit. This was clearly illustrated in a well-known definition of the early period given in the case of *Stratton's Independence* v. *Howbert* as follows: "Income may be defined as a gain derived from capital, from labor, or from both combined, provided it be understood to include profit gained through sale or conversion of capital assets."[8]

[7] R. F. Magill, *Taxable Income*, p. 90 n.
[8] 231 U.S. 399, 34 Sup. Ct. 136 (1913), cited by Magill, *Taxable Income*, p. 96.

Another significant decision bearing on the same point was given in *Merchants' Loan and Trust Co.* v. *Smietanka*.[9] In this case the court said, regarding a contention that the British concept should be applied, that none of the previous American statutes had recognized the principle that gain on an isolated sale should not be taxed and further that in the view of the court "there is no essential difference in the nature of the transaction or in the relation of the profit to the capital involved, whether the sale or conversion be a single, isolated transaction or one of many." It suggested that the adoption of such a principle "would, in a large measure, defeat the purpose of the [Sixteenth] Amendment," and that the court had attempted to determine a definition of income in accordance with "what it believed to be the commonly understood meaning of the term which must have been in the minds of the people when they adopted the Sixteenth Amendment to the Constitution."

In short, the judges felt that the attitude of the average American citizen was that "capital" gains were income and should be taxed as income, along with poker winnings, prizes from quiz shows, and lucky tickets on the Irish sweeps. In this view the courts seem to have simply taken cognizance of the dynamism of enterprise in a rapidly growing economy. In the United States the possibility of making a speculative gain on a quick turnover has been as much the spur for enterprise and daring as the possibility of achieving security of income. An American writer has recently described this environment, and the resulting attitude towards capital gains, in these words:

> The purchase and sale of lands and the accumulation of private fortunes through profits from such transactions became common early in our history.... Later, the rapid succession of economic changes created by the great growth of population and the discovery and exploitation of natural resources produced frequent large increases in the market values of countless business enterprises and pieces of real estate.... In many transactions gains from the sale of capital assets constituted the major type of profit contemplated.... Opportunities for capital gains were in fact recurring.... In this environment

[9] 255 U.S. 509, 41 Sup. Ct. 386 (1921).

RESIDENT INDIVIDUALS 45

capital gains became scarcely distinguishable from ordinary business profits and they became a familiar source of private wealth.[10]

None of the later American cases or amendments to the Internal Revenue Code have disturbed the basic proposition that capital gains are taxed as income in United States. For the most part the special provisions of the Internal Revenue Code relating to capital gains, such as the reduced rate of tax, are in recognition of the fact that the gains so taxed in one year may represent an increment that has accrued over several years and because of this "lumping-up" should be given some relief through a lower tax rate than ordinary income of the year. It is interesting to note in this connection that no distinction whatever was made between capital gains and other income in the tax rates until 1921, and even today such gains are treated as ordinary income if the asset has been held for less than six months.

The Canadian Position

Enough has been said to demonstrate that the English and American theories of income represent two quite different approaches, and further study would reveal other distinctive characteristics. Historically the Canadian position has been an intermediate one, a role in which we not infrequently find ourselves. For our income tax we borrowed our statute law substantially from the United States and our jurisprudence from England. The definition of income contained in the Income War Tax Act enacted in 1917 has an unmistakable resemblance to United States income tax statutes and bears no resemblance whatever to the English act. Yet the interpretation given it has followed with few exceptions the decisions of the English courts.

This is not to say, of course, that in recent times "capital" gains have not been taxed in Canada simply because of slavish adherence to the English cases. It is probably closer to the truth to say that as a matter of policy and custom such gains are not now taxed, a view confirmed by the statement of the

[10]Seltzer, "Special Legal Status of Capital Gains," p. 22.

Hon. D. C. Abbott in his 1950 Budget Speech. Undoubtedly the actual content of the exemption will alter from time to time, and in post-war years transactions formerly disregarded have been brought to tax, the most striking being frequent or substantial transactions in real estate. However, the general position is still that of the British, and the "badges of trade" set down by the Royal Commission would apply equally well in Canada.

The above analysis has brought out at least superficially significant differences in the concept of income in the two leading English-speaking countries.[11] The reader is warned, however, that as we go to press the Chancellor of the Exchequer has just given notice of pending extensions of the British scope of tax.

TAXATION OF INDIVIDUALS IN CANADA

Liability for Tax: Residence

First, what individual is taxable in Canada? The answer to this question turns on the test of residence. Residence happens to be the Canadian test, but there are others. It may be contrasted, for example, with the test of citizenship applied in the United States income tax and the test of domicile, which, as will appear later, is the main test for liability under death duties.

There are few general principles by which "residence" may be determined. It is a question of fact, to be established on the circumstances of each individual taxpayer. A resident is defined in the Income Tax Act to include persons who "sojourn" in Canada for transient or casual visits totalling more than 183 days in a year, but the law does not otherwise establish any general criterion. Generally speaking, common understanding applies. Most people who live in Canada are residents of Canada. They have their homes here, be it a house, apartment, flat, or other abode. Their families are here and their belongings, and apart from short visits outside of the country on business or for holidays they spend their lifetime "residing" in Canada. By inference a person ceases to be a resident when he departs from

[11]For a more exhaustive discussion see F. E. LaBrie, *The Meaning of Income in the Law of Income Tax*, Parts I and II.

RESIDENT INDIVIDUALS 47

the country without leaving a trace of any of these things behind him. On the other hand a "foreigner" can become a resident of Canada for tax purposes by manifesting some of the earmarks of a whole-time resident. He may be deemed to have this status even though in fact he has been present in Canada for only a small part of the year or, under some circumstances, has not been present at all during the year. A person is normally regarded as resident of Canada, for example, if he maintains a place of abode available for his use here and makes visits to Canada during the year, irrespective of the length of the visit. Also generally classed as a resident is a person who visits Canada year after year as a part of his habit of life, irrespective of the fact that he keeps no abode here and may not stay a full six months of the year. A review of the Canadian and English judicial cases will indicate the position taken by the courts in various specific circumstances.

Items Included in Income

Let it be assumed that we have now identified a resident of Canada. The principal characteristic of such a person for tax purposes is that he must pay tax on his whole world income, no matter what its source.

Income received by individuals is classified generally as arising either from "property" or from "offices and employments," using the language of the Income Tax Act. The great bulk of personal income, of course, is that received from "offices and employments," or, in common parlance, salaries and wages. Also included in income are the value of board and lodging where provided by the employer, tips, and any income in kind that forms part of the remuneration of an employment. With some major exceptions noted below allowances for personal and living expenses paid by an employer must also be included in income. No tax is imposed on an employee on his employer's payment on his behalf into an approved superannuation plan, group insurance plan (to the extent of insurance for $25,000), medical service plan, or supplementary unemployment benefit plan. An amount allocated to the taxpayer's account under a profit-sharing plan must be included as income in the year of allocation under law in effect prior to 1961, but an alternative provision was enacted in that year giving substantially the same treatment as for pension plans. Benefits derived by an employee under stock option and stock purchase plans are taxed under a special formula.

Generally speaking, salaries and wages are regarded as net income without any allowances for expenses incurred in earning them. There are an increasing number of statutory exceptions to this rule, which include a deduction granted a clergyman of the rental value of a manse or of rent actually paid for his residence, and of expenses incurred by salesmen and certain ambulant employees of transportation companies (engineers, conductors, bus-drivers, etc.) for meals and lodging while away from home in the course of their employment. Similarly allowances received by a salesman or construction worker for living and travelling expenses and by a clergyman from his congregation for travelling expenses need not be taken into income. Reasonable *per diem* allowances paid to employees other than salesmen for periods of absence from their "home city" are also excluded. This exclusion is only necessary for payments for which the taxpayer does not render an accounting to his employer. The ordinary accountable advance is not regarded as being within the computation of income at all. Exclusion is also granted for union dues, for professional membership dues when required by the terms of the employment to be paid by an employee to maintain his professional status, and for expenditures for travel, office rent, salary of a substitute, or supplies used in an employment where by the terms of the employment the employee is himself required to make such expenditures. An annual amount up to $300 received by a volunteer fireman need not be included in income.

For greater certainty the law lists certain other forms of income, mainly from property, that must be taken into account. The enumeration includes dividends, director's and other fees, annuity payments, superannuation or pension benefits or retiring allowances, amounts received from a registered retirement savings plan, death benefits, interest (on an accrual basis in the case of bonds and debentures), alimony, amounts received from an estate or trust, royalties, rentals, and profit-sharing plan

RESIDENT INDIVIDUALS 49

allocations. Certain benefits that arise to a shareholder through his relationship to a corporation must also be included as income.[12]

Deductions and Exemptions

So much for the items that must be brought into account. Certain other receipts need not be included. There are also certain deductions that may be taken. In general the amounts which need not be included are payments declared to be exempt from tax by a statute of the Canadian Parliament, repayment of War Savings Certificates, war veterans' pensions, workmen's compensation awards, unemployment insurance benefits, cash payments out of a profit-sharing plan (the amount having been previously taxed when credited to the employee), proceeds from the sale by a prospector or developer of a mining claim under specified conditions, and, within limitations, expense allowances received by members of legislatures and municipal councils.

Of the amounts that may be deducted the most significant in the case of employees is a contribution to a superannuation fund by way of payroll deduction, the maximum allowance under the Act being $1,500 a year for current services. An additional allowance is also made for payments of arrears in respect of prior services, the maximum deduction here also being $1,500 a year. No deduction is allowed for payments on life insurance or endowment or annuity contracts except where these are approved as a registered retirement savings plan. Where a taxpayer is not a member of a pension plan such payments may be claimed up to 10 per cent of earned income but not exceeding $2,500; where he is claiming a deduction for pension contributions he may raise his total deduction to $1,500 by payments into a registered retirement savings plan.

Shareholders in mining, petroleum, and natural gas producing companies are allowed a deduction for depletion in respect of dividends on their shares. The maximum rate of such deduction is 20 per cent of the dividend, but is reduced if only a part of the income of the company is from production of minerals, petroleum, or gas.[13] Alimony payments may be deducted

---

[12]See Sections 8 and 81 of the Income Tax Act and the following chapter.
[13]See next chapter.

from income of the year when paid. Tuition fees paid to a university by a student may be deducted from the student's income. As mentioned previously, under specified conditions salesmen, transport employees, and others are allowed to deduct expenses of their employment, and clergymen may deduct amounts in respect of their residences.

The general rule is that all sources of income are aggregated, losses being offset against income, except where the loss is incurred in farming, and farming is not the main source of income. In these circumstances (applicable usually to "gentlemen farmers") the loss may be offset against the main income only up to an amount of $5,000.

The year of income for all individuals except those carrying on a business is the calendar year. Most individuals report on a "cash" basis, i.e., they include as income only money actually received or income in kind actually enjoyed in the year.

Certain other special features of the Canadian income tax on individuals are dealt with in later pages of this chapter.

When total income has been calculated in accordance with the rules described above certain deductions common to all individual taxpayers may be taken to determine "taxable" income.

The personal exemptions now in force were established by Parliament as $1,000 for a single taxpayer and $2,000 for a taxpayer having "married" status. In general the principle on which the larger allowance is granted is the support of a dependent. It may, of course, be claimed by a legally married taxpayer who supports his (or her) spouse. It may also be claimed by a person not supporting a spouse who supports a wholly dependent son or daughter under 21 years of age or a son or daughter 21 or over who is attending school or university or who is wholly dependent by reason of mental or physical infirmity. An unmarried person or a person separated from his (or her) spouse may claim the "married" allowance if he maintains a "self-contained domestic establishment" and actually supports therein a wholly dependent person related by blood, marriage, or adoption. At the present time, except in the case of a spouse, a person is regarded as wholly dependent if he has an income of $950 or less.

RESIDENT INDIVIDUALS   51

The taxpayer supporting children or grandchildren is allowed to deduct $250 for each such child eligible to receive family allowance payments (in general any child under 16 years of age) and $500 for each child 16 years of age or over but under 21. He may also deduct $400 for a child 21 or over if wholly dependent by reason of mental or physical infirmity or if attending school or university. The income of a student attending university may be reduced by the amount of tuition fees paid by him for purposes of this test. Amounts up to $500 actually expended for the support of infirm parents or grandparents, for brothers or sisters under 21 years of age, or brothers and sisters over 21 who are wholly dependent by reason of mental or physical infirmity may also be deducted. The same allowance is granted for such persons who are "in-laws." This deduction must be shared if there is more than one contributor and is limited to $250 is the dependent is a child eligible for family allowances. Double allowances, of course, are not allowed to be taken for dependents, and where a taxpayer has claimed married status in respect of a dependent he may not also claim, except for one minor case, a second allowance for the same dependent under another provision of the law.

Where the taxpayer is 65 years of age or over an additional deduction of $500 a year is granted along with the amounts mentioned above. Thus a single taxpayer in this age group has an exemption of $1,500 and a married taxpayer an exemption of $2,500.

Along with these basic exemptions, usually known as the "personal" exemptions, a taxpayer may also deduct amounts up to 10 per cent of his income for donations to approved charitable organizations for which he can provide receipts. He may also claim deductions for certain medical expenses as established in the Income Tax Act. These may be deducted to the extent that they exceed 3 per cent of the taxpayer's income, and for 1961 and later years no limit is imposed on the amount that may be so deducted, previous maximum restrictions having been repealed. In lieu of this allowance taxpayers who are blind or who are confined to a bed or a wheel chair by reason of a physical infirmity may claim a straight deduction from income of $500.

A standard deduction of $100 a year may be claimed by all taxpayers in lieu of deductions for charitable donations, medical expenses, union dues, and professional membership dues. This may be taken whether or not payments have been made under any of these headings.

The basic exemption of $2,000 given for married status is subject to adjustment where both husband and wife have an income. A husband and wife are not required to file joint returns as they are in England nor is a married man required to include any income of his wife's with his own. But if the wife receives over $250 but less than $1,250 in the year the excess over $250 is deducted from the husband's exemption of $2,000. On the other hand, if she earns $1,250 or more a year both husband and wife must file returns and pay tax as single persons.

TABLE I

GRADUATED RATES OF DOMINION PERSONAL INCOME TAX

| Taxable income | | Basic | Plus this |
Over	But not over	tax	percentage[1]
$	$	$	%
0	1,000		11
1,000	2,000	110	14
2,000	3,000	250	17
3,000	4,000	420	19
4,000	6,000	610	22
6,000	8,000	1,050	26
8,000	10,000	1,570	30
10,000	12,000	2,170	35
12,000	15,000	2,870	40
15,000	25,000	4,070	45
25,000	40,000	8,570	50
40,000	60,000	16,070	55
60,000	90,000	27,070	60
90,000	125,000	45,070	65
125,000	225,000	67,820	70
225,000	400,000	137,820	75
400,000		269,070	80

[1] On excess over amount in left-hand column.

RESIDENT INDIVIDUALS

Rates of Tax

On the balance remaining after deduction of the amounts set out above (taxable income) the individual is required to pay tax at the rates in the preceding schedule on his 1961 income. In addition an old age security tax of 3 per cent of taxable income, but not to exceed $90, is payable by every taxpayer.

A flat 4 per cent tax also applies on investment income from sources outside Canada, in general income other than salaries and wages, superannuation, pensions, or retiring allowances. The first $2,400 is exempt, or if the taxpayer's normal allowances are greater he may deduct the greater amount.

The actual income and old age security taxes payable by a

TABLE II

INCOME AND OLD AGE SECURITY TAXES PAYABLE BY A SINGLE TAXPAYER, A MARRIED TAXPAYER, AND A MARRIED TAXPAYER WITH TWO CHILDREN OF FAMILY ALLOWANCE AGE, 1961

Income	Single taxpayer		Married taxpayer		Married taxpayer with two children	
	Income tax	Old age security tax	Income tax	Old age security tax	Income tax	Old age security tax
$	$	$	$	$	$	$
1,500	44	10				
2,000	99	20				
2,500	166	30	44	10		4
3,000	236	40	99	20	44	14
5,000	591	90	403	90	318	54
10,000	1,840	90	1,544	90	1,370	90
20,000	5,825	90	5,375	90	5,006	90
30,000	10,520	90	10,020	90	9,526	90
50,000	20,965	90	20,415	90	20,140	90
100,000	50,855	90	50,205	90	49,880	90
200,000	119,550	90	118,850	90	118,500	90

NOTE: It is assumed that the taxpayer claims the full standard deduction of $100 in lieu of charitable donations, etc. It is also assumed that all income is either earned or from Canadian investments and that as a result the investment surtax does not apply.

single person, a married person, and a married person with two dependents of family allowance age in 1961 are shown in the preceding table for a representative range of incomes.

Payment of Tax

In the case of individuals whose income is mainly from salary and wages under tables provided by the government 95 per cent or more of the tax on the average is deducted by the employer at the time the remuneration is paid. The balance of the tax is payable with the annual return not later than April 30 of the following year. Individuals receiving less than a quarter of their income from salary and wages must estimate their tax for the year in advance and pay it in quarterly instalments on March 31, June 30, September 30, and December 31. The balance remaining after the last instalment on December 31, if any, is payable with the annual return not later than April 30 of the following year. There are penalties for inadequate or late payments and for late filing or non-filing of returns.

In general the Canadian income tax is on a self-assessment basis, as contrasted with the British, Australian, and American systems under which the taxpayer's liability in many instances is calculated for him by the tax department and he is informed of the amount payable. In Canada the taxpayer files a return on which he has estimated his own tax. This is checked or "assessed" by the Taxation Division, using such independent information as it may obtain from employers and others, and the taxpayer is informed by notice of assessment that his return is confirmed, or otherwise. If additional tax has been found to be payable he may pay without protest or he may appeal the assessment to the Minister of National Revenue and thereafter to the Tax Appeal Board or the Exchequer Court, or both. In certain cases an appeal may be taken from the Exchequer Court to the Supreme Court.

For residents of Quebec an abatement of 13 per cent of the federal tax otherwise payable is allowed because that province levies a personal income tax. Under the new federal-provincial tax arrangements for the period 1962-1966 presumably all provinces must levy a personal income tax at the level of the

RESIDENT INDIVIDUALS 55

enlarged federal abatement, which will be raised to 16 per cent for 1962 and will rise to 20 per cent by 1966. In most provinces the new tax will be collected by the federal administration and should cause little inconvenience for the taxpayer.

Since a resident of Canada is subject to tax on his total income, the Canadian levy will be a second tax on income that has already been taxed abroad. An appropriate deduction from the Canadian tax is allowed to compensate for this dual taxation.

From 1949 to 1952 an individual receiving a dividend from a taxable Canadian company was allowed to deduct from his income tax an amount equal to 10 per cent of such a dividend, with some qualifications, and for 1953 and later years this credit has been raised to 20 per cent. Both these credits are discussed more fully in later pages.

Some Particular Aspects of the Canadian Personal Income Tax

Three phases of the Canadian income tax on individuals deserve special comment. They present problems of which the solution has been peculiarly Canadian.

The first is the method of taxing pensions and other forms of remuneration, other than salary or wages, related to employment. The problem is whether to tax such remuneration when it is being earned (i.e., during the years of employment) or later on when it is being received as income. It must be admitted that there are valid objections against either alternative. If this remuneration is taxed when earned in the working years of a man's life he is being taxed on income which he does not then actually receive. If taxed when received, this means taxing a retired person on what may be his sole support. Apart from these considerations, however, the basic problem is to assure that this form of income is taxed at least once, but only once.

Both these problems were referred in 1945 to the Royal Commission on the Taxation of Annuities and Family Corporations (Ives Commission) for solution. The recommendations of this commission were accepted and implemented by the government almost without reservation in 1946.

The present method of taxing pensions, based on these recommendations, is that the contribution of both the employer and the employee, within limits, may be deducted from income in the year paid into the pension fund. Deductions are allowed for such payments in respect of both current and past service. Under a provision of the Act it is established that the employer's contribution to the fund in respect of the employee's services is not to be included as income of the employee in the year of contribution.

Under the above procedure the inflow into a pension fund from contributions is tax-exempt. During the time the moneys of the employer and employee are in the fund they both earn interest and this interest is also exempt from tax while in the fund. At any given time, therefore, under the present terms of the income tax all the money available in a pension fund is money that has yet to be taxed. The problem, thereafter, is to assure that the money withdrawn from the fund is taxed, and the general rule therefore is that all such receipts are taxable.

There are several different circumstances under which this money may be withdrawn. For one, the employee may leave the fund before he commences to receive a pension, because of dismissal, resignation, or death. When he "withdraws" in this manner he or his beneficiaries will ordinarily receive a lump sum amount in settlement of his accrued rights. In such an event there is no mitigation of the general rule, i.e., that the withdrawal is income in the year received, but a measure of alleviation is given in the rate of tax. The recipient has the option of paying a tax calculated at the "effective" (average) rate of tax of the last three years of income. (This same treatment may be taken for a payment for long service or loss of office, a death benefit, or an employee's benefit under a stock option or stock purchase plan, in the latter case with the additional feature that the rate so determined applies only to the extent that it exceeds 20 per cent.)

Where the employee lives to receive his pension, he is taxable on it in full when received. As mentioned above the fund from which the pension arises is made up of (*a*) his own contribution (if any); (*b*) the interest thereon; (*c*) his employer's contribution; and (*d*) the interest on his employer's contribution. On none of these has tax been paid previously, and since it is clearly recognized that pensions represent postponed remuneration from employment there is no doubt that they should be subject to tax.

Where the pension right carries through to a survivor of the pensioned employee it continues to be taxed as income, and the capitalized value of the future pension payments is included in the estate of the deceased and is also subject to death duty. To alleviate this "double" taxation a deduction is allowed each year of a proportionate part of the death duty in calculating income tax on the pension.

Following many years of agitation by professional and other persons not eligible for the "pension" form of treatment for retirement savings a measure was enacted to meet their needs. Under it, amounts paid under a "registered retirement savings plan" may be deducted up to 10 per cent of income, not to exceed $2,500, if the taxpayer is not claiming any other pension deductions, or, if he is so claiming, up to 10 per cent of income, or a total of $1,500, including such other deductions. In general the payment must go only for purchase of a contract for a retirement income, such income to be taxable on receipt.

This method of taxing profit-sharing plans has proven to be unpopular, and the Minister of Finance in 1960 made public a proposed measure which would extend approximately the same treatment now granted pension plans.

A solution different in principle from that applied to pensions was adopted in 1950 for profit-sharing plans for employees. Previously the law had not specifically provided for such plans, and in setting up rules to cover them it was provided that allocations by the employer to the employee would be taxable as income of the employee in the year of allocation, whether the money was withdrawn or not. The contribution of the employer is to be deductible from his income, the earnings of the plan are to be exempt, and of course the employee is not to be taxed again on withdrawing actual cash benefits for which he has been previously taxed on allocation. It is apparent that under such a system payment of the tax is not postponed to a later time as in the case of pensions.

Certain other "employment-related" benefits are given special tax treatment as well. It was mentioned earlier that death benefits paid by an employer are taxed but are eligible for the alleviation (three-year average effective rate) applicable to lump sum receipts. A further alleviation is granted in the definition of the taxable death benefit; a death benefit is exempt to the extent of the lesser of $10,000 or the salary for the last twelve months of employment.

Benefits under stock-option plans are given special tax treatment. In general the benefit is measured as the difference between the option price and the actual value of the shares at the time of acquisition. The benefit is subject to the three-year average effective rate alleviation, with the additional relief that the rate so determined is reduced by 20 per cent.

Where an employee is a member of a group insurance plan any premium in excess of the amount required to provide insurance for $25,000 is included in his income for the year.

The main description given in the preceding paragraphs has related to the "pension" type of tax treatment. A problem of somewhat similar type arises with contractual annuities. For years the practice was to tax the whole of the proceeds of an annuity as income, following the English precedent. This gave rise to constant representations from taxpayers that a part of the proceeds representing purchase price was capital, had already borne tax, and should not be taxed again. The tax on the full proceeds, therefore, was alleged to be a second tax, at least on part of the annuity.

The taxation of annuities and similar forms of contractual receipts, including endowment policies, is on the basis proposed by the Ives Commission, which is somewhat different from the pension arrangements. Here the process described above for pensions is reversed. No deduction from income is allowed for the cost of the annuity at the time of its purchase, whether it is paid for by instalments or in a lump sum. When the annuity or endowment commences to be received, an amount of each payment representing the return of capital to the annuitant is exempt from tax. This capital element is taken as the present value of the annuity at the time of its commencement. It is spread evenly over the life expectancy of the annuitant and the equal annual amount so calculated is deducted from the actual payment received in each year. The balance of the payment is taxable income. This rule is followed whether in actual fact the annuitant exceeds or falls short of his life expectancy, and no alteration is made in the portion of each payment determined to be taxable using the mortality tables. The effect of this method of taxing annuities and endowments is that when the proceeds are withdrawn in a single amount at the time of vesting there is no income tax. This is also true of the proceeds of a policy of life insurance.

The same general principle (exempting payments out of capital) is applied to receipts by an individual from a trust or estate. The determination of capital in this case, however, is based solely on the facts. The taxpayer receiving the annuity or payment must prove his claim that part or all of his payment was from the capital of the trust or estate.

Another aspect of the personal income tax, perhaps of broader significance than that just discussed, is the manner in which the cash family allowance payments for children have been integrated with the allowance for children granted under the income tax. The Family Allowances Act itself established the principle that as far as possible there was to be no duplication between these two allowances. This mandate has been carried out, under the revised tax structure now in effect, by granting a reduced allowance under the income tax for any child *eligible* for the cash family allowance payment, in general any child under the age of 16. For such a child the income tax allowance is only $250, as compared with an allowance of $500 for any other eligible dependent. The cash family allowance payment is not itself taxable income and no account is taken of it in any way under the income tax other than the adjustment of the deduction for children.

Other countries have encountered the same problem and a variety of solutions have been followed. In England, for example, the family allowance payment must be taken into income but the exemption under the income tax is the same for dependents eligible for family allowances as for those not eligible.

A variety of other provisions relate to special but somewhat unconnected aspects of the personal income tax. Some of these are summarized below.

The author of a literary, dramatic, musical, or artistic work may spread his income from the sale of such a work over two years if he was not engaged in its production for more than two years. If the time of his labours exceeded two years the income from the sale may be spread over three years.[14]

Estates and trusts are taxed as individuals under the Canadian Income Tax Act. Income accruing in trust is taxed at the rates applicable to individuals but without the deduction of the personal exemptions allowed individuals. A deduction is allowed, however, for amounts distributed or made payable in the year to the beneficiaries of the trust out of its income, and in the result the only taxable income is the amount remaining after such distributions have been made. Income once taxed may be distributed to the beneficiaries without further tax thereafter.

Farmers and fishermen are allowed to average their incomes over a period of years and pay a tax for the period as if the income each year had been the average annual income for the period. The first year for which this privilege was granted was 1949, and in that year the farmer or fisherman could elect for the previous three years, giving a four-year average in total, including 1949. In 1950 and later years the period is extended to five years, i.e., the year in which he makes the election and the previous four years. The system is what might be called the "block" system. Once a block of five years has been averaged the privilege may not be used again until a new five-year period has passed.

An individual who is resident in Canada during part of the taxation year is subject to tax in Canada only on his income from Canadian sources, and is allowed a proportionate part of the deductions and exemptions granted a full-time resident in calculating his taxable income.

Sole proprietors or the members of a partnership are taxed on the full earnings of the business for the year, whether distributed or not. In determining such income they qualify for the usual business deductions described in the next chapter, but the taxable income so calculated is taxed at the same rates and

[14]For a full treatment of all averaging devices in use under the Canadian Income Tax Act see John Willis, *The Mitigation of the Tax Penalty on Fluctuating or Irregular Incomes.*

RESIDENT INDIVIDUALS 61

is subject to the same personal and other exemptions as income from salaries and wages. The year of income of the partnership or sole proprietorship is the fiscal year ending in the taxation year, and is subject to the rates, deductions, etc., applicable to that taxation year. Various alleviations are granted where by reason of the winding up of a partnership or withdrawal from a partnership income of more than a period of twelve months falls to be taxed in one year.

SUMMARY

RATES. Throughout the period since 1917 individuals have been subject to progressive graduated rates, which have varied considerably from time to time; rates of tax and illustrations of the tax payable on various incomes are given in the text of the chapter. Since 1933, in addition to the graduated rates on ordinary income, there has been a special tax on investment income. On July 1, 1952, an old age security tax of 2 per cent on taxable income (maximum $30 in 1952, $60 thereafter) came into effect, and was increased to 3 per cent effective July 1, 1959 (maximum $90).

REVENUE

	Revenue in 1959–60 ($000)	Percentage of tax revenue	Percentage of total revenue
Personal income tax[1]	1,566,644	33.0	29.6
Old age security tax	185,550	—	—

[1]Includes gift tax, the amount of which is not available.

STATUTORY REFERENCES. Income Tax Act, Revised Statutes, Canada, 1952, c. 148; Old Age Security Act, *ibid.*, c. 200.

Chapter 3

DOMINION INCOME TAX
RESIDENT CORPORATIONS

IN THE LAST CHAPTER the manner in which nearly 5 million individuals resident in Canada are taxed under the personal income tax was described. It is now proposed to describe the position of resident corporations, which number not more than 2 per cent of individuals but make an almost equal contribution to the national treasury. This description can also be taken as applying in general to business income earned in any form.

The federal corporation income tax was first introduced in 1917 and has been in effect ever since. In addition to the standard corporation tax in both world wars there was a tax on abnormal profits—the Business Profits War Tax in World War I and the Excess Profits Tax in World War II.

Liability for Tax: Residence

As in the case of individuals the test of liability for corporations is residence. Until 1961 this concept rested entirely on the judicial rule that a corporation is resident at the place of its seat of management and control. However, statutory provision was made in that year (effective 1962) deeming a corporation to be resident in Canada if incorporated in Canada and carrying on business in Canada. The exact import of this new measure will depend to a large extent on the meaning given the expression "carrying on business" by the administration and the courts. It is not clear to what extent it will result in double taxation of a form not relieved under the international tax treaties. Only experience with the new rule will gradually clarify these and similar questions.

RESIDENT CORPORATIONS   63

Income of a Corporation

Like the resident individual, a resident corporation is taxed on all its income from any source throughout the world. The tax base is defined generally in the Income Tax Act as the income of the corporation from business and property. The breadth of this definition is given some bounds by the limitation that the income for a taxation year from a business or property is the profit therefrom for the year. Actually, therefore, a corporation is taxed on its profit for the year from business and property.

No detailed outline of the method for determining this profit is set out in the statute. The law does not state, for example, that receipts from sales or services must be included on the one side and outlays for materials and wages and other expenses may be deducted on the other. It simply starts with "profit" as the base of the tax, implicitly relying on the accounting and legal professions, in the first instance, to interpret this concept in the light of generally accepted accounting rules and conventions and the past decisions of the courts of law. Some readers will undoubtedly recall in this connection that in Bill 454, the original "test-run" version of the present Income Tax Act, there was a requirement that income from business and property be determined according to "generally accepted accounting principles." Extensive discussion and examination of this proposal uncovered serious defects in it, not the least being that accountants themselves found it difficult to agree on the nature of the principles which governed their practices. As a result the concept of "profit" was substituted.

If the corporation income tax were simply imposed on profits as the expression is understood by accountants, lawyers, and business men, there would be little more to say about the matter. Such, however, is definitely not the case. The law takes such profits as a point of departure, but considerable adjustments are made before they are regarded as acceptable for tax purposes. While "business" income and "tax" income have in recent years become more closely identified, it is unlikely that they will ever be completely synonymous.

This divergence clearly emerges in the special statutory rules prescribing the methods to be followed in bringing "business" profits into line with "tax" profits. While not all of these rules contemplate treatment different from that which would ordinarily be followed, being given only for the sake of greater certainty, in many instances the reverse is true. The nature of these adjustments is indicated roughly by the headings of the sections under which they appear. One group is headed "Amounts included in Computing Income"; another, "Amounts not included in Computing Income"; a third, "Deductions allowed in Computing Income"; and a fourth, "Deductions not allowed in Computing Income." Still others appear under the heading "Miscellaneous Rules for Computing Income."

Amounts Included and Amounts not Included

On the income or "included" side, the law has little to say of concern to corporations. As was pointed out in the previous chapter, implicit in all Canadian income tax is the understanding that it is only income that is to be taxed, not capital or capital gains. The Act hurdles all the problems inherent in this principle, and for good and sufficient reasons leaves them to be settled by the courts. It imposes a tax on income, and one may search from beginning to end without finding any mention of the fact that capital and capital gains are not taxable.

Of the items that are specifically mentioned for inclusion as income the more important are dividends, interest, income from a partnership or syndicate (a corporation can be a partner), and bad debt recoveries. Reserves set aside in the preceding year for doubtful debts and for amounts received in advance of performance must also be brought into income each year (see below).

While the list of items "not included" as income is fairly extensive for individuals, in the case of corporations it is almost non-existent. The sole provision that might have application to a corporation is the exclusion of income exempt under a statute of the Parliament of Canada, instances of which are difficult to recall.

It is not surprising that the rules governing possible deductions are much more elaborate and extensive. One assumes that this proliferation stems from the inherent eagerness of taxpayers to claim deductions and the traditional reluctance of tax gatherers to allow them.

Deductions Disallowed

The statutory provisions governing the deductions which may not be taken are in themselves an incomplete and even misleading guide. They must be interpreted in the light of the jurisprudence, but even the court decisions leave many areas in obscurity.

The first statutory rule, which is framed as a disallowance of deductions, is confusing because it is the only *general* rule in the statute referring to deductibility. It states that "No deduction shall be made in respect of (*a*) an outlay or expense except to the extent that it is made or incurred by the taxpayer for the purpose of gaining or producing income from property or a business of the taxpayer" (Section 12(1)(*a*)). This then is the prime test which all outlays must pass in order to be deductible. Most of them pass easily, since they fall within the ordinary concepts of commercial and industrial accounting, but there is a wide area of conflict between taxpayers and tax authorities as to the timing of deductions—whether they may be taken in total against the income of a year or amortized over several years—and a lesser area of difference as to the eligibility of an outlay under the basic test of "income-earning" purpose. The former has involved such issues as whether a substantial replacement of a part of a fixed asset—a chimney on a factory or an engine in a boat—represented a repair or a capital addition; the latter has evoked a variety of sophisticated arguments over a century of litigation as to the necessary degree of relationship between an expenditure and its ultimate contribution to the profit of the business. There is undoubtedly a fringe of expenditures which are essential to the establishment and operation of a business which, depending on the liberality or conservatism of one's viewpoint, could be said either to be made or not made for the "purpose of gaining or producing income." Such marginal outlays relate to the commencement, improvement, or preservation of a business and are legion. Examples include the cost of organizing a company, the cost of surveying several alternative sites prior to erection of a fixed asset thereon, the costs of litigation (e.g. under anti-combine legislation) and of legal expenses incurred for a variety of purposes, expenses incurred to obtain contracts or losses suffered as the result of cancellation of contracts, and so on.

The disposition of nearly all these questions has been left to the courts. There is a large and growing volume of Canadian litigation, nearly all of which rests on decisions of the English courts. Several excellent reviews of these decisions have appeared in Canadian literature in recent years, and the reader is referred to these for further elucidation. Suffice it to say here that most tax students, and apparently some jurists as well, are convinced that the judicial interpretations have in the past been too restrictive, and that a new and more realistic attitude toward expenses must be adopted to conform with modern business practices and principles.[1]

The second statutory rule is a disallowance of any deduction for "an outlay, loss or replacement of capital, a payment on account of capital or an allowance in respect of depreciation, obsolescence or depletion except as expressly permitted by this Part" (Section 12 (1)(*b*)).

On the surface this provision appears reasonable enough. Much capital outlay represents an investment in the sense that the asset acquired is of an enduring nature and is not consumed in the operation of the business. The typical example is land. It is therefore right that for tax purposes no deduction be allowed, although for reasons of conservative accounting a business may choose to write down the value of such an investment to a nominal amount. The typical case of capital outlays for which an allowance *is* granted is plant, machinery, and equipment, for which in Canada provision is made through the capital cost allowance system. (See p. 69.)

Unfortunately between these two extremes is a grey area in which outlays are difficult to classify either as capital or as revenue expenditures. And again in this instance the decisions have been left largely to the English courts. The classical dictum is that of Viscount Cave L.C. in *British Insulated and Helsby Cables Ltd.* v. *Atherton*, as follows: ". . . when an expenditure

---

[1] See the bibliography for recent writings, in particular, A. K. Eaton "Where Angels Fear to Tread," *Canadian Tax Journal* 7: 432 (1959).

is made, not only once and for all, but with a view to bringing into existence an asset or an advantage for the enduring benefit of a trade, I think that there is very good reason (in the absence of special circumstances leading to an opposite conclusion) for treating such an expenditure as properly attributable not to revenue but to capital."[2]

Obviously this criterion must be married to the various tests that have been evolved by the courts for determining whether or not an outlay is for a profit-making purpose, and the union has not been a very successful one. There has been a tendency for the courts to attempt first to determine whether or not the outlay is of a capital nature and, if they determine such to be the case, to take it as given that the outlay is not a necessary business expense. The more logical order would be to apply the business purpose rule first, and then the "capital" test. Even under the latter procedure, however, if the outlay were accepted as meeting the business purpose test no allowance could be made for it if it were also found to be of a capital nature unless specific provision can be found in the Income Tax Act or Regulations. Such provisions are still sufficiently restrictive that expenses now regarded as customary incidents of organizing and carrying on a business (several were mentioned above) are not covered. In this respect the present position is unsatisfactory and calls for remedy either by the enactment of new general rules or by the specific inclusion of outlays not now provided for.

Other statutory limitations on deductions disallow expenses incurred for earning exempt income; expenses which are unreasonable in amount, although qualifying as to character; amounts transferred to reserve, contingent account, or sinking fund (a principle adhered to fairly rigidly in Canadian income tax); amounts, other than rent, representing the annual value of property; payments on income bonds; amounts payable to persons not dealing at arm's length but not actually paid within a year.

A statutory rule (the full significance of which will only become apparent with experience) was enacted at the 1960 session. It purports to limit deductions for expenses to the income to which the expense was attributable in the case where the taxpayer received income from more than one source or

[2][1926] A.C. 205, at p. 213.

more than one country. It follows the decision in the Interprovincial Pipeline Case,[3] in which the Supreme Court held that the previous departmental practice was not supported by the law.

Deductions Allowed

The deductions for which positive provision is made under Section 11 are of great significance both to the taxpayer and to the tax authorities, and this section therefore has been the subject of closer study than any other part of the Act. Of the deductions permitted by this section undoubtedly the first in importance is that for capital costs, which appears in subsection (1) (*a*) in the following words: ". . . such part of the capital cost to the taxpayer of property, or such amount in respect of the capital cost to the taxpayer of property, if any, as is allowed by regulation."

It is under this provision that an allowance is granted for what is commonly known as depreciation. But in the use of the words "capital cost" and in the omission of any reference to depreciation, obsolescence, or wear and tear, lies what is probably the most significant break with tradition in the Canadian legislation. The fact that a deduction from income is to be granted a taxpayer for a capital cost incurred to earn that income represents a marked departure from the "engineering" concept of depreciation as compensation for the physical wear and tear on assets actually in use and being worn out. This concept carried with it the corollary that no allowance for depreciation could be granted unless the asset was in use, and furthermore implied that the only capital assets for which the cost might be recovered were physical assets subject to wear and tear. Some capital assets, such as patents, are not of this character at all. It is not suggested, of course, that under the new wording an allowance will be made for all capital costs (e.g., land) but at any rate authority has been given by Parliament for developing a more consistent system of allowances than was possible hitherto.

Arising directly out of this change in concept a radically new system of allowances for capital costs was introduced in 1949 to

[3]Sup. Ct. 59 D.T.C. 1229.

RESIDENT CORPORATIONS   69

replace the former depreciation allowances. The main characteristics of this new system are:

(a) An annual deduction is allowed for the capital cost of an asset whether or not it is being used in earning the income from the business. This plan guarantees the recovery of capital costs from profits and, in effect, grants an allowance for obsolescent or discarded machinery and plant by allowing its original cost to be recovered even though the asset has ceased to be used in the business.

(b) A counterpart of this unconditional allowance for capital cost is that when a taxpayer realizes a value from the sale or other disposition of a capital asset, the amount so realized must be offset against the capital cost allowance which he may claim in the future against assets of that class. The effect therefore is that the value the taxpayer has recovered by the sale may not again be recovered through a deduction from income. This offset against future depreciation is restricted to a maximum amount equal to the original capital cost of the asset; in short, no account is taken of a "capital gain" derived from the sale of an asset at a price in excess of its original capital cost. Where the amount so recovered by a sale exceeds the value yet to be depreciated of assets of that class ("undepreciated value") the excess may in most cases be spread back over the preceding five years. To preclude any tax on the "capital" gain no amount is taken back into income under such circumstances in excess of the amount of depreciation already taken for that asset.

In making a transition to the new plan the capital cost of assets owned by the taxpayer prior to 1949 was taken as the written down ("undepreciated") value at the beginning of the 1949 taxation year, and recapture applies only to capital cost allowances taken after that time. Exceptions to this general rule are made for certain assets on which accelerated depreciation was granted during and after the war; the original intention that there be a recapture of excess depreciation on the sale of such assets has been carried forward under the new system.

(c) The expression "class of assets," used in the above paragraphs, represents a change of some significance in accounting practice for income tax purposes adopted as part of the new plan.

Hitherto there were numerous separate rates for individual types of depreciable assets. These items have now been sorted out into main classes, with a uniform rate applying to the whole of each class.[4] At the same time the diminishing balance system of amortization was introduced, accompanied by an approximate doubling of the rates of write-off. The establishment of classes of assets simplified amortization procedure for tax purposes and facilitated the process of adjusting for the proceeds of disposals. The amount recovered from the disposal of any capital asset is offset against the write-off remaining to be taken for that whole class of assets. In principle the method also represents a departure from the past consistent with the new concept of amortization. No longer are pieces of machinery being "depreciated"; rather the capital cost of assets of approximately the same life is being recovered in computing the profits of the business.

The "recapture" of depreciation has the effect of creating taxable income for the vendor, frequently in substantial amounts, and as a result a new and frequential crucial factor has been introduced in negotiations between purchasers and vendors of fixed assets. The vendor will strive for the lowest valuation of fixed assets and the highest for other assets in order to minimize recapture; the purchaser will strive for the reverse in order to obtain the greatest possible capital cost for write-off. Where purchaser and vendor are not dealing at arm's length, however, this factor does not enter, since the purchaser is allowed to claim as his capital cost only the original cost to the vendor less depreciation taken by the vendor.

In a special budget late in 1960 the Minister of Finance announced a plan for the use of accelerated depreciation for economic stimulus. Double depreciation would be allowed to the taxpayer in 1961, 1962, or 1963 at his option in respect of fixed assets acquired in 1961 for three purposes: (1) to assist new industries "in areas where there is a substantial degree of continued unemployment over the years"; (2) to aid the development of "new products from processing operations not hitherto carried on in Canada"; and (3) to "encourage the production

[4]For the actual classes and the rates of write-off see the Appendix. See also special allowances under Maritime Coal Production Assistance Act and Canadian Vessel Construction Assistance Act.

RESIDENT CORPORATIONS

of new types of goods." Applications for certification for the special allowance are to be addressed to the Minister of Trade and Commerce.

A further step in the same direction was taken in the budget of June 1961. As an incentive for new capital expenditure an increase of 50 per cent in the capital cost allowances otherwise available is to be granted in the first year in respect of new expenditures incurred between June 20, 1961 and March 31, 1963. Such new expenditures will be eligible for the accelerated allowance to the extent that they exceed the lesser of the average expenditures in the last three complete fiscal years or the last year alone of the company prior to June 20, 1961.

In neither of these instances of accelerated depreciation is the total that may be taken to exceed 100 per cent of the cost of the asset.

The "depletion" allowance for a mine or other wasting asset is now granted under 11 (1) (b), which reads: "Such amount as an allowance in respect of an oil or gas well, mine or timber limit, if any, as is allowed to the taxpayer by regulation." With a few important exceptions these allowances are granted in perpetuity. One allowance is granted to the company operating the property and a second is granted to the shareholder on his dividends. The operator's allowance is in most cases expressed as a percentage of income, and the shareholder's allowance is always expressed as a percentage of the dividend.

The rates of allowance for operators are as follows:[5]

(a) *Oil and gas wells:* Operator, 33 1/3 per cent; royalty holder or other person having an interest in the proceeds, 25 per cent.

(b) *Base and precious metal mines:* Operator, 33 1/3 per cent, except that where value of output is 70 per cent or more from gold the operator may take the greater of 40 per cent or $4.00 per ounce.

(c) *Industrial mineral mines (excluding coal):* Operator, 33 1/3 per cent.

(d) *Coal mines:* Operator, 10 cents per ton of coal mined in the year.

Shareholders of companies operating such properties (except

[5]For exact details see Part XII, Income Tax Regulations.

coal mines) are given an allowance varying with the proportion of the company's total income derived from such operations.

The rates established for this purpose are: 20 per cent where 75 per cent or more of the income is from such sources, 15 per cent where 50 per cent to 74 per cent of the income is from such sources, and 10 per cent where 25 per cent to 49 per cent of the income is from such sources.

Other deductions allowed under Section 11 include interest for borrowed money used in the business or in connection with the purchase of property acquired for the business (a deduction otherwise prohibited as an outlay on account of capital), limited outlays for costs of share issue, contributions to an employees' pension plan approved by the Taxation Division (not exceeding $1,500 a year per employee for current services), contributions to make up a deficit in a pension plan, and contributions to an employees' profit-sharing plan and a supplementary unemployment benefit plan. Expenditures on scientific research in Canada, including contributions to a scientific research foundation, may also be deducted in full in the year incurred.

Insurance companies other than life may take a deduction for rebates to policy holders and all companies are allowed a deduction for patronage dividends under the general plan adopted following the Royal Commission inquiry into this contentious phase of taxation.[6]

A group of allowances of significance to the extractive industries are the deductions for "off-property" exploration expenses incurred in searching for minerals, petroleum, or natural gas. The deduction of exploration expenses was limited before the war to expenses incurred for the extension of a known ore body or oil structure; it was not allowed when exploration was "off property." For a time during and following the war this extra allowance was granted by an annual extension, but is now a permanent part of the law. The legislation is unique in that it permits an unlimited carry-over of undeducted amounts against income of later years. In 1953 a deduction for the cost of abandoned lands was also provided.

Until 1953 the deductions for oil exploration were granted only to a company engaged in producing, refining, or marketing

[6]See p. 78.

petroleum, the deductions for mining exploration only to mining companies, but since then mining companies have been allowed to deduct expenses incurred in searching for oil, and vice versa. Provision is now made also for the carry-over of undeducted expenses into an oil company which acquires another oil company by amalgamation through acquisition of shares.

Another deduction of interest to the extractive industries is that granted for taxes paid to a province or municipality specifically on income from mining and logging operations where these come within the requirements established by regulation.

Of more general interest to taxpayers in business is the treatment provided under the new Act for bad and doubtful debts. In each year a deduction may be taken for a reserve for doubtful debts but this reserve must be brought into income in the following year and a new reserve established, based on the experience of the new year. There is also a deduction for bad debts actually written off, but any recoveries made on these debts in a later year must be included with income in that later year. In effect, therefore, there is an annual reappraisal of the reserve for doubtful debts, with the net change representing an addition to or a deduction from income. If recoveries are made for bad debts they must be included in income. The treatment is also applied for amounts set aside which represent income received in advance of performance or to be held for a temporary period, such as sales of milk, bread, transportation, and other tickets, deposits on containers, and so on.

An important rule provided in the statute itself requires the valuation of inventory at the lower of cost or fair market value, or in such other manner as may be permitted by regulation. No alternative methods have been allowed by regulation, and as a result LIFO and similar variations have not been recognized for tax purposes in Canada. Even an appeal to the Privy Council (*M.N.R.* v. *Anaconda American Brass Limited*) failed to achieve recognition for LIFO.

Other miscellaneous statutory rules provide for the restoration to fair market value of transactions between persons not at arm's length at a price other than fair market; for the treatment of outlays under a lease-option, hire-purchase agreement (in general the deduction is limited to the amount that could be claimed if the lessee were the owner of the property); the sale of accounts receivable, the sale of inventory, and the deduction of special reserves for banks and mortgage companies.

The "non-arm's length" concept of the Income Tax Act deserves special mention because of the frequency with which it overrules the ordinary provisions. In general individuals who are related (by blood, marriage, or adoption) and corporations where there is common control, either direct or indirect, by related persons, are deemed not to deal with each other at arm's length. In other cases it is a question of fact. Blood relationship, marriage, and adoption are given statutory definition, and the statute provides for several combinations and permutations of control among corporations.

The instances where the "non-arm's length" rule is employed with greatest effect are the recapture of depreciation, the reduced rate of corporate income tax, and the adjustment of transactions between individuals and corporations. It is also given other uses, as an examination of the statute will disclose.

Taxable Income

As was indicated earlier, all of the foregoing are rules which must be taken into account in adjusting the profits of the business, as determined by recognized accounting methods, to conform with the requirements of the Income Tax Act. This is the first and major step towards calculating the tax. However, certain further deductions are allowed to a corporation in determining the income on which its tax is actually calculated.

These deductions are not numerous, but they are significant. One of the items to be included with income, as mentioned above, is dividends from other corporations. While such dividends must be included in the original reckoning of income they are not, in fact, taxable in the hands of a corporation if received from another Canadian corporation that has paid tax. All such dividends are deducted therefore in determining the taxable income. By an amendment in force since 1950, however, this exemption was restricted where one Canadian company obtains control of another Canadian company after May 10, 1950. In these circumstances the inter-company dividend exemption is

RESIDENT CORPORATIONS				75

limited to the earnings of the controlled company from the time control was assumed, all prior earnings becoming known as "designated surplus." The significance of this change is discussed later in this chapter.

Another allowance in the computation of taxable profits is the deduction of losses. Within limits prescribed in the Act a corporation may now carry forward a loss for five years and deduct it against the income of a later taxation year, or it may carry back a loss of the year immediately succeeding the tax year. The effect of these "carry-over" provisions is to average the income over a much longer term than the annual accounting period of twelve months. Since 1958 the law has barred the carry-over where control of the loss company has changed during the taxation year and where the company ceased to carry on the business in which the loss was sustained.

Corporations, like individuals, are allowed a deduction for charitable donations up to 10 per cent of income. Undeducted amounts may be carried over to the succeeding year.

The method followed in taxing life insurance companies in Canada differs so greatly from the normal rules for corporations that it requires a special rule in the section of the Act devoted to the calculation of taxable income. In general, taxable income of life insurance companies is the net amount credited to shareholders' account during the year, subject to certain deductions. The exact method of determining the taxable income is set forth in the Act.

Rates of Tax

The tax rates in the case of corporations apply to the income of the taxation year, which is the fiscal year of the corporation ending in the calendar year to which the respective provisions of the Act apply. It is now the practice to change the rate as at December 31 and portions of the year falling on one side or the other are taxed accordingly.

For 1961 the rates of corporation profit tax are 18 per cent on the first $35,000 and 47 per cent on the excess. In addition an Old Age Security tax of 3 per cent is levied, giving total rates of 21 per cent and 50 per cent respectively.

The following is a summary of the rates that have applied over the last decade:

Year	Rates (*including old age security tax*)
1949	10% on first $10,000
	33% on excess over $10,000
1952	22% on first $10,000
	52% on excess over $10,000
1953 and 1954	20% on first $20,000
	49% on excess over $20,000
1955 to 1957	20% on first $20,000
	47% on excess over $20,000
1958	20% on first $25,000
	47% on excess over $25,000
1959 and 1960	21% on first $25,000
	50% on excess over $25,000
1961	21% on first $35,000
	50% on excess over $35,000

Corporations subject to tax in Ontario or Quebec are allowed a reduction of tax equal to 9 per cent of income (or 10 per cent where an extra tax is levied by a province for financing universities; Quebec is the only such province) allocated to those provinces under federal rules of allocation. (See chap. IX.)

For certain public utilities (gas, electric, steam) the general rate is reduced to 45 per cent on profit from specified sources.

The right at one time granted to Canadian corporations to file a consolidated return is no longer available. It was withdrawn in 1951.

The introduction of a graduated rate for corporations in 1949 was an innovation in the Dominion tax structure. The lower rate may be taken by only one company in a group of companies having common control or which are related under the non-arm's length concept. The general test for control is ownership or control of 51 per cent or more of the shares. Corporations owned by persons not dealing at arm's length (e.g., brothers, father and son, husband and wife, etc.) are deemed to be related except where there is no common ownership of shares.

Payment of Tax

In Canada corporations have been on an instalment basis for tax payment for years, although it is a different basis from that for individuals. Corporations are required to estimate the profits of their fiscal year six months before the end of that year; they then commence to pay tax in monthly instalments based on their estimate at that time. After nine monthly instalments their fiscal year will have closed and thenceforth they are expected to pay three more monthly instalments representing the balance of the actual tax payable on profits for the year. Penalties are imposed for paying less than the legal amount.

Returns must be filed within six months following the end of the fiscal year of the company, as compared with four months for individuals. The return accompanies the last of the twelve instalments.

Exempt Corporations

Hitherto only the ordinary garden variety of corporation that is resident and carrying on business in Canada has been discussed. There are also special forms of corporate enterprise which have been recognized either by total exemption from tax or by the granting of a special tax status.

Of the totally exempt class the more important are corporations having 90 per cent of their capital owned by a province or municipality, non-profit organizations operated exclusively for social welfare, recreation, or any other purpose except profit, charitable organizations (as defined), boards of trade, chambers of commerce, labour organizations and fraternal benefit societies, and mutual insurance corporations receiving premiums wholly from the insurance of churches, schools, and other charitable organizations. Corporations organized as credit unions carrying on business in only one province have also been extended tax freedom. Federally owned corporations, previously exempt, are now taxable.

Mining companies are granted an exemption from tax during the first three years after coming into production. A similar exemption for three years is granted to new co-operatives.

A personal corporation,[7] which may be described loosely as a family investment-holding company, is exempt from corporation tax, but its income is deemed to be fully distributed each year to the shareholders and is taxed as personal income. Such a corporation loses this status if it carries on any active business.

A tax on only 18 per cent is levied on an investment company, an organization that must have at least fifty shareholders, none of whom holds more than 25 per cent of the shares. It is required to hold 80 per cent of its property in shares, bonds, marketable securities, or cash, to receive 95 per cent of its income from this form of investment but no more than 50 per cent from interest, and to distribute 85 per cent of its income before the end of its fiscal year. Dividends from such companies qualify for the dividend tax credit. A further requirement mooted in a late 1960 budget is that at least three-quarters of gross revenue be in dividends from Canadian companies. Companies not in this position were to be allowed to achieve it in stages in the years 1961 and 1962.

Taxation of Co-operative and Mutual Organizations

The treatment of co-operatives and similar mutual organizations under the income tax law deserves special comment since it has characteristics that are peculiarly Canadian. The present treatment is substantially that recommended in the 1945 report of the Royal Commission on Co-operatives. Canadian co-operatives, which are mainly producers' organizations in the wheat and other agricultural industries, had been exempt from tax under the former Section 4 (*p*) of the Income War Tax Act. This fact, combined with their expansion during the war period, when burdensome tax rates were retarding other forms of business, stimulated a public demand for an inquiry and the appointment of the Royal Commission resulted.

The substance of the Commission's recommendations (one of whose members was a leading exponent of co-operative principles) was that the special status of co-operatives should be abolished and that instead all corporations should be granted the privilege of deducting from their income for tax purposes patronage dividends paid to customers.

[7] See G. McGregor, *Personal Corporations*.

In adopting this recommendation, the government introduced one modification. Any corporation claiming a deduction for patronage dividends could not thereby reduce its taxable income below 3 per cent of the capital employed in the business. The explanation given by the Minister of Finance, Hon. J. L. Ilsley, in his 1946 Budget Speech, for introducing this modification was: "The principle underlying this rule is that amounts set aside out of taxable income to be distributed in proportion to patronage by a co-operative or company which does not pay at least three per cent on the capital employed in its business contain earnings which arise from the employment of capital and ought not to escape entirely."

Against this 3 per cent may be offset any interest paid as a return on capital to the shareholders, and tax need only be paid on the balance not so offset. As a result any corporation, co-operative or otherwise, that pays to its shareholders 3 per cent on the capital employed in the business and distributes the balance of its income in patronage dividends, has no taxable income. Any amount not so distributed is taxable income.

Certain conditions surround the deductibility of patronage dividends. One is that the corporation must have held forth the prospect that dividends would be paid, either in its charter of incorporation, in its contracts with its customers, or by advertisement in a newspaper prior to the commencement of the year of taxation. In general they must be allocated in the taxation year or within twelve months thereafter, in such a form that the customer either receives payment or is entitled to receive payment. The deduction for income tax purposes is for payments on such an allocation. Payments are deemed to be made where there is an actual cash settlement, where certificates of indebtedness are issued for current allocations and matched in the same year by cash redemptions of previous certificates, or where, on application of the customer, the amount is left with the corporation to meet a liability of the customer to the corporation. The law does not require that members and non-members be treated equally, however, and payments for patronage dividends may be deducted where a discrimination has been made in favour of members.

Patronage dividends are included as customer income in the

year of payment, or, where a certificate of indebtedness was taken in lieu of payment, the value of the certificate must be included as income in the year of receipt of the certificate. Patronage dividends on goods purchased for consumption other than in a business are not taxable income—these generally are the dividends paid by the "consumer co-op's."

It was mentioned previously that any new corporations organized as co-operatives are exempt from income tax for their first three years.

The Royal Commission dealt also with related forms of organization, including mutual insurance companies (fire, casualty, and automobile) and credit unions. Both groups were exempt from tax under the law as it existed at the time of the study. At the present time, and pursuant to the Commission's recommendations, such insurance companies are taxable, while credit unions that derive their income primarily from loans to members continue to be exempt. A deduction is allowed to the insurance companies for dividends or refunds to policy-holders or unabsorbed premiums or premium deposits returned or made payable to policy-holders.

Some Tax Problems Arising out of the Relationship between a Corporation and Its Shareholders

So far this chapter has dealt with the manner in which income is taxed when earned by a corporation. Nothing has yet been said of the broad implications of the fact that despite its separate legal personality a corporation in reality does not earn income on its own behalf. It earns it rather on behalf of its owners, the shareholders, to whom, in the final reckoning, belong all the income and property of the corporation remaining after its full liabilities have been met. The fact that a corporation is a perpetual person and, unless dissolved, can hold property of its own to eternity does not alter the fact that it earns income on behalf of its owners.

This "dual personality" of incorporated businesses has invited taxation of income both when earned by the corporation and when received by the shareholder. This is the Canadian and American system as contrasted with the British system under which (until the introduction of the Profits Tax) the whole amount paid by the corporation was treated as a prepayment of the shareholders' tax, and not as an additional tax. A great deal of thought has been given both in Canada and in the United States in recent years to the effects of this so-called "double taxation," and it is generally conceded that one result is to make investment in equities less attractive. Another likely result, arising from the fact that interest on bonds is allowed as a deductable business expense while dividends on shares are not so allowed, is that it tends to encourage loan rather than equity financing by corporations.

Neither these nor the other alleged effects of double taxation are capable of proof or verification, however, and one's acceptance of them depends almost entirely on one's view as to the ultimate incidence of the corporation income tax. Some economists and business men assert that it is the consumer and not the shareholder who bears the tax, but this assertion is extremely difficult to prove. There appears to be a general view that all or most of the tax falls initially on the shareholder, and that the double taxation inevitably has an influence on the attitude of shareholders or prospective shareholders towards investment in equity capital. In Canada a step has been taken toward removal of this "double-tax" feature of the existing structure, which will be described below.

If every corporation distributed its total profits to its shareholders each year as they were earned, no further serious problem in this field of complex relationships would arise. This they do not do, however. Many corporations each year hold back a substantial portion of their earnings, to meet their requirements for working and fixed capital or for other reasons. Each additional increment of such retained profits increases the amount of the undistributed earned surplus of the corporation, and the equity of the shareholders represented by this accumulated undistributed income is frequently found to amount to several times the equity represented by their original subscribed capital.

While such profits are often retained within the corporate structure for justifiable business purposes the ultimate tax ramifications of this action are to postpone personal income tax on the money so retained. However, by the same token, where any amount representing the accumulation of several years enters the stream of taxation in a lump sum in one year, the tax payable under graduated rates will be much greater than if the same amount had been taxed in segments over a period of years. Any event, therefore, which occasions the distribution of substantial earnings accumulated in a corporation over a period of time brings the full shock of progressive rates to bear.

The difficulties inherent in this position are most acute for the owners of closely held corporations whose shares are not generally marketable. The shareholder of a large corporation can in effect "liquidate" his equity, including his portion of the undistributed income to the extent reflected in the market value of his shares, by a sale in the open market. But the shareholder of a closely held corporation with undistributed income on hand does not normally have access to a market for his shares and can obtain cash only by receiving a dividend from the company. When it becomes necessary to distribute all or a substantial portion of the accumulated income at one time, as must be done sometimes on the death of a principal shareholder, the tax blow may be severe. As indicated above, it will normally be considerably in excess of the tax that would have been paid had the income been distributed when earned.

The tax effects of this "lumping-up" of income are encountered by the shareholders of any corporation, large or small, on its winding-up, when a dividend is deemed to be received to the extent of the undistributed income on hand. In reality this again is an acute question only for the smaller corporation, since the large, widely held public companies seldom terminate their affairs.

The problem arising from the fact that the stream of income is taxed before and after it reaches the shareholder has been described as "double taxation." The problem that is encountered when the stream is dammed up and then drained out in a spurt, will be labelled, for want of a better generic title, "undistributed income." In reality they are basically the same, the second representing only an exaggerated manifestation of the first.

A third class of problem arises out of the fact that both the tax structure and the complex nature of corporate financing lend themselves to devices by which undistributed income may be withdrawn from a corporation either as capital or as a nontaxable dividend to another corporation. In either case, if no contrary provisions were made in the law, no tax would be encountered.

The most obvious and effective of such transactions, of course, is simply to redeem the capital stock of the company, thus liquidating all the assets, including the undistributed income. This is the final and effective act, and puts cash directly into the hands of the shareholders, not as income but as a distribution of property. But other transactions, less decisive than a final winding-up, are also of concern to the tax authorities when a company has undistributed income on hand. A principal one is the rearrangement of the capital structure in such a way that a larger claim on the assets of the company is given to some shareholders than to others. Another is the "capitalization" of the undistributed income of the corporation by its transfer from surplus account to legal capital account on the books of the corporation. All that is legally required to effect such "capitalization" is the book entry itself, but the shareholders are usually given evidence of the transaction by the issuance of a stock dividend in proportion to their former holdings. By this simple device a claim of the shareholder on the corporation is reduced from one that would yield him taxable income if satisfied through the normal channel of the dividend route to one that, in the absence of any contrary provision in the law, would provide a tax-exempt payment if satisfied by the redemption of shares.

One marked distinction between the outright redemption of capital stock and the sort of device just mentioned is that the former actually places cash in the hands of the shareholder while the latter only alters the character of funds which the shareholder has a right to receive at some indefinite time in the future. The practical problem faced by legislators in drawing up law to cover this situation is whether to attempt to take a tax at the time that the character of the claim changes, or to run the risk of waiting for an actual distribution of funds and attempting to tax then. Under Canadian law, as the subsequent explanation will reveal, the first alternative has been favoured.

Finally, a word regarding the relationship to this problem of tax-free inter-company dividends. The fact that a dividend can be declared from one company to another without payment of further corporation tax has provided an avenue for the withdrawal of undistributed income under a few basically simple devices. The net result of all such transactions, which will not be discussed in detail here, is to provide the original owners of the company having the surplus with payment for it, or a substantial part of it, in the form of a payment for property, and as such not subject to income tax.

The manner in which these troublesome aspects of company-shareholder relationships are dealt with under the Canadian personal income tax can be given only scant justice in the brief space available. The following summary of present treatment is offered with apologies for its inadequacy.

Since 1949 recognition has been given the presence of double taxation through a dividend tax credit. Under this plan a taxpayer may take a credit against his personal income tax for dividends received from a taxable Canadian corporation equal to 20 per cent of the amount of the dividends. Thus, where dividends are received from a corporation subject only to the reduced rate "double taxation" is eliminated, a result consistent with the original objective, among others, of assisting smaller businesses.

With regard to undistributed income the *general* rule under the Canadian income tax law is that such amounts are taxable when dispersed. This follows simply because all dividends of an operating company, whether paid out of current or past earnings or (because of the virtual impossibility of distinguishing them) paid out of capital or a capital surplus, are taxed as income when received. In general on the winding-up of a company only accumulated earnings are taxed; other distributions are treated as a return of capital or capital surplus.

RESIDENT CORPORATIONS   85

The *general* rule governing the position of undistributed surpluses has been drastically altered, however, by various special provisions. Under the principal of these, a company may at any time pay a tax of 15 per cent on its total undistributed income on hand at the end of its 1949 taxation year. Once having paid tax on this amount, it may pay at any time thereafter a tax of 15 per cent on its undistributed income on hand accumulated after its 1949 taxation year, provided that it has paid out an equal amount of dividends in the same period. Such undistributed income then becomes "tax-paid undistributed income," and is excluded from the calculation of undistributed income for any other purposes of the Act.

The effect of this is that, following any event which under the Act results in a dividend being deemed to be received by the shareholder when there is undistributed income on hand, such as winding-up, share redemption, capitalization, etc., such tax-paid undistributed income will be disregarded in the calculation of the amount of the dividend deemed to be received. If all the undistributed income is tax-paid any of these actions may be taken with no further tax payable by the shareholder. An ordinary dividend, however, will continue to be taxable, even when paid by a company having a wholly tax-paid surplus.

Where a corporation has undistributed income on hand, the following transactions are taken as payment of a dividend to a shareholder: (*a*) the redemption or acquisition of any of its common stock; (*b*) the reduction of its common stock; (*c*) the conversion of any of its common stock into other types of shares or into a debt of the corporation; (*d*) the capitalization of undistributed income. A corporation is deemed to have capitalized undistributed income where it has paid a stock dividend or increased its paid-up capital in other specified ways. Any of these transactions ordinarily results in the imputation to the shareholder of a taxable dividend, but to the extent that the surplus on hand is "tax paid" to the same extent the dividend is exempt from personal income tax to the shareholder.

Various other transactions between company and shareholder are also subject to special tax treatment. The premium paid on redemption or acquisition of preferred shares is exempt in the hands of the shareholder, but for shares issued since February 19, 1953 the corporation must pay a special tax of either 20 per cent or 30 per cent of the amount of the premium, the rate depending on whether the premium was less or more than 10 per cent of the par value.

Loans to shareholders under certain conditions are deemed to be dividends for which no dividend tax credit is allowed, as are other benefits conferred on shareholders by the corporation.

All the above devices are means of giving direct alleviation of the sharp edge of the progressive income tax by substituting a levy paid by the corporation. Since 1950 the law has also included a preventative measure intended to prevent the complete escape of personal income tax through an inter-company dividend and a subsequent winding-up of the receiving company. This measure is known as the "designated surplus" provision, and its main effect is to make taxable at full corporate rates inter-company dividends received from a controlled corporation acquired after May 10, 1950 to the extent of the undistributed surplus on hand at the time control was acquired. This penalty is so severe that it closed the original loop-hole; in practice it is alleviated by having the subsidiary pay the 15 per cent tax on its pre-1949 undistributed surplus before acquisition and pass that surplus tax-free to the parent, which can in turn make a tax-free distribution (through the channels described above) to its own shareholders. A variety of other devices have also been employed, including the redemption of shares through an investment dealer, for which the law provides a 20 per cent charge on the corporation having the designated surplus.

The fact that dividends could be withdrawn free of tax or at a low rate under some of Canada's foreign tax treaties also offered an opportunity for a time of withdrawing designated surplus to another country without tax penalty. This chance was removed by the enactment of a tax of 15 per cent on the corporation having the designated surplus.

The latest major change in the law having a bearing on the transfer of surpluses between corporations is a new series of provisions codifying the consequences of a statutory merger of two or more corporations. Such mergers are possible under the company laws of Ontario, Quebec, New Brunswick, Manitoba, and possibly one or two other provinces, but not as yet under the Dominion Company Act. The tax effect of a merger is that any surplus previously "designated" in the prior corporations ceases to be so in the new entity. A fault in the drafting of the first version of the law made it possible so to arrange the capital structure of the new entity that all undistributed surplus could be withdrawn free of tax through the redemption of preferred shares. A later amendment has imposed a tax penalty, payable by the corporation, of 20 per cent on the undistributed surplus so withdrawn from the corporation.

The proliferation of special provisions relating to corporate surpluses had led to a general request for a complete review of this aspect of the law. Such a review was promised by the Minister of Finance in his 1960 Budget Speech, but no action was taken in the Budget Speech of a year later.

SUMMARY

RATES. On and after January 1, 1961, the rates of tax, including the old age security tax of 3 per cent, are 21 per cent on the first $35,000 and 50 per cent on the excess. Again this a tax rebate will be allowed equal to 9 per cent of income allocated to Ontario and 10 per cent of income allocated to Quebec.

REVENUE

	Fiscal Year 1959–60 ($000)	Percentage of tax revenue	Percentage of total revenue
Corporation income tax[1]	1,142,880	24.0	21.6
Old age security tax	91,336	—	—

[1]Includes revenue from 15 per cent tax on undistributed income.

STATUTORY REFERENCES. Income Tax Act, Revised Statutes, Canada, 1952, c. 148; Old Age Security Act, *ibid.*, c. 200; Regulations issued by Order in Council.

Chapter 4

DOMINION INCOME TAX
NON-RESIDENTS AND FOREIGN INCOME OF RESIDENTS

IN THE PRECEDING CHAPTERS attention has been focussed on the application of the Dominion income tax to individuals and corporations resident in Canada. These are, of course, the main sources of income tax revenue. The tax also applies, however, in various ways to other individuals and corporations not resident in Canada, and as well to foreign income of Canadian residents. These miscellaneous aspects not previously covered will be dealt with in the present chapter.

Since the inception of the Dominion income tax in 1917 non-residents carrying on an activity in Canada have been subject to tax at graduated rates on the income from that activity. In addition a withholding tax at 5 per cent (now 15 per cent) was introduced in 1933 on payments to non-residents not carrying on an activity in Canada (interest, dividends, rents, etc.).

Non-Residents

Non-residents subject to Canadian income tax fall generally into two main classes: first, those who carry on an activity in Canada (either a business activity or the performance of personal services), and, second, those who receive income from Canada without carrying on any activity here. For convenience the first group will be divided into (i) those who carry on business activities and (ii) those who perform personal services.

Income from Business Activities

Business activities performed directly in Canada by non-residents are carried on for the most part by branches of foreign corporations. An enormous volume of business is carried on indirectly in Canada by foreign corporations through their subsidiaries in this country, but this is not of concern in the present context since the subsidiaries would themselves in most cases be classed as Canadian residents and taxed accordingly. The main consequence of the foreign ownership of these Canadian residents is to create some special problems in tax administration. Particularly is it necessary for the tax authorities to be on guard against any artificial transactions between the subsidiary and the parent that are designed to reduce the profits of the subsidiary subject to Canadian taxes. Every effort is made, therefore, to correct the effect of transactions not on an arm's length basis in determining the profits of the subsidiary in Canada.

The foreign corporation operating through a branch in Canada presents a different problem. The Income Tax Act imposes a tax on such a corporation in respect of the proportion of its total income that may reasonably be attributed to the activities carried on through its Canadian branch. The law provides no fixed rules by which the income is to be allocated to the Canadian activities (such as are found in the provincial corporation income tax acts), and such allocation undoubtedly is based on the accepted practices of individual taxpayers, the rulings of the administration, and the decisions of the Tax Appeal Board and the Exchequer Court. The extensive litigation on the concept of "carrying on business" also assists both taxpayer and tax authority in determining liability.

Apart from the statute, the provisions of our tax treaties with the United States, the United Kingdom, and several other countries also have an important bearing on the taxation of foreign businesses operating in Canada. Such tax treaties or conventions often have the effect of modifying national laws that would otherwise apply to international businesses. Scores of them are now in force throughout the world and their pattern is becoming increasingly standardized. The general principles on which they are based have been developing slowly over the years. The League of Nations Fiscal Committee, by drafting a model treaty, did much to advance consideration of international tax problems, and at the same time the increasing familiarity of tax experts with these problems has also led to considerable progress in this field. At the present time (1960) Canada has tax treaties with France, Sweden, New Zealand, Ireland, Denmark, Germany, Netherlands, South Africa, Australia, Finland, Belgium, and Norway.

Because of our close and active commercial relations with the United States and the United Kingdom our tax treaties with these countries are of particular importance. These have a similar pattern. A cardinal principle of both is that one contracting country agrees to tax the profits of a business enterprise of the other contracting country only when that business enterprise has a "permanent establishment" in the territory of the other country. Another principle is that where there is a permanent establishment tax will be imposed only on "industrial or commercial profits," as distinct from investment and other income, and only on such profits as may be attributed to the trade or business carried on in the territory of the other contracting party. The result is that, where a business enterprise of one country has a permanent establishment in the other country, the first country binds itself under the treaty to tax only the industrial or commercial profits of the foreign enterprise that may be allocated to that permanent establishment. There are thus two basic factors that govern: first, the presence of a permanent establishment, and, second, the determination of the industrial or commercial profits attributable to that permanent establishment.

The concept of the permanent establishment is therefore an integral and essential part of the taxation of international business income under the tax treaties. Presumably the reasoning behind its adoption is that the tax authorities of a country would have difficulty in enforcing the collection of tax from a foreign business unless the business had some property or assets within its boundaries. It also recognizes the common-sense view that if a company does have an office or factory in a country there is a fairly strong presumption that it is earning income in that country.

In the Canada–U.S. treaty permanent establishment includes "branches, mines and oil wells, farms, timber lands, plantations, factories, workshops, warehouses, offices, agencies and other fixed places of business of an enterprise." Not included is a subsidiary corporation or an office used exclusively for the purchase of goods or merchandise within the other country. No definition, however, can remove all the problems of interpretation. Some of the more doubtful cases arise between countries which are as close neighbours as Canada and the United States. The travelling circus, for example, using hundreds of thousands of dollars' worth of equipment, enters Canada from the United States, tours the populated areas for several weeks or months and leaves again, after deriving considerable income from Canada. Is the circus a "permanent establishment" in Canada? Another example is that of an American oil exploration company which sends into Canada a crew of men and an array of expensive equipment to spend a year or two roaming over a lease of land looking for oil areas. The fees for such work are high and considerable income is earned from this activity in Canada, even though the only "establishment" here may be a permanent mailing address at an hotel. A third example is the large American construction company that may be engaged in Canada for two or three years on some building project. A fourth is the American aeroplane hired by a Canadian farmer for a considerable fee to dust his fields with insect killer, the aeroplane not making a landing in Canada during the flight. Are the oil crew, the construction project, and the aeroplane "permanent establishments"? The Supplementary Convention of June 12, 1950, with the United States gave answers to several of these questions by providing that the use of substantial equipment or machinery within the country constitutes a permanent establishment.

Problems also arise where the establishment itself definitely comes within the list of those described as permanent but is occupied by the foreign enterprise only for a fairly short period. The question then is: how short a period of ownership or occupation will bring such an establishment into the "permanent" classification?

The expression "industrial and commercial profits" is defined mainly by exclusion, since it is agreed that certain forms of income such as dividends, interest, rents or royalties, management charges, or remuneration for labour or personal services will not be regarded as profits. This exclusion is subject to the reservation that some payments, for example interest, will be regarded as "industrial or commercial profits" where they arise from carrying on a business activity such as banking. The same rule would apply to a company that obtained its income from the business of providing personal services, even though income from personal services is not normally regarded as "industrial or commercial profits." In general it is left to the operation of the internal tax law in each country to determine the nature of taxable profits. Our tax agreement with the United States, for example, does not affect the right of that country to tax as profits the capital gains of Canadians doing business there, even though Canada has no comparable form of tax.

Among the more complex problems are those encountered in determining the income of the permanent establishment. Like the Act itself the treaties contain no rules by which the allocation is to be made, and this is left to be governed by the law or practices of each country. One of the most common practices, and probably the most defensible method, is simply to tax the profits shown by the accounts of the permanent establishment. The treaties authorize the contracting parties to make whatever adjustment of these accounts may be necessary to have them reflect the true picture of profits attributable to the permanent establishment.

In some businesses, however, accounting procedures between head office and branch are such that it is impossible to put them on the basis that would exist were they separate and independent persons. It is often necessary, therefore, to employ whatever basis of allocation may be reasonable in the circumstances. Income is frequently allocated in the same ratio that sales in or revenue from each country bear to the total sales or revenue of the business. This formula presents some difficulties, not the least of which is the exact determination of the place of the sale, a question that has been the subject of considerable litigation. A theoretical objection to this formula is that it allocates to the country in which the sale is made all of the profit from the sale, whereas in fact a part of the profit may have been a manufacturing profit earned in another country. Attempts have been made to meet this shortcoming by introducing other factors in combination with gross sales or gross revenue. These other factors include the value of fixed assets, salaries and wages, capital invested, number of employees, and so on. No single formula fits every case. It is understandable, therefore, that a great variety of rules exists.[1] Under the United States Internal Revenue Code, which, in contrast to the Canadian Income Tax Act, provides statutory rules, there are three principal bases of allocation. These include separate accounting, independent factory price (where goods are sold on an arm's length basis between the factory and the selling branch in the foreign country), and an allocation based on the ratio of property and gross sales in the United States to the companies' total property and gross sales.

Because of the special problems involved in taxing shipping and transportation companies, different methods are usually employed here. Under the Income Tax Act Canada exempts the earnings of companies that are residents of another country, even though they may have a permanent establishment in Canada, if the other country reciprocates by not taxing the earnings of a Canadian company. This same rule is followed in our treaties with both the United States and the United Kingdom.

Income from Personal Services

As in the case of the non-resident business, the income tax liability of a non-resident individual who performs personal services in Canada is limited to the income he earns in Canada. Division C of the Income Tax Act provides that the income to be so taxed will be determined on reasonable principles and that a reasonable proportion of the exemptions granted a resident will be granted to a non-resident.

There are numerous examples of this kind of taxpayer, ranging from the "commuters" in Detroit or Niagara Falls, U.S.A., who work the year round in Windsor or Niagara Falls,

---

[1]Further illustrations of allocation rules may be found in chapter IX, where the provincial corporation income taxes and the federal tax credit are discussed.

Canada, to the lawyer, surgeon, musician, artist, singer, actor, wrestler, or other performer, who may be in Canada for only one or two days in the year. All these, in the precise definition of "employed" in the Act, are performing "the duties of an office or employment" in Canada, and are therefore taxable here.

The tax treaties alter the effects of the tax law by excluding certain of these non-residents from tax liability. These exclusions are particularly significant vis-à-vis the United States, since there is a great deal of transient employment of non-residents on both sides of the border. At present neither Canada nor the United States taxes the earnings of a resident of the other country present for 183 days or less (*a*) if he is an employee of a firm of the other country or of a permanent establishment in the other country of a firm in the first country, or (*b*) if he is not such an employee and his earnings during his temporary stay do not exceed $5,000.

There is a provision to the same general effect in the treaty with the United Kingdom, limited, however, to employees of a firm of the other country. Within this limitation it is parallel with the United States agreement, the only test being that the employee not be present for more than 183 days.

Special treatment is also given under these treaties to certain other forms of personal income. Under both the United Kingdom and United States treaties there is now a provision that the country in which an exchange professor or teacher is visiting for a year or two will not tax his earnings, it being left to his home country to impose a tax; similar treatment is extended to remittances received from the home country by a visiting student or apprentice. A similar provision is in effect for wages, salaries, and pensions of government employees resident or temporarily resident in the foreign country, the home country retaining the right to tax at the source. On the other hand it is agreed that annuities, endowments, etc., paid by an insurance company of one country to a resident of another country, or any pension (including in the United States treaty a government pension) will be taxed by the country of residence of the recipient rather than at the source.

In the Canada–U.S. treaty it is agreed that each country will allow a deduction for charitable donations made to approved charities in the other country, within specified limits.

Income from Other Sources

The second general form of non-resident income subject to Canadian tax differs from that dealt with above in that it does not arise from activities carried on in Canada. Though the owner may never visit this country, income from property owned in Canada or from investments in Canada is subject in general to a flat withholding tax of 15 per cent on the gross amount of the payment. It should be pointed out, however, that in law the tax is applicable to every individual and corporation not having the status of a resident in Canada, so that it will apply to payments to a non-resident corporation, even though it may be carrying on business in Canada. Following changes announced in a budget on December 20, 1960, the forms of payment subject to this 15 per cent withholding tax are:

(*a*) All dividends (except paid by a public utility to a resident of a foreign country in which the public utility carries on its operations, which are exempt).

(*b*) All interest, including interest on bonds of or guaranteed by the government of Canada or a provincial or municipal government (in the case of governmental bonds the 15 per cent rate will apply only on loans issued after December 20, 1960).

(*c*) Payments out of a Canadian estate or trust, with minor exceptions.

(*d*) Rents, royalties, or similar payments, including payments for the use in Canada of property, inventions, trade names, designs, etc., but not including payments for a copyright, or the use of railway rolling stock. (By a special provision a non-resident owning real estate in Canada or receiving a timber royalty from Canada may file an income tax return and pay on the net income from such real estate or royalty at the rates applicable to a resident, taking credit for any withholding tax previously deducted from the remittances.)

(*e*) Alimony payments.

(*f*) Patronage dividends.

(*g*) Payments for motion pictures shown in Canada, but at a rate of 10 per cent instead of 15 per cent.

The tax treaties have modified in some respects the application of this withholding tax. The United Kingdom treaty, for example, provides an exemption from the 5 per cent tax for dividends from a wholly owned subsidiary to the parent corporation in the United Kingdom. Under the United States treaty the 5 per cent rate applied where at least 51 per cent of the voting shares of the Canadian corporation are owned by a United States corporation. Other treaties made similar modifications. However following the changes in late 1960 these treaty provisions have either been abrogated or are in the process of withdrawal by re-negotiation with the countries concerned.

An innovation introduced in a special budget of late 1960 was a tax of 15 per cent on the annual profits of the Canadian branches of non-resident companies. This applies to profits earned after January 1, 1961, and is 15 per cent of taxable income remaining after deducting federal and provincial profits taxes and an amount representing the net increase in capital invested in Canada during the year.

Foreign Income of Canadian Residents

Strictly speaking, a discussion of the treatment of foreign income of Canadian residents should have appeared in chapter II, but it has been postponed to this chapter because of its relevance to the present topic. Like Canada many countries today impose some form of tax on the income of non-residents— a practice which is the reverse side of the shield we have just examined. It is apparent that as a result of this practice the foreign income of Canadian residents is taxed in the foreign country and again in Canada.

The effect of this double taxation is alleviated under the Canadian Income Tax Act (the United States follows the same system) by the allowance of a deduction from the Canadian income tax for income taxes paid abroad on the same income.

The method by which foreign taxes are offset against Canadian taxes is simple. The tax payable in Canada on the total income, including the income from abroad, is calculated first. Of this total tax an amount is then determined that bears the same proportion to the total tax as the income from abroad bears to the total income. In other words, if half the income is from abroad then the desired amount is half the Canadian tax. The tax that has been paid abroad on the foreign income may then be deducted from the Canadian tax up to the limit of the amount so calculated. The object is that the foreign tax (which within limits may include a tax payable in lieu of an income tax) for which a credit is allowed shall not exceed the Canadian tax on the same income. Stated in another way, the Canadian tax on foreign income may be completely offset by the foreign tax on the same income, and to some extent, following a 1960 amendment, by tax paid abroad on other income as well, always with the proviso that the total allowed shall not exceed the Canadian tax.

It might be noted that the "tax credit" system for removing double taxation, while not a Canadian or American invention, is in contrast to the continental European system of excluding certain forms of income from tax at the source by treaty or occasionally by statutory provision. This method also found popularity with the framers of the model tax agreements approved by the League of Nations, and would appear to be to the advantage of a creditor country. But Canada's position as a young debtor nation has favoured the adoption of a tax at the source on certain forms of income going abroad. Particularly has it been to Canada's advantage to tax dividends, interest, and royalties going to non-residents. The means for so doing, as mentioned above, has been the withholding of a gross tax at a flat rate of 15 per cent, with no requirement for the filing of a return by the non-resident and no additional graduated tax if the income exceeds any given amount. It should be added that Canada has accepted the full implications of this system and grants Canadian residents, as a matter of right under the income tax law, the privilege of deducting any tax paid abroad on income subject to Canadian tax up to the amount of the Canadian tax on that income.

The European system, as just mentioned, removes double taxation by arrangements between countries for the mutual exclusion of given forms of income from any taxation by the country where the income has its source. As a result of this system an automatic tax credit for foreign taxes such as that found in the Canadian law is a rare thing in European taxing laws. Furthermore such taxes as are collected by the country of origin are more often levied at the same graduated rates as apply to residents, with the requirement of filing a return, than at a flat rate, as in the Canadian system. Where such taxes are levied (usually where no treaty exists between the country of the taxpayer's residence and the country of source), the absence of an automatic tax credit results inevitably in double taxation.

The British income tax authorities have recently been viewing the tax credit plan with favour. For many years the only tax credit allowed was a limited one for taxes paid to countries in the Commonwealth, although by treaty certain forms of foreign income had been excluded from taxation outside of Britain. In recent years, however, both by treaty and by amendment to the income tax law, the tax credit system has been adopted on a greatly enlarged scale.

The tax treaties, particularly that with the United States, have reduced the instances of double taxation of earned income by eliminating some of the more common circumstances under which it might arise. The tax credit nevertheless comes into frequent use. There are many residents of Canada living in Niagara Falls and Windsor who work in the United States (commuting in the opposite direction from that of the commuters previously mentioned) who are taxed there under United States law and are also subject to tax in Canada as residents of this country. In this case the tax credit is allowed by Canada, the country of residence, calculated in the manner just explained.

The same general rules apply also to Canadian individuals carrying on business outside of Canada or receiving income from investments abroad.

In connection with dividends, the tax treaty with the United Kingdom provides for a reciprocal tax credit that is unique. The United Kingdom has no special withholding rate on dividends paid to non-residents, but for residents and non-residents alike the standard 38.75 per cent rate of income tax applies to dividends distributed by British companies. Under the Canada–United Kingdom tax treaty this 38.75 per cent rate is treated in the same manner as the withholding tax imposed only on non-residents by, say, the United States. For a dividend on a common share the Canadian government has undertaken that a Canadian shareholder of a British company will be allowed a deduction from his Canadian tax in respect of this standard rate and also for the $12\frac{1}{2}$ per cent profits tax. The counterpart of this is that residents of the United Kingdom are allowed to take credit against their tax not only for the 15 per cent Canadian withholding tax but also for the rate of corporation income tax paid in Canada by the corporation of which they are shareholders. This treatment is consistent with the character of the English standard rate paid by corporations as a withholding tax rather than as a separate tax on corporate income.

Double taxation of the profits of Canadian corporations and business enterprises is encountered in two general cases: first, where the corporation receives profits from a branch operating in a foreign country, and, second, where the corporation receives dividends from shares of a foreign company held as part of its investment portfolio, over which it has neither control nor complete ownership. In both these circumstances the tax credit procedure is used.

In the case of the foreign branch there is sometimes difficulty in determining the proper amount of the tax credit because of differences in the rules applied by Canada and the foreign country for determining the foreign income. The foreign country may allocate income to its jurisdiction by one method, while the Canadian tax authorities may adopt another method which they regard as being more suitable. A tax credit is allowed, however, on income which the Canadian authorities agree has been subject to tax both in Canada and abroad, the credit being calculated in the manner described previously.

In the case of dividends received by a Canadian corporation from a controlled foreign subsidiary, the Canadian tax credit provision was extremely complicated until the budget of 1949. A tax credit was allowed not only for the foreign withholding tax, if any, but also for the corporation tax paid in the foreign country by the subsidiary. In 1947 this system of tax credits was extended through a foreign holding company to taxes paid by subsidiaries of that holding company. To be eligible the foreign holding company must have received at least 75 per cent of its income from dividends of its own subsidiaries. Such corporation relationships were referred to colloquially as "sons" and "grandsons" of the Canadian company. By a complicated calculation the Canadian company was enabled to take a deduction for a portion of the dividends received from abroad in respect of taxes deemed to have been paid on such dividends under the foreign corporation tax by the "sons" and "grandsons."

A 1949 amendment to the tax law entirely eliminated this complicated tax credit calculation and substituted in its place the right to exclude from Canadian income all dividends received from a controlled subsidiary. A further step was taken in the 1951 budget with the extension of this privilege to dividends from companies of which more than 25 per cent of the shares are owned. In effect this change extends to foreign dividends the general practice in respect of inter-company dividends in Canada, except for the limitation in the foreign field for the degree of ownership. This automatic exemption of dividends from abroad where as little as 25 percent ownership exists is a unique feature of Canadian law and gives Canadian business operating abroad a considerable advantage over entities of other countries.

Corporations as well as individuals also receive income in the nature of rentals, royalties, or similar payments from abroad. Where these have been subject to a withholding tax a credit is allowed against the Canadian corporation income tax.

Foreign Business Corporations and Non-Resident-Owned Investment Corporations

Special treatment is given certain corporations whose activities are carried on largely outside of Canada or who do no active commercial business in Canada.

One such class of company is that known as the foreign business corporation, which is entirely exempt from tax under the Income Tax Act. The principal qualification for such exemption is that the corporation shall carry on all its essential business activities outside of Canada. The company may be incorporated here and may have substantial business offices here but the purpose for which it was organized is carried out entirely in another country. The better-known instances are two or three large Canadian corporations operating public utilities in foreign countries. Following an amendment in 1959, however, no corporations will be recognized for exemption as foreign business corporations which were not in existence before April 10, 1959.

A second class of corporation of a quite different character that qualifies for special taxation under the Income Tax Act is the non-resident-owned investment corporation. Such a company must be owned to the extent of at least 95 per cent by non-resident persons, trustees of non-resident persons, or corporations owned by non-resident persons. Its income must be limited to the return from investments (bonds, shares, debentures, mortgages, etc.), from the lending of money, from rents, etc., and from estates or trusts. It may not carry on any commercial or business activity in Canada. Such a company is not exempt from tax but is subject to a reduced rate of 15 per cent, a device which in effect anticipates the payment of the withholding tax that would otherwise apply on its investment income leaving Canada. When actual payments are made to the non-resident owners no withholding tax is collected.

Summary

RATES. The rates of graduated tax are as given in chapter II. The general rate of withholding tax at the present time is 15 per cent (for exceptions see text).

REVENUE

	Fiscal year 1959-60 ($000)	Percentage of tax revenue	Percentage of total revenue
Non-resident withholding tax	73,353	1.5	1.4

STATUTORY REFERENCE. Income Tax Act, Revised Statutes, Canada, 1952, c. 148.

Chapter 5

DOMINION DEATH DUTIES AND GIFT TAX

DEATH DUTIES were first imposed by the Dominion in 1941, applicable to estates of persons dying on and after June 14, 1941, under the Succession Duty Act. This legislation was replaced by the Estate Tax Act from January 1, 1959. Gift tax was first imposed in 1935 under the Income War Tax Act.

Today, under the terms of the Tax Sharing Agreements, the federal tax is the only levy in eight provinces. Additional provincial duties are also imposed in Ontario and Quebec.

The gift tax preceded the succession duties by some six years, having been introduced first in 1935. Its initial purpose was to discourage the watering-down of income by the dispersal among several persons of the assets which produced that income. It continues to serve that purpose today, but in addition has been integrated with the death duties, which in one sense can be regarded as a gift tax applicable at the time of demise.

General Character of Death Duties

There are two distinct general forms of tax on property passing at death. One of these is the "estate" duty; the other, the "succession" duty.

The "estate" duty is imposed on the value of the property passing at the time of death, including joint property, life insurance, gifts, and so on. The rate depends only on the total amount of such property, no account being taken of who receives it or how much anyone receives. It can be regarded loosely as a debt of the deceased to the state that comes due at the moment of his death and it must be met out of his estate before his beneficiaries obtain their bequests.

A "succession" duty, on the other hand, is a tax on the beneficiary in respect of the amount that he receives from the estate. In its simplest form a succession duty is graduated in rate only in accordance with the amount of the bequest, but in most jurisdictions employing this form of levy the rates are also modified to take into account the relationship of the beneficiary to the deceased. In theory the liability for a succession duty falls on the individual successor and the payment comes out of his individual bequest.

Arguments have been advanced in support of both types of levy. The estate duty is commended for the simplicity achieved by basing the tax calculation simply on the aggregate of the property passing at death. But it is criticized because it takes no account of "ability to pay," all successors in effect being taxed at the same rate no matter how small or large their benefit from the estate. The succession duty is supported because of its apparent recognition of ability to pay, since the rate of tax depends on the size of the individual succession. It arouses criticism because of the administrative complications encountered, particularly in establishing liability where a complex series of successions is provided in a will. Some additional inconvenience arises also because of the necessity of calculating a tax on each of the parts of the estate under the succession duty, rather than simply on the total as under the estate duty.

So deeply ingrained is the acceptance of ability-to-pay as the best criterion for a tax that academic writers have generally lent almost unquestioning support to a succession duty. It is worth while pointing out, therefore, that in actual practice the distinction between the two forms of duty is often more apparent than real. This situation arises simply out of the manner in which testators often will their property and executors administer the estate after death. It is quite a common practice for a testator to provide that bequests in amounts specified in his will are to be paid to named beneficiaries ($1,000 to Aunt Harriet, $500 to his favourite charity, $500 to his college, etc.), the balance of the estate after these specific bequests have been paid to go to other named beneficiaries. Under such a direction in a will an executor will pay the specific bequests to the beneficiaries in the amount stated, and the duty payable on these bequests will come out of the balance of the estate, along with the duty on that balance. This is done because, even though formally the succession duty may be imposed on the successor, in actual practice the executor is made responsible for its payment, and having distributed the bequests in the amount required by the will he must look to the balance of the property in his possession to pay the duty on these fixed bequests. In many wills so drawn he is, in fact, directed to pay the duty from the balance of the estate.

The effect of this common arrangement is to completely thwart any pretensions to taxation in accordance with ability-to-pay. The final incidence of the duty is all on the residual beneficiary or beneficiaries, who unfortunately are often the closest relatives of the deceased (because testators tend to leave small specific bequests to their more remote legatees, and the balance to their nearest beneficiaries). The recipients of the specific bequests will have paid no duty whatever.

Of course where the testator simply directs that his estate is to be distributed in certain proportions to his beneficiaries (i.e., one-quarter to one person, one-quarter to a second, and one-half to a third) without providing for specific bequests in stated amounts, the executor is in a position to allot to each beneficiary his appropriate duty, and the principle of ability-to-pay operates as intended. It has, of course, been argued against the application of this principle to succession duties that the actual amount of the bequest received is a very rough guide to ability to pay, since a beneficiary receiving a small bequest may be enjoying a large income and be able, in fact, to pay a high duty. This, however, would seem to be a general criticism applicable to any tax that rests on a single criterion of ability-to-pay.

Both the estate and the succession duty are in use today in leading tax jurisdictions. For example, the national governments of both the United States and the United Kingdom impose estate duties exclusively (the only remnant of a succession duty in the British system, the legacy duty, was repealed in 1948), while the American states employ either or in some cases both forms of tax, the succession duty generally being known as an "inheritance" tax. In Australia both the Commonwealth and the state governments impose estate duties. In Canada both forms of duty have been in effect since January 1, 1959; the federal government imposes an estate tax and the provinces (Ontario and Quebec) levy succession duties. Prior to 1959 the federal tax was in the succession duty form as well, but was changed to an estate tax largely for greater simplicity.

The Dominion Estate Tax

To any person acquainted with the general character of the Canadian income tax the main principles of the Canadian estate tax will be immediately familiar. Persons domiciled in Canada are taxed on their whole estate; non-domiciled persons are taxed only on their Canadian assets. The position differs from the income tax only in the substitution of the concept of domicile for that of residence.

As a basis for tax liability domicile is used infrequently; it is in fact encountered almost exclusively in death taxation. Much has been written to clarify its meaning, but for the layman it remains an obscure concept. As contrasted with residence, which implies a home in fact, domicile appears to imply a legal, abiding, and permanent home, or a home in law. In the concept of domicile a person is regarded as having one home to which he is attached by law, no matter where he may at the time be resident. The subtleties of this distinction may be pursued by the reader in any standard text on death taxation, and for present purposes, since it is true of the vast majority of mankind, it will be assumed that persons are domiciled where they reside. It will only be necessary to remember that there are exceptions to this generalization in individual instances.

The similarity with the income tax is not limited to the basis of liability in the Estate Tax Act but is apparent as well in the details of the tax calculation.

For domiciled persons the scheme is as follows:
1. Determine the aggregate net value of the whole estate.

2. Deduct the exemptions to obtain the aggregate taxable value.

3. Calculate the tax on the aggregate taxable value in accordance with the single schedule of progressive rates.

For non-domiciled persons the calculation involves only two main steps:

1. Determine the aggregate net value of the Canadian assets of the estate.

2. Calculate the tax on such value at a flat rate of 15 per cent.

Estates of Domiciled Persons

Aggregate net value. The computation of the amount of the estate of a deceased person that comes within the ambit of the tax is the first and one of the most vital steps. Division B of the Act is devoted to this computation. The net is spread wide; ". . . all property, wherever situated, passing on the death of such (domiciled) person" and "all property, of which the deceased was, immediately prior to his death, competent to dispose," are to be included. And even this broad scope is widened further to sweep in certain property owned or controlled by the deceased during his lifetime which he disposed of prior to his death. The principal example of this extension is the inclusion of all gifts made by the deceased within three years prior to his death, a provision of such finality that one must automatically count in all such gifts in the reckoning of property passing at death.

Various other forms of property and transactions in such property are brought into the computation by special provisions. The list, as set forth in Section 3 of the Act, includes:

1. Property transferred as a *donatio mortis causa*; usually personal property transferred on the death-bed, the gift being conditional on death.

2. Gifts with reservation of benefit. A typical instance would be the gift of a home made on condition that the donor be allowed to occupy it until his death. Where there is any such reservation the whole amount of the gift is to be included in the estate.

3. Settlements with reservation of interest. A typical instance would be the gift of a business with the reservation that an annuity be paid the donor out of the profits until his death.

4. Joint property to the extent of the beneficial interest of the deceased at death. The most frequently encountered example of joint property is the residence held in the name of husband and wife. Whereas under the former Succession Duty Act such property was excluded from the estate only to the extent that persons other than the deceased had contributed value towards its purchase, under the Estate Tax Act the sole test is the legal ownership at the time of death.

5. Transfers for partial consideration. Where the deceased has transferred property within three years prior to his death for less than its full value the benefit so conferred shall form part of his estate.

6. Annuities and pensions to the extent of the beneficial interest accruing to other persons on the death. Periodic payments of this type are capitalized in accordance with approved tables and their present value is included in the estate.

7. Death benefits from an employer to beneficiaries of the deceased whether paid voluntarily or under an arrangement.

8. Proceeds of life insurance to the extent the policy was owned by the deceased at the time of his death. If the policy has been transferred or assigned to another person prior to death the proceeds are not included in the estate. This represented a major departure from the Succession Duty Act, under which only that portion of a policy which could be established had been paid for by another person was excluded from the estate.

The proceeds of a life insurance policy taken on his life by a company controlled by the deceased are given special mention. If the proceeds are payable to the spouse or child or to the estate of the deceased they are fully taxable; if they are payable to the company they are included in the estate to the extent of the excess of the proceeds over the net profits of the last five years of the company, the latter presumably as a recognition of the insurable interest of the company in the deceased.

9. Transfers in consideration of marriage in the three years prior to death, and rights of dower and curtesy arising on the death.

Other provisions in Section 3 which bear on the computation of aggregate net value include: (*a*) a clarification of the position of a general power of appointment; it is to be included only if exercised at death or within 3 years of death; (*b*) a broadening of the definition of an *inter vivos* gift to include such transactions as the artificial creation of debts enforceable against the deceased and payable at the time of his death and the forgiveness of a legitimate debt by the deceased at his expense on his death; (*c*) a general catch-all for benefits conferred by a corporation controlled by the deceased.

One of the most radical changes in the Estate Tax Act, which is not evident from a review of its provisions, is that real property of the deceased outside Canada is to be included with aggregate net value. Formerly it was omitted in conformance with almost universal usage that real property is taxed where it has its situs.

Certain amounts which need not be included or deductions which may be made are covered by Sections 4 and 5. They are very few. To the extent that there has been a *bona fide* sale to another person of property passing on the death of the deceased it may be excluded from his estate. Debts, encumbrances, and reasonable funeral, probate, and like court fees may be deducted, but not charges of solicitors and executors.

A final and vital aspect of the determination of aggregate net value should be mentioned here before passing on. This is the matter of valuation. In general, as under the Succession Duty Act, property of the deceased is valued as at the time of death. A special division of the Estate Tax Act—Division F—supplies rules for certain forms of property and property ownership. These rules relate to the non-deductibility of future income tax, to listed securities, to the shares of closely held companies, to certain forms of debt, to property disposed of *inter vivos*, to shares of companies where there has been a stock dividend and also where the company has been the beneficiary of an insurance policy. In this same Division are found the reliefs for quick successions: 50 per cent for a second death within one year, diminished by 10 per cent in each of the following four years with no relief after the fifth year.

No provision is made for an alternative date of valuation under the Canadian law such as that found in the United States estate tax.

Aggregate taxable value. From the aggregate net value of the estate of a domiciled person certain deductions may be taken in determining the value subject to tax.

The principal deductions are comparable to the personal exemptions granted under the income tax; they are the amount which may be subtracted from the estate to leave a taxable residual. Varying with the character and number of dependents of the deceased, they are granted whether or not any bequests are made under the estate to such dependents. The following is a simplified presentation of what are rather complex provisions in the law:

Basic deduction
1. In the general case.................................. $40,000
2. Where the deceased is survived by (*a*) a widow, or (*b*) an infirm widower and dependent child................ $60,000

Dependent children deduction
In addition to the basic deduction there is allowed:
1. Where no spouse survives, for each dependent child of the deceased....................................... $15,000
2. Where the $60,000 basic deduction is applicable, for each dependent child of the deceased............... $10,000

Despite the fact that the basic deduction is only $40,000 no estate of $50,000 or less is subject to estate duty. This creates a "notch" area immediately in excess of $50,000 which is alleviated by a rule that the tax shall not exceed one half the difference between $50,000 and the amount of the estate.

In addition to these "personal" exemptions deductions are also allowed for charitable bequests, for normal and reasonable gifts and for war veterans and other exempt pensions.

Rates of tax. The balance remaining after the above deductions have been made is subject to tax in accordance with rates set out in Division D of the Act. Table III sets out the schedule in abbreviated form.

In Table IV some examples are given of the amount of duty payable under these rates on estates of various sizes and under various assumptions as to beneficiaries. No account is taken in these calculations of the abatement for estates in Ontario and Quebec. Tables in the appendix give illustrations of the actual tax payable on the estate of deceased persons domiciled in these two provinces.

TABLE III

FEDERAL ESTATE TAX RATES IN EFFECT FROM JANUARY 1, 1959

Taxable value	Tax on lowest amount	Rate on excess
$	$	%
0– 5,000	—	10
5,000– 10,000	500	12
10,000– 15,000	1,100	14
15,000– 20,000	1,800	16
20,000– 40,000	2,600	18
40,000– 60,000	6,200	20
60,000– 100,000	10,200	22
100,000– 150,000	19,000	24
150,000– 200,000	31,000	26
200,000– 275,000	44,000	28
275,000– 350,000	65,000	30
350,000– 450,000	87,500	32
450,000– 550,000	119,500	34
550,000– 650,000	153,500	36
650,000– 750,000	189,500	38
750,000– 850,000	227,500	40
850,000– 950,000	267,500	42
950,000–1,100,000	309,500	44
1,100,000–1,300,000	375,500	46
1,300,000–1,550,000	467,500	48
1,550,000–1,800,000	587,500	50
1,800,000–2,000,000	712,500	52
Over 2,000,000	816,500	54

Credits against tax. The tax calculated in accordance with the schedule given in Table III may be reduced by the offset of abatements or credits under three headings: (1) provincial taxes; (2) gift taxes; and (3) foreign taxes.

The abatement for provincial taxes is simple in form but complex in operation. Quebec and Ontario are the only provinces in Canada which continue to levy succession duties, and with respect to property deemed to have its situs in those provinces under the federal situs rules there is an automatic abatement of one-half of the federal duty. The federal rules for determining situs for this purpose are contained in the Estate

TABLE IV

DUTY PAYABLE UNDER DOMINION ESTATE TAX IN PROVINCES OTHER THAN ONTARIO AND QUEBEC

Aggregate net value	Estate to widow	Estate to widow and 2 children under 21	Estate to widow and 4 children under 21	Estate to widower with no children
$	$	$	$	$
50,000	—	—	—	—
75,000	1,800	—	—	5,300
100,000	6,200	2,600	—	10,200
150,000	16,800	12,200	8,200	21,400
200,000	28,600	21,800	19,000	33,600
250,000	41,400	36,200	31,000	46,800
300,000	55,200	49,600	44,000	60,800
350,000	69,500	63,600	58,000	75,500
400,000	84,500	78,500	72,500	90,700
500,000	116,300	109,900	103,500	122,900
600,000	150,100	143,300	136,500	157,100
700,000	185,900	178,700	171,500	193,300
800,000	223,700	216,100	208,500	231,500
900,000	263,500	296,900	247,500	271,700
1,000,000	305,300	340,300	288,500	313,900
1,500,000	534,700	525,100	515,500	544,300
2,000,000	785,300	774,900	764,500	795,700

Tax Act (Sec. 9 (8)) and differ in several instances from the common law rules followed by the provincial governments in levying tax. Inconsistencies arise as a result, with an abatement being granted where no tax is levied by the province, and *vice versa*.

The credit for gift tax arises from the fact that, where gift tax has been paid on a gift which subsequently is included in an estate under the three-year rule, an offset against the Estate Tax may be taken for the gift tax paid on the same property.

The credit for foreign taxes of course arises only where property has been taxed by a foreign jurisdiction. Under the Estate Tax Act credit is allowed as a matter of statute, whereas formerly it was granted only through the operation of tax treaties between Canada and other countries. For the foreign tax credit it has been necessary to provide rules of situs in the statute, and for this purpose the same rules as enacted for the provincial tax credit are used.

Before passing on to the treatment of non-domiciled estates at least one further aspect of the arrangements governing domiciled estates should be mentioned. This is the matter of liability for payment of duty. This is markedly different from the position under the Succession Duty Act, under which the legal liability fell on the successor, but in practice was paid by the executor. Under the Estate Tax Act liability is in two parts:

1. a liability on the executor to pay tax on the whole estate out of any property passing through his hands, and

2. a liability on the successor to pay tax on property received directly by him to the extent that the tax on such property has not been paid by the executor. An instance would be a life interest for a substantial annuity where the property in the hands of the executor is less than the amount of the duty. Under these conditions the successor is liable, and may spread the tax over six annual instalments.

Estates of Non-Domiciled Persons

Much of the previous description of the scope of the Estate Tax applies for non-domiciled persons in so far as such a person dies leaving assets having a Canadian situs. The principal differences arise in respect of deductions, exemptions, and rate of tax. No deductions are allowed in determining aggregate value of the property except to the extent that they were "secured by and charged upon" such property. A mortgage on real estate would be an example of such a debt. No exemptions comparable to the personal exemptions are allowed, except that where the amount of the property is less than $5,000 no duty is payable.[1] And the rate of tax, as mentioned earlier, is a flat 15 per cent on the aggregate value of the Canadian assets.

Where the property has also been subject to a provincial tax an abatement of one-half the federal rate is allowed with respect thereto.

For this tax rules of situs have been provided to determine whether property is situated within or without Canada. These follow closely the rules established in the death tax treaties between Canada and foreign countries, and differ in some respects from those used for the provincial and foreign tax credits.

Gift Tax

The primary purpose of the gift tax is to protect the revenues derived from the income tax and from the succession duties although a small amount of incidental revenue is also produced. It protects the former by discouraging the transfer of income-earning property, such as stocks and bonds, from wealthy persons (who would otherwise pay at a high rate of tax on their yield) to less wealthy persons (who would pay at a lower rate). Similarly it protects succession duty revenue by discouraging the making of gifts during a person's lifetime for the purpose of avoiding succession duties at the time of his death.

The gift tax is an annual tax. It is imposed on gifts made in any one year by a person resident in Canada or by a personal corporation in Canada. A "gift" is defined to include any transfer, assignment, or other disposition of property by way of gift. It also includes direct or indirect dispositions such as the creation of a trust or the creation of an interest in property. The liability to tax is not affected by the fact that the property disposed of is situated outside of Canada.

[1]Under the Canada–U.S. Death Tax Convention signed in February, 1961, this exemption was increased to $15,000 for American domiciliaries having property in Canada.

Since the principal purpose of the tax is to discourage the dispersal of income-earning assets of very wealthy persons but not to discourage true charitable giving, the exemptions are quite liberal. No account need be taken of any gift of $1,000 or less made within the year. A person may give away as many gifts of $1,000 or less to as many individuals or institutions as he

TABLE V

RATES OF GIFT TAX

Where the aggregate taxable value is		
Over	Not over	Percentage
$	$	
	5,000	10
5,000	10,000	11
10,000	20,000	12
20,000	30,000	13
30,000	40,000	14
40,000	50,000	15
50,000	75,000	16
75,000	100,000	17
100,000	150,000	18
150,000	200,000	19
200,000	250,000	20
250,000	300,000	21
300,000	400,000	22
400,000	500,000	23
500,000	600,000	24
600,000	700,000	25
700,000	800,000	26
800,000	1,000,000	27
1,000,000		28

wishes without being subject to tax. But any gift or aggregate of gifts exceeding $1,000 to any individual institution or person must be brought into account. Where gifts in excess of $1,000 have been taken into account no duty need be paid, however, until in the aggregate they exceed either $4,000 or, alternatively, one-half of the taxpayer's income of the previous year after deduction of the income tax payable thereon. In addition the taxpayer may make any amount of gifts to charitable organizations in Canada and to any government in Canada. A gift to a spouse or child of the taxpayer of an interest in real property may be made without tax in an amount not exceeding $10,000. Only one such gift may qualify for exemption. No account is taken of gifts which do not become effective until the death of the donor since such gifts are subject to estate tax. As stated previously in the section on estate tax, where any disposition had been taxed under the gift tax within three years prior to death, the amount of the gift tax is allowed as a credit against the estate tax.

The rates of tax are set out in Table V. The "aggregate taxable value" is the amount of gifts remaining in the aggregate after deducting all gifts under $1,000, all the charitable and other gifts previously mentioned, and the greater amount of $4,000 or one-half of the previous year's income after tax.

SUMMARY

RATES. Estate tax is at graduated rates varying with the size of the estate. Gift tax is at graduated rates depending on the amount of the gift.

REVENUE

	Fiscal year 1959–60 ($000)	Percentage of tax revenue	Percentage of total revenue
Death taxes*	88,431	1.9	1.7
Gift tax	†		

*Net revenue after deducting credits allowed on Quebec and Ontario estates.
†Revenue from the gift tax is included with personal income tax revenue.

STATUTORY REFERENCES. The Estate Tax Act, 1958, c. 29; Income Tax Act, *ibid.*, c. 148, Part IV.

CHAPTER 6

DOMINION COMMODITY TAXES
THE CUSTOMS TARIFF,
THE GENERAL SALES TAX

THE CUSTOMS TARIFF

FROM earliest times the customs tariff has played an important part (until the twentieth century the leading part) in the revenue systems of, first, New France, later, British North America and, since 1867, the Dominion of Canada. The landmarks in this long history are: 1662, the first recorded tariff in New France; 1774, the Quebec Revenue Act; 1778, the Declaratory Act; 1813, the introduction of the general tariff ($2\frac{1}{2}$ per cent) in Upper and Lower Canada; the loss of the preferences in the British market and the final abandonment of the Navigation Laws in the 1840's; 1854, the Reciprocity Treaty with the United States; 1858, the Cayley Tariff; 1859, the Galt Tariff; 1866, the expiration (by abrogation) of the Reciprocity Treaty; 1867, the introduction of a national tariff with Confederation; 1879, the National Policy; 1897-8, the introduction of the British Preferential Tariff; 1907, the general revision setting the basic pattern for the present tariff; 1911, the rejection of reciprocity with the United States; 1913, the first West Indies Trade Agreement; 1920, the second West Indies Trade Agreement; 1925, the third West Indies Trade Agreement; 1932, the Ottawa Empire Trade Agreements; 1934, United States Reciprocal Agreements Act passed by Congress; 1935, United States–Canada Trade Agreement (effective January 1, 1936, the first Canada–United States agreement in seventy years, i.e., since 1866); 1937, United Kingdom–Canada Trade

CUSTOMS TARIFF, GENERAL SALES TAX 117

Agreement; 1938, second United States-Canada Trade Agreement; 1940-5, War Exchange Conservation Act and other temporary wartime changes; 1948, General Agreement on Tariffs and Trade (Geneva Agreement); periodic revision to the General Agreement since 1951.

General Character of the Tariff

It would be a presumption for the writer to attempt to discuss in detail the ramifications of the customs tariff. The triumphs of penetrating the labyrinth of specific and *ad valorem* duties, preferential rates, bound margins, etc., will be reserved for the tariff expert. He alone may venture into the maze with any confidence. The main purpose here will be served if the reader is given a few general impressions of the tariff as it stands today.

The elemental facts about the present tariff may be stated briefly. In basic form it has undergone no fundamental change since the revision of 1907. It is a "three-decker" affair with separate schedules of rates under the British Preferential Tariff, the Most Favoured Nation Tariff (prior to 1948 the Intermediate Tariff), and the General Tariff. Until 1935 the greatest volume of goods entered under the General Tariff, applicable to countries with which Canada has no trade agreement. After the trade agreement with the United States came into force, however, imports from that country were transferred to the intermediate classification and the General Tariff became of negligible importance. This trend has continued in recent years, particularly since further countries were given the benefit of the reduced rates under the Geneva Agreement, GATT, in 1948. The British Preferential rates are of course limited to imports from countries within the British Commonwealth.

The countries which came under the three levels of rates in 1960 were as follows:

British Preferential Countries

Africa, South, Union of (including the Mandated Territory of South West Africa)
Australia, Commonwealth of
British non-self-governing Colonies and Protectorates

British West Indies
Cameroons, Mandated Territory of the
Ceylon
Eire
Great Britain and Northern Ireland, the Kingdom of
India
Malay States
New Zealand (including Western Samoa and the Cook Islands)
Pakistan
Rhodesia (Federation of Rhodesia and Nyasaland)
Tanganyika, Mandated Territory of
Togoland, Mandated Territory of

Most Favoured Nation Countries

Argentine Republic	Honduras
Austria	Hong Kong
Belgium, Colonies and Possessions	Iceland
Bolivia	Iran
Brazil	Iraq
Burma	Italy
Chile	Japan
China	Lebanon
Colombia	Liberia
Costa Rica	Lichtenstein
Cuba	Luxembourg
Czechoslovakia	Mexico
Denmark	Netherlands, Netherlands Indies,
Dominican Republic	Curaçao, and Surinam
Ecuador	Nicaragua
Egypt	Norway
Ethiopia	Palestine
Finland	Panama
Formosa	Paraguay
France, Colonies and Possessions	Peru
Germany, Western	Philippine Islands
Greece	Poland
Guam	Porto Rico
Guatemala	Portugal
Hawaii	Russia
Haiti	Salvador, El

CUSTOMS TARIFF, GENERAL SALES TAX

Samoa, American
Spain
Sweden
Switzerland
Syria
Turkey

United States of America
Uruguay
Venezuela
Virgin Islands, U.S.A. (St. Croix, St. John, and St. Thomas)
Yugoslavia

Principal General Tariff Countries

Abyssinia
Afghanistan
Albania
Bulgaria

Germany (other than Western)
Hungary
Roumania
Thailand

Extent of the British Preference

No general *indicia* give an exact measurement of the degree of preference under the British Preferential rates. But a rough idea can be gained from a comparison between the actual rates that prevail on some of the major imports under this schedule and the corresponding rates under the other two schedules. Particularly significant are the rates on machinery and woolen and cotton textiles, of which a considerable volume is imported from the United Kingdom. (See Table VI.)

The Tariff as a Revenue Source

The analysis of customs revenue for selected years since 1925 in Table VII illustrates the following general characteristics of the modern Canadian tariff as a revenue source:

1. Almost no revenue is derived from industrial raw materials, which come in free from all countries. The one notable exception is bituminous coal, on which a small duty produces a fairly large yield. Generally speaking the tariff applies to manufactured or semi-manufactured goods.

2. On the average almost a third of the customs revenue comes from the important iron and steel group. Protective duties have been levied since the 1880's, and at some periods these duties have been quite high. However, Canada's primary iron and steel industry meets little more than half the over-all

TABLE VI

RATES ON SPECIFIC IMPORTS UNDER THE THREE TARIFF SCHEDULES

Tariff item		B.P. rates	M.F.N. rates[1]	General rates
27	Coffee, green, m.o.p.	free	2¢ lb.	5¢ lb.
28a	Tea	free	2¢ lb.	8¢ lb.
77a	Cocoa beans	free	$1.50 cwt.	$3.00 cwt.
135	Sugar (96% raw)	28.712¢ cwt.	$1.28712 cwt.	$1.28712 cwt.
169	Books (novels, etc.)	free	22½%	25%
287	Chinaware	free	35%	35%
318	Window glass	free	7½%	17½%
427 427a	Machinery, n.o.p.—of a kind made in Canada	10%	22½%	35%
	—of a kind not made in Canada	free	27½%	35%
438a	Cars, trucks and buses	free	17½%	27½%
439	Bicycles and tricycles	20%	27½%	30%
522(3)	Cotton fabrics, coloured	17½%	22½%	35%
554b	Woollen fabrics	20% plus 20¢ per lb. (not to exceed 60¢ per lb.)	27½% plus 38¢ per lb.	40% plus 40¢ per lb.
568	Knitted goods	20%	35% plus 25¢ per lb.	45% plus 30¢ per lb.
611a	Boots and shoes	20%	27½%	40%
711	All goods not specifically enumerated	15%	25%	25%

[1]Under GATT, rates lower than M.F.N. rates apply on most of these items.

requirement during a period of expansion such as the present, and the excess is met by imports mainly from the United States. At such times American steel does not have much trouble in surmounting the moderate rates now levied. The full effect of a period of capital expansion on revenue from this group was shown in 1956, when revenue reached a peak of $218 million.

CUSTOMS TARIFF, GENERAL SALES TAX 121

A corollary of this characteristic of the iron and steel group is that under depressed conditions the Canadian capacity is usually more than adequate to meet the slackened demand, and in the past imports have fallen drastically. The result is that in practice this largest single source of customs revenue has been extremely volatile, a fact graphically demonstrated by the drop from $62 million in 1929 to $12 million in 1934, and the sharp spurt from $62 million in 1946 to $218 million in 1956.

3. The textile group is the second largest source of revenue, but it is considerably more stable than iron and steel, since it is related to consumer rather than capital expenditure.

4. Substantial revenues are still derived from some of the old stand-by items, such as sugar, coffee, and spirits. In connection with the latter, however, it is important to bear in mind the exceptional circumstance that the tariff on spirits is the counterpart of the domestic duty. If the usual system were followed of taxing all excised goods sold in Canada, irrespective of their source, at a uniform rate, the additional tariff on imported spirits would appear as a quite moderate rate and the customs revenue would be correspondingly reduced. The protective difference between the internal excise duty on spirits of $13.00 per proof gallon, and the British Preferential rate on imported spirits, is only 50 cents per gallon at the present time.

The reader may discover other characteristics of the tariff as a revenue source in Table VII.

Summary

RATES: Various, see Customs Tariff.

REVENUE

	Fiscal year 1959-60 ($000)	Percentage of tax revenue	Percentage of total revenue
Net customs duties	525,722	11.0	9.9

STATUTORY REFERENCES. The Customs Tariff, Revised Statutes, Canada, 1952, c. 60.

TABLE VII

Customs Revenue by Main Sources for Selected Years
(millions of dollars)

Year[1]	1925	1929	1934	1938	1955	1956	1957	1958
1. Total[2]	120.2	198.9	70.8	101.7	479.8	577.7	554.2	517.0
2. Agricultural and vegetable; food	17.7	19.9	12.6	13.7	27.9	31.5	32.6	36.2
Fruits	2.3	4.5	3.7	3.2	7.0	8.4	8.3	8.7
Sugar and products	8.3	6.2	3.6	3.6	8.0	8.2	8.5	11.2
Coffee	.6	.6	.5	.5	1.9	2.0	2.2	2.3
Tea	2.5	2.7	1.5	1.6	.03	.03	.04	.04
3. Agricultural and vegetable; non-food	14.3	29.6	7.8	11.3	28.4	29.9	27.7	44.4
Alcoholic beverages	12.1	27.0	6.4	6.8	17.0	17.2	15.2	31.8
Rubber and products	—	—	.4	.6	6.2	7.4	6.7	7.0
4. Animals and animal products	3.6	5.2	2.3	2.7	8.4	9.9	10.5	10.7
5. Fibres, textiles and products	25.5	32.0	11.6	13.4	53.3	61.4	64.1	65.2
Cottons	7.4	6.9	3.2	3.8	16.4	19.1	19.9	21.0
Silks	4.9	6.6	1.0	.8	1.6	2.0	2.2	2.3
Woolens	8.5	9.8	4.3	4.9	12.1	15.0	15.8	13.8
Artificial silk	—	2.9	1.4	1.4	14.0	15.2	16.4	17.6

[1]Fiscal years ended March 31 up to and including 1938; remaining years calendar years.
[2]Gross revenue before refunds; will not agree therefore with revenue figures given elsewhere.   Source: Dominion Bureau of Statistics, annual report, *Trade of Canada.*

TABLE VII (*continued*)

Year[1]	1925	1929	1934	1938	1955	1956	1957	1958
6. Wood, wood products and paper	5.9	9.1	3.2	4.2	18.2	21.5	22.2	23.2
Paper and manufactures	2.5	3.7	1.4	1.9	9.4	11.4	11.5	11.9
7. Iron and products	26.0	62.1	12.3	26.1	162.0	218.5	204.5	176.6
Rolling mill products	3.3	5.4	1.0	3.4	10.8	18.3	14.9	11.6
Engines and boilers	2.0	5.1	1.3	2.0	10.6	12.6	13.5	10.2
Machinery (excluding agricultural)	5.3	12.5	2.7	7.5	47.1	65.0	64.6	53.6
Vehicles and parts	8.2	24.9	3.6	6.6	45.7	57.1	45.8	42.0
8. Non-ferrous metals and products	7.1	13.4	3.6	7.2	57.1	67.5	64.4	59.3
Electrical apparatus	3.8	6.8	1.7	3.7	39.7	45.6	43.6	38.9
9. Non-metallic minerals and products	9.8	13.8	10.6	13.7	26.5	30.8	28.2	25.9
Coal and products (mainly bituminous)	4.9	6.6	7.4	9.5	5.8	7.3	6.0	4.4
10. Chemicals and allied products	2.7	3.7	3.0	3.5	22.4	24.6	25.2	26.9
11. Miscellaneous commodities[2]	6.7	10.0	3.7	6.1	75.2	82.1	74.8	48.7

[1] Fiscal years ended March 31 up to and including 1938; remaining years calendar years.
[2] Includes additional and special duties which cannot be allocated to any special group or commodity.

The General Sales Tax

The general manufacturers' sales tax was first introduced by the Dominion in 1920, and with some alterations has been in effect ever since. The rate reached a low point of 1 per cent in 1930, remained unchanged at 8 per cent from May 2, 1936, to April 11, 1951, and on the latter date was increased to 10 per cent. Effective April 10, 1959 the rate became 11 per cent. From January 1, 1952 until April 10, 1959, 2 percentage points of the rate had been collected as an old age security tax. When the rate was increased in 1959 the additional one per cent was allocated to the old age security tax revenue.

The general sales tax is the most significant of what are known in the Dominion tax structure as excise taxes and is today by far the leading source of revenue among such taxes.[1]

Excise Taxes and Duties Distinguished

Mention has been made of the fact that the sales tax is an *excise tax*. Another important group of Dominion levies are known as *excise duties*. To clear up the inevitable confusion between these similar terms it will be as well to describe each at this point.

To begin with, in law they are distinguishable by the fact that the excise taxes are imposed under the Excise Tax Act (the old Special War Revenue Act) while the excise duties are levied under the Excise Act. Another and more basic difference is that excise duties are levied on commodities in the possession of the Crown, and which remain in the possession of the Crown until the duty is paid, while the excise taxes are required to be paid by a person on the performance of some action by him, such as the manufacture and sale of goods. Another difference is that the excise taxes are generally at *ad valorem* rates while the duties are specific taxes on weight or volume. The excise taxes are imposed on a wide range of commodities while the duties fall only on tobacco and alcoholic products. The taxes apply alike

---

[1] For a detailed discussion of the sales tax see John F. Due, *The General Manufacturers Sales Tax in Canada;* see also *Conference Data Papers* issued by Canadian Tax Foundation.

to home and imported products, in the latter case in addition to the tariff duty. On the other hand it is a distinctive feature of the excise duties on spirits and tobacco products that the excise duty as such applies only to products of domestic manufacture, while the tariff alone is levied on imported products, at a rate which compensates for the internal duty and also includes some element of protection. A further distinction is that evidence of payment of the excise duty usually appears on the dutiable article, e.g., the stamp on a package of cigarettes; but the excise taxes, with one or two exceptions, are "hidden" in the sense that the consumer is given no indication of the presence of the tax. Finally, there are marked differences in the manner in which the taxes and duties are administered. The taxes are collected through a system of licensing and self-assessment by the manufacturer while the duties involve extremely close supervision over all aspects of manufacture, which must be carried on in bonded premises under the control of the revenue authorities. This distinction in collection procedure is more fully discussed in a later chapter.

Nature of the Sales Tax

Turning now to the sales tax, the first point to be noted is that it is a manufacturers' tax, by which is meant that it applies only on the price at the factory, no matter at what point the tax is collected. As such it may be contrasted with a wholesale sales tax or a retail sales tax, imposed respectively at the point of wholesale or retail sale. While it applies to domestic goods on the manufacturer's "sale price," in the case of imported goods it applies to the duty paid value, which is the imported value plus the customs duty. Its scope is universal. It embraces all goods produced or manufactured in Canada or imported into Canada, except goods which are specifically granted exemption under the statute (most staples and implements of production are exempt). The liability for payment of the tax falls on the vendor at the time of sale or delivery of the goods to the purchaser. A system of licensing of manufacturers and wholesalers plays an important part in the administration of the tax.

As a manufacturers' tax the Canadian levy has characteristics different from those of the retail taxes imposed by certain of the provinces and many of the American states. Manifestly it has the advantage of being easier to collect than the retail tax since it taps the spring almost at its source where there are the fewest outlets and individual payments are for larger amounts. Nevertheless it presents other problems not encountered under a retail tax, the most troublesome undoubtedly being the determination of the sale price to which it applies. The final price to the consumer can be accepted as the base for a retail tax, but different considerations arise when the base is a point considerably removed from the final consumer. The determination of sale price therefore is one of the major problems encountered, and of course is of great significance in determining the proper amount of tax.

Sale Price

The general definition of "sale price" given in the Act is as follows:

... "sale price" for the purpose of determining the consumption or sales tax, means the aggregate of
  (i) the amount charged as price before any amount payable in respect of any other tax under this Act is added thereto,
  (ii) any amount that the purchaser is liable to pay to the vendor by reason of or in respect of the sale in addition to the amount charged as price (whether payable at the same or some other time) including, without limiting the generality of the foregoing, any amount charged for, or to make provision for, advertising, financing, servicing, warranty, commission or any other matter, and
  (iii) the amount of excise duties payable under the *Excise Act* whether the goods are sold in bond or not,
and, in the case of imported goods, the sale price shall be deemed to be the duty paid value thereof.[2]

Although the Act does not even suggest that the sales tax should be imposed on an amount less than the sale price, a long

[2]Excise Tax Act, s. 29.

established administrative practice has the effect of setting aside the sale price in many cases where the manufacturer sells to a person other than a wholesaler.

In order to equalize the amount of tax paid on goods sold by a manufacturer to a retailer (or to a user) with the tax which would be payable if the goods had been sold to a wholesaler, the Department authorizes payment of the sales tax on the "established wholesale price." In practice this concept permits a manufacturer to use as the tax base in respect of sales to retailers and users the price at which he sells like goods in representative quantities to independent wholesalers.

The Regulations define "established wholesale price" as:

(i) the price for which the manufacturer regularly sells his taxable goods of like quality, quantity, value and packaging in representative quantities in the ordinary course of business to *bona fide* independent wholesalers in the zone or territory in which the sale is made, or

(ii) the price established by the larger or largest dollar volume of sales to *bona fide* independent wholesalers, by the manufacturer who regularly sells at more than one price his taxable goods of like quality, quantity, value and packaging in representative quantities in the ordinary course of business to *bona fide* independent wholesalers in the zone or territory in which the sale is made, or

(iii) either price, as defined, less one or more of the following, where applicable

  (*a*) cash discount at the rate actually taken on sales that constitute the major portion of the dollar volume of sales to the wholesalers, or

  (*b*) cash discount at the rate actually taken on the larger or largest dollar volume of sales in any case where cash discount at more than one rate is taken on sales that constitute the major portion of the dollar volume of sales to the wholesalers, or

  (*c*) transportation prepaid or allowed on sales to the wholesalers, subject to compliance with the provisions of Regulation 27, Transportation.[3]

[3]Regulations under the Excise Tax Act, July, 1959.

In the absence of an established wholesale price, for example, where a manufacturer sells his goods only to retailers, or to retailers and users, the Deputy Minister may determine the value for tax. Special rules governing the determination of sale price for specific goods have been issued by the Department, as indicated in the Regulations. These cover a variety of items including candy; soft drinks; wines; clothing of all kinds, except boots and shoes; footwear of materials other than rubber; fur articles; ladies' handbags and luggage; canvas goods; furniture; greeting cards; jewellery, watches, and clocks; watch expansion bracelets; electric lamps; radios, television sets, and record players; sewing machines, refrigerators, stoves, washing machines, ironers, and clothes dryers; monuments and concrete burial vaults; drugs, pharmaceuticals; proprietary medicines; toilet goods; and motion picture films. In some of these the price to the consumer is taken as the starting point and reduced by a percentage discount representing the mark-down determined as necessary to reduce it to the level of the price at the factory.

Another problem arises where the vendor and purchaser are interrelated, associated, or affiliated concerns. In this case the Regulations provide that ". . . the established wholesale price of either of them shall be the value on which the tax is payable by the manufacturer, except where determined otherwise by the Minister under the provisions of section 37 of the Act."

Other important rules governing the tax base and the timing of payment are dealt with in the following excerpts from the Regulations:

Computation of tax on the established wholesale price or on the determined wholesale value becomes effective only from the date its use is commenced and never with retroactive effect.

Under the method of tax computation outlined by this Regulation the tax shall be payable by the manufacturer on shipment of his taxable goods from the manufacturing premises, whether on sale, consignment (except salesmen's samples), or for stock in the manufacturer's own branches, warehouses or retail stores, except (for sales tax purposes only) shipments to a branch being operated under a wholesaler's licence, and the tax shall be paid on or before the last day of the month following the month during which the shipment was made.

Where a manufacturer has paid tax or has incurred liability for payment of tax under this Regulation on shipment of his taxable goods from the manufacturing premises no allowance will be permitted in respect of changes in the tax nor for adjustment of price on the goods shipped previously. Moreover, where a manufacturer who has paid tax or has incurred liability for payment of tax under this Regulation by reason of shipment of his taxable goods from his manufacturing premises to his own branch or warehouse then sells the goods out of the branch or warehouse at a price lower than the established wholesale price or the determined wholesale value on which the tax was payable, no adjustment is permissible.[4]

Another class of case requiring a pragmatic determination of the manufacturer's sale price, fortunately limited, is where the goods are sold by a licensed wholesaler. There is little problem for the wholesaler when the goods are imported since the tax applies on the duty paid value in accordance with the general rule. Where the wholesaler is the vendor of domestic goods, however, he must collect the tax not on his own selling price but on his purchase price. This may be determined by either of two methods. The first is based on the actual cost of taxable goods as charged by the manufacturer to the wholesaler. Purchase invoices and import entries must be retained for audit if this system is followed. Under the second method an attempt is made to arrive at a presumed cost to the wholesaler by deducting from his gross sales of taxable goods a margin representing his expenses and mark-ups. This margin is calculated on the experience of the two years preceding the year of sale. A wholesaler must use one base consistently; he is not allowed to transfer each year from one base to another.

In the case of liquor and tobacco products subject to excise duty the sale price includes the duty. Formerly the excise tax on matches, playing cards, and wines was included in the sale price of these articles but recent amendments to the definition of sale price have excluded these taxes from the base.

[4] *Ibid.*

Licensing System

Where a tax is levied prior to the point of final sale to the consumer, as is done with a manufacturers' tax, care must be taken to assure that it is collected only once on each article. This problem of "pyramiding" is overcome under the Canadian sales tax by a system of licensing. All enterprises in Canada classified by the Department of National Revenue as manufacturers or producers of taxable goods are required to obtain a licence from the Department, while those not so classified, either because they are not manufacturers or producers or because they manufacture exempt articles, may not obtain such a licence. These licences not only provide the Department with a Tax Roll; they also have another unique function. They establish a charmed circle of tax exemption, within which materials and semi-manufactured goods may move from one licensed manufacturer or wholesaler to another licensed manufacturer or wholesaler and no tax need be collected. It is only when the purchaser does not hold a licence that the tax must be collected by the vendor. This system allows the free purchase of raw materials and semi-finished manufactured goods, prevents the tax from being collected more than once, and gives the vendor an automatic signal when it should be collected, i.e., he collects it when the purchaser has no licence.

Manufacturers, producers, and some wholesalers are licensed, while retailers are not. Sales from the licensed group to unlicensed wholesalers and retailers are therefore subject to tax. The licensing of new wholesalers has been restricted since September 1, 1938, and wholesalers now starting business are licensed only if 50 per cent of their sales are of exempt goods and they have provided a bond ranging from a minimum of $2,000 to a maximum of $25,000. This practice suggests that the licensing of wholesalers is now regarded only as an administrative convenience to avoid making refunds of tax on their exempt sales, although wholesalers' licences issued prior to the above date have not been cancelled.

In issuing sales tax licences many delicate decisions are required of the Department. While manufacturing or producing is generally understood to be a process in which a new product is created, there are borderline cases where the degree of manufacturing or production carried on is so slight that it is almost necessary to draw a line on some arbitrary basis. The Act has been interpreted to include as manufacturing or producing, along with the ordinary processes of manufacture, the assembling of components into a completed article, lumbering, mining, fishing and farming, and the production of any goods by mixing or blending. It has been ruled, for example, that blending oils, spices, dyes, etc., salting peanuts, and retreading used tires are manufacturing processes. The Act provides that every printer, publisher, lithographer, engraver, dresser or dyer of furs, every person who makes, repairs, or remodels fur garments, every packer of olives, every commercial artist, and every person who wraps, packs or boxes candy and confectionery (except a retailer) must be licensed. On the other hand there are activities where the change resulting from the process is so slight as to rule them out of the general category. For example, the blending of tea, the roasting and grinding of coffee, the cutting and threading of pipe, the washing and sterilizing of rags, and the repackaging of bulk goods in different or smaller packages have been ruled not to constitute manufacturing or production.

Many large enterprises throughout the country are not subject to the tax as manufacturers because their business is quite clearly not of a manufacturing nature. These are mainly the service industries, including transportation, amusements, communications, and financial institutions. Such industries, of course, pay tax on any of their own purchases not specifically exempted. For administrative convenience and as authorized under the Act the Department exempts any producer of taxable goods who sells exclusively by retail and whose annual sales do not exceed $3,000. Also exempt are blacksmiths, dentists, dental mechanics, druggists, milliners, opticians, portrait photographers, plumbers, shoemakers, custom tailors and dressmakers, and certain show-card and sign makers; however if those in the enumerated classes manufacture goods which are not made to individual specifications the exemption will be withdrawn if annual sales of such goods exceed $3,000.

Payment of Tax

On domestically produced goods the sales tax is payable by the end of the month following the month in which a taxable sale has been made. A taxable sale by a manufacturer or wholesaler occurs at the time of delivery to the purchaser or at the time when property in the goods passes, whichever is the earlier. Physical delivery of the goods is, of course, the most easily recognized of the two events, and delivery of goods to a common carrier without lien, C. O. D., or draft against bill of lading, is *prima facie* evidence of delivery. However, goods put in transit with a draft for the purchase price attached to the bill of lading are apparently not regarded as having been delivered until the draft is paid and the documents forwarded to the receiver. The one exception to the general rule that the whole tax is due on delivery or transfer of title is where goods are to be paid for by instalments, in which case the tax is to be paid at the time of each instalment in the same proportion that the instalment bears to the total sale price.

The consumption of goods by the manufacturer, even though they were not produced by him to be sold, constitutes a taxable sale. This would include, for example, printing done for his own use, or the putting to some other use of materials purchased for a manufacturing process. Certain other forms of consumption and transfer are also regarded as sales under the Act (Section) 31.

In the case of imported goods the tax must be paid at the time the goods are imported or taken out of warehouse for consumption.

Exemptions

Exemptions from the sales tax are quite extensive. Most of the staples of life, most of the equipment for and products of the natural resources industry, most building materials, and machinery and apparatus used directly in the process of manufacture (see below) are exempt. A detailed list of all the items, as contained in Schedule 3 of the Act, runs to several pages. The general groups include raw and prepared foodstuffs, farm products and materials and equipment used on the farm, portable engines for use on the farm or in logging, products of the mine or quarry, products of and materials and equipment used by fishermen, certain religious and charitable articles, newspapers, magazines, periodicals and books, certain articles when purchased or imported by diplomats of other countries (a privilege generally granted by all countries), building materials, fire brick and refractories, processing materials, machinery and apparatus used directly in the process of manufacture or production, electricity, all fuel for lighting or heating, and other miscellaneous articles. Samples of any taxable goods to be distributed gratis are exempt from tax, and the customary containers of tax-exempt goods are also exempt.

From the point of view of both the revenue and the taxpayer these exemptions are of major importance. In calculations prepared by the Department of Finance for the Joint Committee of Parliament on Old Age Security[5] it was estimated that to restore all exempt goods to taxable status would increase the revenue from the sales tax by $300 million, a significant addition when compared with the actual revenue in 1950 of $400 million. The five main groups of exempt goods were described in these estimates as (1) foodstuffs; (2) fuel, including electricity; (3) building materials; (4) manufacturing machinery and apparatus; and (5) farm machinery. A sixth group included all other exempt goods, running to hundreds of small items. It was estimated that the value of sales in these groups exempt from tax (at 1950 manufacturers' prices) was as follows:

		(millions)
(1)	Food	$1,450
(2)	Fuel	700
(3)	Building materials	850
(4)	Manufacturing machinery	380
(5)	Farm machinery	320
(6)	Miscellaneous	100
	Total	$3,800

[5] Minutes of Proceedings and Evidence, no. 23, Wednesday, May 24, 1950.

The general effect of these exemptions has been to limit the scope of the tax largely to consumer expenditures on clothing, house furnishings, semi-durable goods (cars, etc.), liquor, and tobacco. They have undoubtedly had the effect of reducing or largely eliminating the regressivity of the tax, owing particularly to the exclusion of foodstuffs.

The exemption of machinery and apparatus and complete parts therefor, used in the manufacture or production of goods, is of fairly recent origin, having been introduced only in 1945. A distinction has been made in this exemption between goods used directly in the process of manufacturing and other machinery and apparatus. Office equipment and motor vehicles are specifically excluded from the exemption, and regulations of the Department have delineated the equipment and apparatus which comes within it. Service industries do not qualify since they do not manufacture goods, although public utilities are treated as manufacturers to the point where distribution of their product commences.

Another exemption of cost goods that raises interesting problems from time to time is the exclusion of "materials (not including grease, lubricating oils, or fuels for use in internal combustion engines) consumed or expended directly in the process of manufacture or production of goods."

Owing to the fact that producers and manufacturers of exempt goods may not obtain a licence unless the Act grants an additional specific exemption, the parts and materials for such goods are automatically subject to tax. This follows because only by being licensed can a manufacturer obtain his supplies and materials free of tax. For this reason in the case of many of the exempt goods parts and materials have been specifically included in the exempt list as well.

Provincial governments may purchase goods free of tax when they are for provincial use and not for resale or use by any board, commission, railway, public utility, university, etc., controlled or operated by the province.[6] Public hospitals and institutions for the care in residence of children or aged, infirm,

---

[6]Municipalities may purchase certain specified capital goods free of tax.

or incapacitated persons, receiving a Dominion or provincial government grant, are also extended this exemption. The full tax is payable on all purchases from the public by departments of the Dominion government. Half rates of tax are granted in respect of articles manufactured and produced by the labour of the blind, deaf, and dumb, in institutions devoted to care of persons so afflicted.

Refunds and drawbacks of tax are given under certain conditions. Of these undoubtedly the most important is the complete remission of tax on all goods exported from Canada. Refunds may also be claimed by an unlicensed wholesaler, jobber, or other dealer on goods on which he has paid tax when he sells such goods to a licensed manufacturer or wholesaler who is entitled to purchase exempt from tax. On returned goods not replaced the manufacturer may refund the sales tax to the purchaser and claim a credit for such refunds on a later report. Application for refunds, for the return of overpayments or payments in error must be made by the taxpayer within two years after payment of the tax.

In summary, the Dominion government sales tax is a manufacturers' tax normally imposed on and collected by the manufacturer of goods of domestic origin or imposed on the duty paid value and collected at the time of entry for consumption of imported goods. Most of the staples of life and many of the capital goods of industry are exempt from this tax. Its principal incidence now falls upon consumer expenditures for clothing, household furnishings, and semi-durable and durable goods. It has no counterpart in either the American or the British tax systems although the purchase tax in the United Kingdom has some features in common. The closest parallel to the Canadian sales tax is that levied by the Commonwealth government in Australia, although even here there are significant differences.

Summary

RATE. 11 per cent (since April 10, 1959), of which 3 per cent is earmarked for old age security.

REVENUE

	Fiscal year 1959–60 ($000)	Percentage of tax revenue	Percentage of total revenue
Net sales tax (after deducting refunds)	732,658	15.4	13.9
Old age security tax	270,000	—	—

STATUTORY REFERENCES. Excise Tax Act, Revised Statutes, Canada, 1952, c. 100; Regulations under the Excise Tax Act, July, 1959; Old Age Security Act, Revised Statutes, Canada, 1952, c. 200.

CHAPTER 7

DOMINION COMMODITY TAXES
EXCISE TAXES, EXCISE DUTIES, AND MISCELLANEOUS TAXES

FREQUENT REVISIONS of the Dominion commodity taxes in recent years have produced a relatively simple tax structure composed of the general sales tax, the excise taxes, and the excise duties. The general sales tax has been described in the preceding chapter, and it is intended here to discuss the remaining two groups and some other taxes of minor importance.

EXCISE TAXES

A limited number of excise taxes were first introduced under the Special War Revenue Act in 1915 and levies of this form have been imposed ever since by the Dominion. Like the sales tax, the excise taxes are manufacturers' taxes, and the description of the general characteristics of this form of levy in the preceding chapter applies to them as well almost without modification. Every manufacturer or importer of any taxable goods must be licensed, and the tax applies either at the time of sale of a taxable article by the licensed manufacturer, or at the time of importation. Where the article is also subject to the general sales tax, the excise tax and the sales tax apply separately to the same value. There are today no retail sales taxes in the Dominion tax system. The repeal of the retail jewellery tax in 1949 ended one of the few experiments in this field in the fiscal history of the federal government. For a time following 1951 defence requirements necessitated the reimposition of several taxes repealed in the post-war period and substantial increases in the rates of existing taxes were made, but recent changes have restored a relatively simple structure with a few main sources of revenue.

Excise Taxes, Duties, Miscellaneous

Any deviations from the general pattern of the manufacturers' excise tax or any special characteristics of a particular tax will be noted in the following description. To give as accurate a presentation as possible, in most instances the text of the Excise Tax Act is reproduced in full. For convenience the Schedule is rearranged in the order of taxes imposed at 10 per cent and those imposed at 15 per cent.

1. 10 per cent rate

The following articles and commodities are subject to the 10 per cent rate:

(a) *Toilet articles* (Schedule I, Section 2): Articles, materials or preparations of whatever composition or in whatever form, commonly or commercially known as toilet articles, preparations or cosmetics, which are intended for use or application for toilet purposes, or for use in connection with the care of the human body, including the hair, nails, eyes, teeth, or any other part or parts thereof, whether for cleansing, deodorizing, beautifying, preserving or restoring, and including shaving soaps and shaving creams, antiseptics, bleaches, dipilatories, perfumes, scents, and similar preparations.

(b) *Lighters* (Schedule I, Section 3): Devices, commonly or commercially known as lighters, which produce sparks, flame, or heat, whether or not in combination with other articles on the separate or combined value, as the case may be; a minimum tax of 10 cents is provided.

(c) *Slot machines* (Schedule I, Section 4): Coin, disc, or token operated slot machines or amusement devices of all kinds.

(d) *Smokers accessories* (Schedule I, Section 6): Tobacco pipes; cigar and cigarette holders and cigarette rolling devices.

(e) *Matches* (Schedule I, Section 8).

(f) *Clocks, watches, ornamental articles, and jewellery* (Schedule I, Section 9):

(i) Clocks and watches adapted to household or personal use, except railway men's watches, and those specially designed for the use of the blind, and alarm clocks where the sale price by the Canadian manufacturer or the duty paid value of those imported does not exceed ten dollars.

(ii) Articles of all kinds made in whole or in part of ivory, jet, amber, coral, mother of pearl, natural shells, tortoise shell, jade, onyx, lapis lazuli, or other semi-precious stones.

(iii) The following articles, namely: articles commonly or commercially known as jewellery, whether real or imitation, including diamonds and other precious or semi-precious stones for personal use or for adornment of the person; goldsmiths' and silversmiths' products except gold-plated or silver-plated ware for the preparation or serving of food or drinks.

2. 15 per cent rate

Radios, television sets and record players (Schedule I, Section 5):

(*a*) Phonographs, record playing devices, radio broadcasting receiving sets or any combination of the foregoing and tubes therefor; any apparatus or device that enables a person to hear programmes of music distributed by any means whatever or radio broadcasting programmes distributed by any means whatever; but this paragraph does not include any article coming within paragraph (*b*) of this section. (A minimum tax of $2 is provided for radios.)

(*b*) Television receiving sets and tubes therefor; any apparatus or device that enables a person to see, or to see and hear, television programmes distributed by any means whatever or television radio broadcasting programmes distributed by any means whatever.

(*c*) Electron tubes, not including cathode ray tubes, the duty-paid value of which, as the case may be, does not exceed five dollars per tube. (A minimum tax of 10 cents per tube is provided.)

(*d*) Cathode ray tubes for television receiving sets.

3. *Excise Taxes on Playing Cards, Wines, Tobacco Products, etc.*

This is a more or less related group of taxes, by Mrs. Grundy's standards. Certain of them, particularly those on tobacco products, are also orphans in the Excise Tax Act. Prior to World War II cigarettes and tobacco suffered the imposition only of excise duties, to be described in the latter part of this chapter, but a part of the wartime increases were imposed in the form of excise taxes. This procedure was adopted to avoid the entire disruption of the basic tobacco tax structure in the Excise Act and to avoid the increased expense for manufacturers entailed in requiring them to tie up more funds in excise stamps, a feature of the excise duties.

The actual rates of this group of taxes are as follows:

(a) *Playing cards* (Section 27): For every 54 cards or fraction of 54 in each package, 20 cents per pack.

(b) *Wines* (Section 28): Wines of all kinds containing 7 per cent or less of absolute alcohol by volume, 25 cents per gallon; non-sparkling wines containing more than 7 per cent of absolute alcohol by volume but not over 40 per cent of proof spirits, 50 cents per gallon.

(c) *Sparkling wines*, including champagne (Section 28): $2.50 per gallon.

(d) *Cigarettes* (Schedule II): On each five cigarettes or fraction thereof, $2\frac{1}{2}$ cents.

(e) *Manufactured tobacco, including snuff* (Schedule II): For each pound, 80 cents.

(f) *Cigars* (Schedule I, Section 7): 15 per cent (the value of the cigar to which the 15 per cent rate applies to include the excise duty).

Summary

RATES. With some exceptions mentioned in the text the current rates are 10 and 15 per cent on the manufacturer's price.

REVENUE

	Fiscal year 1959–60 ($000)	Percentage of tax revenue	Percentage of total revenue
Cigarettes, tobacco, and cigars	185,503	3.9	3.5
Automobiles	64,281*	1.4	1.2
Radios, television sets, and phonographs	17,759	.4	.3
Other	19,026	.5	.4
Total	286,568	6.0	5.4

STATUTORY REFERENCES. Excise Tax Act, Revised Statutes, Canada, 1952, c. 100; Regulations under the Excise Tax Act, Circular no. ET1, July 1, 1959.

*Repealed June, 1961.

Excise Duties

Several of the provinces imposed excise duties on liquor and tobacco before Confederation, and they have been an important source of revenue for the Dominion since 1867.

In 1960 the rates of excise duties, all of which may be found in the Schedule to the Excise Act, were as follows:

1. *Alcoholic Products*

(a) *Spirits distilled in Canada*: Per proof gallon, $13. (It was noted previously that the excise duty applies only to spirits of domestic manufacture; imported spirits are subject to a tariff duty of $13.50 per proof gallon under the British Preferential Tariff and at higher rates under the other tariffs.)

(b) *Canadian brandy*: Per proof gallon, $11.

(c) *Beer*: 38 cents per gallon.

(d) *Other spirits*: Reduced rates are provided for spirits used in certain products. Spirits used in the manufacture of patented medicines, extracts, essences, pharmaceutical products, and perfume, are taxed at a reduced rate of $1.50 per proof gallon. The same rate is granted for spirits purchased by licensed druggists for use in prescriptions for medicines and pharmaceutical products. For spirits used in chemical compositions approved by Order in Council the reduced rate is 15 cents per gallon. In any case where the spirits taken into a bonded manufactory are imported an additional duty of 30 cents per gallon applies along with the rates given immediately above. Spirits used in the manufacture of vinegar are exempt from duty and a draw-back of 99 per cent of the duty is given on spirits used in a governmental or university scientific laboratory or for any other scientific research not of a private character and also when used in *bona fide* public hospitals. Spirits used in the treatment of domestic wines and in the manufacture of any article subject to a special excise tax are also exempt.

2. *Tobacco Products*

(a) *Cigarettes*: The excise duty on standard cigarettes (those described as weighing not more than $2\frac{1}{2}$ pounds per thousand)[1]

[1] 3 pounds per thousand after April 1, 1962.

is $4 per thousand. On cigarettes which contain more tobacco the duty is $5 per thousand. In equivalent terms the additional excise *tax* on cigarettes (2½ cents for each five cigarettes) is $5.00 per thousand. The total duty and tax applying to cigarettes therefore is $9.00 per thousand, or nine-tenths of a cent per cigarette.

(b) *Manufactured tobacco*: Products under this category, including snuff, pipe tobacco, and cigarette tobacco for "roll your own," whether produced from foreign or domestic leaf, are subject to an excise duty of 35 cents per pound. In addition these products bear an excise *tax* of 80 cents per pound, making a total excise tax and duty levy of $1.15 per pound.

(c) *Cigars*: A duty of $2 per thousand (plus a *tax* of 15 per cent).

Some International Comparisons

In view of the leading and traditional place of alcoholic and tobacco products in the tax systems of Canada, the United States and the United Kingdom some international comparisons are of interest. For example, the Canadian duty of $13 per proof gallon is lower than the United States federal rate on spirits of the same strength. Making allowance for the difference between the size of the gallon and the standard of proof, the American rate is about $14.37 on a Canadian gallon of Canadian proof. On the other hand the British duty on spirits is approximately $29.50 per proof gallon. On the usual 25-ounce container of 30 underproof spirits sold in Canada these rates work out respectively at $1.42 (Canada), $1.57 (United States), and $3.45 (United Kingdom).

Having introduced the term, a side note on the mysterious subject of "proof" might also be in order at this point. The expression "proof" is said to have had its origin in the days when, with nominal tax rates in force, the precise measurement of alcoholic content was not essential, and a rough and ready test was devised. This was known as the "gunpowder test," and involved saturating gunpowder with the spirits and then igniting the powder. If a flash was produced by the gunpowder on ignition the spirit was "overproof"; if not, it was "underproof."

EXCISE TAXES, DUTIES, MISCELLANEOUS   143

Today, of course, in the well-equipped laboratory of the modern distillery the measurement of alcoholic content is made with scientific precision. The exact and precise test, as defined in the Excise Act (Section 3 (*f*)) is as follows: "... 'proof spirits,' or 'spirits of the strength of proof,' means any spirit having the strength of proof by Sikes' hydrometer, that is, any spirit which at the temperature of fifty-one degrees Fahrenheit weighs exactly twelve-thirteenths of the weight of an equal measure of distilled water at the same temperature."

For the layman this technical definition represents a considerable regression in ease of understanding from the old gunpowder test, and it is comforting to know that proof can be expressed more simply in terms of volume. Spirits of the strength of proof in Canada are spirits which contain by volume 57.1 per cent of alcohol at 60° F. A bottle of proof spirit therefore is a little better than half (or about four-sevenths) pure alcohol by volume. Spirits containing a greater or less proportion by volume are described as being "overproof" or "underproof" by a certain percentage. Thus a liquor that is "30 per cent underproof" (or "70 per cent proof") has an alcoholic content by volume 30 per cent less than 57.1 per cent, or 40 per cent. This happens to be the alcoholic content of spirits sold in Canada at the present time. It compares with a pre-war content of about 43 per cent (24.7 per cent underproof), or approximately 7.5 per cent by volume higher than the present strength. Correspondingly a liquor that is "30 per cent overproof" (or "130 per cent proof") would have an alcoholic content by volume of 30 per cent more than 57.1 per cent, or 74.2 per cent.

The same standard of proof applies in England, and British spirits for some years have been 30 per cent "underproof." In the United States, however, the *standard* of proof is lower, being only 50 per cent by volume, which is 12.4 per cent underproof by the Canadian standard. The usual strength today in the United States is 85 to 90 per cent proof, which on the American standard of proof gives an alcoholic content by volume of 85 to 90 per cent of 50 per cent, or 42.5 to 45 per cent. This is slightly higher than the prevalent Canadian content by volume of 40 per cent.

For beer the present duty of 38 cents per gallon in Canada may be compared with a rate of about 35 cents per equivalent gallon in the United States and about 41 cents in the United Kingdom. On the typical 12-ounce bottle these gallonage rates work out to 2.9 cents in Canada, 2.6 cents in the United States, and 3.0 cents in the United Kingdom.

In the case of cigarettes the Canadian rate on the standard package of twenty cigarettes is 18 cents and the United States federal rate on the same package is 8 cents. In both countries many of the lesser jurisdictions also impose special cigarette taxes or else the cigarettes are subject to a general retail tax, and in Canada the 11 per cent sales tax also applies. To the smoker in the United Kingdom, however, any Western Hemisphere rates would appear purely nominal. As part of the drive to reduce imports of dollar tobacco the tax on cigarettes has been kept at a very high rate in the post-war period and in 1960 was something like 43 cents per packet of twenty cigarettes, more than double the Canadian rate.

Summary

RATES. The principal rates on alcoholic products are now $13 per proof gallon for spirits and 38 cents per gallon for beer. On standard cigarettes the excise duty is $4 per thousand ($9.00 per thousand including the excise tax) and on manufactured tobacco 35 cents per pound ($1.15 per pound including the excise tax).

REVENUE

	Fiscal year 1959–60 ($000)	*Percentage of tax revenue*	*Percentage of total revenue*
Tobacco products	146,176	3.0	2.8
Alcoholic beverages	193,058	4.1	3.6
Licences	34	—	—
Less refunds	−4,061	—	—
Net total	335,207	7.0	6.3

STATUTORY REFERENCES. Excise Act, Revised Statutes, Canada, 1952, c. 99.

Other Dominion Taxes

Insurance Premiums

A tax of 10 per cent is imposed under the Excise Tax Act on premiums paid by a resident of Canada to an unlicensed British or foreign company in respect of insurance on property situated in Canada. This levy is administered by the Department of Insurance. In 1959–60 the revenue was only $18,000.

Export of Electricity

Prior to October 1, 1959, under the Electricity and Fluid Export Act a tax of 3/100 of 1 cent was imposed on each kilowatt hour of electricity exported from Canada. From that date the tax has been levied under Part II of the Excise Tax Act. This is a control measure rather than a revenue tax, and collections have been less than one million dollars per annum.

Chapter 8

CONSTITUTIONAL LIMITATIONS ON PROVINCIAL TAXATION

THE FOLLOWING CHAPTERS are a discussion of the provincial tax system. So vital has been the influence of the constitutional limitations on its development, however, that a knowledge of this background is essential to an understanding of its existing form. The present chapter will be devoted therefore to a brief appraisal of this influence.

The constitutional basis of the taxing power in Canada was established in 1867 under the British North America Act. It restricted the provinces to "direct taxation within the province" and granted unrestricted power to the Dominion to raise funds "by any mode or system of taxation." The full text of the provisions governing the provinces is as follows:

Section 92. In each Province the Legislature may exclusively make Laws in relation to Matters coming within the Classes of Subjects next hereinafter enumerated; that is to say, . . .

(2) Direct taxation within the Province in order to the Raising of a Revenue for Provincial Purposes . . . .

(9) Shop, Saloon, Tavern, Auctioneer, and other Licences in order to the raising of a Revenue for Provincial, Local, or Municipal Purposes.

Section 121 also indirectly relates to the manner of imposing taxes, and reads as follows: "All Articles of the Growth, Produce, or Manufacture of any one of the Provinces shall, from and after the Union, be admitted free into each of the other Provinces."

Section 124 preserved certain lumber dues to the province of New Brunswick and Section 125 provided that "no lands or Property belonging to Canada or any Province shall be liable to taxation."

Direct Taxation

The circumstances that resulted in this allocation of taxing power have frequently been explored in other writings, and need not be fully reviewed here. Suffice it to say that however obscure the intentions of the framers of the constitution may have become with the passage of time in regard to other matters, their disposition of financial powers is singularly unequivocal. Every fact and every authority demonstrates that their purpose was to allot the main financial resources to the federal government. The Royal Commission on Dominion-Provincial Relations summed up this view in the following words:

All that is certainly known is that the framers had large plans for the new Dominion and they proposed a strong central government with ample financial powers to carry the program through. The financial settlement which gave the Dominion the unrestricted taxing power, and the exclusive use of the most important revenue sources of the time [nearly four-fifths of the former provincial revenues were given to the new Dominion government] is the most significant evidence of the leading role cast for the new federal government and of the responsibilities which it was expected to assume.[1]

As a corollary one might say that if no further evidence were available the very restriction of the provinces to direct taxes, which were extremely unpopular at the time of Confederation, would in itself be sufficient to prove this purpose. In the light of the subsequent development of the income tax to its present commanding stature this limitation seems like no restriction at all, but every coin must be valued in its own realm. No one foresaw in 1867 that the income tax would achieve the important role it has recently played in national finances. It was then only an infant in swaddling clothes, giving little promise of its subsequent healthy growth. The levy that spelled direct taxation for the average Canadian of the period was the property tax, and all the evidence indicates that there was a profound and ready distaste for even this tax in many parts of British North America. In fact the theory that the provinces were given direct

[1] *Report of the Royal Commission on Dominion-Provincial Relations*, Book I, p. 36.

taxation because it was so unpopular and that this arrangement was accepted because of the restricted functions they were expected to perform is borne out by several speeches and documents of the period.

Apart from these considerations the division probably seemed natural and logical enough at the time if only on the grounds that the three main tax sources of the day were the customs duties, excise duties, and property taxes, and when the first two had been given to the federal government under the terms of union there was left only the third for the provinces.

To give the Fathers of Confederation their due, an objective analysis of the forms of taxation at their disposal does not suggest any alternative arrangement that would conform to the basic and desirable requirement of restricting the incidence of a provincial tax to the residents of that province. One could easily argue that the final arrangement was entirely realistic if only because a direct tax, alone of all taxes, may be imposed within the limits of the province without any great danger of its incidence spreading beyond the provincial boundaries. The more remote the tax is from the final point of its incidence the greater is the likelihood that it will fall on a resident of another province. This point may easily be appreciated by considering the ultimate incidence of a general manufacturers' sales tax imposed, say, in Ontario or Quebec. It is evident that such a levy would fall eventually on residents of all or most of the provinces of Canada.

There may also be something in the fact that the influential economist of the day was John Stuart Mill, who, as will be seen in a moment, had a great deal to say concerning direct and indirect taxation.

Judicial Interpretation

While the British North America Act determined the general division of taxing powers, it was left to the Judicial Committee of the Privy Council to delineate the exact limitations of these powers. The first decision on these powers was given in 1881. The case was *Citizens' Insurance Co. of Canada* v. *Parsons*,[2]

[1](1881) 7 App. Cas. 96.

which served to clear the air of whatever doubts there may have been of the respective powers of the two levels of government. It established that no conflict existed between the general powers given to the Dominion on the one hand and the exclusive powers given to the provinces on the other. The Dominion had power to levy every sort of taxation but the provinces were restricted to direct taxation within their geographical limits. This view was subsequently confirmed by the Privy Council in *Bank of Toronto* v. *Lambe*[3] and *Caron* v. *The King*.[4] These decisions settled that the Dominion and provincial taxing powers might overlap in the field of direct taxation and that any resulting double taxation was not contrary to the British North America Act.

The two levels of government are not completely free in their respective spheres, however. Each must exercise its taxing power in such a way as not to impair or destroy the powers given the other government under the constitution. This principle was established in the decision in *Great West Saddlery Co.* v. *The King*[5] and confirmed in *Caron* v. *The King*.

In giving its decisions on the nature of direct taxation, almost from the first case the Judicial Committee of the Privy Council adopted the definition that appears in John Stuart Mill's *Principles of Political Economy*, which by now should be familiar to every tax student in Canada. Mill defined a direct tax as "one which is demanded from the very person who it is intended or desired should pay it." He defined an indirect tax as one which is imposed on one person in the expectation that he will recoup himself from another person, for example, the customs or excise.

The history of this definition in the legal cases has been described by Kennedy and Wells in the following words:

This definition was at first selected by the Judicial Committee not with the intention of making it a binding legal definition but because it seemed to embody with sufficient accuracy the understanding of the words likely to have been present in the minds of those who passed the British America Act. As decision followed decision, however, the definition adopted with diffidence in the earlier decisions almost

[3] (1887) 12 App. Cas. 575. [4] [1924] A.C. 999. [5] [1921] 2 A.C. 91.

crystallized into a binding legal definition of the words 'direct taxation,' and in *Cotton* v. *The King*, Lord Moulton, speaking for the Judicial Committee, laid it down quite plainly in words which their Lordships have subsequently re-affirmed: "These decisions have established that the meaning to be attributed to the phrase 'direct taxation' in section ninety-two of the British North America Act, 1867 is substantially the definition quoted above from the treatise of John Stuart Mill and that this question is no longer open to discussion."[6]

The cases in which this concept was developed merit further brief consideration. (Those dealing with provincial succession duties are discussed in a later chapter.)

The question was early faced in *Attorney-General for Quebec* v. *Reed*.[7] The tax in question was a stamp duty of 10 cents on court exhibits or on actions related thereto. Here their lordships by a process of reasoning that would bemuse a freshman student in economics arrived at two conclusions regarding the nature of a direct tax. The first was as follows: "The best general rule is to look to the time of payment; and if at the time the ultimate incidence is uncertain, then, as it appears to their Lordships, it cannot, in this view, be called direct taxation within the meaning of the second section of the ninety-second clause of the act in question." The second was that any special circumstances of the transaction in which the tax was involved had no bearing on the general question. Included under this heading would be an agreement among the parties, for example, to the effect that one of them was to bear the amount of the tax, rather than the other. It is only the general and ordinary incidence of the tax that is to be considered.

The court introduced an additional refinement in *Bank of Toronto* v. *Lambe*. Whereas the *Reed Case* had left the impression that the tax must be considered indirect if its ultimate incidence was uncertain at the time of payment, in the *Lambe Case* the Privy Council decided that for a tax to be considered indirect not only must there exist a doubt that the tax did not rest with the first payer, but also the method by which the tax

[6]W. P. M. Kennedy and D. C. Wells, *The Law of the Taxing Power in Canada*, p. 49.
[7](1884) 10 App. Cas. 141.

was passed on must be clear and self-evident. If this method is "an obscure and circuituous one" then the tax must be considered a direct tax.

The right of the provinces to impose licences on brewers was confirmed in *Brewers' and Maltsters' Association of Ontario* v. *Attorney-General for Ontario*.[8] The court held these licences not to be indirect taxes, on the grounds that they were demanded from the very person whom the legislation intended or desired should pay them.

By the turn of the century the court had almost fully developed its concept of direct taxation, and in several subsequent cases applied it without the introduction of any radical changes. The most recent decisions, including that rendered in 1949 in *Attorney-General for British Columbia* v. *Esquimalt and Nanaimo Railway Co.*,[9] appear only to have further confirmed these principles. A list of most of the Privy Council cases dealing with taxation is appended to the present chapter. The more significant of these in the period between the *Lambe Case* and the case last cited, omitting those referring to succession duties, are *Attorney-General for Manitoba* v. *Attorney-General for Canada*, 1925, *The King* v. *Caledonian Collieries*, 1928, *City of Halifax* v. *Fairbanks' Estate*, 1928, *Attorney-General for British Columbia* v. *Kingcome Navigation Co. Ltd.*, 1934, and *Atlantic Smoke Shops Ltd.* v. *Conlon*, 1943.

Practically all of these cases contain an excellent review of the past decisions and the developing significance of the concept of direct taxation. Typical of these is the summary given by Lord Cave in the *Fairbanks Case*.

The framers of that act evidently regard taxes as divisible into two separate and distinct categories, namely, those that are direct and those which cannot be so described, and it is to taxation of the former character only that the powers of a provincial government are made to extend. From this it is to be inferred that the distinction between direct and indirect taxes was well known before the passing of the Act; and it is undoubtedly the fact that before that date the classification was familiar to statesmen as well as to economists, and that certain taxes were then universally recognized as falling within

[8] [1897] A.C. 231.   [9] [1950] A. C. 87.

one or the other category. Thus, taxes on property or income were everywhere treated as direct taxes. . . . On the other hand, duties of customs and excise were regarded by everyone as typical instances of indirect taxation. When therefore the Act of Union allocated the power of direct taxation for provincial purposes to the province, it must surely have intended that the taxation, for those purposes, of property and income should belong exclusively to the provincial legislatures, and that without regard to any theory as to the ultimate incident of such taxation. To hold otherwise would be to suppose that the framers of the Act intended to impose on the provincial legislature the task of speculating as to the probable ultimate incidence of each particular tax which it might desire to impose, at the risk of having such tax held invalid if the conclusion reached should afterwards be held to be wrong.

What then is the effect to be given to Mill's formula above quoted? No doubt it is valuable as providing a logical basis for the distinction already established between direct and indirect taxes, and perhaps also as a guide for determining as to any new or unfamiliar tax which may be imposed in which of the two categories it is to be placed; but it can not have the effect of disturbing the established classification of the old and well-known species of taxation, and making it necessary to apply a new test to every particular member of those species. The imposition of taxes on property and income, of death duties and of municipal and local rates is, according to the common understanding of the term, direct taxation, just as the exaction of the customs or excise duty on commodities or of a percentage duty on services would ordinarily be regarded as indirect taxation; and although new forms of taxation may from time to time be added to one category or the other in accordance with Mill's formula, it would be wrong to use that formula as a ground for transferring a tax universally recognized as belonging to one class to a different class of taxation.[10]

A significant aspect of the decisions is that the Privy Council has laid down that the classification of taxes into one category or the other must follow the general understanding of the distinction between direct and indirect taxes as it existed at the time the act was drafted. It is assumed that this understanding was somewhat similar to that contained in Mill's oft-quoted definition. Great importance has been attached in the cases

[10][1928] A.C. 117, at pp. 124, 125.

to the intent of the legislators in passing any particular statute, and also to the form of the legislation. The Judicial Committee would appear to have said that where the act imposes the tax on the purchaser, and where there is no clear and self-evident means by which that purchaser may pass on the tax to another person, that tax is a direct tax. The mechanical procedure for *collecting* the tax is provided in practice by appointing the seller as an agent of the Crown for this purpose. This would not seem, however, to have a direct bearing on the legality of the tax, as long as it is *imposed* on the purchaser.

In this connection the charging provisions of the provincial statutes imposing gasoline taxes are of great interest. It is evident that considerable care has been taken in drafting these and similar acts to meet the basic requirement of the Privy Council decisions. The provincial gasoline tax acts are of particular interest, because in practice, as a matter of administrative convenience, the taxes are actually collected from the gasoline refiners.

Newfoundland: ". . . every consumer shall pay to the Minister a tax of — cents a gallon on all gasoline, except tax exempt gasoline purchased or received by such customer."

Prince Edward Island: "Every purchaser shall pay to the Provincial Treasurer, for the use of Her Majesty in the right of the Province of Prince Edward Island, a charge or tax at the rate of — cents per gallon on all gasoline purchased or delivery of which is received by him."

Nova Scotia: "In order to the raising of a revenue for provincial purposes every purchaser shall pay to the Minister for the use of Her Majesty in the right of the Province of Nova Scotia, a charge or tax at such rate not exceeding ——— cents a gallon as the Governor-in-Council from time to time fixes and determines on all gasoline purchased or delivery of which is received by such purchaser."

New Brunswick: "Every consumer shall pay to the Minister for the use of the Crown in the right of the Province, a tax, to be known as the gasoline tax, in respect of all gasoline purchased by or delivered to, the consumer, at such rate, not exceeding — cents a gallon, as the Lieutenant-Governor-in-Council may from time to time determine."

Quebec: "(1) No person may buy gasoline in this Province, for his own use or for that of his family, agent, employee, partner or employer, without paying a duty equal to ——— cents per gallon, imperial measure.

"(2) Such duty shall be paid by the purchaser and shall be collected by the vendor in the manner indicated by the Minister, and shall be remitted to the Bureau by the vendor.

"(3) The vendor shall act, in such case, as agent for the Bureau, and he shall remit to it the said duty at the times determined by the Minister."

Ontario: "Every purchaser of gasoline shall pay to the Minister for the use of the Crown in right of Ontario, a charge or tax at the rate of — cents per imperial gallon on all gasoline purchased or delivery of which is received by him."

Manitoba: "Every purchaser shall pay to Her Majesty for the public use of the government a tax equal to — cents on every gallon of gasoline purchased by him in the province."

Saskatchewan: "Unless exempted by the regulations every purchaser shall pay, for the use of Her Majesty in the right of Saskatchewan, a tax in respect of the use of gasoline of which he is the purchaser, such tax to be computed at the rate of ——— cents per gallon on all such gasoline."

Alberta: "Every purchaser shall pay to the Minister for the use of the Crown, in the right of the Province of Alberta, a charge or tax on all fuel oil purchased by him or delivery of which is received by him. . . ."

British Columbia: "Every purchaser shall pay to Her Majesty for the raising of a revenue for Provincial purposes at the time of making the purchase a tax equal to — cents per gallon of the gasoline purchased by him . . . which tax shall be levied and collected in the manner provided in this Act or the regulations."

Contrast with the United States

It is an interesting commentary on the ingenuity and resourcefulness of the legal mind that a serious constitutional limitation on the powers of the *federal* government in the United States in imposing direct taxes has also been overcome by legislative action or judicial interpretation.

In the United States under the constitutional disposition of the taxing power the federal government is allowed to impose direct taxes only if they are "apportioned among the several states which may be included within this Union, according to their respective numbers," nor may any "capitation, or other direct, tax" be imposed, "unless in proportion to the census or enumeration herein before directed to be taken."[11]

The early judicial view of this limitation was that it allowed only real estate and poll taxes, but the income tax imposed during the Civil War was upheld as being not a direct tax but an excise tax or duty, a field in which the federal power is limited only by the requirement that the tax or duty be generally applicable. A later attempt in 1894 to tax incomes was held to be unconstitutional, but fifteen years later a tax on corporate income, imposed as an excise tax on corporation franchises, was held by the Supreme Court to be within the federal power. This uncertainty regarding the income tax was finally removed in 1913 by the 16th Amendment which gave Congress full power to impose a tax on income without regard to the original constitutional limitations. Certain other federal levies are presumably still brought within the pale by the device of imposing them as excises. For example, a case involving the constitutionality of the federal gift tax was settled by the Supreme Court in 1929 in favour of the federal government on the ground that the tax imposed was not a direct tax but an excise tax.

Taxation within the Province

To conform to the constitutional limitations provincial taxation in Canada must not only be direct but must also be "within the province." In practice this requirement is met if the subject-matter of the tax, whether persons or property, is within the province.

Persons, including artificial persons and corporations, are liable if found in the province. The case of *Bank of Toronto* v. *Lambe* early settled this point. The decision said in part: " ... clause 2 of section 92 does not require that persons to be taxed by Quebec are to be domiciled or even resident in Quebec. Any person found within the province may be legally taxed there if taxed directly."

The question whether a natural person is "within the

[11]United States Constitution, Act 1, Sec. 2, par. 3, and Sec. 9, par. 4.

province" or not is easily settled. The location of a legal person or a corporation is not self-evident, however, and a great deal of litigation has evolved from the obscurities of this aspect of provincial taxation. In general it has been settled that business enterprises are located in the province if they carry on business in the province. Property, which falls into the two broad classifications of immoveable and moveable, is also taxable if located in the province. The situs of immoveable property, which for the most part takes a concrete physical form, such as land, presents fewer complications than does the situs of moveable property. Some of these problems are discussed later in connection with provincial succession duties, which have given rise to many of them. In passing it is interesting to note that the inclination of the provinces to overcome these difficulties by legislation was curbed by early court decisions which determined that the common law must govern in determining the location of property.[12] As a result the rules of situs that now apply have been the outgrowth of litigation and may be found only in the decisions of the courts.

Licensing Powers

With regard to the provincial powers under clause 9 to impose "Shop, Saloon, Tavern, Auctioneer, and other Licences in order to the raising of Revenue for Provincial, Local, or Municipal Purposes," it would appear from the cases that these words confer a fiscal power and not simply a regulatory one. In short, the provinces and municipalities are not constitutionally barred from imposing licences for revenue purposes. While the courts have not ruled consistently on the matter[13] it is also now fairly well established that the power is a general one, and that the licences that may be imposed do not have to be of the same class as those mentioned in the clause.

Whether or not the licences imposed under clause 9 of Section 92 must come within the limitations of clause 2, i.e.,

[12]See particularly *The King* v. *Lovitt*, [1912] A.C. 212.
[13]Compare *Severn* v. *Regina*, (1878) 2 S.C.R. 70, and *Brewers' and Maltsters' Association of Ontario* v. *Attorney-General for Ontario*, [1897] A.C. 231.

direct taxation within the province, has not been finally determined by the Privy Council. One Canadian authority, however, has interpreted the decision in the case of *Shannon* v. *Lower Mainland Dairy Products Board*[14] to mean that clause 9 "empowers the imposition of indirect as well as direct taxes by way of license fees."[15]

Proposed Amendment of the B.N.A. Act

The question of the constitutional limitations on the provinces received considerable attention in the Dominion Parliament in 1936. At that time the Dominion government had given an undertaking to the provinces that it would obtain an amendment to the British North America Act which would allow them to impose an indirect sales tax. An extremely interesting debate ensued in which the main participants were Hon. Ernest Lapointe, Hon. C. H. Cahan, and Hon. R. B. Bennett in the House of Commons and, in the Senate, Rt. Hon. Arthur Meighen and Hon. Raoul Dandurand.

The government had just concluded a conference with the provincial governments at which the undertaking had been given to seek this amendment. The provincial governments had been unanimous in requesting it since they were still unsure of their constitutional grounds regarding the retail sales tax. Up to that time the imposition of such a tax had been tried only in Alberta under the Ultimate Purchasers Tax Act (1936), which, as events turned out, was withdrawn in the following year. New Brunswick had also enacted a more restricted tax under chapter 10A of the Corporation Tax Act, which was never proclaimed. Saskatchewan was to enact a tax in the following year which is still in effect, and other provinces were prepared to follow suit. There was still considerable uneasiness, however, over their constitutional rights and also over their ability to enforce and administer a direct retail purchases tax imposed on the purchaser. The Dominion had therefore undertaken to petition the Imperial Parliament to amend the British North

[14][1938] A.C. 708.
[15]V. C. MacDonald, "The Licensing Power of the Provinces."

America Act so as to allow the provinces to impose a retail sales tax in the form of an indirect tax on the vendor. While sharing most of the general administrative difficulties associated with any retail sales tax, if levied as an indirect tax the new tax would have the advantage in that the retailer would be legally liable for payment of the tax and could be sued for payment. It would then be his responsibility to recoup the amount of the tax from the purchaser.

The specific resolution submitted by the Government requested that a petition be presented to the Imperial Parliament to amend the British North America Act, and to provide as follows:

(1) Section 92 of the British North America Act 1867, is amended by adding thereto as clause 2A the following:

    2A Indirect taxation within the province in respect of:
        (i) retail sales, other than of all alcoholic beverages, spirits, malt, tobacco, cigarettes and cigars, which are subject to customs and excise duty or tax in Canada or other than of all goods and articles for delivery without the province;
        (ii) the patronage of hotels, restaurants, and places of amusement or entertainment;
    in order to the raising of a revenue for provincial purposes.

(2) The said clause 2A shall be deemed to have retroactive effect with respect to provincial legislation in force at the passing of this Act.

In introducing the resolution Mr. Lapointe explained that its purpose was to widen the field of taxation available to the provinces and to remove doubts as to the validity of taxes which were already being levied by some of them. He acknowledged that the Privy Council decisions, particularly in *Attorney-General for British Columbia* v. *Kingcome Navigation Co. Ltd.* had practically settled the general law with regard to direct and indirect taxes but he felt that it was still difficult to come to a definite decision in connection with some specific taxes. He further defended the proposed change on the ground that the provinces would not have sufficient revenues without using this form of taxation, that in the United States the individual states had this power, and that, furthermore, it was the unanimous wish of the Canadian provinces that it be granted to them.

ON PROVINCIAL TAXATION 159

Mr. Cahan and Mr. Bennett, replying for the Opposition, reviewed the Privy Council cases and argued that there was no inconsistency or confusion and that with a little perseverance the provinces could find their way along the road indicated by these decisions. Mr. Bennett also objected to the amendment on the grounds that it represented an invasion of the Dominion's constitutional rights and strongly expressed the view that the Dominion should not detract from its own powers. He questioned the necessity of the part of the resolution dealing with the tax on theatres, places of amusement, restaurants, and so on, giving it as his opinion that the provinces already had full authority in this field.

Several other speakers engaged in the debate in the Commons, including Hon. Charles Dunning, the then Minister of Finance.

The resolution was subsequently adopted on division and sent to the Senate. Here it was flayed mercilessly by Rt. Hon. Arthur Meighen. He attacked the manner in which it was proposed to effect the amendment and also attacked the purpose of the amendment itself on several grounds. The spearhead of his offensive appeared to be that once the provinces were given the powers requested in the resolution they would proceed to establish tariff walls around their boundaries by imposing high sales taxes on the produce of other provinces. He expressed this view forcefully in such words as "this address should be entitled 'an address to provide for the inevitable dissolution of Confederation.'" "If this resolution is passed and acceded to there will be no way of escape from nine tariff walls in Canada. The Government proposes to surrender the first and most sacred citadel of Confederation and cannot avoid that surrender if it insists upon the passing of the resolution in its present form."

Other Opposition senators followed Mr. Meighen in speaking against the measure, although it was ably supported by Hon. Raoul Dandurand, Rt. Hon. George B. Graham, and other Government senators. Eventually, however, the resolution went to the Senate Banking and Commerce Committee. No minutes were kept of the proceedings in this committee but from subsequent remarks in the Senate it would appear that the senators heard representatives of both the provinces and the commercial interests. The motion reappeared in the Senate some two weeks after the initial debate, and in re-introducing it the Government moved an amendment to meet the criticism made by Mr. Meighen. This amendment took the following form: " . . . that the said address be amended by adding at the end of paragraph 1 of Clause 2A the following: provided that such taxation does not favour or discriminate against the sales of any goods or articles of the growth, produce or manufacture of any province or of any country."

Mr. Meighen renewed his eloquent protestations against the motion. He stated that the amendment did not meet his objections, and made an impassioned plea to the Senate to defeat the motion on the grounds that increased taxation would result in more unemployment and that the net result would be most harmful. Objections were again voiced on other grounds by further speakers and on division the motion was defeated almost three to one, 40-15. It is not recorded that any further action was taken by the House of Commons in the matter.

The possibility of such an amendment was not mooted again until the 1945-6 negotiations with the provinces. It is interesting to note in passing that the Royal Commission on Dominion-Provincial Relations was opposed to any further extension of the sales tax in the provincial field. Its report said: "The Commission appreciates the full strength of the argument against the tax [the sales tax] and hopes that its general recommendations are of such a character as to remove any demand for its imposition except by the Dominion." It went on to suggest, however, that any constitutional doubts regarding certain provincial taxes should be removed: "In connection with excise taxes a question of jurisdiction was raised. Provinces are obliged to frame their taxes on such things as fuel oil or gasoline so as to conform to the courts' definition of direct taxes. It is claimed that in some cases the result is inefficiency and expense in collection. It would be in keeping with the general tenor of Plan 1 that, if the provinces withdraw from certain fields of taxation, they should have full power conferred on them to levy taxes on certain named commodities which would include fuel oil and gasoline."[16]

No action was taken on this recommendation and the proposal for an amendment to allow the imposition of an indirect retail sales tax was revived and became part of the overall plan finally submitted by the Dominion to the provinces in May 1946.[17] When the Dominion failed to gain the agreement of all provinces, it went no further with this proposal in 1946 or 1947. However at the federal-provincial conference of December 4-7, 1950 it undertook to sponsor an amendment to the British North America Act in a form to be agreed upon with the provinces that would permit them to levy an indirect retail sales tax. Despite the acceptance by several provinces of a wording proposed by the Dominion, failing universal agreement the matter was again dropped. Nothing more was heard of it until the request was renewed by the Premier of Ontario at a federal-provincial conference in mid-summer, 1960. He later dropped the matter and when Ontario enacted a tax in 1961 it was in the usual direct form. Again the issue has come and gone.

PRIVY COUNCIL DECISIONS BEARING ON DIRECT AND INDIRECT TAXATION

(a) *Taxes held to be valid*

1. *Bank of Toronto* v. *Lambe*, (1887) 12 App. Cas. 575. The Quebec act, 45 Vict., c. 22, which imposed taxes on banks varying with the paid-up capital, and the number of places of business, was held to constitute direct taxation.

2. *Brewers' and Maltsters' Association of Ontario* v. *Attorney-General for Ontario*, [1897] A.C. 231. The Liquor License Act (Revised Statutes, Ontario, 1887, c. 194, s. 51 (2)), requiring every brewer and distiller to obtain a licence thereunder to sell wholesale within the province was held to be valid.

3. *Canadian Pacific Railway* v. *Workmen's Compensation Board of British Columbia*, [1920] A.C. 184. It was held that assessments on employers made by the Workmen's Compensation Board for the purpose of the accident fund administered by the Board were direct in character.

[16]Book II, p. 162. [17]*Plenary Conference Discussions*, p. 385.

4. *Burland* v. *The King*, [1922] 1 A.C. 215. The Quebec statute which taxed transmissions within the province of the moveable property of domiciled decedents situate outside the province was upheld.

5. *City of Halifax* v. *Fairbanks' Estate*, [1928] A.C. 117. The Judicial Committee here decided that a business tax, imposed under a city charter on occupiers of real property, and based on the capital value of the premises, was a direct tax.

6. *Attorney-General for British Columbia* v. *Kingcome Navigation Co. Ltd.*, [1934] A.C. 45. The Fuel-oil Tax Act (1930) of British Columbia, which imposed a tax upon every consumer of fuel oil according to the quantity which he had consumed, was held to be *intra vires*.

7. *Attorney-General for Manitoba* v. *Forbes*, [1937] A.C. 260. In this case the tax on wages imposed by the Special Income Tax Act (1933) of Manitoba, was held to be an income tax, and therefore a direct tax.

8. *Atlantic Smoke Shops Ltd.* v. *Conlon*, [1943] A.C. 550. A New Brunswick retail tobacco tax was held to be a direct tax.

9. *Attorney-General for British Columbia* v. *Esquimalt and Nanaimo Railway Co.*, [1950] A.C. 87. A provincial tax on timber lands in British Columbia was held to be a direct tax.

(b) Taxes held to be invalid

1. *Attorney-General for Quebec* v. *Queen Insurance Co.*, (1878) 3 App. Cas. 1090. The imposition of a stamp duty on policies of insurance, renewals, and receipts, by Quebec (39 Vict., c. 7) was held to constitute indirect taxation.

2. *Attorney-General for Quebec* v. *Reed*, (1884) 10 App. Cas. 141. In this case a provincial act which imposed a duty of 10 cents upon every exhibit filed in court was held to be *ultra vires*.

3. *Cotton* v. *The King*, [1914] A.C. 176. It was held that the tax imposed by the Succession Duty Act (1906) of Quebec was indirect for the reason that the executor was required to pay it.

4. *Attorney-General for Manitoba* v. *Attorney-General for Canada*, [1925] A.C. 561. The Judicial Committee held it was *ultra vires* the Manitoba Legislature to enact chapter 17 of its statutes for 1923 entitled "an Act to provide for the collection of a tax from persons selling grain for future delivery."

5. *Attorney-General for British Columbia* v. *Canadian Pacific Railway Co.*, [1927] A.C. 934. In this case it was held that an act of the Legislature of British Columbia, the Fuel-oil Tax Act (Revised

Statutes, British Columbia, 1924, c. 251), requiring that every person who shall purchase within the province fuel oil for the first time after its manufacture in, or importation into, the province, shall pay a tax thereon, was *ultra vires* the Legislature.

6. *The King* v. *Caledonian Collieries Ltd.*, [1928] A.C. 358. The Mine Owners' Tax Act of Alberta (13 Geo. 5, c. 33) purported to impose upon every mine owner, as therein defined, a percentage tax upon the gross revenue of his mine during each preceding month. It was held that the tax was not direct taxation.

7. *Macdonald Murphy Lumber Co.* v. *Attorney-General for British Columbia*, [1930] A.C. 357. In this case it was held that a provincial tax on timber which is cut within and exported from the province is an export tax and indirect.

8. *Lower Mainland Dairy Products Sales Adjustment Committee* v. *Crystal Dairy Ltd.*, [1933] A.C. 168. Provincial levies on dairy farmers, in the adjustment of returns from products sold, were held to be indirect.

9. *Provincial Treasurer of Alberta* v. *Kerr*, [1933] A.C. 710. It was held that the Alberta Succession Duties Act contained no clause excluding personal liability of an executor and that the duties imposed were accordingly indirect.

10. *Attorney-General for Alberta* v. *Attorney-General for Canada*, [1939] A.C. 117. An Act Respecting the Taxation of Banks (1937) of Alberta was not in a true sense taxation to raise revenue for provincial purposes since it imposed a prohibitive rate of tax.

Chapter 9

PROVINCIAL INCOME AND CORPORATION TAXES

Personal Income Taxes

IN 1960 only Quebec was levying a personal income tax, although this source was traditional among Canadian provinces. British Columbia led the way in 1876, Prince Edward Island followed in 1894, Manitoba in 1923, and most of the other provinces joined them during the 1930's. Under the Wartime Tax Agreements these levies were all withdrawn with respect to incomes of calendar years from 1941 to 1946 inclusive, and under the Tax Rental Agreements of 1947, 1951, and 1956 their suspension has been guaranteed up to and including the calendar year 1961 in all provinces but Quebec.[1]

Both Ontario and Quebec were free to impose their own taxes on incomes after 1946, following expiry of their Wartime Tax Agreements, but neither used this authority. The Ontario legislature enacted an Income Tax Act to impose a tax equal to the 5 per cent credit against its own levy which has been offered by the Dominion since 1947. Concurrently an Income Tax Agreement Act was passed authorizing the Provincial Treasurer to enter into an agreement with the Dominion for the latter to collect this tax, the levy to come into force on entry into the agreement. However, on the entry of Ontario into a tax rental agreement with the Dominion in 1952 the province gave up its right to impose a tax on personal incomes of 1952 to 1956, and under the succeeding arrangements for 1957 to

[1]See Historical Review, chap. 1.

1961 again chose to leave its tax in suspense in return for compensation from the federal government.

For the period 1962 to 1966 a totally different regime is in prospect. With the onus placed on provincial governments under the new federal-provincial arrangements to impose their own taxes it is to be assumed that in 1962 there will be ten such levies in effect. These will likely follow the model of the federal act, since such identity has been made a condition of collection by the federal government on behalf of the provinces, and will levy rates which will absorb the full amount of the federal abatement. The abatement, set at 13 per cent for 1961, will rise to 16 per cent in 1962 and thence by 1 percentage point each following year to 20 per cent in 1966. Some provinces will no doubt collect their own taxes, but most will enter into agreements for collection by Ottawa. Unfortunately in mid-1961 final details had not been settled and the reader can only be warned of impending events.

Details of the only provincial tax in effect in 1961, that of Quebec, were as follows:

Exemptions: $2,000 for persons having married status; $1,000 for persons having single status; $250 for dependents qualified for family allowances and $500 for other dependents. An additional $500 is granted for taxpayers 65 years of age or over. A standard deduction of $100 is allowed and from January 1, 1961, all other allowances, such as those for medical expenses, are to be the same as under the Dominion Act.

Rates: Graduated from 2.5 per cent of the first $1,000 of taxable income to 13.2 per cent on the excess over $400,000. The resulting tax exceeds the Dominion credit of 13 per cent for most middle and upper income taxpayers.

A dividend tax credit equal to 15 per cent of the federal credit is allowed, and distributions of tax-paid undistributed surplus are subject to a special rate of 2.25 per cent.

Summary

RATES. Quebec only, as given in text.

REVENUE. In fiscal year 1958–9 Quebec revenue was $47,773,000, representing 13.1 per cent of tax revenue and 8.6 per cent of total revenue.

STATUTORY REFERENCE. Provincial Income Tax Act, 1954, c. 17.

CORPORATION TAXES

Income Taxes

Provincial corporation income taxes were in effect in British Columbia and Prince Edward Island before World War I, but were introduced first in most provinces in the early thirties. All were suspended for incomes of the years 1941 to 1946 under the Wartime Tax Agreements, but were re-introduced in 1947. In Ontario and Quebec a 7 per cent profits tax applied from 1947 to 1951, and the terms of the 1947 tax agreement with the other eight provinces provided that they impose a 5 per cent tax, under a uniform act, on profits of the same calendar years. Its purpose was to allow the non-agreeing provinces to tax their corporations without undue discrimination.

In 1952 this position was changed by the withdrawal of the uniform tax in the eight agreeing provinces and by the repeal of the Ontario tax under its Tax Rental Agreement with the Dominion. The uniform tax was, in effect, absorbed into the federal rate through an increase in that rate. At the same time provision was made for a credit to any corporation equal to 5 per cent of its income allocated to Quebec, irrespective of whether any tax had been paid to the province. This credit was increased to 7 per cent, the full Quebec rate. Later in the negotiations for the 1957–61 arrangements with the provinces the relief was increased to 9 per cent in the form of an abatement, and on this basis Ontario joined Quebec in levying a profits tax. For 1957 the Quebec rate was increased to 9 per cent, and a new Ontario tax was imposed at a rate of 11 per cent. For 1960 these taxes were in effect at rates of 11 per cent and 10 per cent, the Quebec rate having been increased to 10 per cent to take advantage of a raise in the federal abatement applicable where an extra tax is imposed by a province for financing universities. For 1961 the Quebec rate has been increased to 12 per cent, the additional 2 per cent being required to finance a newly introduced scheme of hospital insurance.

As with the personal income tax the prospect for the period 1962 to 1966 is for the introduction of corporation profits taxes in all ten provinces. A federal abatement of 9 per cent has been enacted for the period, and provision made for federal collection under agreement with any individual province wishing such an arrangement. Federal collection will only be undertaken where the provincial levy is in substantially the same form as the federal.

Ontario–Quebec–Federal Taxes in 1961

In considering the provincial taxation of corporation profits there is an advantage in relating the major aspects of the legislation to the federal corporation profits tax. If in every respect all three levies were identical there would be no implications for a corporate taxpayer except for the additional tax burden represented by the excess of the provincial rate over the federal abatement. This fortunately is the position in Canada following changes made by Quebec to apply in 1961. Prior to that time the Ontario tax and federal abatement had been on almost identical bases, but Quebec followed rules with regard to liability to tax, computation of profits, and allocation of income which were substantially different. These main differences were removed in 1961, so that all three levels of the tax—Ontario, Quebec, and federal—may now be discussed in terms of the federal abatement. This examination will be relevant for the future shape of things, since it is to be expected that the new provincial corporation profits taxes in the other provinces will follow the pattern described below.

1. *Liability to tax.* Under the federal abatement rules the first step in allocating income to a province is to determine whether there is a permanent establishment in the province carrying on activities that give rise to an income in that province.

The regulations[2] under the federal act set out the general

[2]Income Tax Regulations, Part IV.

rules by which this fact may be determined. The rules in brief are that if there is no permanent establishment outside of the province the whole of the income will be attributed to the permanent establishment in the province; if there is no permanent establishment in the province none of the income will be attributed to the province; if there are permanent establishments both within and without the province income will be allocated among the various permanent establishments on the basis of further rules set out in the regulation. "Permanent establishment" is defined to include "branches, mines, oil wells, farms, timber lands, factories, workshops, warehouses, offices, agencies and other fixed places of business." The regulation also provides that an employee or agent authorized to enter into contracts or to fill orders from a stock in his possession will be regarded as a permanent establishment, and that the use of substantial machinery or equipment in a particular place at any time in a taxation year will also constitute a permanent establishment for that year. However, an agent who maintains an office solely for the purpose of *purchasing* merchandise for a corporation will not be regarded as a permanent establishment of that corporation. Where a taxpayer otherwise having a permanent establishment in a province owns land in a province the land will also constitute a permanent establishment.

It will be recognized that these rules are similar to those now embodied in the international treaties, and much of the description in chapter IV is also applicable here.

Liability to tax under the Ontario and Quebec measures follows these same rules, except that Quebec has retained the right to tax a corporation whether or not it has a permanent establishment in Quebec if it "has business dealings through a subsidiary or a commission agent, broker or other independent agent, or maintains an office solely for the purchase of merchandise." This is a vestige of a former rule under which companies were held liable if they obtained orders or made sales in Quebec through an employee or agent, even though they had no office in the province.

2. *Nature of income subject to tax.* For the abatement income

is determined under the Dominion act in so far as it relates to corporations. The explanation that has been given previously of the nature of the Dominion tax on corporate income is therefore equally applicable to the tax abatement provisions.

Until 1961 substantial differences in profit computation arose from the retention of the straight line system of depreciation in Quebec (as contrasted with the diminishing balance-capital cost allowance system under the federal law) and from the absence of a provision for the carryover of losses in the Quebec law. Both these differences were removed by legislation enacted late in 1960 which brought the Quebec law into line with that of the Dominion. The Ontario law has been on identical terms with the federal abatement (except for unimportant differences) from its inception in 1957.

3. *Allocation of income.* Of crucial importance in the regional taxation of income is the method or methods adopted for allocating the appropriate income to each jurisdiction where a corporation carries on business under several jurisdictions. It was here that the most marked differences previously arose between the federal (and Ontario) rules and those of Quebec. The 1961 Quebec changes removed these differences as well.

Under the federal rules only income attributable to operations of a corporation in a province is treated as income of that province. As indicated above, the *sine qua non* of tax liability is that there be a permanent establishment in the province. If this test has been satisfied, the problem remains to determine the income of the establishment. The rules given in the regulation under the act prescribe the manner in which this is to be done.

The general rule under the federal regulation requires that the income be allocated in the ratio that the gross revenue and the salaries and wages of the permanent establishment bear to the total gross revenue and salaries and wages of the corporation. This formula gives a weighting to the ultimate *indicia* of direct income-earning activities (i.e., sales); also, through the wages and salary factor, to activities which are less directly connected with the ultimate transaction. It would, for example, allocate to a factory in one province a portion of the income of the corporation even though no sales were made in that province, thereby giving effect to the concept of a "manufacturing profit" supported by the decision of the Privy Council in the *International Harvester Case*.[3] The permanent establishment to which the gross revenue is to be attributed is specifically provided in the regulation. The main sections read as follows:

(4) For the purposes of determining the gross revenue for the year reasonably attributable to the permanent establishment in the province within the meaning of paragraph (*a*) of subsection (3), the following rules shall apply:

(*a*) where the destination of a shipment of merchandise to a customer to whom the merchandise is sold is in the province, the gross revenue derived therefrom shall be attributable to the permanent establishment in the province;

(*b*) where the destination of a shipment of merchandise to a customer to whom the merchandise is sold is in a province in which the taxpayer has no permanent establishment, if the person negotiating the sale may reasonably be regarded as being attached to the permanent establishment in the province of the taxpayer, the gross revenue derived therefrom shall be attributable to that permanent establishment;

(*ba*) where the destination of a shipment of merchandise to a customer to whom the merchandise is sold is in another country in which the taxpayer has no permanent establishment,

  (i) if the merchandise was produced or manufactured, or produced and manufactured, entirely in the province by the taxpayer, the gross revenue derived therefrom shall be attributable to the permanent establishment in the province, or

  (ii) if the merchandise was produced or manufactured, or produced and manufactured, partly in the province and partly in another place by the taxpayer, the gross revenue derived therefrom attributable to the permanent establishment in the province shall be that proportion thereof that the salaries and wages

---

[3]*International Harvester Co. of Canada Ltd.* v. *Provincial Tax Commission et al.*, [1949] A.C. 36. Other leading cases relating to liability and allocation of income under provincial laws are *In re the Income Tax Act, 1932, and Proctor and Gamble Co.*, [1938] 2 D.L.R. 597; *Firestone Tire and Rubber Co.* v. *Commissioner of Income Tax*, [1942] S.C.R. 476; *Provincial Treasurer of Manitoba* v. *Wm. Wrigley (Jr.) Co.*, [1950], A.C. 1.

paid in the year to employees of the permanent establishment in the province where the merchandise was partly produced or manufactured (or partly produced and manufactured) is of the aggregate of the salaries and wages paid in the year to employees of the permanent establishment where the merchandise was produced or manufactured (or produced and manufactured);[4]

Note that the principal rule is that gross revenue is to be allocated to the permanent establishment in the province to which the merchandise is shipped, which in general is the province in which the purchaser resides. Where there is no permament establishment in the province of the purchaser the revenue is allocated to the province of the permanent establishment to which the salesman is attached. Other rules cover the rendering of services and the sale of timber.

Special ratios are established for insurance corporations (net premium income), banks (salaries and wages, loans and deposits), loan and trust companies (revenue from loans on property in province, revenue from loans in other provinces where there is no permanent establishment, and other gross revenues), railways ("equated track miles" and gross ton miles), airlines (fixed assets and revenue plane miles), grain elevators (grain received and salaries and wages) and bus and truck transporation (miles travelled and salaries and wages), pipeline operators (miles of pipe and salaries and wages) and ship operators (port-call-tonnage and salaries and wages) in some cases one of the factors being given a different weighting than the others. These special provisions override the general, and are provided because of the impossibility of devising universal rules that will effect a reasonable allocation in every set of circumstances.

One aspect of these rules should be mentioned. The ratio contemplated in them is the ratio of provincial factor to the corresponding factor for the company covering all its operations, including those outside of Canada. The effect therefore is to divide the total income into a pie of which a part represents the foreign income and another part the Canadian income, the latter being divided again into smaller segments of provincial income.

[4]*Income Tax Regulations*, Part IV s. 402(4).

In this respect the Ontario and Quebec law differs from the federal abatement rules, since they tax world income, including foreign income, and allows a tax credit at the full rate of 11 or 12 per cent for income allocated to jurisdictions outside the respective province.

Quebec now follows the rules of allocation just outlined with the exception that goods exported from Canada will be allocated to a Canadian establishment whether or not the firm has an establishment in the foreign country, whereas under the federal rules the allocation would not be made to Canada if there were an establishment abroad, but to that establishment.[5]

SUMMARY

RATES.   12 per cent in Quebec; 11 per cent in Ontario.

REVENUE[1]

	Fiscal year 1958–9 ($000)	Percentage of tax revenue	Percentage of total revenue
Quebec	81,720	22.3	14.7
Ontario	144,430	39.6	22.3

[1]General note on provincial revenue figures: data given in this and the following chapters are based on compilations prepared by the Dominion Bureau of Statistics. Fiscal years ended nearest to December 31, 1958, are given as fiscal year 1958–9.

STATUTORY REFERENCES. *Quebec*, Corporation Tax Act, 11 Geo. 6, c. 33; *Ontario*, Corporations Tax Act, Revised Statutes of Ontario, 1960, c. 73; Part IV, Regulations Under the Income Tax Act, Order-in-Council P.C. 1954–1917, published in *Canada Gazette*, Part II, Jan. 12, 1955, as amended.

Other Corporation Taxes

Quebec imposed the first special provincial taxes on corporations early in the 1880's; by the end of the century they were being imposed by all the provinces. Withdrawn in all the provinces under the Wartime Tax Agreements, they have been in effect in Quebec for the whole period since 1947 and in Ontario as well except for the five years 1952 to 1956. The end of the tax rental agreements will leave all provinces free to

[5]For further details on Quebec rules see Order-in-Council No. 521, effective Jan. 1, 1961.

re-impose such taxes in 1962. These special taxes were developed originally as a substitute for the general property tax; today the principal forms in effect in Quebec and Ontario are the taxes on capital and place of business, but a variety of other bases are also in use.

First, a brief note on the precise character of a "corporation tax." This nomenclature has been borrowed from the Dominion-provincial taxation agreements, where it was necessary to make an exact delineation of the taxes that would be suspended by the province. The nature of a tax on corporation income, just discussed, is fairly self-evident. The following definition from the taxation agreement, however, will indicate the precision of language required for an exact identification of a "corporation" tax:

> ... "corporation tax" means ... a tax or fee other than a tax on net income but including a tax on gross revenue or gross receipts or any part thereof, the imposing of which singles out for taxation or for discriminatory rates or burdens of taxation corporations, or any class or classes thereof, or any individual corporation or any class of persons that is composed mainly of corporations, either formally or in effect, by imposing a tax or fee on or in respect of any act, matter or thing or activities or operations mainly done by, or affecting, or carried on by corporations, or otherwise, except
> (i) a bona fide and reasonable provincial licence, registration, filing or other fee; but no fee or class of fees first charged or imposed after the first day of January, 1957, shall exceed $400.00 per annum for each corporation and no fee charged or imposed on or prior to the said day which is in excess of $400.00 per annum for each corporation shall be increased by more than sixty per cent and no fee charged or imposed on or prior to the said day which is less than $400.00 per annum for each corporation shall be increased by more than sixty per cent or to $400.00, whichever is greater;
> (ii) the fees charged for the incorporation of a company;
> (iii) a licence fee or other fee or tax for specific rights, benefits or franchises granted by a municipality, or where they are to be exercised or enjoyed only in territory not included in any municipality, by any authority (including the Province) having jurisdiction in such territory;

(iv) any assessment under The Workmen's Compensation Act;
(v) a business or occupancy tax based on floor space or on the rental or assessed value of property, imposed by a municipality, or in territory not included in any municipality by any authority (including the Province) having jurisdiction in such territory; or
(vi) any royalty or rental on or in respect of natural resources within the Province;
(vii) a bona fide and reasonable business or occupancy tax imposed by a municipality or in a territory not included in a municipality by any authority (including the Province) having jurisdiction in such territory on the gross revenue or gross receipts within the municipality or territory from all or part of the business of:
   (A) a telephone, electric light, electric power, gas, street railway, bus, or closed circuit television company, in lieu of taxes imposed on power lines, pole lines, towers, cables, wires, conductors, conduits, equipment, mains, tracks or other like property or improvements at a rate not in excess of five per cent of the gross receipts or gross revenue subject to the tax; or
   (B) of any other corporation if
      (I) the tax is imposed under legislation enacted prior to June 27, 1946,
      (II) the tax is in lieu of such a tax based on floor space or upon the rental or assessed value of property,
      (III) the tax is imposed on a corporation or class of corporations that is subject to the said tax under legislation enacted prior to June 27, 1946, and
      (IV) the rate of tax is not in excess of the general tax rate; and
(viii) a licence fee in respect of personal property of a corporation imposed in lieu of a personal property tax that could be levied upon the personal property of the corporation under or pursuant to a provincial statute enumerated in Appendix "B" if
   (A) the licence fee does not exceed the amount that the corporation could be required to pay as a personal property tax in lieu of which the licence fee is imposed, and
   (B) payment of the licence fee exempts the corporation from liability to pay the personal property tax in lieu of which the licence fee is imposed;
(ix) a fee or other charge that is not a tax on net income, gross revenue

or gross receipts that is applied as part of the liquor control system of the Province;
(x) a tax upon the premiums of insurance companies carrying on business within the Province in respect of insurance on persons resident or property situated in the Province;
(xi) a fee based on the premiums of fire insurance companies carrying on business within the Province in respect of property situated in the Province, charged for the maintenance of an office of the Province commonly known as the office of the Fire Marshal, sufficient to meet the costs incidental to such maintenance but not exceeding one per cent of such premiums.

Some aspects of this definition are worthy of comment. It will be noted, for example, that simply because a corporation pays a tax that tax is not automatically a corporation tax. To qualify as such, a tax must be a levy aimed in form or effect exclusively at corporations. Further, a fee or charge of an appropriate amount for a registration, franchise, or services, even though paid only by corporations, is not a tax, nor is a royalty or rental paid to a province in respect of its natural resources.

As indicated above, the general corporation taxes in Quebec and Ontario are on paid-up capital and places of business, and they apply to all companies unless otherwise provided. Certain companies are subject to special charges and exempt from the general in Quebec; banks and insurance, loan, navigation, telegraph, telephone, express, tramway, railway, sleeping-car, trust, gas and electric, gasoline, real estate, liquor, brewery, tobacco, and extra-provincial persons or partnerships not taxed under any other provisions of the Act. All the above companies are also subject to the 12 per cent profits tax.

In Ontario the corporation taxes are related to the profits tax through a provision under which the profits tax may be offset against the liability for corporation taxes. The effect is that the corporation taxes become a minimum charge payable by corporations. Special taxes are levied in Ontario on banks, railways, telegraph companies, railway express companies, car companies, hotels, and insurance companies. For the "paid-up capital" tax the concept is broader than the ordinary sense of the term, and along with paid-up capital stock includes surplus and reserve funds (less reserves for depreciation), indebtedness of a capital nature, including bonds, mortgages, debentures, income bonds and debentures, liens, notes and any other security on the property or any part of it. An allowance is made for the deduction of good-will, trademarks, patents, franchises, etc., to the extent that in the opinion of the provincial treasurer they have no value.

In Table VIII the rates and the basis of taxation are given both for the general levies on paid-up capital and places of business and for the special levies paid in lieu of these general charges in both provinces.

Quebec imposes substantial levies of a similar form on corporations under an Act to Ensure the Progress of Education in addition to the taxes imposed under the Corporation Tax Act. Revenues from these taxes are assigned by statute to the Education Fund for the support of education in the province. For 1961 the following taxes were in effect under this Act: (*a*) petroleum refineries: ⅓ of 1 per cent on paid-up capital; (*b*) telephone companies having a paid-up capital over $1,000,000: ⅓ of 1 per cent per annum on their paid-up capital; (*c*) pulp and paper companies, on wood cut for use in the manufacture of pulp, paper, or by-products thereof: 15 cents per cord (imposed both on holders of leased timber limits and owners of wooded territory); (*d*) hydraulic power companies, on electricity generated within the province: 15 cents per thousand kilowatt-hours (imposed both on lessees and owners of hydraulic powers within the province). The Quebec Hydro Electric Commission is also required to pay an annual amount of $2.8 million into the Fund.

Insurance Premium Taxes

Since 1957 all provinces have imposed a tax on the premium income of insurance companies. From the first agreements in 1940 such levies were classed as corporation taxes and debarred to the agreeing provinces, but in 1956 the federal government,

TABLE VIII

Corporation Taxes in Quebec and Ontario

Scope of tax	Quebec — Basis of tax	Rate	Ontario — Basis of tax	Rate
General rates on all companies except those below	Paid-up capital Place of business: In Montreal or Quebec In other municipalities (Where capital less than $25,000 these charges are reduced to $25 and $20 respectively.)	1/10 of 1% $50 each $25 each	Paid-up capital Offices No designated office	1/20 of 1% $50 $50
Banks	Paid-up capital Reserve fund and undivided profits Head office in Montreal or Quebec Other offices	1/10 of 1% 1/10 of 1% $50 $25	Paid-up capital Reserve fund and undivided profits	1/5 of 1% 1/10 of 1%
Insurance cos.	Premium income	2%	Premium income	2%

Loan cos.	Companies with fixed capital:
	  Paid-up capital and invested moneys
	  Also taxes on places of business varying with fixed capital
	Companies without fixed capital: rate varies with invested moneys
		
		1/20 of 1%
			General rates	

Navigation cos.[1]	Same as general rates		General rates	
Telegraph cos.	Annual flat tax	$5,000	Money invested in province	1%

[1]Additional taxes are imposed on capital invested and on places of business where these companies operate hotels.

TABLE VIII (*Continued*)

	Quebec		Ontario	
	Basis of tax	Rate	Basis of tax	Rate[1]
Telephone cos.	Paid-up capital: $100,000 or more Under $100,000	1/5 of 1% 1/10 of 1%		
Express cos.	Per 100 miles of track or fraction thereof used in province (Maximum tax $10,000)	$800	Per 100 miles of track or fraction thereof used in province	$800
Tramway cos.[1] Railway cos.[1]	Gross revenue Main or branch line: Single track—per mile Other track—per mile	1% $60 $40	Operating over 150 miles: (*a*) Track in municipalities: Per mile for one track Per mile for other tracks (*b*) Track outside municipalities: Per mile for one track Per mile for other tracks Operating over 30 but under 150 miles: Per mile Operating under 30 miles: Per mile	 $60 $40 $40 $20 $15 & $5 respectively $10 & $5 respectively
Sleeping or parlour car cos.	Capital invested in rolling stock used in province Places of business at general rates ($50 & $25)	1/3 of 1%	Capital invested in cars in province	1%

[1]Additional taxes are imposed on capital invested and on places of business where these companies operate hotels.

AND CORPORATION TAXES

TABLE VIII (*Continued*)

	Quebec		Ontario	
	Basis of tax	Rate	Basis of tax	Rate
Gas & electric cos.	Paid-up capital Places of business at general rates	1/5 of 1%	General rates	
Gasoline cos.	Paid-up capital Places of business at general rates	3/8 of 1%		
Real estate cos.	Same as general rates except capital tax reduced to 1/20 of 1% where business only holding vacant lots			
Liquor cos.	Paid-up capital Other than Canadian cos. pay tax on sales Places of business at general rates	3/8 of 1% 1/5 of 1%	,,	
Brewery cos.	Paid-up capital Places of business at general rates	1/5 of 1%		
Tobacco cos.	Paid-up capital Places of business at general rates	1/5 of 1%	,,	
Partnerships, associations, firms or persons having principal place of business outside Canada and not otherwise taxed under Act	Gross earnings Places of business at general rates	1/10 of 1% ($50 & $25)	,,	

during the negotiation of new arrangements, undertook to withdraw its own tax and allow the provinces to enter the field. Such taxes have been in effect in Ontario and Quebec since the end of the war, and the resumed taxes in the eight other provinces follow the same pattern. They apply at a rate of 2 per cent on premium income in respect of business transacted in the provinces, premium income in most cases being defined as gross premiums less return premiums and premiums for re-insurance.

SUMMARY

RATES. On paid-up capital: *Quebec*, various, mainly 1/10 of 1 per cent; *Ontario*, various, mainly 1/20 of 1 per cent; on places of business: *Quebec*, various, ranging from $25 to $100 each; other bases used for special cases; *Ontario*, $50 per establishment. *All provinces*, insurance premiums, 2 per cent.

REVENUE

	Fiscal Year 1958–9 ($000)	Percentage of tax revenue	Percentage of total revenue
Newfoundland	284	2.1	.5
P.E.I.	77	2.6	.6
Nova Scotia	785	4.4	1.0
New Brunswick	615	2.7	.9
Quebec	25,313	6.9	4.5
Ontario	14,360	3.9	2.2
Manitoba	1,125	6.9	1.5
Saskatchewan	642	1.2	.4
Alberta	1,887	6.7	.8
British Columbia	2,568	2.1	.9

STATUTORY REFERENCES. *Newfoundland*, The Insurance Companies Act, 1957, c. 76; *P.E.I.*, The Premium Tax Act, 1957, c. 27; *Nova Scotia*, Insurance Premiums Tax Act, 1957, c. 4; *New Brunswick*, Premium Tax Act, 1957, c. 14; *Quebec*, Corporation Tax Act, 11 Geo. 6, c. 33; Progress of Education Act, 10 Geo. 6, c. 32; *Ontario*, Corporations Tax Act, Revised Statutes of Ontario, 1960, c. 73; *Manitoba*, The Insurance Corporations Tax Act, 1957, c. 32; *Saskatchewan*, The Insurance Premiums Tax Act 1957, c. 23; *Alberta*, Insurance Corporations Tax Act, 1957, c. 35; *British Columbia*, Insurance Premiums Tax Act, Revised Statutes of British Columbia, 1960, c. 198.

Provincial Corporation Fees

In addition to the corporation taxes previously described all companies incorporated in a province must pay a fee for incorporation based on their capital (paid-up, authorized, etc.). An annual registration fee may also be charged. In most provinces these annual fees have been nominal, but in the Maritime Provinces they were used in the past to a considerable extent as an additional source of revenue from corporations. At the present time, however, the provisions of the statutes under which they are imposed—the Companies' Tax Act in Prince Edward Island, the Domestic, Dominion, and Foreign Corporations Act in Nova Scotia, and the Companies Act in New Brunswick—have been modified in accordance with the limitations imposed by the Tax Rental Agreements. In no province is any significant revenue derived from this source.

Another unimportant levy, falling principally on insurance corporations, may also be mentioned. Under an act called in most provinces the Fire Prevention Act (in Ontario the Fire Marshal Act, and in British Columbia the Fire Marshal Tax Act) authority is granted for levying a tax on premium income, mainly of fire insurance companies, for the support of a provincial office for the prevention of fires. This levy is usually limited to $\frac{1}{4}$ or $\frac{1}{8}$ of 1 per cent of the premium income, although in some provinces it may be slightly higher.

STATUTORY REFERENCES

Newfoundland, The Companies Act, Revised Statutes, Nfld., 1952, c. 168; *Prince Edward Island*, An Act to Provide for the Licencing or Registration of Certain Corporations and Persons, 1957, c. 20; *Nova Scotia*, Companies Act, Revised Statutes, Nova Scotia, 1954, c. 41; Domestic, Dominion and Foreign Corporations Act, *ibid.*, c. 74; *New Brunswick*, Companies Act, Revised Statutes, New Brunswick, 1952, c. 33; *Quebec*, Companies Act, Revised Statutes, Quebec, 1941, c. 276; Companies Information Act, *ibid.*, c. 281, Extra-Provincial Companies

Act, *ibid.*, c. 279; *Ontario*, Corporations Act, Revised Statutes of Ontario, 1960, c. 71; Corporations Information Act, *ibid.*, c. 72; *Manitoba*, The Companies Act, Revised Statutes, Manitoba, 1954, c. 43; *Saskatchewan*, The Companies Act, Revised Statutes, Saskatchewan, 1953, c. 124; *Alberta*, The Companies Act, Revised Statutes, Alberta, 1955, c. 53; *British Columbia*, Companies Act, Revised Statutes, British Columbia, 1960, c. 67.

Chapter 10

PROVINCIAL SUCCESSION DUTIES

SUCCESSION DUTIES were first levied in 1892 by Ontario, Quebec, New Brunswick, and Nova Scotia. In 1893 they were introduced by Manitoba, in 1894 by Prince Edward Island and British Columbia, in 1905 (on becoming provinces) by Saskatchewan and Alberta. Newfoundland also had imposed death taxes for some years prior to union with Canada in 1949. All but the Ontario and Quebec statutes are repealed at present under the terms of the Dominion-provincial Tax Rental Agreements in respect of deaths occurring between April 1, 1947, and March 31, 1962. Under the revised federal-provincial tax arrangements for 1962–6 the provinces will all be enabled to return to the field. However it is unlikely that many will do so because of the federal offer to continue a direct payment in lieu of revenues to any province that leaves its tax in suspense.

The death duties being levied in Ontario and Quebec in 1961 were in addition to the Dominion duties described previously, although an abatement of the federal duty substantially avoids duplicate taxation in these provinces. The same general arrangement will apply if and when other provinces enter the field.

The hybrid character of the provincial levy as a combined succession and estate duty was evident in the earliest legislation. While the original duties, modelled after New York and Pennsylvania inheritance taxes, were succession duties in form, the rates imposed under them were determined (where there was a graduation by size) by reference to the aggregate value of the estate passing, as they would be under an estate duty. This confusing admixture was further confounded by the introduction of a variation of rates and exemptions by classes of beneficiary.

The original Ontario act, for example, exempted amounts going to beneficiaries of the direct line if the total estate did not exceed $100,000 and exempted collateral heirs and strangers if the estate did not exceed $10,000. The rates applicable to the part of the estate going to direct heirs were $2\frac{1}{2}$ per cent when the estate exceeded $100,000 but did not exceed $200,000, and 5 per cent on the amount over $200,000. The rate on the part going to collateral heirs was 5 per cent and on the part going to other beneficiaries was 10 per cent. It will be noted that the only graduation of rates by the size of the estate in the Ontario act appears in the schedule applying to direct heirs, and in some provinces there was no graduation even on this basis. Under the original Quebec act there were five classes of beneficiaries for whom the rates were 1 per cent, 3 per cent, 6 per cent, 8 per cent, and 10 per cent, irrespective of the size of the total estate. Manitoba in 1893 was the first province to introduce a graduated rate schedule which rose from 1 per cent in the lowest bracket to 10 per cent on estates over $1,000,000.

Writing on this subject in 1902 R. A. Bayly, one of the early students of provincial succession duties in Canada, made the following pointed observation on the system that had already been adopted at that time:

It should be distinctly recognized that the English and American systems differ: and that it is dangerous, if not impossible, to engraft portions of the English Acts upon the Ontario Act, as they are based on different principles.

If it is considered that the English system of "Estates Duty" is the form in which the tax should be imposed in Canada, then let us have an Act modelled after the Imperial Finance Act, 1894; or if the American system be preferred, then why not follow the Transfer Tax Act of New York: but the hotch-potch which we have at present in Ontario reminds one of the famous stew which Jerome's Three Men in a Boat, on their memorable voyage up the Thames, concocted from all the scraps they could find.

It is neither American, English nor Canadian.[1]

In 1905, three years after Bayly had written the above passage, Ontario gave a new complication to the hybrid character of these duties by adding a tax at graduated rates varying with

[1]R. A. Bayly, *Succession Duty in Canada*, p. iv.

the size of the individual succession. This innovation was quickly adopted by most of the other provinces, and the pattern thus established has survived substantially unchanged to the present time. The taxes in effect in Ontario and Quebec today have altered little from the original form except that in Quebec there are now only three classes of beneficiaries.

Constitutional Development

Underlying and in part associated with these structural aspects of the succession duty was the struggle of the provinces to delineate the constitutional limits of their taxing powers in this field. As we have seen, they were confined to "direct taxation" imposed "within the province." The first of these, the restriction to direct taxation, was the least difficult hurdle to surmount. The Judicial Committee early established in the *Reed* and *Cotton* decisions[2] that a death duty was indirect if imposed on the executor, administrator, or trustee, without the right of recovery from the beneficiary. The provincial legislation was adapted to these decisions by the device of imposing the tax directly on the beneficiary, although as a result of the *Kerr* decision[3] in 1933 new doubt was cast on the form of several of the provincial statutes and amendments were immediately introduced to remove any further question.

The limitation to taxation "within the province" has presented a challenge calling for the exercise of much greater ingenuity. Courts have laid down the general principle that to be *intra vires* the province must impose a tax on "subject matter," that is, on persons or things, within the province, and the efforts of the provinces were directed to finding the largest possible content for the subject matter of their legislation. A tax imposed on property actually situated (having its "situs") in the province was early established to be within their competence.[4] They have since had unquestioned right to tax all property, both real and personal, actually situated in the province as long as the tax is imposed on the property, and not on the succession to the property. In this form the succession duty differs little from a

[2]*Attorney-General for Quebec* v. *Reed*, (1884) 10 App. Cas. 141. *Cotton* v. *The King*, [1914] A.C. 176; also *Burland* v. *The King*, [1922] 1 A.C. 215.
[3]*Provincial Treasurer of Alberta* v. *Kerr*, [1933] A.C. 215.
[4]*The King* v. *Lovitt*, [1912] A.C. 212; *Toronto General Trusts* v. *The King*, 1919] A.C. 679.

property tax payable at the time of death as a condition of the transmission of the property. Furthermore, real property, by long-established convention, occupies a special and universally accepted status for death duty purposes. It is subject to tax only in the jurisdiction in which it is located, even though both the decedent and the beneficiary may reside in another jurisdiction.

The principal bone of contention has therefore been the personal property of the deceased located outside of the province of his domicile. Personal property usually includes all property other than real property, the principal examples being insurance, bonds, shares, mortgages, bank deposits and so on. From the beginning the provinces exhausted every resource to bring such personal property, no matter where located, within the subject matter of their tax. The earliest attempts were directed simply at taxing property of a decedent domiciled in the province as property having its situs in the province, relying on the maxim *mobilia personam sequuntur* (moveable property follows its owner). In 1908, however, the Privy Council in the *Woodruff Case*[5] determined that it was beyond the constitutional powers of a provincial government to tax property as such when located outside the province, and later cases destroyed any grounds for the theory that the situs of property outside the province could be brought into the province on the *mobilia personam sequuntur* rule.

When the direct avenue of approach was thus blocked, the provinces fell back on the less direct method of taxing the transmission of the property in the province rather than the property itself. There followed some unsuccessful experimentation under the Quebec Act using wording which the courts held in the *Cotton Case* to apply only to the transmission of property situated in the province, but when the defect was remedied the statute was upheld by Privy Council in the case of *Burland v. The King*.[6]

This decision clearly established the right of a province to tax extra-provincial personal property subject to transmission within the province. Further, a dictum contained in this judg-

---

[5] *Woodruff v. Attorney-General for Ontario*, [1908] A.C. 508.
[6] *Burland v. The King*, [1922] 1 A.C. 215.

ment indicated the view of the court that to qualify as being "within the province" a transmission should be between a decedent domiciled in the province and a beneficiary also either domiciled or ordinarily resident in the province. This dictum was embodied as law in the *Kerr Case* referred to previously. The portion of the decision relevant to this point is as follows: "In their Lordships' opinion, the principle to be derived from the decisions of this Board is that the Province, on the death of a person domiciled within the Province, is not entitled to impose taxation in respect of personal property locally situate outside the Province, but that it is entitled to impose taxation on persons domiciled or resident within the Province in respect of the transmission to them under the Provincial law of personal property locally situate outside the Province."

In brief, the person subject to the tax, the beneficiary, must be within the province. In the clear light of this definitive statement the existing statutes of many of the provinces appeared to be in difficulty, since two different and irreconcilable bases of tax were being employed under them simultaneously. Amendments were made to several of them following the *Kerr Case*.

One circumstance in which no province imposed a tax has not yet been mentioned. It has not ordinarily been the practice of any province, nor for that matter of the Dominion, to tax persons domiciled or resident in the province when they receive a bequest from an estate in another jurisdiction. Although most of the evidence suggests that it would be within the rights of any government to impose it, such a tax would probably not be practicable because of the difficulty of enforcing collection. The taxing authorities would have no indication of the passing of property such as they have where the decedent dies in the province or the property is situated in the province.

The position that emerged from the legislation and litigation described above may be summed up as follows:

1. The provinces can impose death duties as long as the liability rests on the beneficiary and not on the executor.

2. They can impose a tax on any form of property situated in the province, no matter where the decedent or beneficiary is domiciled or resident.

3. They can impose a tax on the transmission of personal property located outside the province where both the decedent and the beneficiary are domiciled or resident in the province.

4. They probably could impose a tax on the receipt of a benefit from outside the province by a person resident in the province, but in fact have not imposed such a tax.

Overlapping Taxation

The inevitable result of this evolution was that personal property has been exposed to double taxation in Canada. First, personal property was subject to tax in the province where the property was located (the province of situs). As previously stated, this right has never been challenged. Secondly, it was subject to tax in the province where the deceased and the beneficiary were domiciled, by means of the tax on the transmission. The stormy history of Canadian provincial succession duties is dominated by the conflict between these two principles of "situs" and "domicile." No permanent solution was ever found for this problem as long as all provinces were in the field.

Apart from this general conflict of principle, there were serious uncertainties in the past about the determination of the actual situs of various forms of intangible property. Such property, being mainly the evidence of ownership or debt, has no self-evident or factual location, and situs must be determined by legal fictions often somewhat artificial. There has been constant litigation as to the situs of deposits in a branch bank, real estate mortgages, negotiable instruments, bonds and shares of incorporated companies, and simple contract debts. It appears to have been established in the *National Trust Case*[7] that "a provincial legislature is not competent to prescribe the conditions fixing the situs of intangible property." As a result situs was required to be determined in each case by reference to the general principles of the common law and these principles have only gradually emerged as the result of constant litigation. Particularly contentious has been the situs of shares of incorporated companies. The leading case in this field has been *Brassard*

[7] *The King* v. *National Trust Co.*, [1933] 4 S.C.R. 670.

v. *Smith*[8] which established situs as the place where the shares can be "effectively dealt with." This rule has been followed by the provinces.

It would be unfair to leave the impression that no efforts were made to resolve the conflicts that bedevilled provincial succession duties. In 1922 the Conference of the Commissioners on Uniformity of Legislation in Canada delegated to the Nova Scotia representatives the task of drawing up a uniform act based on situs (as opposed to domicile). Their investigations resulted in a recommendation the following year that the Alberta Act (then employing only the situs rule) be made the basis of discussion, but no further concrete results appear to have been achieved. The next move came in 1925 when Premier Bracken of Manitoba convened a meeting in Winnipeg, attended by representatives of Ontario and the four western provinces (Quebec and the Maritimes abstaining) to discuss the possibility of adopting a uniform act. A committee established to draft both a uniform act and a model reciprocal agreement as an alternative submitted the fruits of its labour to an inter-provincial conference held in Ottawa in 1926, but again no concrete results appear to have been achieved. A conference of the four western provinces alone held a few months later to work out a limited regional solution was also unproductive.

Somewhat more encouraging results were achieved for a temporary period by means of reciprocal provincial agreements. Under these arrangements the Canadian provinces adopted methods for avoiding double taxation of property among themselves, and also by themselves and foreign jurisdictions, very similar to those now in effect under the Dominion's income tax and succession duty conventions with foreign countries. Where there was double taxation the province of domicile undertook to allow a deduction from its duties for any duty paid on the same estate to the other party to the agreement. Ontario had entered into such an agreement as early as 1906 with the United Kingdom, and the other provinces followed suit, probably in consideration of the statutory allowance granted by that country under the Finance Act of 1894.

[8] [1925] A.C. 371.

Ontario also led the way in developing inter-provincial agreements, and by 1925 was allowing credits to its domiciled estates for duties paid to most of the other provinces, in some cases without reciprocity. In that year, however, Ontario cancelled all credits for duties except in the case of those paid to Nova Scotia, British Columbia, and Alberta, although during the late twenties and early thirties it entered into reciprocal agreements with Prince Edward Island and New Brunswick for the immunity of certain forms of property. During this period Ontario did not at any time have an agreement with Quebec, although attempts were made to bring one about (this was not to be achieved until a decade and a half later, in 1945). Some of the other provinces had also entered into reciprocal agreements but Manitoba, Saskatchewan, and Quebec had never entered into agreements with another province.

All this ground so hardly won was lost almost overnight in 1937. Alberta led off by cancelling its agreements with the other provinces and repealing the concession for United Kingdom duties. Ontario in a few weeks followed suit, except that it retained the United Kingdom allowance, and with the other provinces joining the parade there very shortly remained only a reciprocal agreement between British Columbia and New Brunswick and the concession granted by most provinces for duties paid to the United Kingdom. In 1943 the United Kingdom cancelled its agreements with Ontario and Manitoba.

On the withdrawal of all the provinces but Ontario and Quebec from the field of succession duties under the Tax Rental Agreements these problems of conflicting principles have disappeared, at least temporarily, in these jurisdictions. A further progressive step was also taken in 1945 when Ontario and Quebec entered into a reciprocal agreement on the "duty-credit" basis. This agreement, dated January 17, 1945, is still in effect, but has become less significant in view of the 1946 amendment under the Ontario Act (Section 7) giving the Lieutenant-Governor-in-Council power to designate any other jurisdiction imposing succession duties in respect of which Ontario will allow a credit against the Ontario duty when the property has been subject to double taxation. By regulation this allowance has been extended to duties paid in the following: the United Kingdom, the Union of South Africa, the Commonwealth of Australia, Eire, the Dominion of New Zealand, the provinces of Canada, the District of Columbia, and each of the United States of America.

Present Quebec and Ontario Duties

As mentioned above, the provincial rates of duty applicable to the individual succession depend on (1) the aggregate value of the estate, (2) the amount of the individual succession, and (3) the relationship of the deceased to the beneficiary. Under the provincial acts beneficiaries are divided into only three classes. In Quebec Class 1 includes all lineal ancestors and descendents, husband, wife, father- and mother-in-law, son- and daughter-in-law, and children (or parents) by adoption. In Ontario Class 1 is a narrower group, being limited to grandfather, grandmother, father, mother, husband, wife, child, son- and daughter-in-law. In both provinces the remaining relatives are in Class 2, and strangers in Class 3.

Exemptions

Exemptions from duty in the two provinces are set out in Table IX. There are general exemptions based on the size of the estate, general exemptions for small amounts of succession, and individual exemptions by class of beneficiary. Individual bequests to successors of any class are totally exempt if the amount of the estate is less than the amounts shown for the particular class. If the total amount of the estate is more than the amounts shown, the total amount of the succession is dutiable. An important exception to this general statement is the $10,000 exemption for Class 1 beneficiaries in Quebec, which, since December 1951, is *deductible* where the dutiable estate does not exceed $50,000.

In 1959 Ontario made a marked departure from its traditional pattern of exemptions for preferred beneficiaries. In place of the previous exempt limit of $50,000 it provided exemptions which take into account the dependent status of close beneficiaries of the deceased.

TABLE IX

Exemptions under Quebec and Ontario Succession Duties

	Quebec	Ontario
General exemptions		
Estates	none	if less than $5,000
Successions	none	if less than $500
Specific exemptions		
Class 1 beneficiaries	$10,000 plus $1,500 for each surviving child, deductible if estate does not exceed $50,000	exempt if total estate is less than $60,000, increased by $10,000 for each dependent child of a widow (see text)
Class 2 beneficiaries	exempt if total estate is less than $1,000	exempt if total estate is less than $10,000
Class 3 beneficiaries	dutiable in both provinces except for bequests not exceeding $1,000 to employees of 5 years' standing	

The new allowances are in two parts: "dependents' allowance" and "individual dependent allowance." The first exempts the whole estate if it falls below the limit; the second exempts the individual bequest if the estate is taxable.

Dependents' Allowance
Where a beneficiary is:

Widow	$60,000
Widow with dependent child or children	$60,000 and $10,000 for each such child
Infirm husband and dependent child or children	$60,000 and $10,000 for each such child
Dependent orphan children	$15,000 for each such child

Individual Dependent Allowance

Widow	$60,000
Infirm husband with at least one dependent child	$60,000
Dependent child where there is also a widow or infirm husband	$10,000
Dependent orphan child	$15,000

In general these exemptions follow the pattern of the federal Estate Tax Act. The resemblance is superficial, however, since under the federal act these amounts are true deductions from the dutiable estate, leaving a taxable residual, whereas under the Ontario Act they are amounts beyond which the *total* value becomes dutiable. This has had the effect of creating a very substantial penalty for amounts only slightly in excess of the exemption, which has been relieved by a "notch" provision which prevents the duty from reducing the net estate or benefit below the exemption.

Rates of Duty

The rates of duty applicable under the Quebec and Ontario statutes are in the form of dual schedules, one establishing a rate based on the total amount of the estate and the other a rate based on the amount of the individual succession. The sum of the two rates gives the amount applicable to the individual succession. The first rate is determined by the total amount of the estate, including tax-exempt real property outside of the province. In Ontario the exempt bequests for charitable and other purposes are deductible in determining both rates of tax, but not in Quebec. There are three such sets of rates, one set for each class of beneficiary. The rates based on the size of the total estate and the rates based on the amount of the individual succession increase the more remote the relationship of the beneficiary to the deceased. In Ontario the rates as given in the schedule are subject to a surtax of 15 per cent, 20 per cent, and 25 per cent for beneficiaries of Class 1, Class 2, and Class 3 respectively. The rate schedules are given in the Appendix in Tables XVI and XVII. These rates apply to the total amount of the estate if it falls within the bracket, not just to the part of the total estate that falls within the bracket. In the Appendix will also be found tables (XVIII and XIX) showing some actual instances of the combined Quebec-plus-Dominion and Ontario-plus-Dominion duties for a representative group of estates.

The Ontario Act: Some Specific Details

The Ontario Act imposes a duty (Section 5) on property having its situs in Ontario and also on a person receiving a transmission of property in Ontario. In addition it imposes a tax on every person to whom there has been a "disposition" of property in Ontario—in effect a transfer in the form of a gift or any act benefitting him directly or indirectly—within five years prior to the death, the duty to be payable on the death of the person making the disposition. Dispositions made since 1892 with any reservation to the donor (e.g., the right to enjoyment of the income therefrom) are taxable on the death of the donor. The Ontario Act also imposes a duty on every disposition made outside of Ontario during the lifetime of the decedent where both the decedent and the beneficiary lived in the province at the time of the disposition and also at the time of the death of the decedent.

"Property," for the purposes of the Ontario Act, includes joint property (except the share contributed by the survivors), any annuity, income, or other interest which the deceased purchased or contributed (to the extent of his contribution), insurance moneys payable on the death, property over which deceased had power of appointment, any property passing prior to death regarding which the decedent reserved any rights during his lifetime, and similar inclusions. All such property is to be valued as at the date of death, without any adjustment for subsequent increase or decrease in value.

Exemptions are allowed for certain bequests in addition to those outlined above. These include the unlimited deduction of charitable and educational bequests and gifts made to governments, the value of pensions going to survivors of the deceased out of a pension plan of the Dominion government or the provincial and municipal governments of Ontario, and any non-commutable contractual annuity or an annuity purchased by the deceased and payable to a close relative, to the extent of $1,200 a year on one person and $2,400 per year on the aggregate of persons. In the case of "interests in expectancy" (a deferred right to income or capital after all prior rights have been exhausted) the duty may be paid either at the time of the death or at the time of the actual receipt of the expectancy.

The Ontario law has a provision to alleviate the problem of payment of duty on an annuity or other right to income from an estate. By this provision the payment of duty may be spread over ten years, unless either the period of the annuity or the life expectancy of the beneficiary is less than ten years, in which case the shorter period will apply.

The Quebec Act: Some Specific Details

The scope of the Quebec duty is very similar to that of Ontario. A duty is imposed on "all property, moveable or immoveable, the ownership, usufruct or enjoyment whereof is transmitted owing to the death" (Section 3) and also on "every transmission within the Province, owing to a death of a person domiciled therein, of moveable property locally situate outside the province at the time of such death" (Section 24). Gifts made within five years of death are taxable as part of the estate, along with all gifts made during the lifetime of the decedent where he reserved, in whole or in part, until his death, any control, ownership, or enjoyment over the property given. There are the usual provisions to bring into the estate joint property, life insurance proceeds, gifts in contemplation of death, and so on. Exemptions are granted without limit for donations for charitable, educational, and other purposes, but these do not affect the rate of duty as under the Ontario Act. The Civil Code that governs property rights in Quebec gives rise to differences in the nature of devolutions which are distinctive to that province, but which will not be discussed here.

Summary

RATES. Under the Ontario and Quebec duties rates are graduated in accordance with (1) the size of the total estate, (2) the amount of the individual succession, and (3) the relationship of beneficiary to the deceased.

REVENUE

	Fiscal year 1958–9 ($000)	Percentage of tax revenue	Percentage of total revenue
Quebec	22,270	6.1	4.0
Ontario	33,518	9.2	5.2

STATUTORY REFERENCES. *Quebec*, Succession Duties Act, 7 Geo. 6, c. 18, and 13 Geo. 6, c. 32; *Ontario*, Succession Duty Act, Revised Statutes, Ontario, 1960, c. 386.

Chapter 11

PROVINCIAL CONSUMPTION AND EXPENDITURE TAXES

Gasoline Taxes

SINCE THE TWENTIES the motor vehicle has been playing an increasingly important role in provincial finances in Canada. With the vast distances over which roads must be built and the demand for ever-improved high-speed arteries, highway expenditures are a major item in every provincial budget. At the same time gasoline taxes and motor vehicle licences, which provide a ready means of levying a toll on highway users, provide a correspondingly large share of provincial revenues. Gasoline taxes were first imposed in Alberta in 1922, in Manitoba and British Columbia in 1923, in Prince Edward Island and Quebec in 1924, in Ontario in 1925, in Nova Scotia and New Brunswick in 1926, and in 1928 in Saskatchewan. Today provincial gasoline taxes are at a record peak, and account for one-quarter to one-third of the retail price of gasoline. Rates have risen in nearly every province in the post-war period, as the following summary shows:

RATES OF PROVINCIAL GASOLINE TAX IN POST-WAR PERIOD
IN CENTS PER GALLON

Nfld. 1949, 14¢ per gal.; 1954, 15¢; 1955, 17¢; 1960, 19¢
P.E.I. 1946, 10¢; 1947, 13¢; 1957, 16¢
N.S.   1946, 10¢; 1946, 13¢; 1951, 15¢; 1955, 17¢; 1961, 19¢
N.B.   1946, 10¢; 1946, 13¢, 1954, 15¢; 1961, 18¢
Que.   1946, 8¢; 1947, 11¢; 1950, 13¢
Ont.   1946, 8¢; 1947, 11¢; 1957, 13¢
Man.   1946, 7¢; 1947, 9¢, 1956, 11¢; 1961, 14¢
Sask. 1946, 8¢; 1947, 10¢; 1953, 11¢; 1957, 12¢; 1961, 14¢
Alta. 1946, 7¢; 1947, 9¢; 1951, 10¢; 1961, 12¢
B.C.   1946, 7¢; 1947, 10¢; 1961, 13¢

In addition to gasoline these taxes usually apply also to other products of petroleum, natural gas, or coal, in liquid form, which are capable of operating an internal combustion engine. These generally include diesel oil, benzol, benzine, and distillate, but not kerosene. Certain of these products are also used for heating purposes but are not taxed when so used.

As invariably is the case, exemptions are granted for certain uses or classes of users. The exclusions differ from province to province, but the general aim is to limit the tax to fuel purchased for operating motor vehicles on the public highways, and other uses are either totally exempt or subject to rebate of a substantial portion of the tax. The principal tax-exempt uses include consumption on the farm (tractors, combines, etc.), in the mine and forest (bulldozers, loaders, etc.), in fishing boats, and in industry generally, where gasoline is consumed either for internal combustion engines, for heating, or as a direct component in a manufacturing process. Rebates are also given for shipments to points outside of the province. Exemptions are provided either by refunds on application of the exempt user or else by the issue of a licence to certain consumers which enables them to purchase gasoline free of tax. Gasoline sold to such licensed consumers is coloured purple or some other distinctive shade by means of a harmless chemical. This means of identification allows inspection of the contents of the tank of any motor vehicle to detect the unauthorized use of tax-free gas.

The incidence of these refunds and exemptions varies markedly between provinces. In the east they amount to only 10 or 15 per cent of the tax otherwise collectible, but in Saskatchewan and Alberta half or more of the gas is tax-free, owing to the extensive use of exempt fuels in tractors and other mechanized equipment on the farm.

In Manitoba in addition to the tax imposed directly on gasoline there is a safe-guarding levy under the Motive Fuel Users Tax Act. This tax applies to any fuels not taxed as gasoline which are actually used to provide motive power. In general for "non-road" use, including boats and aeroplanes, a special rate of 2 cents per gallon is levied. In British Columbia a special tax of 1 cent per gallon is imposed on marked (coloured) gasoline sold for use other than in motor vehicles (the Coloured Gasoline Tax Act) and a tax of ½ cent per gallon on fuel oil for general consumption, including heating (Fuel-Oil Tax Act).

A recent trend in nearly all provinces has been towards the charging of a higher tax on diesel oil used on highways. This has followed studies which have indicated that vehicles of this type were not bearing sufficient tax at the ordinary rate. These extra charges range from 2 cents to 8 cents per gallon. Mention should also be made of the licence fees that are imposed on all companies and individuals handling gasoline in every province. These serve the purpose of control and regulation but do not produce a substantial revenue.

Summary

RATES (in cents per gallon; special diesel oil rates, where levied, are given in brackets). Newfoundland, 19; Prince Edward Island, 16; Nova Scotia, 19 (27); New Brunswick, 18 (23); Quebec, 13; Ontario, 13 (18½); Manitoba, 14 (17); Saskatchewan, 14 (17); Alberta, 12 (14); British Columbia, 13 (15).

REVENUE

	Fiscal year 1958–9 ($000)	Percentage of tax revenue	Percentage of total revenue
Newfoundland	4,695	35.1	7.5
Prince Edward Island	2,214	74.4	17.6
Nova Scotia	14,698	81.6	19.4
New Brunswick	11,602	51.5	16.3
Quebec	89,577	24.5	16.1
Ontario	52,771	14.5	8.2
Manitoba	14,339	88.7	18.7
Saskatchewan	20,241	38.0	14.3
Alberta	25,098	89.3	10.6
British Columbia	28,845	23.1	9.8

STATUTORY REFERENCES. *Newfoundland*, Gasoline Tax Act, Revised Statutes Newfoundland 1952, c. 38; *P.E.I.*, Gas Tax Act, Statutes, Prince Edward Island 1961, c. 13; *Nova Scotia*, Gasoline Tax Act, Revised Statutes Nova Scotia 1954, c. 109; *New Brunswick*, Gasoline

Sales Act, Revised Statutes New Brunswick 1952, c. 98; *Quebec*, Gasoline Tax Act, Revised Statutes Quebec 1941, c. 83; *Ontario*, Gasoline Tax Act, Revised Statutes Ontario 1960, c. 162; Motor Vehicle Fuel Tax Act, *ibid.*, c. 248; *Manitoba*, Gasoline Tax Act, Statutes Manitoba 1955, c. 55; *Saskatchewan*, Fuel Petroleum Products Act, Revised Statutes Saskatchewan 1953, c. 62; *Alberta*, Fuel Oil Tax Act, Revised Statutes Alberta 1955, c. 125; *British Columbia*, Gasoline Tax Act, 1958, Revised Statutes of British Columbia 1960, c. 162; Coloured Gasoline Tax Act, *ibid.*, c. 63; Motive-fuel Use Tax Act, *ibid.*, c. 251; Fuel-Oil Tax Act, *ibid.*, c. 158.

Retail Sales Taxes

Eight of the Canadian provinces—all but Manitoba and Alberta—now levy a retail sales tax of general application. Except in Quebec they are known by such names as the Social Service, Hospital, or Education Tax. Such a tax was first imposed in Alberta in 1936 under the Ultimate Purchasers Tax Act; it was suspended in 1937 and has not been reimposed since. Saskatchewan introduced the retail sales tax in 1937, Quebec in 1940, British Columbia in 1948, New Brunswick in 1950, Newfoundland in 1950, Nova Scotia in 1959, Prince Edward Island in 1960, and Ontario in 1961. The Canadian position now parallels that in the United States where some thirty-five states and several large cities levy 1 to 3 per cent taxes of this type.

Limitations of a Direct Tax

In the past the Canadian provinces have been disinclined to resort to this type of taxation, one reason being the constitutional restrictions on their fiscal powers. Under the present status they are barred from imposing an indirect retail sales tax in the form used by many of the American states. It was pointed out earlier in the general discussion of provincial powers that retail sales taxes qualify as direct taxation only when they are imposed on the final consumer who buys for his own use or consumption, and not for resale. The direct sales tax has minor problems of enforcement compared to an indirect tax that can be imposed on the vendor in respect of his sales, but these are unimportant by comparison with the complications which arise from other causes, particularly the granting of extensive exemptions.

Experience indicates that, whether imposed as a direct or an indirect tax, the successful collection of a retail sales tax requires top-notch efficiency both in planning and in execution. Revenue arises from hundreds or thousands of sources, as contrasted with the much reduced area requiring supervision in the case of the manufacturers' excise. This situation requires not only strict supervision to prevent leaks but also a greater degree of public education in collection procedure, particularly where a large number of articles are exempt from the tax. These administrative aspects have been discussed in detail by officials and also by Professor Due in his Foundation Tax Paper.[1] One of the worst problems encountered in imposing a manufacturers' tax—the determination of the sale price to which the tax applies—is not as troublesome, however, under a retail tax. Whereas the manufacturers' tax is interposed at an arbitrary point on the route to the consumer, the retail tax applies on the final consumer price paid which, in most cases, is an identifiable market price. Adjustments are required to be made but are limited.

Scope of Tax

In a sense it is somewhat misleading to call these taxes "retail taxes," particularly in view of the popular conception of a retail sale. One ordinarily thinks in this connection of the bright display windows and well-laden shelves of the stores in the local shopping district. Actually the retail taxes in the Canadian provinces are of much broader application. They are more properly described as taxes imposed on every person who purchases goods for his own use or consumption and not for resale. They apply, for example, to all the machinery, equipment, and apparatus used in a factory, since these are regarded as being consumed by the manufacturer and not purchased for

[1] G. H. Shink, "The Sales and Use Tax Laws of the Province of Quebec," pp. 336-46; R. M. Burns, "Problems in the Introduction of a Consumer Purchase Tax," p. 324; L. F. Detwiller, "Provincial Sales Tax," pp. 60-81; John F. Due, *Provincial Sales Taxes*.

resale.[2] They also apply to almost all materials and supplies purchased by the service industries where they are used up in providing the service (e.g., cleaning fluid). The universal test of liability is, Does the purchaser use or consume the property himself or does he pass it on by resale to another person? In keeping with this test any materials bought to be manufactured into an article of a different character for resale are exempt from tax. An interesting exception to this general rule is found in Quebec, where industries are granted an exemption on their purchases of taxable articles in the same proportion as their sales made outside the province bear to total sales. If, for example, one-half of a company's sales are made outside of Quebec, the company pays tax on only one-half of the value of its taxable purchases. This relief is limited to two-thirds, however, so that a company must pay tax on at least one-third of its taxable purchases.

Articles subject to tax under the provincial statutes embrace the broadest possible field. In Quebec it is charged on purchases of "moveable property" and in the other provinces on "tangible personal property," or simply on "goods." In principle the Quebec definition appears to make liable purchases of intangible property such as bonds and stocks, since it seems to have been necessary to exempt such purchases by specific provision under the statute. This is a wider initial definition than is used in the other provinces but in fact the exclusion of intangible property reduces it to the same general scope.

The tax is payable by the purchaser at the time of the sale if the goods are purchased within the province and at the time of receipt if the goods are from outside the province whether brought in, ordered in, or in any other manner caused to be delivered to the consumer. Mail order goods would undoubtedly be the largest of this class of goods, although in the provinces where equipment and machinery is taxable this type of purchase would be a heavy source of revenue.

[2]A departure has been made in New Brunswick, Nova Scotia, Prince Edward Island, and Ontario where, following the Dominion's example, an exemption has been granted for machinery used directly in the process of manufacture or production of goods for sale.

Where goods are purchased within the province the tax is collected by the retailer. Where they are received from outside the resident of the province is required by statute to pay the usual tax, a provision most difficult to enforce in practice. Goods and merchandise passing out of the province to a non-resident user are not subject to tax. In every case it is only a sale, i.e., an exchange of value, that constitutes a taxable transaction. *Bona-fide* gifts are not taxable.

In administering the tax a licensing system very similar to that described for the Dominion sales tax is used. This system enables manufacturers to purchase materials for manufacture or processing free of tax, although as mentioned previously in several provinces all other machinery, equipment, and materials purchased by them not for resale are subject to tax.

Exemptions from Tax

Exemptions from the taxes are numerous. These undoubtedly complicate the collection problem since it would be a much simpler matter in practice to have the rate apply to every sale and avoid the vexing problem for the retailer of determining when to collect and when not to collect. It is, of course, socially desirable that certain essentials of life be exempt, and on this ground food is excluded in all provinces. Other exemptions reflect the elimination of double tax where other special levies are imposed (e.g. gasoline) or the granting of a preferred position to certain groups in society (e.g. farmers). The following is a brief summary of the exemptions in the various provinces.

Gasoline: Nfld., P.E.I., N.S., N.B., Que., Ont., Sask., B.C. *Food*: all provinces. *Small sales*: Nfld.—under 17¢; P.E.I.—under 25¢; N.S.—15¢ or less; N.B.—14¢ or less; Que.—10¢ or less; Ont.—under 17¢; Sask.—14¢ or less; B.C.—less than 15¢. *Drugs and prescriptions*: Nfld., P.E.I., N.S., N.B., Que., Ont., Sask., B.C. *Farm equipment and supplies*: Nfld., P.E.I., N.S., N.B., Que., Ont., Sask., B.C. *Fuels*: P.E.I., N.S., N.B., Ont., Sask., B.C.; Que.—coal and firewood. *Alcoholic products*: Que.—beer; Ont.—draft beer. *Tobacco products*: N.B., P.E.I., Que. *Soaps and laundry material*: Sask. *Catalysts*: P.E.I., N.S., N.B., Ont., B.C. *Motor vehicles*: N.S. *Books*: P.E.I., N.S., N.B.,

Que., Ont., Sask. *Newspapers, magazines, and periodicals* (by subscription): P.E.I., N.S., N.B., Ont., Sask. *Children's clothing*: P.E.I., N.S., N.B., Que., Ont., B.C. *Children's footwear*: P.E.I., N.S., N.B., Que., Ont., B.C. *Machinery and apparatus for production*: P.E.I., N.S., N.B., Ont. *Electricity*: N.B., P.E.I., Ont. *Vessels and fishing supplies*: Nfld., P.E.I., N.S., N.B., Que., Ont., Sask. *Sales to Dominion Government*: Nfld., Que., B.C. *Meals*: P.E.I.—$1.00 or less; Nfld.—prepared meals under 17¢; N.S.—$1.00 or less; N.B.—$1.00 or less; Que.—all meals; Ont.—$1.50; B.C.—where they are less than $1.01. *School supplies*: P.E.I., N.S., N.B., Que., Ont., Sask.

Summary

RATES. Newfoundland, 5 per cent; Prince Edward Island, 4 per cent; Nova Scotia, 5 per cent; New Brunswick, 3 per cent; Quebec, 4 per cent; Ontario (Sept. 1, 1961), 3 per cent; Saskatchewan, 3 per cent; British Columbia, 5 per cent.

REVENUE

	Fiscal year 1958–9 ($000)	*Percentage of tax revenue*	*Percentage of total revenue*
Newfoundland	8,033	60.1	12.9
Nova Scotia	1,661	9.2	2.2
New Brunswick	7,942	35.3	11.2
Quebec	62,941	17.2	11.3
Saskatchewan	21,667	40.7	15.3
British Columbia	84,488	67.6	28.6

STATUTORY REFERENCES. *Newfoundland*, Social Security Assessment Act, Revised Statutes Newfoundland 1952, c. 41; *Nova Scotia*, Hospital Tax Act, Statutes Nova Scotia 1958, c. 4; *New Brunswick*, Social Services and Education Tax Act, Revised Statutes New Brunswick 1952, c. 213; *Quebec*, Retail Sales Tax Act, Revised Statutes Quebec 1941, c. 88; *Ontario*, The Retail Sales Tax Act, 1960–1, Statutes of Ontario, 1961, c. 91; *Saskatchewan*, Education and Hospitalization Tax Act, Revised Statutes Saskatchewan 1953, c. 61; *British Columbia*, Social Services Tax Act, Revised Statutes British Columbia 1960, c. 61.

Tobacco, Liquor, and Meals Taxes

Tobacco Taxes

Similar in form to the general retail sales taxes just described are the special taxes on retail sales of certain goods. Of these the tobacco taxes are of first importance. This tax was first imposed in Quebec and New Brunswick in 1940, in Prince Edward Island in 1942, and in Nova Scotia in 1958. In all four provinces the tax is now levied on cigarettes at 1/5 of a cent per cigarette or a flat charge of 4 cents for a package of 20. On other tobacco products an ad valorem rate is levied at 5 per cent in Nova Scotia and 10 per cent elsewhere.

Liquor Taxes

Taxes on liquor levied in several provinces are described in chapter 12.

Meals Tax

The Quebec meals tax, or to give it its proper name, the "Hospital Duty," was first imposed in 1926, applicable to hotels and restaurants; in 1941 its scope was broadened to include dining cars and most other establishments. The rate is 5 per cent on the price of each meal costing $1.00 or more served in any establishment where, for monetary consideration, food is served. Establishment is defined to include a hotel, a restaurant, any railway train or ship in the province, and any other premises in the province where, for monetary consideration, food is served. It does not include establishments commonly known as boarding-houses, or educational, charitable, hospitalizing, or sheltering institutions, or other similar institutions. Also excluded from the scope of the tax are meals served to employees in an establishment maintained by their employer. The tax charged on the price of the meal must be shown on the bill as a separate item. The price of the meal to which the tax applies includes any charge for beer, wine, or other beverages consumed with it, and, since May 1, 1961, has been extended to apply to the consumption of liquor in certain establishments without a meal.

All revenues from the duty are paid into the Public Charities Fund, from which grants are made for the support of hospitals and other institutions in the province. The municipalities are authorized to impose a similar duty under the same act.

SUMMARY

RATES. Tobacco tax (Prince Edward Island, Nova Scotia, New Brunswick, and Quebec): 4 cents per package of 20 cigarettes; other tobacco: 10 per cent in Prince Edward Island, New Brunswick, and Quebec; 5 per cent in Nova Scotia; meals tax (Quebec): 5 per cent of the price of the meal if the meal is $1.00 or more.

REVENUE

	Fiscal year 1958-9 ($000)	Percentage of tax revenue	Percentage of total revenue
Tobacco taxes			
Prince Edward Island	290	9.8	2.3
New Brunswick	1,725	7.7	2.4
Quebec	20,233	5.5	3.6
Meals tax (Quebec)	5,924	1.6	1.1

STATUTORY REFERENCES. *P.E.I.*, Health Tax Act, Revised Statutes, Prince Edward Island, 1951, c. 71; *Nova Scotia*, Hospital Tax Act, c. 4, 1958; *New Brunswick*, Tobacco Tax Act, Revised Statutes, New Brunswick, 1952, c. 231; *Quebec*, Tobacco Tax Act, Revised Statutes, Quebec, 1941, c. 87; Hospital Duty Act, *ibid.*, c. 89.

AMUSEMENT AND PARI-MUTUEL BETS TAXES

These taxes were introduced during and after World War I and have been in effect in most provinces since. All provinces except Saskatchewan and Alberta impose a tax in one form or other on the price of admission to places of amusement. In eight of the provinces there are also taxes on pari-mutuel bets placed at race tracks. Provincial governments now stand alone in both these fields, wartime federal taxes having long since been repealed.

Rates and Scope of Amusement Taxes

The rates of provincial amusement taxes are now almost uniformly 10 per cent of the admission price. This rate applies, with minor variations for lower priced tickets, in all provinces but Newfoundland, New Brunswick, and Quebec. In Newfoundland there is a flat rate of 5 cents per ticket, in New Brunswick the rate is 11 per cent, and in Quebec, $12\frac{1}{2}$ per cent (although in fact this is a composite provincial-municipal rate, 5 per cent for the municipality, 5 per cent for the Public Charities Fund and $2\frac{1}{2}$ per cent for the province). Municipal taxes are also levied in Newfoundland and Saskatchewan.

In most provinces there are also licences for the operation of a theatre or place of amusement based on the number of seats or some similar criterion.

In their usual form these taxes are simply a surcharge on the price paid for gaining entrance to premises where entertainment is being provided (e.g., a theatre), or where it is possible to participate in an amusement (e.g., a dance-hall). In most provinces there is a minimum tax charged on complimentary passes. In Ontario, Manitoba, and British Columbia the tax has been extended to include an element similar to the cabaret tax formerly imposed by the Dominion. In Ontario the general 10 per cent rate on admissions to theatres, concerts, etc., is imposed on the charge for meals or refreshments served in conjunction with any dance, performance, or entertainment. The same practice has been followed in Manitoba, where the 10 per cent rate applies to the bill payable as the charge for eatables where dancing is provided therewith.

In defining places of entertainment or amusement a wide net is cast. In addition to the obvious places such as theatres, concert halls, and dance-halls, there are also usually included circuses, carnivals, grand-stand shows, side shows, amusement parks (and sometimes the "rides" and amusement devices therein), skating rinks, roller-skating rinks, race tracks, any hall or grounds used for wrestling, boxing, or any other outdoor or indoor athletics, games, or sports.

Exemptions from the Amusement Taxes

An inevitable feature of this form of tax is the long list of amusements and entertainments that are exempt. The principal exemption is for events having a charitable purpose. In view of the widespread adoption of public shows, entertainments, and "bingos" for charitable purposes the administration of this exemption calls for diplomacy of the highest sort. Most worthy citizens become utterly lawless when their charitable instincts are aroused.

Amateur sports, games, and entertainments are usually exempt. One need only recall the storm that has raged on the subject of amateur vs. professional sports in recent years to appreciate the quandary of the tax collector in attempting to be fair and impartial in this field. Other less contentious exemptions normally granted include those to agricultural fairs, art exhibitions, educational lectures, and amateur musical concerts. Minimum amounts for tickets are also exempt. The amounts vary from province to province, but most are between 30 and 60 cents.

A novel feature of the Ontario legislation provides for the refunding only of a portion of the tax equal to the proportion that the proceeds actually turned over to charity bears to the total gross proceeds. It would appear that under this plan if half the proceeds actually are disbursed to charities, only half the tax is refunded.

All provinces regulate the collection of the amusement taxes through a licensing system, which normally requires either a licence or a certificate of exemption to be obtained before the performance may be put on. The censorship of films is also closely associated with movie tax administration in some provinces.

Pari-Mutuel Bets Taxes

Of the same class as the amusement taxes are those levied on pari-mutuel bets. They are imposed as a percentage of bets placed on a pari-mutuel machine at a licensed race track in the province. In Prince Edward Island, where interest in the sport of kings is surprisingly keen, the tax is 5 per cent. Nova Scotia has 6 per cent and New Brunswick 5 per cent. Quebec levies a rate of 12½ per cent (less the track take of 5 per cent); Ontario, 6 per cent; Manitoba, 10 per cent; Saskatchewan and Alberta, 5 per cent; and British Columbia, 12 per cent.

Summary

RATES. Admission taxes in general are at a 10 per cent rate, except for Newfoundland (5 cents per ticket) and New Brunswick (11 per cent). Pari-mutuel bets taxes are imposed in Prince Edward Island, Nova Scotia, Quebec, Ontario, the Prairie Provinces, and British Columbia at rates from 5 per cent to 12 per cent.

REVENUE

	Fiscal year 1958-9 ($000)	Percentage of tax revenue	Percentage of total revenue
Newfoundland	120	.9	.2
Prince Edward Island	78	2.6	.6
Nova Scotia	405	2.2	.5
New Brunswick	361	1.7	.5
Quebec	6,419	1.8	1.1
Ontario	9,907	2.7	1.5
Manitoba	667	4.1	.9
Saskatchewan	103	.2	—
Alberta	1,066	3.8	.5
British Columbia	2,899	2.3	1.0

STATUTORY REFERENCES. *Newfoundland*, Cancer Control Act, c. 40, 1953; *P.E.I.*, Amusement Tax Act, c. 3, 1952; *Nova Scotia*, Theatres and Amusements Act, Revised Statutes, Nova Scotia, 1954, c. 288; *New Brunswick*, Theatres, Cinematographs and Amusements Act, Revised Statutes, New Brunswick, 1952, c. 228; *Quebec*, Amusement Tax Act, Revised Statutes, Quebec, 1941, c. 85; Licence Act, *ibid.*, c. 76; *Ontario*, Hospitals Tax Act, Revised Statutes, Ontario, 1960, c. 178; Race Track Tax Act, *ibid.*, c. 341; *Manitoba*, Amusements Tax Act, Revised Statutes, Manitoba, 1954, c. 4; *Saskatchewan*, City Act, Revised Statutes, Saskatchewan, 1953, c. 137; Town Act, *ibid.*, c. 138; Horse Racing Regulation Act, *ibid.*, c. 349; *Alberta*, Amusements

Act, Revised Statutes, Alberta, 1955, c. 13; *British Columbia*, Amusement Tax (Hospital Construction Aid Tax Act), Revised Statutes, British Columbia, 1960, c. 179; Pari-Mutuel Betting Tax Act, *ibid.*, c. 274.

Chapter 12

PROVINCIAL LIQUOR AND MOTOR VEHICLE REVENUES
AND MISCELLANEOUS TAXES

Liquor Fees, Taxes, and Profits

ALTHOUGH provincial brewery, distillery, saloon and retail licences were one of the earliest forms of revenue, receipts from this source have only been substantial since the 1920's when the retail sale of spirits in Canada was brought under the monopoly of provincial Liquor Control Boards. Sales of beer and wine also are allowed now only under conditions laid down by these boards. No province has complete prohibition, but it is optional in local areas by vote.

Development and Nature of Liquor Control

The sale of intoxicating liquors in Canada has been subject to some form of government control from earliest times. In the French régime the problem became serious in the fur trade, and the sale of liquor to the Indians was early prohibited "on account of the fury of these people when in a state of intoxication." After Confederation, and until World War I, control or prohibition of sale was regulated by local option under powers given to local areas under the Canada Temperance Act, a Dominion statute, and under similar provincial acts. Sentiment for prohibition on a provincial and even national scale was increasing in the years before World War I. Several provincial plebiscites were taken on the question and in 1898 there was a Dominion-wide plebiscite on a proposal for a national prohibition law. While this plebiscite showed a majority in favour of prohibition the number of voters participating was only 44 per cent of the total electorate and Sir Wilfrid Laurier, the prime minister of the day, did not feel that this was sufficient to demonstrate clearly the general will of the country.

Despite these provincial and national plebiscites no break was made with the local option system until the middle of World War I when in 1916 and 1917 all provinces except Quebec passed prohibition laws. Quebec followed suit in 1919. The prohibition was absolute and complete in every province except Quebec, where the ban only extended to spirits.

Prohibition survived in all provinces for varying periods following the war but was gradually replaced by provincial monopoly control over public sale and distribution. This step came first in 1921 in Quebec and British Columbia. Manitoba followed in 1923, Alberta in 1924, Saskatchewan in 1925, Ontario and New Brunswick in 1927, and Nova Scotia in 1930. Prince Edward Island abandoned prohibition only in 1948, when the result of a plebiscite was in favour of government control of liquor sales by a majority of more than two to one. Today, therefore, in all provinces the manufacture, distribution, and sale of intoxicating beverages are under the control of the provincial governments (this is in addition to the control exercised by the Dominion excise administration).

In general, spirits are sold by the bottle only through government-operated liquor stores. Except in New Brunswick, Quebec, and British Columbia permits are required. Charges for these permits are nominal, ranging from 25 cents to $2.00, and they are issued annually to anyone of age and of sound mind and not otherwise disqualified. Bottled beer and wine may also be obtained at these provincial outlets in all provinces, and in some there are, in addition, retail outlets maintained by the breweries, by other licensed dispensers or, in the case of Ontario, by native wineries. Quebec has the most liberal laws for the sale of beer. In that province it may be sold by the bottle through such outlets as grocery stores. In most provinces (with the exception of Prince Edward Island and New Brunswick) beer is also sold by bottle or glass in hotels, taverns, beer parlours, or clubs for immediate consumption. In several provinces licences are also granted for the serving of liquor and wine in "cocktail bars" and dining rooms, in hotels, taverns, and lounges.

While the profit derived from the sale of alcoholic beverages through provincial outlets is not tax revenue in the narrowest sense it may be regarded as such if only because in jurisdictions where liquor control does not exist the same revenue is obtained indirectly through a tax. In addition to whatever social objectives may be served by liquor control, therefore, there is the substantial advantage that the sale of liquor through government stores provides a convenient method of collecting a particular form of provincial tax. However, although from this point of view the profit margin may be regarded as a tax, its nature as a trading profit makes it almost impossible to draw any conclusion as to the weight of the charge made by the provinces through their mark-up.

Only in two provinces is there any special tax on the purchase of liquor in addition to the mark-up. In Quebec a tax is payable on every bottle of spirits purchased at a government liquor store. The tax, levied under the Alcoholic Liquor Act, amounts to 5 cents on a bottle of 13 ounces or less, 10 cents on a bottle of 13 to 27 ounces, and 15 cents on a bottle over 27 ounces. In Prince Edward Island there is a Health Tax of 10 per cent payable on the price of every purchase at a government liquor store. Most provinces levying a general retail sales tax apply it to the price of alcoholic beverages (sometimes exempting beer) and in Nova Scotia a special rate of 5 per cent (the general rate being 3 per cent) has been enacted.

Taxes on Brewers, Distillers, and Vendors

Taxes as such do play a prominent role, however, in those provinces where beer may be purchased directly from breweries by the owners of licensed taverns and beer parlours for public sale. In these circumstances the mark-up that would apply had the sale been made through a government outlet is replaced by a form of tax. Ordinarily this levy is a double-sided affair, one part being a graduated licence fee on the brewer who makes the beer and the other a similar charge imposed on the licensed retail vendor.

In Quebec, for example, every brewer in the province must be licensed, and a flat fee is payable both on the application for and on the granting of the licence. In addition to these fees substantial duties are imposed on the sale of beer by a brewery to one of the licensed outlets mentioned below. Every gallon of beer sold by a brewery for consumption in the province is subject to a duty of $14\frac{1}{2}$ cents, payable to the Liquor Commission.

The province also levies a duty in the form of a licence fee on the application and granting of licences for the sale of alcoholic beverages for public consumption. These licence fees vary in amount depending on the nature of the establishment, which may be trading-post, boat, dining car, banquet, grocery store, tavern, club, café, restaurant, hotel, or inn. In addition, on the purchase of beer for resale these licensed establishments must pay to the brewery a duty of 5 cents per gallon on draft beer, 4 cents per dozen of small bottles, and 7 cents per dozen of large bottles. These duties do not apply to wine and spirits, which must be purchased by the licensed establishment from the provincial liquor stores, and are therefore subject to the usual retail mark-up and the special tax previously mentioned. Substantial duties are also charged on the transfer of any right conferred by a permit.

The system in effect in Ontario is very similar. Licences must be taken out by provincial brewers, the charge being $1,500 per annum. In addition every brewer must pay a fee of $16\frac{1}{2}$ cents per gallon where annual production is less than 2 million gallons and $18\frac{1}{2}$ cents per gallon where it is more than 2 million gallons. Brewers outside of the province must pay the higher gallonage charge. Fees are also imposed for the opening of brewers' retail stores and central beer warehouses. Ontario is the only province that grants permits for the sale of native wine through outlets owned by the wine manufacturers. Licence fees for such outlets are a combination of a flat fee plus a charge of $10\frac{1}{2}$ per cent on gross value of sales plus a flat amount per store operated.

As in Quebec licences are granted for sales through hotels, taverns, restaurants, etc., the fee being in most cases a combination of a fixed amount and an amount varying with the gallonage sold, in the case of beer, or calculated at a percentage of purchases by the establishment, in the case of wine and spirits. The gallonage charge on beer is graduated according to the amount of beer sold and the *ad valorem* rate on liquor and wine purchases is 10 per cent. The various schedules covering the wide assortment of outlets are quite extensive and may be found in the regulations issued under the Ontario Liquor Control Act.

In Manitoba brewers pay a graduated annual licence fee and a tax of $12\frac{1}{2}$ cents per gallon of beer sold in the province; licensed outlets pay a flat fee plus 5 per cent of the cost of beverages sold. In Saskatchewan all beer must be purchased through the provincial liquor control stores at the usual price and therefore no gallonage tax is levied. In Alberta brewers must pay a fee of $1,500 and vendors a charge of 4 per cent on sales. In British Columbia brewers and distillers pay a licence fee of 1 per cent of the assessed value of their land and improvements, and licences are granted also for dining-rooms, dining-lounges, lounges, and public houses. Fees are a flat rate plus 2 per cent of the cost of beer and liquor purchased.

At the present time Nova Scotia and Newfoundland allow the sale of beer through outlets other than government liquor stores. A gallonage tax ranging from $7\frac{1}{2}$ cents to 40 cents plus a per barrel charge on draft is levied on beer sold through private establishments (taverns and dining-rooms) and there are also fees for licences to operate such an establishment. In both Prince Edward Island and New Brunswick all purchases of spirits, beer, or wine must be made at government stores and, as previously mentioned, in Prince Edward Island a tax of 10 per cent of the retail price is collected under the Health Tax Act. In Newfoundland beer may be sold both through taverns and through outlets established by the breweries. A commission is charged by the Liquor Control Board on both types of sale at approximately $1.20 per case of 2 dozen bottles.

Summary

RATES. The provincial revenues are derived from the trading profit on direct sales through provincially owned outlets and from licences, fees, and taxes for the right to manufacture, vend, or consume alcoholic beverages.

PROVINCIAL LIQUOR AND REVENUE[1]

	Fiscal year 1958-9 ($000)	Percentage of total revenue
Newfoundland	3,933	6.3
Prince Edward Island	1,363	10.7
Nova Scotia	12,019	15.9
New Brunswick	7,481	10.5
Quebec	46,458	8.3
Ontario	72,982	11.3
Manitoba	11,371	14.8
Saskatchewan	12,452	8.8
Alberta	19,574	8.3
British Columbia	27,139	9.2

[1]Includes profits, taxes, fees, etc.

STATUTORY REFERENCES. *P.E.I.*, Temperance Act, Revised Statutes Prince Edward Island, 1951, c. 159; Health Tax Act, *ibid.*, c. 71; *Newfoundland*, Alcoholic Liquors Act, Revised Statutes Newfoundland, 1953, c. 93; *Nova Scotia*, Liquor Control Act, Revised Statutes Nova Scotia, 1954, c. 155; *New Brunswick*, Intoxicating Liquor Act, Revised Statutes, 1952, c. 116; *Quebec*, Alcoholic Liquor Act, Revised Statutes, Quebec, 1941, c. 255; *Ontario*, Liquor Control Act, Revised Statutes, Ontario, 1960, c. 217; Liquor Licence Act, *ibid.*, c. 218; *Manitoba*, Liquor Control Act, Statutes Manitoba, 1956, c. 40; *Saskatchewan*, Liquor Act, Revised Statutes, Saskatchewan, 1953, c. 348; Liquor Exporters Taxation Act, *ibid.*, c. 60; *Alberta*, Liquor Control Act, Statutes Alberta, 1958, c. 37; Liquor Licensing Act, *ibid.*, c. 38; *British Columbia*, Government Liquor Act, Revised Statutes of British Columbia, 1960, c. 166.

MOTOR VEHICLE LICENCES AND FEES

All provinces were requiring motor vehicles to be licensed prior to World War I. Operators' licences and special charges on commercial carriers are a more recent development, not having been introduced in most cases until the twenties.

As indicated earlier, motor vehicle and related licences now account for a substantial revenue in all provinces, a fact attributable in part to the very high per capita registration of motor vehicles in Canada (one for every 3.5 persons). The general pattern of revenue from this source is similar in all provinces. First, there are fees for the compulsory registration of any person operating a vehicle on the public highways; second, there are fees for the compulsory registration of any vehicle being operated on the public highways; and, third, there are added charges on commercial carriers (buses, transports, etc.) for the privilege of operating a business of carrying freight or passengers on the public highways.

While the charges for operators' licences are a flat amount of $1.00 to $5.00 per annum,[1] a variety of bases are used for the registration and carrier charges for vehicles, each presumably reflecting the judgment of the provincial authorities as to the fairest basis for levying a contribution towards the maintenance of a registry and the upkeep of the provincial highways. For example, the general registration fee for both private and commercial vehicles in Quebec and the eastern provinces is based on the weight of the vehicle but the additional charges on public carriers are calculated on a great variety of bases, including receipts, mileage, ton miles, passenger capacity, passenger miles, etc. In Ontario the charge for compulsory registration under the Highway Act is based on horsepower (as measured by cylinders) in the case of private passenger vehicles and on gross weight in the case of commercial vehicles. In addition commercial freight carriers must pay a licence fee based on gross weight under the Public Commercial Vehicle Act, and passenger carriers a monthly fee under the Public Vehicle Act calculated at a fraction of a cent on each "passenger-mile" travelled in the province in the previous month.

In the Prairie Provinces the wheelbase of the vehicle appears to have gained favour as the criterion for the annual registration fee, and gross weight carrying capacity or passenger miles travelled in the province as the bases for the additional charges on commercial carriers. In British Columbia there is a flat

[1] In some provinces where the higher rates apply they are for a period of more than one year; in Alberta and British Columbia, for example, the $5.00 fee covers a five-year period, and in Saskatchewan the licence period is two years.

primary registration fee for all vehicles and an annual fee determined by weight; in addition, public carriers pay a licence fee based on seating capacity for passenger vehicles and on freight capacity for freight vehicles.

In Table X an attempt has been made to reduce the variety of rates and bases for the annual registration fee to a comparable form for three standard types of motor vehicle. The table shows the total charge payable in 1961, whether described as a licence, registration, marker, or other charge, in each of the ten provinces on a standard passenger car, a pick-up truck, and a van. No charge is included for the operator's licence (ranging from $1.00 to $5.00) or for payments into an Unsatisfied Judgment Fund, or similar fund, as required in Prince Edward Island, Ontario, Alberta, and possibly other provinces. In Saskatchewan no amount is included for the compulsory insurance, the charge for which is payable at the time of registration.

TABLE X

Provincial Charges in 1961 on Registration of Motor Vehicles

	Passenger car	Pick-up truck	Van
Newfoundland	$18.00	$25.00	$245.00
Prince Edward Island	19.50	20.80	168.50
Nova Scotia	22.68	21.60	194.25
New Brunswick	23.00	29.00	155.00
Quebec	25.50	39.75	136.00
Ontario	25.00	20.00	179.00
Manitoba	19.00	30.00	225.00
Saskatchewan	15.00	25.00	200.00
Alberta	15.00	45.00	150.00
British Columbia	22.50	30.00	180.00

Summary

RATES. Various bases of charge, including weight, horsepower, wheelbase, and carrying capacity.

Revenue

	Fiscal year 1958-9 ($000)	Percentage of total revenue
Newfoundland	1,575	2.5
Prince Edward Island	647	5.1
Nova Scotia	5,082	6.7
New Brunswick	4,433	6.2
Quebec	35,505	6.4
Ontario	58,981	9.1
Manitoba	6,577	8.6
Saskatchewan	6,998	4.9
Alberta	11,474	4.8
British Columbia	14,984	5.1

STATUTORY REFERENCES. *Newfoundland*, Highway Traffic Act, Revised Statutes of Newfoundland, 1952, c. 94; *P.E.I.*, Highway Traffic Act, Revised Statutes, Prince Edward Island, 1951, c. 73; Public Vehicle Act, *ibid.*, c. 134; *Nova Scotia*, Motor Vehicle Act, Revised Statutes, Nova Scotia, 1954, c. 184; *New Brunswick*, Motor Vehicle Act, 1955, c. 13; Motor Carrier Act, Revised Statutes, New Brunswick, 1952, c. 148; *Quebec*, Motor Vehicles Act, Revised Statutes, Quebec, 1941, c. 142; *Ontario*, Highway Traffic Act, Revised Statutes, Ontario, 1960, c. 172; Public Commercial Vehicles Act, *ibid.*, c. 319; Public Vehicles Act, *ibid.*, c. 337; *Manitoba*, Highway Traffic Act, Revised Statutes, Manitoba, 1954, c. 112; *Saskatchewan*, The Vehicles Act, Statutes of Saskatchewan, 1957, c. 344; *Alberta*, Vehicle and Highway Traffic Act, Revised Statutes, Alberta, 1955, c. 356; Public Service Vehicles Act, *ibid.*, c. 265; *British Columbia*, Motor Vehicle Act, Revised Statutes, British Columbia, 1960, c. 253; Department of Commercial Transport Act, *ibid.*, c. 101.

MISCELLANEOUS TAXES, LICENCES, AND FEES

Property Taxes

Following Confederation provincial property taxes were first imposed in British Columbia in 1876 and in Prince Edward Island in 1877. Prior to World War I Saskatchewan and Alberta introduced moderate taxes on land for the support of education and the Maritimes also used land taxation for road financing.

During World War I practically every province (Quebec being a notable exception) derived special revenues from real property taxes through levies on its municipalities. These taxes were retained after the war in varying degree, particularly in the western provinces, but in recent years they have been disappearing rapidly. The property tax has today achieved the distinction in Canada of being exclusively a municipal levy, and today forms the backbone of the local government tax structure.[1] Saskatchewan, the last province to use the source for general purposes, repealed its tax in 1953. Some provinces impose property taxes of limited application on land in unorganized territories not subject to a municipal rate or on other special classifications of land such as mineral, oil or forest bearing land. The latter are dealt with in chapter 13, "Provincial Revenues from the Public Domain."

In a province by province review of provincial land taxes commencing with Newfoundland it can be said that no tax of this type is in effect in that province today.

Almost the first to enter the field and among the last to leave it, Prince Edward Island in 1948 repealed a tax on all land and buildings outside of incorporated municipalities which had been in effect since 1877, except for a break between 1882 and 1894. This had been one of the oldest property taxes in Canada, originating as a provincial levy because of the comparative lack of development of municipal institutions on the Island. At the same time a poll tax and a horse tax under the Roads Act were repealed, and a provincial tax on personal property suspended in 1941 under the Wartime Tax Agreements was again suspended in 1947 under the new agreement.

Both Nova Scotia and New Brunswick impose directly taxes of minor importance on undeveloped land. In New Brunswick a Wild Lands Tax is payable where five hundred acres or more is held by any one owner, and in Nova Scotia a similar levy is imposed under the Land Tax Act, applicable only on land where more than a thousand acres is occupied by one owner. The former is at a rate of 3 cents per acre; the latter at 1 per cent of assessed value.

[1]See chapter 14.

Quebec has never imposed a provincial property tax, and Ontario has only a limited tax applicable to land and improvements situated outside of an organized municipality under the Provincial Land Tax Act (first levied in 1925). Generous exemptions for mining claims, timber limits under Crown lease or licence, and other properties are given.

In Saskatchewan, the levy under the Public Revenues Act was the last provincial property tax, imposed by and for the benefit of the province and levied on the assessed value of real property in cities, towns, municipalities, and local improvement districts. A uniform assessment of properties had been established for this tax, the province itself determined the rates of tax to be levied, and collection was carried out by the municipalities for the province. The rates varied depending on whether the property was in a rural municipality, in a city, town, or village, in a local improvement district or was land held under a grazing lease. This tax expired December 31, 1952.

In Alberta the Social Services Tax Act and the Wild Lands Tax Act, and the Education Tax Act, all of which imposed provincial property taxes of long standing, have been repealed since World War II. There now remains only the Grazing Lease Taxation Act, a levy equal to the amount of rent payable under the grazing lease.

As an aside, Alberta is one of the few governments ever to have adopted a tax based on the single-tax principles of the noted publicist and humanitarian, Henry George. It will be recalled that Henry George argued that almost all the world's ills could be cured by a sole tax imposed on the increased value of land resulting from development and settlement, and from this thought sprang the single tax movement. In Alberta the principles advocated by George were adopted in 1913 but were applied in practice with circumspection. Under the Unearned Increment Tax Act a tax of 10 per cent was levied on the increase in value of a parcel of land at the time of its registration over the value at which it was entered at the time of the last previous registration. From the calculation of value were excluded all improvements on the land and any irrigation or other construction works carried out since the land was last registered. The Act came into force with respect to transfers of land following October 25, 1913 and established the methods of valuing any interest in land created either before or after that date. Enforcement of the tax was assured by the stipulation that no land might be registered until the unearned increment tax had been paid. With its repeal in 1956 vanished one of the last links with Henry George in Western Canada.

British Columbia, which has had the longest experience of any province with property taxes of all forms, today imposes a tax only on real estate outside of organized municipalities. All but ½ of 1 per cent of the area of the province is as yet unorganized, however, and revenue from this source is therefore considerably more important than the "wild land" taxes in other provinces. Under the Taxation Act farm lands are taxed at ½ of 1 per cent (exclusive of improvements), improved forest and tree-farm land at 1 per cent (improvements taxable), and wild land at 3 per cent (improvements taxable). For the support of education outside of school districts the province also levies a tax under the Public Schools Act. The basis is land plus 75 per cent of the assessed value of improvements.

SUMMARY

REVENUE. In fiscal year 1958–9: Ontario, $2,200,000; British Columbia, $6,100,000; other provinces, unimportant.

STATUTORY REFERENCES. *Nova Scotia*, Land Tax Act, Revised Statutes, Nova Scotia, 1954, c. 144; *New Brunswick*, Wild Lands Tax Act, Revised Statutes, New Brunswick, 1952, c. 250; *Ontario*, Provincial Land Tax Act, Revised Statutes, Ontario, 1960, c. 313; *Alberta*, Revised Statutes, Alberta, Grazing Lease Taxation Act, c. 36, 1960; *British Columbia*, Taxation Act, Revised Statutes, British Columbia, 1960, c. 376; Public Schools Act, *ibid.*, c. 319.

Land Transfer Taxes

Most provinces charge fees on the registration of the transfer of title to property. In Quebec, Ontario, and Alberta in addition to these fees taxes are also imposed on the transfer itself. The levy in Quebec, although at a higher rate than in the other provinces, is much more limited in scope. It applies only to transfers of property effected by a trustee under the Dominion Bankruptcy Act or by a liquidator under the Dominion Winding-up Act. In Ontario and Alberta the tax applies to all transfers of land. In both provinces the tax applies to the true consideration for the transfer for sale whereas in Quebec it applies to the greater of the consideration for the transfer or the value of the property as shown on the municipal valuation roll. The purchaser is liable for payment of the tax, which is usually collected through the land registry offices.

These taxes were first imposed in Ontario in 1921, and in Quebec in 1925.

Summary

RATES. Quebec, $2\frac{1}{2}$ per cent; Ontario, $\frac{1}{5}$ of 1 per cent; Alberta, $\frac{1}{5}$ of 1 per cent on value to $5,000 and $\frac{1}{10}$ of 1 per cent on value over $5,000 plus, on subsequent transfers, $\frac{1}{5}$ of 1 per cent on increases in value not exceeding $5,000 and $\frac{1}{10}$ of 1 per cent on increases of more than $5,000.

REVENUE. In fiscal year 1958-9: Ontario, $4,174,000; other provinces, unimportant.

STATUTORY REFERENCES. *Quebec*, Property Transfer Duty Act, Revised Statutes, Quebec, 1941, c. 79; *Ontario*, Land Transfer Tax Act, Revised Statutes, Ontario, 1960, c. 205.

Security Transfer Taxes

Quebec and Ontario alone of the provinces impose taxes on the transfer of securities. They were introduced in Quebec in 1906 and in Ontario in 1911. Until its repeal in 1953 there was also a federal levy in the same form. The revenue from this source is not great in the two central provinces but because of the fact that the two largest security exchanges are located there the taxes have more than ordinary significance.

These taxes apply to the value or sale price at which a transfer is made of any share or bond or any debenture or debenture stock. In both provinces they extend not only to changes of ownership consummated within the province but also to orders for sale to be executed outside of the province, and to deliveries of shares in the province where the sale or transfer has been executed outside the province. The tax applies on the price at which the securities were exchanged; if a change in ownership is effected otherwise than by a sale, the base of the tax is the current market price. Failing a current market price the Provincial Treasurer may determine the value for tax. Ontario exempts the sale, transfer, or assignment of any bond, debenture, or share of the Dominion of Canada or of any province of Canada, and both provinces exempt the first issue of shares of any corporation and the transmission of any securities upon a death. Payment of the tax is usually made by purchase of special stamps.

SUMMARY

RATES. Ontario and Quebec rates are the same, as follows:

(a) *Bonds, debentures, or debenture stock:* on each $100 par value, 3 cents.

(b) *Shares:* On value under $ 1 $\frac{1}{10}$ cent per share
On value $1 to $ 5 $\frac{1}{4}$ cent per share
On value $5 to $ 25 1 cent per share
On value $25 to $ 50 2 cents per share
On value $50 to $ 75 3 cents per share
On value $75 to $150 4 cents per share
Over $150   4 cents per share plus $\frac{1}{10}$ of 1 per cent of value over $150

REVENUE. In fiscal year 1958–9: Quebec, $1,410,000; Ontario, $2,632,000.

STATUTORY REFERENCES. *Quebec,* Security Transfer Tax Act, Revised Statutes, Quebec, 1941, c. 78; *Ontario,* Security Transfer Tax Act, Revised Statutes, Ontario, 1960, c. 364.

Hospital Insurance Charges

With the inauguration of a jointly sponsored federal-provincial scheme of hospital insurance under the Hospital Insurance and Diagnostic Services Act in 1958 charges for financing the provincial portion of costs have appeared in several provinces.

By 1961 all provinces had instituted plans, but not all included a direct charge, since methods of financing the provincial share included charges in the general budget, earmarked taxes, and hospital insurance premiums. Most plans are supported as well by appropriations from general revenue.

The status of special charges at mid-1961 is set out for the provinces below.

Newfoundland: No general charge made, but an annual premium is levied for persons having access to "cottage" hospitals.

Prince Edward Island: Monthly premiums of $2.00 for single persons and $4.00 for married are charged.

Nova Scotia: A Hospital Tax, in the form of a 3 per cent retail sales tax, was introduced on January 1, 1959 (rate increased to 5 per cent in 1961).

New Brunswick: Monthly hospital premiums of $2.10 and $4.20 were introduced on commencement of the New Brunswick scheme in July, 1959, but following election of a new government in June, 1960, the premiums were suspended. No specific charge for hospital service had been re-introduced at the time of writing.

Quebec: No earmarked charges are imposed, but when hospital insurance was introduced in January, 1961, the corporation profits tax was increased by 2 per cent and the personal income tax was raised.

Ontario: Monthly premiums of $2.10 and $4.20 were being charged in 1961. It had been announced that these might be increased.

Manitoba: Monthly premiums of $3.00 and $6.00.

Saskatchewan: Annual hospitalization tax of $17.50 and $35 for single persons and families respectively in 1960 were increased to $24 and $48 for 1961, bringing them to the common level of $2 and $4 per month in other provinces; one third of revenue from 3 per cent sales tax goes for hospitalization.

Alberta: Mill rate levied on property for a portion of the costs of the plan.

British Columbia: The yield of 2 per cent of the 5 per cent provincial retail sales tax assists with hospital insurance.

Miscellaneous Licences, Fees, Dues, etc.

The present and preceding chapters of this book have described tax sources that would account for 90 per cent or more of the revenue in each of the Canadian provinces. There are innumerable additional individual sources of revenue under acts that impose licences, fees, or minor taxes in respect of a great multitude of affairs. Simply to enumerate these would consume several pages without giving any clear impression of their character. Present needs therefore must be satisfied by a bare statement that these additional sources include licences and fees for various businesses, occupations, and professions, permits for engaging in various forms of activity, etc. Fairly complete information on these miscellaneous sources is given in the standard tax services and, of course, may also be obtained directly from the provincial governments. One tax of which particular mention might be made is the tax on long distance telephone calls levied in Nova Scotia. It is charged at the rate of 5 cents for each 50 cents or fraction of 50 cents of the bill.

CHAPTER 13

PROVINCIAL REVENUES FROM THE PUBLIC DOMAIN

THE IMPORTANCE of the public domain in Canada varies considerably from one province to the next, but all have revenues in some form or other from this source. In the provinces richly endowed with natural wealth the sale or rental of these resources has been an old and stable support to the public purse since before Confederation, and periodically a new bonanza, such as the post-war petroleum findings in Alberta, provides a welcome assistance to hard-pressed provincial treasuries.

The resources of a country as broad as Canada show a marked variety; a brief list from east to west would include iron ore and pulpwood in Newfoundland, coal in Nova Scotia, timber and pulpwood in New Brunswick, gold, copper, asbestos, timber, pulpwood, and water-power sites in Quebec, gold, copper, nickel, iron, uranium, and pulpwood in Ontario, some timber, minerals, and petroleum in Manitoba and Saskatchewan, coal, petroleum, and timber in Alberta, and timber, lead, zinc, silver, and gold in British Columbia. All provinces derive a revenue also from game and fishing licences, fur royalties, sale of land, and other miscellaneous sources.

Whatever the form of the natural resource the method of taxing its exploitation for the benefit of the people presents a set of problems that is distinctive in tax administration. Where the provincial share is in the form of a rental or royalty the determination of the amount and form of the charge is of theoretical and practical significance. The constitutional limitation of the provinces to direct taxation applies here as elsewhere, and in at least one case, that of the Alberta Mine Owners' Tax,[1] a levy on a

[1]*The King* v. *Caledonian Collieries Ltd.*, [1928] A.C. 358.

natural resource was declared to be an indirect tax beyond the powers of the province. On the other hand these levies often take the form of a special income tax on the profits made from the use of the natural resource, and to the usual problems of determining net taxable profit, ordinarily complicated enough, there are added the further difficulties of isolating the profit made solely from one form of activity.

It would appear desirable before discussing the levies actually imposed by the Canadian provinces to provide the answers to a few fundamental questions in this field. It is necessary to be reasonably certain that we know (1), what constitutes a natural resource of a province; (2), what taxing rights a province has in respect of its natural resources; (3), what are the limitations on the exercise of these rights through the charging of a rental or royalty; (4), what other forms of charge a province may make in respect of its natural resources.

1. *Natural Resources of the Province*

For guidance in delineating this concept it will be necessary to rely on the definitions contained in the present Tax Rental Agreements, since it is apparent that only here for the first time in Canada has an attempt been made to set forth a consistent series of terms relating to it. These definitions do not in themselves represent an original contribution to this field of legal terminology but rather draw together in a codified form principles and practices that do not appear together elsewhere. It might be mentioned that these concepts appear in the agreements because, it being agreed that the provinces were to be left free to impose appropriate levies on natural resources, it was to the advantage of both parties to give certainty to the exact bounds of this freedom.

Close analysis introduces some refinements into the notion of "natural resources of the province" as held by the man-on-the-street. To his mind this expression undoubtedly refers to almost everything on, in, and above the earth in its natural state. While this idea serves well enough for ordinary purposes, consideration of the statute and case law in seeking a basis for delineating taxing powers leads to the conclusion that the only resource that is legally a resource "of the province" is one in respect of which the province has retained rights of ownership. As a result natural resources of the province are defined in the tax agreements to mean "lands and waters, and any rights to or interest in lands and waters, *vested in the Crown in right of the Province*, including forests, minerals, petroleum and natural gas on or in such lands and waters and rights vested in the Crown in the said right to take wild animals and fish on or in such lands and waters."[2]

In this sense, therefore, a mineral deposit is only a natural resource if the province has retained the rights of ownership to that mineral deposit. While the province has broad powers, such as the authority to establish regulations for the working conditions of a mine and even to close a mine if these are not followed, such powers are not those of ownership. They are derived from the general powers of the government to make regulations for the public welfare.

In the same vein, a fish or a bird or an animal is only a natural resource of the province as long as it is on land, in water, or in the air over land the title to which has been retained by the provincial government or in respect of which the provincial government has retained the game rights, even though the ownership of the property has passed to another person. While at first it may seem to be an unusually artificial distinction that a deer is a natural resource while it is on a Crown preserve and ceases to be so if it crosses over into a farmer's property, this distinction is, in law, a very real one and is of vital significance in the delineation of the rights of the province. Again it should be repeated that the absence of proprietary rights does not affect the province's authority to regulate for the general good. Any province, acting for the general welfare of its citizens, has full power to restrict or prohibit the hunting or taking of any game or fish. But this authority does not rest on a proprietary interest. The following analogy may help to clarify this statement; it is not necessary for a provincial government to own all motor vehicles travelling on the public highways in the province before it can determine and prescribe the maximum speed at

[2]Dominion-Provincial Tax Sharing Agreements, clause 13(1)(*n*).

which such motor vehicle may legally travel, nor is it necessary that it own all such motor vehicles before it can impose a charge for the licensing of them.

From this concept of a natural resource it follows that the natural wealth of a province and the natural resources in respect of which the province has retained a proprietary interest may be different quantities. In Nova Scotia, for example, of about 9,000 square miles of occupied forest land in the province over 8,200 square miles are privately owned, and as a result produce little revenue to the province. In Quebec and Ontario timber stands and mineral deposits have in days gone by been sold or granted outright to private owners. In Alberta some of the recent oil discoveries have been on lands purchased prior to the return of the natural resources to the province in 1930, the mineral rights belonging to the surface owner, and of course one of the reasons that the Mine Owners' Tax was held *ultra vires* was that the province did not own the resources in the twenties. Similar instances could be drawn from other provinces. It would be misleading to leave the impression, however, that these are more than isolated cases. Generally speaking, the forest or mineral rights have been retained for the Crown in all provinces, even though ownership of the surface land may be in private hands.

2. *Rights of the Province*

This definition of natural resources, with its emphasis on proprietary rights, leads to a logical conclusion, namely, that what the province owns it has the right to sell. Furthermore this right is guaranteed under clause 92, Section 5, of the British North America Act, which gives to the provinces "The Management and Sale of the Public Lands belonging to the Province and of the Timber and Wood thereon." To the extent, therefore, that the province is owner of the natural resources it is free to sell the title to such resources, which essentially means the right of exploitation. The sale price need not take any set form. It may be a single lump sum payment; it may be an amount calculated in relation to each unit of production forthcoming during the life of the natural resource; or it may be a combination of both of these forms. Where the payments are geared to the use of or production from the natural resource they are usually known as rentals or royalties.

3. *Rentals and Royalties*

The most typical instance of a rental is the charge made to a hydro-electric power company for the right to use a Crown-owned site at a place where hydraulic power may be generated. (Many power sites are privately owned in some provinces, and of course the province may not impose a true rental under such circumstances.) While these rentals are often dependent on the amount of water put through the turbines or the amount of electrical energy produced, in the concepts of the tax agreements it is not in respect of the ownership of the water that the province charges the rental, but rather in respect of the right given to an individual or corporation to have access to such water on a site owned by the province. There are, of course, other forms of provincial property for the use of which a person will be willing to make a payment. The distinguishing feature of the rental, therefore, is that it represents compensation to the province in return for certain rights of use or occupancy where the natural resource itself is not consumed or used up or changed in form.

The definition of "rental" as used in the Tax Sharing Agreements is clearly in this sense. It is described as "a charge imposed on a person in respect of the occupation or use by him of a natural resource, whether improved or unimproved, including the use of water or water-power sites, without severance, taking, extraction or removal thereof or of any part thereof, the real intent and purpose of which charge is to compensate for the value of such occupation or use."[3]

Having described the rental, it becomes easy to introduce the royalty, which is similar to a rental in that it is a charge for the use of a natural resource. But it differs from a rental in one marked respect—it applies where there is an actual physical removal or change of the natural resource. The typical examples are the charges made for cutting down trees, extracting minerals, catching fish, shooting fur-bearing animals, etc., on Crown

[3]Clause 13(1)(*q*).

property. It is a necessary qualification of a royalty, however, that as a compensation to the province for the use or destruction of its natural resource it must not exceed the appropriate amount that will repay the province for the value of the resource which it owns. What is the value of a natural resource of the province? It is the value of that resource *in place*, before extraction, processing, or manufacturing. In short, the value of a mineral is the value of that mineral in the ground before it has been extracted or refined or manufactured in any way; the value of a tree is the value of that tree in the forest before axe or saw has been laid to it.

The exact definition of royalty which appears in the agreements gives effect to this principle. Anyone familiar with the common parlance of the mining and lumbering industries will appreciate that it gives the expression a much more precise and definitive meaning than it usually carries. The definition follows,

Royalty means a charge
(i) required to be paid by a person in respect of any right conferred on or vested in him to sever, take, extract or remove any thing forming part of the natural resources of the Province including therein timber, mineral ore, petroleum and natural gas, and wild animals or fish, the right to take which forms part of the said natural resources,
(ii) the amount of which is determined by reference to the quantity or value or both of the thing that he severs, takes, extracts or removes or alternatively, in the case of mineral ore, the value at market prices of the minerals contained therein, after extraction therefrom, and
(iii) the real intent and purpose of which is to compensate the Province for the value in whole or in part of the said thing prior to its severance taking, extraction or removal. . . .[4]

This definition requires some study before its full meaning is clear. Its three essential elements can be compressed into the following generalizations: (*a*) a royalty must be a charge for the right to exploit a resource; (*b*) it must vary appropriately with the amount of the resource exploited; and (*c*) it must only compensate the province for the value of the resource, bearing

[4]Clause 13(1)(*r*). A proviso to the definition excludes a charge based on profits or gross receipts unless appropriate deductions are made from the net profits or gross receipts for the valud added by processing and manufacturing to work back to the value before such processing or manufacturing.

in mind always that natural resource here includes only forest, mineral, and other properties owned by or reserved to the Crown.

In practical terms it is contemplated under paragraph (ii) of the definition that either a "volumetric" royalty (a fixed amount per ton or per thousand board feet, etc.) or an "ad valorem" royalty (a fixed percentage of a given value of production) will be imposed. However, the proviso (see note 4) also contemplates that a royalty may be levied in respect of the gross receipts or net profits, and where this is done appropriate adjustments must be made to exclude the value added by processing or manufacturing.

4. *Alternatives to Rentals or Royalties: Profits Taxes*

Designed for the same purpose, but considerably different in form, are the specialized income taxes on mining and logging profits imposed by some provinces. Whereas a royalty is a charge for the sale of a natural resource owned by the province, these taxes are of the same general form as an income tax but imposed on a specialized form of income. They have the advantage that they are fully within the powers of direct taxation, whether the rights to the natural resources have been retained or not. In the non-agreeing provinces they must meet only the test of direct taxation. In the agreeing provinces their imposition would be barred had not an exception been made in the agreements which permits them if they meet certain defined qualifications.

The principal interest of these taxes lies in their attempt to isolate the profit earned in one phase of a continuous process. In the case of mining this objective is usually achieved through excluding by one or more methods the profit deemed to be earned from milling and processing the ore after it leaves the pithead of the mine. The formula contained in the tax agreements for determining "income derived from mining operations" is of particular interest in this connection, and is reproduced here because most of the agreeing provinces that impose this form of tax have adopted verbatim in their taxing statutes the definition in the agreements containing these qualifications. It duplicates almost exactly the tax base employed under the Ontario Mining Tax, discussed later, and may indeed be said to have had its origin in the Ontario form of tax. The definition follows:

"Income derived from mining operations" means the net profit derived or deemed to have been derived from mining operations by a person engaged therein with or without an allowance in respect of depletion and if such a person received net profit or gain from sources other than mining operations either by reason of the carrying on by him of the processing of mineral ore extracted by him or otherwise, the net profit to be deemed to have been derived by him from mining operations shall not exceed that portion of the total net profit or gain received by him from all sources, determined by deducting from the said total the aggregate of
(i) the returns received by him by way of dividends, interest or other like payments from stock, shares, bonds, debentures, loans or other like investments,
(ii) the net profit, if any, derived by him from, and attributable in accordance with sound accounting principles to, the carrying on of any business, or derived from and so attributable to any source, other than mining operations and the processing and sale of mineral ore or products produced therefrom, and other than as a return on investments mentioned in section (i), and
(iii) an amount by way of return on capital employed by him in processing mineral ores or products derived therefrom, equal to eight per cent of the original cost to him of the depreciable assets including machinery, equipment, plant, buildings, works and improvements, used by him in the processing of mineral ore or products derived therefrom but the amount to be deducted under this section shall not be in excess of sixty-five per cent, nor less than fifteen per cent or such greater percentage (not in excess of sixty-five) as the Province may determine, of that portion of the said total net profit remaining after deducting therefrom the amounts specified in sections (i) and (ii);[5]

This definition does not lend itself easily to synopsis but an attempt will be made. It addresses itself first to a simple operation where the ore is only raised to the surface and then sold without any further processing. This is quite a rare circumstance, but if it occurred the whole income would be regarded as

[5]Clause 13(1)(*f*).

mining income. The definition realistically goes on to cover the more normal case where processing is carried on at the mine, in which case provision must be made for isolating the purely mining profit from the profit made on processing. This is accomplished by working back from the final total profit of the company by a process of elimination. First, investment income is eliminated, then profits earned from carrying on any other form of business than mining are deducted, and, finally, a profit on processing operations is excluded, calculated at an assumed rate of 8 per cent on the amount of depreciable assets used in such processing. There are thus three essential exclusions: (a) investment income, (b) profit from any other business (such as customs smelting), and (c) an assumed profit on processing. In respect of the third deduction both maximum and minimum limits are operative. In no case is it to be more than 65 per cent of the total profit nor on the other hand is it to be less than 15 per cent, although in the discretion of the Province it may be any rate within this range. The maximum assures that in every case there will be some income subject to tax as mining income. The minima are an attempt to assure that a proper weighting is given in the processing profits for research and invention which may not be properly reflected in the amount of physical equipment employed in processing a complex ore.

The possibility of imposing a tax of similar form and intent on profits from logging operations is also contemplated in the agreements, and the characteristics of such a tax are now spelled out in the same detail as the mining profits tax. The general purpose of such a levy must be to tax only profits derived from the cutting and transporting of the trees to the place of processing, whether it be to the foot of the ladder in the pond of a big pulp or lumber mill or to the yard of a small sawyer performing only elementary cutting operations.

Under the Income Tax Act provision is made for a deduction from income subject to Dominion tax for provincial taxes on logging as well as on mining profits, whether imposed by an agreeing or non-agreeing province. While mining taxes are fairly common, as will appear in the following pages, in 1961 only Ontario and British Columbia were levying a tax on logging profits. The former is charged at a rate of 9 per cent. The latter, which came into effect on October 1, 1953, is 10 per cent of annual profits in excess of $25,000.

Provincial Mining Taxes and Royalties

With this introduction to the theoretical aspects of the subject it is now possible to consider some of the actual levies imposed by the Canadian provinces on their natural resources, touching first on minerals.[6]

The character of these levies inevitably reflects the nature of the resources, which are by no means uniform either in type or in extent. In Newfoundland the principal mineral revenues come from mining profits taxes on iron ore in Labrador, base metals at Buchans on the mainland, and charges for iron ore mined on Belle Isle. Many promising mineral deposits are in sight, including copper and asbestos, most of which will bear the mining profits tax rate of 5 per cent. Prince Edward Island is almost entirely devoid of either mineral or forest wealth. In Nova Scotia there are extensive coal deposits from which the province derives a revenue under the Mines Act through a royalty of $12\frac{1}{2}$ cents per long ton. There are also royalties under the same Act for gold (35 cents per oz.), silver (2 cents per oz.), copper (4 cents per unit), iron (5 cents per short ton), lead (2 cents per unit), and zinc (2 cents per unit), a unit being defined as each 1 per cent of metal contained in a ton of ore sold, concentrated, smelted, or shipped. The Lieutenant-Governor-in-Council may determine royalties for other minerals. Authority is granted also for the substitution of a profits tax at graduated rates on income from mining operations for the above royalties (other than coal) by agreement, but it is believed that this alternative has been used infrequently, if at all. Since 1952 the province has obtained revenue from its substantial gypsum

[6]The following information on mining practices has been abstracted largely from *The Mining Laws of Canada* (4th ed.) a publication of the Mines Branch of the Department of Mines and Technical Surveys, prepared by Arthur Buisson and obtainable from the Queen's Printer, Ottawa. Revised information has been supplied where available.

deposits through a Gypsum Mining Income Tax Act levied at a rate of 33⅓ per cent. The gypsum rights in the province have all been alienated to private owners, so that the straight royalty was beyond provincial powers.

New Brunswick's mineral resources are limited, but recent base metal discoveries prompted the enactment of a Mining Tax Act in the form authorized under the Tax Sharing Agreement. The rates of tax under this act are as follows: on profits over $10,000 but not over $1,000,000, 7 per cent; on profits over $1,000,000 but not over $5,000,000, 8 per cent; on profits over $5,000,000, 9 per cent.

In Quebec, where there are extensive deposits of both precious and base metals, the precedent established by Ontario in 1907 has been followed and since 1925 all revenues from mineral exploitation have been derived from a tax on mining profits under the Mining Act. The sole and unimportant exception is a tax of 10 cents an acre on undeveloped mineral lands. There are no "volumetric" royalties (per ounce, per ton, etc.) of the usual type found in most provinces.

Profits subject to the mining tax are determined in accordance with rules established under division 3 of the Mining Act. In general they are to be calculated by deducting from the gross value of the output sold, utilized, or shipped during the year appropriate allowances which will leave as a residual the profit on such output. These deductions include the cost of transportation of the output, the working expenses of the mine, cost of the necessary power and light for the operation of mines, mills, and plants, cost of explosives, insurance, depreciation on buildings and equipment at a rate not exceeding 15 per cent, expenditures during the year on development work (sinking shafts or making further excavations), and, by discretion of the Lieutenant-Governor-in-Council, a deduction for prospecting expenses. No allowance is made for depletion and no mines are exempt, except those having profits under $10,000.

This Quebec tax differs in one important respect from that suggested in the agreements (and also from the Ontario tax) in that no attempt is made to eliminate profits attributable to processing as distinct from mining profits. In short, there is nothing in the Quebec definition comparable to the deduction of 8 per cent on assets employed in processing. Nor is income from investments or other business operations excluded. Mines in Quebec are also subject to the ordinary corporation profits tax (see chapter 9) but in computing profits so taxed a deduction is allowed for the amount of mining tax paid.

The Quebec mining tax rates are as follows:

On profits over $10,000 but not over $1,000,000	4 per cent
On profits over $1,000,000 but not over $2,000,000	5 per cent
On profits over $2,000,000 but not over $3,000,000	6 per cent
On profits over $3,000,000	7 per cent

The position in Ontario regarding mineral taxation is very similar to that in Quebec. As mentioned earlier, Ontario adopted a profits tax in 1907 and does not now impose any other royalties, with one or two unimportant exceptions. There is a moderate acreage tax on mineral lands, and an output tax on natural gas. Under the Assessment Act the municipalities also are authorized to impose a profits tax for municipal purposes.

The Ontario tax in the main provided the outline for the concept established in the Tax Rental Agreements. It is a tax on mining profits proper, determined by eliminating extraneous income and making an allowance for profits from milling, concentrating, and other processing. Like the Quebec law, and by contrast to the agreement definition, the Ontario statute starts with gross receipts (rather than with net profits) and provides for all deductions that may be made in arriving at net mining profit. Three general cases are contemplated, and provision is made for each. The first is where the ore is simply raised to the pit-mouth and sold without processing; the second is where the ore, mineral, or mineral-bearing substance is not sold but is treated for or by the owner either upon the premises or elsewhere. The third case is an extension of the second, and anticipates the contingency that there is no means of ascertaining the market value of the ore at the pit-mouth or that there is no established market price or value for the ore. In this contingency the profit is to be ascertained by deducting from the gross value of the output of the year, as determined by the mine assessor, amounts which will leave a residual representing the profits on mining operations. These deductions are similar to those listed for Quebec. As in the adjoining province, while provision for depreciation up to 15 per cent per annum is made, there is no allowance for depletion.

As indicated previously the two marked differences between the two statutes, which are similar in almost every other respect, are that in Ontario an adjustment is made to eliminate processing profits by a deduction representing 8 per cent on assets employed in milling, concentrating, or other processing.

In Ontario, as in Quebec, mines earning less than $10,000 a year are exempt. Mining companies are subject to the provincial corporation profits tax but a deduction is allowed in computing taxable profits for the mining tax paid. Relief is also given for taxes on their income paid to municipalities under the Assessment Act. The municipal tax is based on the same income and formerly was levied at statutory rates. The rates must now be approved by the provincial government.

The Ontario rates are as follows:

On profits over $10,000 but not over $1,000,000	6 per cent
On profits over $1,000,000 but not over $5,000,000	8 per cent
On profits over $5,000,000	9 per cent

The Ontario acreage tax applies to all mining concessions or claims in the province at the rate of 10 cents per acre per annum. There are certain unimportant exclusions from the tax by definition, and outright exemptions are also granted for mining rights in municipalities laid out as townsites or subdivided into lots or parcels, mineral rights in land for the production of natural gas or petroleum in southern Ontario, and agricultural lands used for farming purposes during the preceding year. In all cases the exemption does not extend to mining rights that are severed or held apart or separate from the surface rights.

Under Part 2 of the Mining Tax Act, Section 27, a tax is also imposed on every person producing natural gas. There are two rates. A rate of 2 cents per thousand cubic feet applies where the natural gas is exported from Canada and a rate of $\frac{1}{2}$ cent per thousand cubic feet applies where it is consumed in Canada.

In Manitoba the 8 per cent profits tax under the Mining Royalty and Tax Act has also substantially replaced volumetric royalties. This statute follows in part the Ontario and Quebec acts but embodies the tax agreement definition of income from mining operations. The net mining profit is first ascertained by deducting from the gross revenue of the mine a long list of mining expenses similar to those enumerated above for Quebec and Ontario, such as cost of transporation of the output to market, working expenses of the mine, salaries and wages of employees, operating costs of milling, smelting, and so on. Depreciation is allowed up to a rate of 15 per cent per annum as in Ontario and Quebec. Following the agreement definition further adjustments are made to eliminate the profits on processing activities by deducing an amount equal to 8 per cent of the cost of depreciable assets used in processing. This deduction has, of course, a maximum of 65 per cent of the net profit and minima in the discretion of the Province. No allowance is made for depletion.

As a concession to new mines the general 8 per cent rate is moderated on the income of the first two years. For the first year the rate is reduced to 6 per cent, for the second to 7 per cent, and thereafter the full 8 per cent applies.

With the extension eastward into Manitoba of the prairie oil discoveries, royalties from this source have begun to appear as a revenue in the provincial budget. The charge is $12\frac{1}{2}$ per cent of production. Manitoba since 1955 has also adopted a device to obtain a tax revenue from oil and other mineral deposits forming part of private land. Under the Mineral Taxation Act a levy is charged on the owner of such lands in a producing area based on the value of the deposit. Similar charges have been in effect for some time in Alberta and Saskatchewan.

In Saskatchewan authority is given under the Mineral Resources Act to issue regulations fixing the royalties, fees, dues, or charges for leases, permits, mineral rights, etc. and the actual charges in effect are contained in these regulations. For example the Quartz Mining Regulations give the charges in effect for "hard-rock" mining. There are alternative levies under these regulations, one an *ad valorem* royalty, and the other a tax on profits, the lesser being payable. The royalty is 5 per cent of the market value of the mineral content of ores sold during the year. The profits tax is $12\frac{1}{2}$ per cent of income from mining operations as defined in the Tax Sharing Agreements. No allowance is granted for depletion in calculating either charge. A concessional rate of tax is made for mines commencing operations since January 1, 1947, at the following rates:

On profits over $10,000 but not over $100,000	3 per cent
On profits over $100,000 but not over $500,000	5 per cent
On profits over $500,000 but not over $1,000,000	7 per cent
On profits over $1,000,000	$12\frac{1}{2}$ per cent

Section 18 of the Alkali Mining Regulations establishes a royalty on alkali and products therefrom to be calculated in accordance with a formula, and royalties are also provided for under regulation in respect of Quarriable Substances, Subsurface Minerals, and Petroleum and Natural Gas. The latter have become an important source of revenue in recent years. A levy of 8 per cent is charged on the sale value of natural gas and an *ad valorem* rate is imposed on the sale value of the output of oil wells graduated with the average daily production of the well. The schedule of charges is as follows:

Monthly Production (bbls.)	Royalty
0– 600	5%
600– 900	30 bbls. plus 13% on excess over 600 bbls.
900–1500	69 bbls. plus 17% on excess over 900 bbls.
1500–4950	171 bbls. plus 18% on excess over 1500 bbls.
4950 and over	16% of total production

Under the Mineral Taxation Act there are also taxes on

acerage and on the assessed value of minerals contained in mineral lands. For purposes of these levies the province is divided into non-producing and producing areas. Any acreage held in non-producing areas is subject to an annual acreage tax of 3 cents per acre. Mining properties in a producing area are valued annually by the mining assessor at the fair value of their mineral content and the tax is levied at a rate not exceeding ten mills on the dollar of the assessed value. Non-producing properties in a productive area pay at a rate of 50 cents per acre. Operators of mineral properties paying a royalty may offset such royalty against the Mineral tax.

In Alberta, of course, petroleum now holds the centre of interest. The principal levy on this increasingly valuable resource is an *ad valorem* royalty on the gross output of oil wells on Crown lands. The schedule of charges is as follows:

Monthly Production (bbls.)	Royalty
0– 600	5%
600– 750	30 plus 14% on excess over 600 bbls.
750– 950	51 plus 17% on excess over 750 bbls.
950–1150	85 plus 18% on excess over 950 bbls.
1150–1500	121 plus 19% on excess over 1150 bbls.
1500–1800	$12\frac{1}{2}$ of production
1800–4050	225 plus 20% on excess over 1800 bbls.
over 4050	$16\frac{2}{3}$% of production

It is interesting also that the province has recently borrowed from forestry a technique generally followed in disposing of timber stands. When a new producing field has been proven in the province the discoverer is now required to return approximately one-half the area to the province. At the appropriate time all comers are allowed to bid for the right to work the properties through competitive tenders. As a result of the adoption of this system the province had received several hundred millions of dollars in addition to royalty which are payable on production from the properties.

In Alberta the natural gas royalty is 15 per cent of the value of output with a minimum of $\frac{3}{4}$ cents per one thousand cubic feet. Most of the other royalties are *ad valorem* also, the common rate being $2\frac{1}{2}$ per cent, which applies to the value of copper, gold, silver, lead, zinc, and other unspecified quartz minerals. On coal the royalty is 10 cents per short ton if mined under Crown lease and 7 cents per short ton under Crown agreement of sale, on salt 40 cents per short ton, and on other quarriable materials at comparable rates. As explained earlier, all of these royalties apply only when the natural resources are being extracted from Crown lands.

Like the other western provinces Alberta also imposes under the Mineral Taxation Act a tax on the owners of mineral lands. There are two charges under this Act. The first applies to every owner of any mineral property at a rate determined annually on the minerals in, on, or under the property at a rate which has been $1\frac{1}{2}$ cents per acre for some years. The second, which is in addition to the first, applies on the assessed value of the *principal* mineral at a rate to be fixed by the Lieutenant-Governor-in-Council. For some years this rate has been 8 mills. A further tax is imposed on oil and gas resources under the Oil and Gas Resources Conservation Act to provide revenues for the operation of the Conservation Board. The rate applies to the assessed value of petroleum properties in the province but is not to exceed 10 mills on the dollar. In recent years it has been only slightly in excess of 1 mill.

In British Columbia the principal mineral tax is a levy of 10 per cent on income from mining operations imposed under the Mining Tax Act.[7] This tax is based on the definition contained in the agreements. A charge of 25 cents an acre on Crown-granted mineral claims is also payable under certain circumstances.

Under the Coal Act there is a royalty of 25 cents a ton on coal delivered from the location of the mine (this was levied formerly under the Taxation Act), and under the Petroleum and Natural Gas Act a royalty on the value at the well-head of 15 per cent on natural gas and $12\frac{1}{2}$ per cent on other products

[7]First $25,000 of profit exempt.

is charged. Quarriable materials, excepting marble, bear 5 cents a cubic yard under the Land Act; marble taken out in slabs or blocks is $1 per cubic yard. A tax on the assessed value of coal lands is imposed under the Taxation Act at 7 per cent for Class A and 2 per cent for Class B, but lands held under a lease or licence from the Crown under the Coal and Petroleum Act or the Coal Act are exempt. A Mineral Property Taxation Act passed in 1957 and proclaimed only in respect of iron ore properties was held invalid by the Supreme Court of British Columbia and has not been operative. However in 1960 by Order-in-Council under the Mineral Act a royalty on iron ore was provided for in its place.

Other Revenues from Minerals

While of primary importance as revenue sources the taxes and royalties just described are the last in point of time of a sequence of charges paid by a miner or oil producer. They become effective only if and when production has been achieved, and are preceded by fees, licences, lease rentals, and so on which all must pay for the right to search or acquire minerals.

To begin with, in most provinces a nominal annual fee ($5 to $10) must be paid by an individual to qualify as a prospector. Companies also must pay, although on a scale usually running to a maximum of $75 or $100. In some provinces there is an additional charge for qualification as a "miner" after a claim has been proven. For the recording of each claim found by a licensed miner there is another fee ($5 to $10 a claim).

Of more significance is the charge imposed by the province for a "lease" of the mineral-bearing property, which carries the right to extract the minerals in the property. Leases are generally for a period of 21 years, renewable for similar periods. The "rental" is usually by the acre, although not uniformly so. Special arrangements prevail for certain deposits, such as petroleum.

The first stage here is usually the granting of a right to carry on geological or geophysical work over an area of several thous-

FROM THE PUBLIC DOMAIN 245

and acres (a reservation), for which there is a flat charge. In Alberta it is $250 for each reservation (not to exceed 100,000 acres) for the first four months, 7 cents an acre for two renewal periods of three months, and 8 cents an acre for two further three-month renewal periods. For further periods of revenue the rates are considerably higher. Generally similar charges are made in the other provinces, and substantial deposits must be made as a guarantee that work will be carried out on the reservation. In Alberta, when oil has been found in an area, the part of the proven territory that is not required to be returned to the province may be taken under lease for an annual charge of $1.00 per acre. In Manitoba this charge is 50 cents per acre on producing properties; on non-producing properties it is 50 cents per acre under the primary lease and $1.50 per acre under secondary lease. In Saskatchewan the charge is 50 cents an acre the first year and $1 thereafter; and in British Columbia $1 per acre.

Various other minor charges for examination of records, registration of transfers or assignments of claims, application for rental of lease, settling of disputes, etc., also contribute to provincial revenues from minerals.

Provincial Forest Charges and Taxes

While in detail no less complex, forestry charges are in principle markedly contrasted to the profits taxes now almost universally adopted for mining.[8] In forestry the basic charge and main source of revenue is simply a price paid to the province for the purchase of trees growing on Crown lands. Since trees are generally a visible quantity capable of ready valuation the fixing of a just price is fairly simple by comparison with the valuation of a mineral body of uncertain quality and extent. This difference probably accounts for the divergence in approach to these two principal natural resources among the provinces.

The price fixed for the trees on Crown land, in the nomen-

[8]For an exhaustive review of Canadian forestry charges, see *Forestry Tenures and Taxes*, A. M. Moore, Canadian Tax Foundation, Toronto, 1957.

clature of the earlier part of the chapter, is a volumetric royalty. It is a charge "the real intent and purpose of which is to compensate the province for the value in whole or in part of the said thing [the tree] prior to its severance, taking, extraction or removal." In practice, however, only in British Columbia is the expression "royalty" used, the other provinces employing such terms as stumpage, Crown dues, bonus dues, etc. In form the charges are usually calculated at a rate per thousand board feet for saw-logs and at a rate per cord for pulpwood. They become payable after the trees are felled and scaled by experienced and impartial scalers, who are licensed by the government to perform this work.

This description represents an over-simplification, since in practice the royalty may be made up of one, two, or even three constituents. To begin with, in every province there are basic charges payable on all trees taken on Crown lands (sometimes with variations for type, grade, location, etc.), which are established by statute or Order in Council. For convenience these may be described as Crown dues (in British Columbia they are officially "royalties" and in New Brunswick "stumpage"). With unimportant exceptions no one may cut trees on Crown land without paying these dues, so that in effect they are a bedrock price for the purchase of Crown-owned trees.

In addition to these basic charges the royalty usually includes a sum determined by competitive public tender for stands as they are made available by the province. The actual arrangement entered into between the buyer or lessee and the province varies—it may be in the form of a timber berth, a pulpwood berth, a timber sale, a timber permit, etc.—but with some exceptions the payment provisions are similar. A payment over and above the Crown dues represents the additional value placed on the timber because of exceptionally high quality, easy accessibility, heavy market demand for lumber or pulp, and various other factors.

In most provinces there is an "upset" price fixed for the stand on auction (i.e., a minimum below which the province will not entertain tenders). Buyers or lessees usually bid over this price, depending, of course, on the strength of the competition for the stand. In this case, therefore, there are three elements in the royalty: (1) the Crown dues, (2) the upset price, and (3) the bonus price paid over the upset price. Sometimes the upset price will include the Crown dues, but the three elements are distinguishable, nevertheless. All these elements are expressed normally in terms of so much per thousand board feet for saw-logs or so much per cord for pulpwood.

This composite royalty is by far the major source of revenue, but there are others. In all the provinces there is a ground rent, which entitles the operator to entry onto the land and gives him legal protection against cutting of the timber on his limit by unauthorized persons. This charge is payable annually at $1 per square mile in Ontario, $10 per square mile in New Brunswick, $10 per square mile in Manitoba and Quebec, $20 per square mile in Saskatchewan, and $30 in Alberta. In British Columbia there are a variety of such charges. For timber and pulpwood the ground rent is $140 per square mile and $70 per square mile respectively west of the Cascade Mountains, while east of the Cascades it is respectively $100 per square mile and $50 per square mile.

In Quebec and New Brunswick there are "acquisition" charges which appear to replace some or all of the element of the royalty representing the excess over Crown dues payable in other provinces. In Quebec special licences are granted to assist small industries, carrying a minimum acquisition charge of $500 per square mile for a maximum holding of 50 square miles. In New Brunswick the minimum acquisition charge is $40 per square mile.

The most radical departures from the general scheme of forestry charges outlined above are found in British Columbia, as exemplified in the "forest management" and "tree farm" arrangements. These are complex in detail, and the reader wishing further information should consult official provincial sources or *Forestry Tenures and Taxes*, by A. M. Moore.

As indicated earlier, a relatively new venture in this field appeared in Ontario in 1950 with the enactment of a 9 per cent tax on logging profits.[9] A similar tax at a 10 per cent rate was enacted in British Columbia in 1953.[10] This form of tax in no way affects the stumpage dues for timber limits. Its basic purpose is to obtain for the province a share of the gain made in cutting and removing forest resources. Where paper or other finished products are made the allocation of part of the final profit to the logging operation requires complex and somewhat arbitrary determination.

British Columbia also reveals an unusual levy in the Esquimalt and Nanaimo Railway Grant Tax. This applies at a rate of 25 per cent on sales of land from the valuable grants given the railway at the time of its construction.

Charges are also levied on the operators for the support of fire protection in the province. These charges are usually by the acre or by the square mile. Expressed uniformly as a charge per square mile they work out to $6.40 in New Brunswick ($12.80 on privately owned "wild" lands over 500 acres in extent), $6.40 in Alberta, $12.80 in Ontario, and $38.40 in British Columbia (lower rates for forest management licences). In Saskatchewan and Manitoba the operators are assessed one half the cost of government outlay on fire protection. In Quebec fire protection is under the charge of individual protective associations established by the companies and operated under government supervision. Timber operators are usually subject as well to general property taxes. There are also special taxes, such as the timber area tax in Alberta (2 cents per acre). A 1 per cent tax on the assessed value of land held under lease, timber berth, etc., for which no stumpage is payable, was enacted in 1953 in British Columbia.

OTHER MISCELLANEOUS REVENUES

Space will permit only the mention of other revenues from natural resources, including water-power rentals and storage charges (significant particularly in Quebec and British Columbia),

[9]Logging Tax Act, Revised Statutes, Ontario, 1960, c. 224.
[10]Logging Tax Act, Revised Statutes of British Columbia, 1960, c. 225.

fur royalties (in Quebec, Ontario, Manitoba, and the other provinces to a lesser extent), game and fishing licences (in Ontario hunting and trapping licences produced $2 million and angling licences alone $2½ million in 1959–60, and the other provinces all had some revenues from this source), and land sales and miscellaneous licences and permits.

Summary

RATES. Mining profits taxes are at rates of 5 per cent in Newfoundland; graduated rates of 7, 8 and 9 per cent between $10,000 and $5,000,000 in New Brunswick; 4, 5, 6, and 7 per cent between $10,000 and $3,000,000 in Quebec; 6, 8, and 9 per cent between $10,000 and $5,000,000 in Ontario; 8 per cent in Manitoba; 3 per cent to 12½ per cent between $10,000 and $1,000,000 in Saskatchewan; and 10 per cent in British Columbia. Logging profits taxes are 9 per cent in Ontario and 10 per cent in British Columbia. Rentals, royalties, stumpage dues, and other charges are also imposed at various rates on mineral and forest resources, water-power sites, game, fish, etc.

REVENUE

	Fiscal year 1958–9 ($000)	Percentage of total revenue
Newfoundland	1,593	2.6
Prince Edward Island	23	.2
Nova Scotia	1,285	1.7
New Brunswick	3,567	5.0
Quebec	29,848	5.4
Ontario	31,619	4.9
Manitoba	3,730	4.9
Saskatchewan	23,945	16.9
Alberta	118,320	50.1
British Columbia	44,768	15.1

STATUTORY REFERENCES. *Newfoundland*, The Mining Tax Act, Revised States, Newfoundland, 1952, c. 43; various special acts governing concessions in Labrador and Newfoundland; *P.E.I.*, Oil and Minerals Act, Revised Statutes, Prince Edward Island, 1951, c. 103; *New Bruns-*

wick, Crown Lands Act, Revised Statutes, New Brunswick, 1952, c. 53; Forest Service Act, *ibid.*, c. 93; Mining Act, *ibid.*, c. 146; Mining Income Tax Act, 1954, c. 10; *Nova Scotia*, Mines Act, Revised Statutes, Nova Scotia, 1954, c. 179; Gypsum Mining Income Tax Act, 1954, c. 114; Petroleum and Natural Gas Act, *ibid.*, c. 215; *Quebec*, Quebec Mining Act, Revised Statutes, Quebec, 1941, c. 196; Lands and Forest Act, *ibid.*, c. 93; Water Course Act, *ibid.*, c. 98; *Ontario*, Mining Tax Act, Revised Statutes, Ontario, 1960, c. 242; Mining Act, *ibid.*, c. 241; Public Lands Act, *ibid.*, c. 324; Assessment Act, *ibid.*, c. 23; Crown Timber Act, *ibid.*, c. 83; Logging Tax Act, *ibid.*, c. 224; *Manitoba*, Mining Royalty and Tax Act, 12 Geo. 6, c. 52; Mines Act, Revised Statutes, Manitoba, 1954, c. 166; Mining Royalty and Tax Act, *ibid.*, c. 169; Mineral Taxation Act, 1954, c. 19; Crown Lands Act, *ibid.*, c. 57; The Forest Act, *ibid.*, c. 90; *Saskatchewan*, Mineral Taxation Act, Revised Statutes, Saskatchewan, 1953, c. 59; Mineral Resources Act, 1959, c. 84; The Forest Act, 1959, c. 96; *Alberta*, Mineral Taxation Act, Revised Statutes, Alberta, 1955, c. 203; Mines and Minerals Act, *ibid.*, c. 204; The Forests Act, *ibid.*, c. 118; Oil and Gas Conservation Act, 1957, c. 63; *British Columbia*, Mining Tax Act, Revised Statutes, British Columbia, 1960, c. 247; Taxation Act, *ibid.*, c. 376; Placer Mining Act, *ibid.*, c. 285; Mineral Act, *ibid.*, c. 244; Coal Act, *ibid.*, c. 260; Land Act, *ibid.*, c. 206; Petroleum and Natural Gas Act, *ibid.*, c. 161; Forest Act, *ibid.*, c. 153; Water Act, *ibid.*, c. 405; Logging Tax Act, *ibid.*, c. 225; Mineral Property Taxation Act, *ibid.*, c. 245; Mineral Tax Act, *ibid.*, c. 247.

Chapter 14

MUNICIPAL TAXATION IN CANADA

IN ADDITION TO the Dominion and the ten provinces there are in Canada some 4,255 municipalities, containing over 90 per cent of the population, each endowed with a power to tax. They encompass the whole area of the provinces of Nova Scotia and New Brunswick and all the densely populated areas in the other provinces. Only the northern and uninhabited regions of the central and western provinces are not organized, but in British Columbia there are large unorganized areas throughout the province. In Prince Edward Island, because of the smallness of the territory, all the area outside of the one city and the seven towns has remained under the general jurisdiction of the provincial government.

Municipal organizations fall into two main groups, urban and rural. The principal classes in the urban group are cities, towns, and villages. Organizations known by these names are found throughout Canada, although requirements for incorporation in any one class vary to such an extent that what passes as a city in one province may be only a town in the next. Rural municipalities on the other hand are officially known by a variety of names. In Newfoundland they are called Rural Districts, in Nova Scotia they are known as Counties and Municipalities, in New Brunswick as Counties, in Quebec as Parishes and Townships, in Ontario as Townships, in Manitoba and Saskatchewan as Rural Municipalities, in Alberta as Municipal Districts, and in British Columbia as Districts. Many such units are in fact heavily populated, particularly where adjacent to large cities.

The term "county" is applied to rural units of government in five provinces—Nova Scotia, New Brunswick, Quebec, Ontario, and Alberta—but the structure of the county differs in these provinces. In Nova Scotia and New Brunswick the entire province is divided into counties. There are 18 in Nova Scotia, 12 of which constitute single municipalities with the remaining 6 divided into 2 municipalities each. Urban units of government in Nova Scotia are located geographically within a county but form no part of it politically and are entirely independent of county administrations except as to joint expenditures.

The province of New Brunswick is divided into 15 counties, each of which is a single municipality. All the urban municipal organizations which lie within the boundaries of the counties are autonomous units of government but, with the exception of Fredericton, they have representation on the county council.

In the provinces of Quebec and Ontario only the more southern parts are organized into counties which, in turn, are divided into separate areas of rural and urban autonomous local government units. In these two provinces the county forms a second tier of government superimposed on the basic government units of which the county is comprised.

In Quebec a county includes all the territory within its geographic boundaries less the area occupied by any city or town. Thus a Quebec county municipality structurally consists of village municipalities and townships or parishes and, on occasion, some unorganized territory as in the counties of Abitibi, Chicoutimi, and Portneuf, for example.

In Ontario, cities and "separated" towns only are excluded from the county administration[1] but these enter into agreements with the county on matters of joint expenditure. Thus in Ontario the territory of a county is wholly divided up into townships, villages, and towns. A "separated" town in Ontario is one which, by special legislation, has been separated from the county within which it is geographically located. There are 8

---

[1]An exception is made in the case of the municipalities comprising Metropolitan Toronto, all of which are separated from the county for municipal purposes.

such towns in the province and in their relationship to the county they have the same detached status as that of a city.

In Alberta, the County Act of 1950 provides for a county form of government which combines under one county council all the functions of school boards and municipal councils for the whole territory enclosed within the county boundaries. There are now 12 such counties in Alberta.

Embryonic forms of rural municipal government are also provided for newly settled districts of some provinces. These are known as Improvement Districts in Saskatchewan, Alberta, and Ontario, and as Local Government Districts in Manitoba. While not organized as municipal corporations these units ordinarily function as such under the direct control of the provincial governments and may collect land taxes much as do the municipalities.

Most of the 4,250 Canadian municipal organizations, in addition to levying taxes for their own purposes, must also levy taxes for the support of school boards and other organizations. Many of these ancillary organizations are almost autonomous, and have the power to requisition funds from the municipality and are entitled to receive the full amount of their requisition, whether or not the municipality has been able to collect that amount of revenue.

In Table XII organized municipal governments in Canada in 1960 are classified by type and by province. Neither improvement districts nor school districts are included.

Local taxation had advanced farthest in Ontario at Confederation. Here it had evolved from a simple tax on selected forms of property first levied in 1793 to a fully developed levy on real and personal property and income by 1867, an advance reflecting a remarkable development of organized municipal government in this province. Some of the Maritime municipalities had property and income taxes, but municipal organization was itself retarded. However, the rapid tempo of urbanization following 1900 in both the east and the west was financed mainly by real property taxes, supplemented usually by poll taxes and taxes on personal property and income. Failure of

TABLE XII

MUNICIPALITIES IN CANADA BY TYPES OF ORGANIZATION AND BY PROVINCES, 1960

Province	Cities	Towns	Villages	Total urban	Rural	Total local municipalities	Counties (2nd tier)	Total incorporated municipalities
Newfoundland	2	36	—	38	4[1]	42		42
Prince Edward Island	1	7	16	24		24		24
Nova Scotia	2	40	—	42	24	66		66
New Brunswick	6	20	1	27	15[2]	42		42
Quebec	42	152	336	530	1,132	1,662	76	1,738
Ontario	30[3]	157	154	341	573[4]	914	39[5]	953
Manitoba	6	35	37	78	112[6]	190		190
Saskatchewan	11	105	369	485	296[7]	781		781
Alberta	9[8]	86	156	251	48[9]	299		299
British Columbia	32	3	55	90	30	120		120
TOTALS	141	641	1,124	1,906	2,234	4,140	115	4,255

[1]Does not include 2 local improvement districts and 31 community councils.
[2]Does not include 57 local improvement districts.
[3]Excludes the Municipality of Metropolitan Toronto.
[4]Does not include 24 improvement districts.
[5]Includes the Municipality of Metropolitan Toronto.
[6]Includes 5 units of self-government officially known as "suburban municipalities." Does not include local government districts.
[7]Does not include 12 improvement districts.
[8]Does not include Lloydminster which is included with Saskatchewan.
[9]Does not include 4 improvement districts and 2 special areas but includes 12 counties.

SOURCE: Dominion Bureau of Statistics; Provincial Annual Reports of Municipal Statistics; Canadian Almanack and Directory.

the personal property tax, however, had led to its virtual abandonment by the end of the century in Ontario and the western provinces. It was replaced by business taxes imposed on various bases (assessment, rental value, square footage, etc.). On the heels of this development, prior to World War I there appeared in the western municipalities a form of Single Tax or site valuation (exemption in whole or in part of improvements). The agitation spread to eastern Canada although there were no conspicuous defections from the general tax on real property. By the end of World War I, however, when property values had seriously dropped most western municipalities were bringing improvements back on the tax roll.

One of the major changes in municipal taxation in the intervening years has been the disappearance of the municipal personal income tax. It was last levied in Ontario in 1936. Quebec and Montreal taxes of this type, in effect for a short period before World War II, were withdrawn under the Wartime Tax Agreements and have not since been re-enacted. Similar taxes in New Brunswick and Nova Scotia are suspended (1941 through 1961) under the Wartime and Tax Rental Agreements. The personal property tax is still used in the Maritime municipalities and to some extent in the municipalities of Manitoba[2]; poll taxes are also still employed in the Maritimes and to a lesser extent elsewhere.[3] Significant recent developments include the adoption of municipal sales taxes during the thirties in Montreal and Quebec City,[4] and the adoption of taxes on electricity and gas bills in Winnipeg. Of considerable significance also has been the abandonment of provincial taxes on real property within organized municipalities. Alberta, Prince Edward Island, and Saskatchewan have all repealed old and established land taxes in recent years.

Grants from provincial governments for specific or general purposes or in lieu of taxes repealed under Dominion-provincial agreements are an important source of revenue in some provinces, along with returns from publicly owned utilities.

[2]For a discussion of personal property in Canada see *Local Finance*, no. 4, March 1960, The Canadian Tax Foundation.
[3]*Ibid.*, no. 5, May 1960.
[4]*Ibid.*, no. 6, September and no. 7, November 1960.

Payments received from the federal government in lieu of taxation on Crown property are also important in some municipalities. However, the real property tax remains the principal source of local revenues throughout Canada.

In 1959 it is estimated that the 4,000 or so Canadian municipalities collected around $1.6 billion of current revenue. Of this amount about $1.2 billion came from taxes, and of the total tax revenue about $1 billion, or about 84 per cent, came from taxes on the owners of real property. The balance of the tax revenue was from business, sales, poll, and other miscellaneous taxes.

The Property Tax

The property tax in most Canadian municipalities today is almost exclusively a tax on real estate. In parts of the Maritimes, however, and in some of the rural municipalities of Manitoba the personal property tax still represents an important source of local revenue.

In general the real property tax has two main divisions: (a) a tax on the owners of property, and (b) various taxes on the occupiers of property. Of the two the former is by far the more important source of revenue, and will be discussed first.

The annual levy on the owners of real property in a municipality is the base of the Canadian municipal revenue system. The tax rate is expressed either as a "mill rate" or as a percentage. A tax rate of, say, 50 mills means that every $1,000 of property assessment will be taxed $50. Thus a property assessed for $5,500 to which a tax rate of 50 mills is applied will be taxed for $275—$5.5×50. The same tax rate expressed as a percentage would be 5% and would be levied on every $100 of assessed value to produce the same result as a 50 mill tax rate. The manner of "striking" the mill rate each year is outlined in chapter 17. The features of the tax to be discussed here, therefore, are those relating to the determination of its amount and the manner of its administration.

The Tax Base

Two elements in real property may be distinguished: (a) land, and (b) improvements (buildings, etc.). Generally speaking "land" is the original property before any value has been added thereto by permanent works, fixtures, or buildings, while "improvements" are any such additions to the original land. In most of the statutes governing such matters, however, "land" or "real property" is defined to include both the land and the improvements, and the problem of distinguishing them arises only where an exemption or different rate of assessment is granted for improvements.[5] In the New Brunswick Municipal Tax Act (Section 1(c)(i)), for example, the term "real estate" includes "land and buildings or other things erected on or belonging to it." Under the Nova Scotia Assessment Act (Section 1(i)) real property is "land and land covered with water, and whatever is erected or growing upon or affixed to land." The Cities and Towns Act in Quebec (Section 488) defines "taxable immoveables" to include "lands, constructions and workshops erected thereon and all improvements made thereto as well as machinery and accessories which are immoveable by destination." Under the Ontario Assessment Act (Section 1(i)) a more elaborate definition of "land," "real property," and "real estate" embraces land covered with water; all trees and underwood growing upon land; all mines, minerals, gas, oil, salt quarries, and fossils in and under land; all buildings, or any part of any building, and all structures, machinery, and fixtures erected or placed upon, in, over, under, or affixed to land.

In the eastern provinces generally, as these definitions of land, real estate, or real property suggest, no provision is made in law for differentiating between land and improvements in the tax base. In Ontario and Newfoundland, however, the value of property is required to be entered on the assessment roll with the values of land and buildings shown separately, and again as a unit, including all the land and improvements, both at their full assessed value.

In the western provinces and British Columbia, however, improvements are either totally exempt from tax or are entered on the assessment roll at a value lower than their full assessed value. This practice stems from the boom days in the West when every inducement was being given to permanent residence. It also reflects the influence of the Single Tax movement,

[5]See below, p. 264.

which took the western provinces by storm prior to World War I and achieved such a success that for a brief time several of the cities abandoned all other taxes and concentrated exclusively on land. Today this era is almost forgotten, but its influence is still seen in the exemption granted for buildings and other improvements in most of the rural municipalities (farm buildings are generally not taxed) and the reduced valuation at which buildings are entered on the assessment roll in urban municipalities. The most common level at which buildings are assessed is 60 to 66⅔ per cent of full value, but in some of the cities having their own charter it is even lower. The recent status of preferred assessment of buildings and improvements in these provinces is summarized in the following passage:

In Manitoba, buildings are assessed at two-thirds of their value. In Saskatchewan, cities and towns assess buildings and other improvements at "not more than sixty per cent of their fair value"; and villages and rural municipalities assess these at sixty per cent. As a result, cities and towns in Saskatchewan assess improvements at from thirty to sixty per cent of value. In Alberta, towns and villages may exempt from taxation the whole or any fraction of the value of buildings and improvements; in cities the fraction varies between 50 and 75 per cent; rural municipalities tax these at two-thirds of their value. As a result of this provision, one town confined its property taxes to land and business in 1942. The percentage assessed in other towns and cities varied from 50 to 100 but most of them were 66 2/3. The municipalities of British Columbia are empowered to tax buildings and other improvements at any fraction of their value up to three-quarters.[6]

While in essence these special exemptions and assessments are simple enough, in practice they present a problem of definition and valuation. It is perhaps not too difficult a matter to draw a line by definition between land and improvements, but it is a matter of considerable complexity to disentangle the respective values of land and the buildings on the land.[7] In the matter of definition, according to an American authority, "the Canadian experience has introduced little by way of refinement and the matter has received far less discussion than in

---

[6]M. A. Cameron, *Property Taxation and School Finance in Canada*, p. 9.
[7]The valuation problem is discussed later, p. 265.

Australia. In the Prairie Provinces the term 'improvement' is usually synonymous with 'building' and indeed the latter word sometimes appears in the statutes."[8] British Columbia includes as improvements "Aqueducts, tunnels (excluding mine-workings), bridges, dams, reservoirs, roads, transformers, and storage tanks of whatever kind or nature."

One Alberta definition, found in the City Act and typically western, is:

"Improvements" and "building and improvements" mean,—"all buildings or any part of any building and all structures and fixtures erected upon, in, over, under or affixed or attached to any land and includes all machinery, equipment and appliances which constitute an integral part of the building or other structure".

An equally complex problem arises in isolating the exact municipal tax base in the provinces[9] where no tax is levied on personal property. Generally speaking personal property may be described as all property that is not real property, and in practice its taxability therefore depends on whether or not it falls within the definition of real property. Most of the contentious disputes in this regard arise out of the question of whether certain personal property, such as a piece of machinery, apparatus or equipment, is "affixed" to real property, and therefore, by definition, part of such property. An enormous volume of litigation has turned on this question, and some general principles have been worked out by the courts.[10] In general it would appear that if the personal property is physically attached to land or buildings the burden of proof that it is not part of such land or buildings rests on the person who avers that the property is personalty. And if the fixtures rest only by weight, the burden of proof lies with the person who asserts that the property is realty. The problem of isolating the exact municipal tax base is even more complicated in British Columbia. In that province, tenants, "fixtures, machinery and similar things" *must* be assessed as improvements for purposes of school taxa-

[8]H. M. Groves, "The Property Tax in Canada and the United States," p. 27.
[9]The word "province" is used here and elsewhere throughout this chapter only as a handy way of referring to the municipalities in that province.
[10]See, for example, *Stack* v. *T. Eaton Co. et al.*, per Meredith C.J., [1902] 4 O.L.R., at p. 335.

tion—subject to certain exemptions—and *may* be assessed for municipal purposes if the local council so chooses.

Valuation of Property

The Canadian municipal property tax is a tax on the capital value of property.

The significance of this statement may be best demonstrated by the example of the only important exception to it, the city of St. John's, Newfoundland. Here the English and European method of assessment based on the "rental" value of property is still employed. Under this system an *annual* value for the property is established at the amount for which it should rent. Vacant property is subject to a special tax but owner-occupied property is assessed to the owner at its rental value and taxed in the usual way. Complicated rules are devised for estimating this value, and the actual rent paid is seldom the basis of the assessment. Since the annual rental value of a premises is only a fraction of its capital cost the tax rate employed under this system must be very much higher than under the capital value method, to obtain the same revenue. In St. John's, for example, the annual rate of property tax in 1959 was 20 per cent, which is the same as 200 mills.

By comparison, under the Canadian system, which follows the American, the property is valued, whether it is occupied or not, at its "actual value," and the owner will pay an annual tax (expressed usually in mills) on that value. It need hardly be said that the determination of a fair value for the property subject to tax is a matter of vital concern to both the taxpayer and the taxing authorities. To determine the amount of a person's income is a relatively simple arithmetical operation compared to the valuation at market prices of his home or his office or his factory. Few aspects of tax administration call for as rare a combination of experience, judgment, and sense.

This job of valuation falls to the assessor. An extensive literature on the science (or art) of assessing pays tribute to the crucial role he plays in the administration of the property tax. In general he is under obligation by statute to make an annual assessment. Theoretically, therefore, he must view all property in the municipality once a year and, taking into account all the various complicated factors involved, place a true value on it for that year. In fact, the physical impossibility of carrying out this requirement, no matter how large the assessor's staff, results in an actual assessment being made perhaps every two, five, or ten years, with annual assessments in the interim mainly confirming earlier valuations. The practical effect is that seldom does the assessed value of property more than approach its true value. It is generally moving upward or downward considerably more slowly than the market trend and in fact it is regarded as desirable that assessments should not fluctuate as violently as property values often do.

Several basic principles have now been established by jurisprudence and practice to be recognized in assessing. Of those established by the courts the most important is undoubtedly the "willing-buyer willing-seller" formula. This suggests a price established by the free play of bargaining between a seller willing to sell but not anxious to, and a buyer willing to buy but acting without any compulsion from the duress of particular circumstances. Other rules developed by the higher courts for reaching actual or true value have been summarized by a Canadian expert as follows:

1. No item of real property can possess more than one real or actual value.

2. The purpose for which the real or actual value is to be determined does not affect or influence the results.

3. To state the value of anything in terms of money is to express the opinion that the thing valued is susceptible to being exchanged for the amount of money stated. To express the value of anything in terms of money with a provision that it can never be exchanged for the amount of money stated is as offensive to the intellect as a promissory note in the body of which is incorporated a declaration by the debtor that he will never be willing or able to pay the debt.

4. Qualities which are imparted to a thing by the owner but which cannot be transferred to another along with the thing do not affect the value of it.

5. Any particular and perhaps profitable use which the owner of a thing makes of it does not increase its value; it is the use which can be made of the thing by others which determines the value.

6. Replacement cost is not a measure of value; it merely constitutes a ceiling over which value cannot normally go.[11]

While these general rules provide an over-all guidance approved by the courts (although in fact there have been departures in litigation involving major properties, e.g., the *Sun Life* case), for practical purposes the assessor must often look to more mundane details. He must consider the type, location, use, age, condition, and original and replacement cost. He must take into account also the value of adjacent property, recent sales of which may provide some basis for valuation on "willing-seller willing-buyer" terms. He should have knowledge of valuations of the property made for insurance and mortgage purposes, and be capable of taking into account the general outlook for the neighbourhood. Many intangibles should properly be taken into account in assessing property. The alternative or potential uses for the property are a factor in valuation. A race track or a golf course located within a municipality may be valued, for example, on the basis of its potential value as building lots. Specific formulae employed for valuing more complex types of property are the additions and betterments method (basically a net worth valuation), the stock and bond method (the value of a company's stocks and bonds is assumed to reflect the value of its assets), cost less depreciation (greater emphasis on cost as indicative of market value), cost of replacement, and capitalized earnings. The last has been urged by many as representing the only true basis of valuation, the argument being advanced that the only measurement of the value of an asset is the income that it will earn. Undoubtedly some attention is paid to this aspect in making valuations in Canada, but the use of the income method alone, unaided by other approaches to the determination of value, has been rejected by authorities here.

More recently increasing emphasis has been placed in real estate valuation on "scientific" rules. The common character-

[11]O. Lobley, "Municipal Taxation," a lecture delivered on March 30, 1948, at McGill University, in the series "The Fundamentals of Real Estate Practice." A brief but good discussion of the legal and other rules governing assessment in Canada is given in *Report of the Commission to Investigate Taxation in the City of Fredericton*, chapter III, and of course the standard work on the subject for the expert is H. E. Manning, *Municipal Taxation in Canada*.

istic of such methods is the establishment of a unit value for property of each given class, and the adjustment of this unit value for factors such as corner influence and depth of lot. Some methods attempt to take into account even light and ventilation factors.

The scientific approach is generally regarded as an advance, although the element of personal judgment on the part of the assessor is still large enough to substantially affect the valuation. This appears to be inevitable. The best system and the most carefully prepared assessment manuals cannot remove entirely the personal attitudes of the assessor. As a result the basis of valuation of property even within the same municipality undoubtedly varies with the particular bias of individual assessors. Since it is a universal statutory requirement that every property in the municipality be assessed in just proportion to all other property it is not surprising that the most common ground for the appeal of assessment is that the owner feels himself to have been the subject of discrimination.

It is even less surprising that between one municipality and another or one province and another very marked differences in valuations are found. Where a county or provincial tax is levied on real property or where a provincial grant is made on the basis of property assessments equity can only be served by reconciling these differences. In addition to the differences otherwise expected it is recognized that where the assessment of property is the basis of a levy on the municipality by a higher level or second tier of government there is an incentive for under-assessment. This also holds true if assessment is the basis for payment of a grant; the poorer a municipality appears to be, the larger the grant it is likely to obtain. As a corrective measure uniform assessments are made or demanded by a provincial assessment authority in some provinces, or other less direct steps may be taken to encourage uniformity in others.

In Saskatchewan, where the last provincial property tax expired only on December 31, 1952, municipal assessments are made throughout the province under the direction of provincial officials, except in the three largest cities. In Alberta since 1949 the provincial Director of Assessment has been authorized to supervise the assessing in any town, village, or municipal district at the request of the local council, and in 1947 in Manitoba there was created a Provincial-Municipal Assessment Branch in the Department of the Municipal Commissioner which directs assessments in all municipalities but cities and suburban areas. Ontario in the same year set up an Assessment Branch in the Department of Municipal Affairs to assist local assessors with their problems but there is no standardized procedure which has to be followed under provincial direction. For county purposes only, all Ontario counties must equalize the assessments of all the municipalities within their jurisdiction and to assist the county councils in this work most counties have now appointed county assessors.

The uniform assessment of the municipalities comprising the Municipality of Metropolitan Toronto, first used in 1954, and the enactment of legislation in British Columbia in 1953 requiring a uniform municipal assessment for school taxes, are recent marked examples of the trend towards uniformity.

As indicated above, the general rules for assessment are subject to a special modification where it becomes legally necessary to value buildings and improvements separately from the land. One of the most heated controversies aroused by the single tax movement was on this question. It was argued by many that the value of any land was so inextricably bound up with the value of the buildings on it that it was impossible to separate the two. The valuation of the land on which a commercial building is located at, say, the corner of St. Catherine and Windsor in Montreal or Queen and Yonge in Toronto, it must be agreed, would represent a delicate bit of surgery. In practice, however, land is valued separately everywhere in Canada even though in some parts only the total property value has to be shown on the assessment roll. But in the western municipalities and in Ontario and Newfoundland the land and building assessments must be shown separately. Theoretically the value of the land should as nearly as possible be determined as the difference in the value of the total property and the value of the improvements alone. To what extent assessors are able to approach this theoretical ideal in practice is probably difficult to determine.

Exempt Property

Valuing property in the community is the main part of the assessor's job, but another important part is to make sure that every parcel of land and every building is located and brought on to the assessment roll. Apparently in this respect he is not always successful, if American experience is any guide in Canada.[12] Land maps and land record cards, which are constantly inspected and revised, and in some cases even aerial surveys, are used in the pursuit of elusive real estate.

While some property thus escapes taxation by involuntary exemption the amount is now likely to be insignificant compared to that exempted by statute. The bulk of this belongs to the Crown (exempt under Section 125 of the B.N.A. Act) and to schools, churches, hospitals, charities, and, in some cases, to industry. A substantial amount of real property in the form of improvements is also exempted. Accurate figures for all of Canada are not available, but an idea of the position in seven

TABLE XIII

TAXABLE AND TAX-EXEMPT ASSESSMENTS

Municipalities in	Assessed value of taxable real property	Exempt real property
	($000)	($000)
Nfld.	N/A	N/A
P.E.I.	29,590[1]	10,050[2]
N.S.	490,747	301,582
N.B.	359,101	N/A
P.Q.	6,448,193	1,866,895
Ont.	7,047,527	1,317,711
Man.	885,557	165,327[3]
Sask.	1,025,689	560,323
Alta.	1,316,770	257,713
B.C.	1,415,936	1,349,937

[1]Excludes $34,615,000 on which school taxes only are levied.
[2]Incomplete total.
[3]Excludes rural municipalities.
SOURCE: Dominion Bureau of Statistics Memorandum, *Financial Statistics of Municipal Governments*, 1957. Actual.

[12]Cameron, *Property Taxation and School Finance*, pp. 22-3.

of the provinces is given in Table XIII by a comparison for 1950 of taxable and tax-exempt assessments.

This table indicates a marked variation between provinces; an even greater variation exists between individual municipalities. In many municipalities the extent of exempt property is viewed with increasing concern as municipal budgets expand, and there is constant agitation for the removal or modification of the privilege, particularly that granted to property owned by other governments. In 1950 the Dominion government introduced a plan that was intended as a permanent solution to the problem created by abnormal concentrations of its property. While not abandoning its constitutional exemption the Dominion originally undertook to pay grants equivalent to full taxes on 75% of the approved value of federal property wherever this exceeded 4% of the total value of all taxable and federal property. This percentage was established as the national average of its property and any concentration in excess of that average was regarded as creating special local problems. This federal programme of grants was instituted by the Municipal Grants Regulations of 1950 which were superseded in 1951 by the Municipal Grants Act. Amendments to this act in 1955 increased the grants to the equivalent of full taxes on the full value of federal property in excess of 2% of taxable property and in 1957 the 2% limitation was also removed. Thus today, the federal government pays grants in lieu of full taxation on the full approved value of all federal land and buildings to all municipal and other local taxing authorities wherever normal municipal services are performed. Provincial government practices are not as generous as the federal, but there is a growing trend towards payment of full taxes on administrative and business offices; the 1952 step by Ontario in this direction being a significant example. Exemptions for industry are largely a heritage of an earlier day when special tax inducements were freely granted. Opinion is now generally against such practices.

Business and Other Occupancy Taxes

Special taxes on businesses in many provinces are based on some feature of the premises occupied by the business, and are levied on the occupier, in addition to the property tax on the premises payable by the owner.[13] In Ontario municipalities, for example, the business tax is calculated by applying the general rate of municipal tax to a proportion of the assessed value of the property, the proportion varying from 10 per cent to 150 per cent, depending on the type of business. A similar system is used in Halifax, but in that city the proportion of the real property assessment is 50 per cent and is the same for all types of business. In Quebec, Manitoba, and Alberta levies based on the rental value of the premises are most common, and a charge based on a unit of measurement such as the square feet of floor space is employed in Saskatchewan and is authorized as an alternative method of assessment in the towns and villages of Alberta. Flat rate and gross revenue taxes are used in the province of Quebec and in the Maritime Provinces. Business taxes on the rental value basis were introduced to British Columbia in Vancouver and New Westminster in 1948, and since then Victoria, Prince Rupert, and Cranbrook have adopted this form of taxation. Business taxes, again on a rental basis, were first used in Prince Edward Island in Charlottetown in 1953, in this case as an alternative to the personal property tax.

Occupancy taxes on residential properties are less numerous. Several municipalities in the province of Quebec are authorized to impose them at a percentage rate on the actual rental paid. In Montreal, for example, such taxes are charged as a "water tax" at the rate of 8 per cent. In Halifax and Fredericton occupancy taxes are imposed on a fraction of the assessed value of the premises and in Medicine Hat on rental value. (See Table XXI in the Appendix.)

Property Tax Administration

The function of the assessor, one of the main cogs in municipal tax machinery, has already been discussed. His formally prescribed duty is to compile the assessment roll, which is "an official list showing the assessment valuation of each parcel of real property in an assessment district, with descriptions of properties, and names of all known owners."

[13]See R. M. Clark, *The Municipal Business Tax in Canada.*

He is a salaried official of the municipality (not an elected one as are many assessors in the United States) and usually serves indefinitely at the pleasure of the council. There are, of course, wide variations from this general description. In the bigger cities the assessor is in charge of a large staff, or there may be several official "assessors" and an assessment commissioner co-ordinating their activities. In very small centres the assessor may be hired only on a part-time basis, and may be a person of no particular skill who performs the work in his spare time.

When the assessment roll is completed and the tax rate struck, a "tax roll" showing the amount of tax payable on each property is prepared (it is sometimes consolidated with the assessment roll). The municipal "collector" then proceeds to notify each property owner of his tax and to collect the tax. This is his main duty, and in the provinces where there is also a municipal treasurer (e.g., Ontario) there is a tendency to question the necessity of the collector's office. The municipal treasurer is the chief receiving officer, chief disbursing officer, and chief custodian of the funds of the municipality. The collector turns over to the treasurer the returns from the tax payments and also makes a declaration of the taxpayers in arrears. In a sense he acts as agent for the treasurer, which has probably given rise to the suggestion that his work might be done directly by the office of the treasurer. Some smaller municipalities have consolidated the two offices, and indeed there is a trend toward placing in one person the responsibility of assessor, collector, and treasurer. Sometimes this consolidation also includes the position of clerk, an official who often plays a key role in financial and tax administration in the smaller centres.

School Levies

The real property tax in almost every Canadian municipality is in part a levy for general purpose and in part a levy for the support of the school board or school commission of the municipality. All of the above discussion of the real property tax applies, therefore, with equal validity to the school levy as well as to the general levy. The one feature of the school levy worth mentioning is that usually a higher rate is applied to "separate" school supporters than to the constituents of the predominant religion in the municipality. Only in a few instances are taxes levied directly by school boards.

Retail Sales Tax

Most of the larger Quebec municipalities and school authorities have introduced retail sales tax in recent years. The taxes in Montreal and Quebec are older than the provincial tax, having been introduced respectively in 1935 and 1940. The fact that these centres account for 10 to 15 per cent of the total population of Canada gives such levies a position of particular importance in municipal taxation.

The rate of municipal tax in Quebec is uniformly 2 per cent. Since 1940 the province has also imposed a 2 per cent tax. In 1949 in Montreal an additional special tax of 1 per cent, which has since been increased to 2 per cent, was levied for educational purposes. Other cities have followed this lead. The total tax, therefore, in most cities has been 6 per cent (2 per cent for each level of government plus 2 per cent for education), and in 1961 legislation was introduced to make the educational tax uniform throughout the province as part of the provincial rate.

Economical and efficient administration of these taxes has been obtained by the centralization of all collection in the hands of the province. Further simplification has also been achieved by imposing all levies on the same basis. Exemptions are fully uniform, and regulations issued for the provincial tax also govern for the municipal taxes. For this reason the description of the provincial sales tax in Quebec[14] applies equally to the municipal tax.

One special problem of enforcement is encountered where sales taxes are levied by a jurisdiction as small as a municipality. Such taxes are authorized to be imposed only on residents of the municipal area in respect of goods purchased or used by them. Where the purchaser gives an address outside the

[14]See chapter XI.

municipal area the tax is therefore not collected; if a resident brings goods into the municipality it rests entirely with him to report the fact and pay the proper tax. The possibilities of abuse inherent in this system are obvious. They have been curtailed as far as possible by the expansion of the taxable area to the extreme limits of normal habitation of persons shopping in the area, so that Montreal and Quebec City taxes apply in all the suburban localities of both cities. Proceeds of the tax collected in this broad taxable area are allocated to the constituent parts on a population basis.

The taxes in the Quebec municipalities are the only general retail sales or use charges levied by municipal governments in Canada. Other municipal sales taxes even of limited application are rare in Canada, a conspicuous exception being the tax on sales of gas and electricity in Winnipeg. The rate is 5 per cent for commercial users and $2\frac{1}{2}$ per cent for domestic.

Poll Taxes

Of all forms of tax the most ancient is undoubtedly the poll tax. In Canada today it is almost exclusively a municipal levy, and even so is used to any appreciable extent only by the municipalities of the Atlantic Provinces. In Newfoundland, poll tax may range under the Local Government Act from $5 to $10 and this form of tax is still quite an important source of revenue. St. John's has authority to levy a poll tax up to $20 but does not employ the tax. Corner Brook levies $10 per head. For municipal purposes in Prince Edward Island, towns may levy a poll tax up to $10 and villages up to $5. For school purposes, the range is $3–$20. Charlottetown levies $25 on males and $12 on females. In New Brunswick the towns and smaller bodies are required by statute to raise one-sixth of their total municipal levy by such a tax, or the tax may be at a fixed rate of not less than $3 or more than $10 per person for municipal purposes. For school purposes the range is from $1 to $6. In the city of Fredericton the relatively high rate of $15 is imposed. In Nova Scotia poll taxes are also used for both general and school purposes. The Assessment Act allows a maximum rate of $50 to be imposed but rates may vary with the amount of property assessment. In the city of Halifax the rate is $20. Some British Columbia municipalities adopted the provincial tax of $5, which before its repeal in 1952 applied only where no local tax was levied, but all poll taxes were finally repealed in British Columbia in 1957. Alberta followed suit by abolishing the tax in 1958. A poll tax of $4 is still on the Manitoba statutes but no municipality in that province levies the tax. In Saskatchewan a poll tax of $5 may be levied under the City Act and Town Act but in Uranium City private legislation enables that municipality to impose a $20 poll tax.

In general such taxes are administered on a catch-as-catch-can basis, and there is considerable controversy regarding their practicability and fairness. Where they are a charge for a service that cannot be obtained until the charge is paid, e.g., a medical insurance plan, there is a good expectation of uniform collection. Municipal poll taxes, however, apply usually to persons (sometimes limited to males) between the ages of 21 and 60 residing in the municipal area who have paid no other local tax. Their selectivity, therefore, makes them most difficult to administer. Proper enforcement requires a good deal of investigation, which apparently many municipalities do not feel is warranted for the collection of a tax that is usually of nominal amount only.

Other Taxes and Charges

In Saskatchewan the amusement tax is used exclusively by the municipalities, there being no provincial charge, and in Quebec the proceeds are shared with the province. In some Quebec municipalities (Montreal, Verdun, Three Rivers) a water tax, based on rental value of the premises, is charged, and in Quebec City a special tax is levied for garbage collection. In every municipality a considerable revenue is derived from licences of various kinds. These include licences for stores, restaurants, taverns, bars, theatres, dance halls, bowling alleys, and other places of public entertainment, beauty salons, barber shops, pawn shops, brokers' offices, boarding houses, private hospitals, dry cleaning establishments, laundries, undertaking parlours, bicycles, buses, taxis, gasoline pumps, hawkers, peddlers, and for a variety of other enterprises.

OTHER REVENUES

In recent years grants from provincial governments for education and for general municipal purposes have become increasingly important, and in many municipalities surpluses from the operation of publicly owned utilities—street railways, water works, hydro-electric, gas, and telephone companies—are a significant item in corporation budgets. Unfortunately space will not permit a general discussion of provincial-municipal financial relations, but the reader wishing full information on this important aspect of the subject (or indeed on the whole range of problems now faced by municipal government in Canada) will be richly rewarded by looking into the several excellent and up-to-date reports and studies now available.[15]

LOCAL IMPROVEMENT CHARGES

No mention of charges for local improvements has been made in this description of municipal taxation since these are regarded as payment for specific benefits or services received and not as tax levies for general purposes.

MUNICIPAL TAXATION IN NEWFOUNDLAND

The position of municipalities and municipal taxation is so distinctive in Newfoundland that it deserves special attention in this general chapter. It can be said that until 1942 St. John's was the only municipality in Newfoundland, and even today it is not a fully developed municipality in the usual sense of the term. It has a mayor and council elected by the city voters, and carries on the usual functions of a municipal government except for police, fire prevention, and education. The city is policed at the expense of the provincial government, which also

---

[15]Nova Scotia, *The Reorganization of Provincial-Municipal Relations in Nova Scotia* (1949), a report of the Nova Scotia Municipal Bureau, by D. C. Rowat.
New Brunswick, *Report of the Commission to Investigate Taxation in the City of*

bears the cost of fire protection, except for a nominal contribution from the city council. Education in St. John's, and indeed throughout the province, is for the most part denominational, supported mainly by grants from the provincial government.

Today there are, in addition to St. John's, several dozen local units of an elementary form, organized under the gradual fulfilment of a plan projected by the Commission of Government. Several of these were incorporated under separate acts of the Newfoundland legislature, although all similar municipal councils are now incorporated under the general Local Government Act, 1956.

The new local councils are of three kinds, the town council, the rural district council, and the community council. A town council may be established in any settlement where there are 1,000 or more inhabitants, a rural district council where there are two or three adjacent settlements having in all over 1,000 inhabitants, and a community council for settlements of less than 1,000 inhabitants.

The functions of the town and rural district councils are in practice limited almost entirely to the building and maintenance of roads, but in some cases they also include the supplying of water, sewerage, and street lighting. Local school boards are also organized to supervise the schools, and although the bulk of revenue requirements for both the municipalities and school boards comes from the provincial government these entities are empowered to tax and are given every encouragement to use their authority.

Fredericton (1947), J. R. Petrie, Chairman; *Report of the Royal Commission on Rates and Taxes Act* (1951), R. J. Love, Chairman.

Ontario, *Municipal Finance*, a report prepared by the Committee on Municipal-Provincial Relations (1950); *Decisions and Recommendations of the Ontario Municipal Board* (January 1953), L. R. Cumming, Chairman; *Report of the Ontario Provincial-Municipal Relations Committee* (First Report, December 19, 1952; Second Report, February 4, 1953, Progress Report, July 7, 1953), H. J. Chater, Chairman.

Manitoba, *Report of the Provincial-Municipal Committee* (1953), Hon. D. L. Campbell, Chairman.

Saskatchewan, *Report of the Committee Investigating Provincial-Municipal Relations* (1950), G. E. Britnell, Chairman.

Alberta, *Report of the Royal Commission on Taxation* (1948), J. W. Judge, Commissioner.

British Columbia, *Report of the Commission of Inquiry into Education Finance* (1945), M. A. Cameron, Commissioner; *Report of the Royal Commission on Provincial-Municipal Relations* (1947), H. C. Goldenberg, Commissioner.

The tax structure both of St. John's and of the newer municipal councils differs in many respects from those of the municipalities in the other Canadian provinces. Let us look at St. John's first.

The principal tax in St. John's, providing slightly less than half the total revenue, is called the City Tax. It is a property tax, but imposed not on the capital value of the property but on its rental value. (The property tax in the other Canadian municipalities is almost without exception imposed on the capital value rather than on the rental value.) The St. John's tax applies to both land and buildings and is payable by the owner, the rate having been fixed at 20 per cent for some years. As in the other provinces land and buildings used for purposes of public worship, education, or charity are exempt. Other taxes providing lesser revenues are the tax on vacant land and the ground landlord's tax, the latter in effect a tax on absentee landowners. There is also a water tax, based on rental values.

Next in order of importance for revenue is the municipal Business Tax, based on rental value. This was enacted in 1951, and replaced the Stock Tax, which had applied at the rate of 1 per cent on the value of the inventory of every business in St. John's, determined, according to the statute, as the average of the inventory outstanding at the end of each calendar month in the year. This latter form of levy has largely disappeared in the other Canadian municipalities.

Other important tax sources are the entertainment tax, a poll tax which the municipality is authorized to impose at a rate not to exceed $10 per person and a fuel oil tax at a rate of 1 cent per gallon. An unusual tax levied in St. John's is a charge of 2 per cent on fire insurance premiums payable by the insured.

The general tax picture in the newer municipalities is similar to that of St. John's in some respects, the conspicuous difference being the broad reliance on a form of poll tax in lieu of the property tax. Every encouragement is being given by the province for the utilization of the real property tax, and recent legislation, such as the Assessment Act, 1958 and the Local School Tax Act, 1957 has been directed to this end. This effort is gradually meeting with success, although as yet many of the other sources available to the municipalities, and in particular the poll tax, are more important in their revenues.

The poll tax (correctly known as a Municipal Service Fee), referred to above as a principal source of revenue in the local councils, varies in amount from $5 to $10. It applies to all males over 21 who reside or are employed in the municipality for three months in any financial year and all females over 21 who reside in or are employed in the municipality and have an income of $600 or more. It also applies to all persons, companies, and firms not resident in the municipality which own more than $100 worth of property in the municipality.

Other taxes imposed by all or almost all of the newer municipalities include:

(*a*) A stock tax similar to that imposed in St. John's, which may be at a rate between ⅛ of 1 per cent and 1 per cent.

(*b*) Business taxes which may be based on "business done by the operator" in a municipality where there is no real property tax, and which otherwise are based on the assessed value of the business property.

(*c*) An entertainments tax, usually at 5 cents per ticket.

(*d*) Taxes ranging from $5.00 to $10.00 on commercial vehicles (taxis, transports, etc.) and from $2.50 to $5.00 on private vehicles, and a bicycle tax.

(*e*) A tax not exceeding $1 per ton on coal or 1 cent per gallon on fuel oil.

(*f*) $1 per year on main lines of telephone companies.

(*g*) A tax of 2 per cent of the premiums on fire insurance payable by the person paying the premium.

(*h*) Licences and permits for hawkers and peddlers, building contractors, circuses, commercial travellers, bowling alleys, billiard rooms, juke boxes, and slot machines.

Summary

RATES. Property taxes are normally expressed as so many mills on the dollar, and may range from 11.5 to 200 mills, the actual burden of the tax being affected as well by the percentage of true value at which property is assessed. Several Quebec cities tax retail sales 2 per cent, and in Montreal, Quebec City and other centres the School Board has been authorized to impose an additional 1 or 2 per cent (giving a total of 5 or 6 per cent, including a 2 per cent provincial tax). Business taxes are general in Canadian municipalities. For some typical municipal tax rates see Table XX in Appendix.

REVENUE

	Fiscal year 1958–9* ($ million)	Percentage of tax revenue	Percentage of total revenue
Real and personal property	997	88.1	77.4
Sales tax	58	5.1	4.5
Other tax revenue	77	6.8	6.0
Total tax revenue	1,132	100.0	87.9
Privileges, licences, and permits	23		1.8
Public utility contributions	42		3.3
Other revenue	91		7.0
Total	1,288		100.0

*Fiscal years ended nearest to December 31, 1958.

STATUTORY REFERENCES

Newfoundland, Local Government Act, Statutes of Newfoundland, 1961, Act No. 55; Assessment Act, *ibid.*, 1958, Act No. 18; *P.E.I.*, The School Act, Revised Statutes, Prince Edward Island, 1951, c. 145; Town Act, *ibid.*, c. 162; Village Service Act, Statutes of P.E.I., 1954, c. 39; *Nova Scotia*, Assessment Act, Revised Statutes, Nova Scotia, 1954, c. 15; Municipal Act, Statutes of Nova Scotia, 1955, c. 7; Education Act, Revised Statutes, Nova Scotia, 1954, c. 235; *New Brunswick*, Municipal Tax Act, Revised Statutes, New Brunswick, 1955, c. 14; Schools Act, *ibid.*, 1952, c. 204; *Quebec*, Cities and Towns Act, Revised Statutes, Quebec, 1941, c. 233; Municipal Tax Exemption Act, *ibid.*, c. 221; Education Act, *ibid.*, c. 59; The Municipal Code; *Ontario*, Assessment Act, Revised Statutes, Ontario, 1960, c. 23;

Municipal Act, *ibid.*, c. 249; *Manitoba*, Municipal Act, Revised Statutes, Manitoba, 1954, c. 173; *Saskatchewan*, City Act, Revised Statutes, Saskatchewan, 1953, c. 137; Town Act, *ibid.*, c. 138; Village Act, *ibid.*, c. 139; Rural Municipality Act, *ibid.*, c. 140; Local Improvement Districts Act, *ibid.*, c. 141; School Assessment Act, *ibid.*, c. 172; Saskatchewan Assessment Commission Act, *ibid.*, c. 148; The Rural Municipality Act, Statutes, Saskatchewan, 1960, c. 50; *Alberta*, Assessment Act, Revised Statutes, Alberta, 1955, c. 17; Municipal District Act, *ibid.*, c. 215; School Act, *ibid.*, c. 297; Special Areas Act, *ibid.*, c. 317; The Electric Power and Pipe Line Assessment Act, Statutes of Alberta, 1961; *British Columbia*, Municipal Act, Revised Statutes of British Columbia, 1960, c. 255; Assessment Equalization Act, *ibid.*, c. 18; Public Schools Act, *ibid.*, c. 319; Taxation Act, *ibid.*, c. 376.

See also the special charters under which most of the cities are organized: Charlottetown, P.E.I.; Halifax and Sydney, N.S.; Saint John, Moncton, Fredericton, N.B.; Montreal, Quebec City, Three Rivers, Que.; Toronto, Hamilton, Ottawa, Ont.; Winnipeg, St. Boniface, Portage la Prairie, Man.; Calgary, Edmonton, Alta.; Vancouver, Victoria, B.C.

CHAPTER 15

ENACTMENT OF THE TAX LAWS OF THE DOMINION

THE BUDGETARY SYSTEM, THE ESTIMATES

IN THE PREVIOUS CHAPTERS dealing with taxation in Canada today the whole phenomenon has been taken more or less for granted as part of the ordained course of human affairs. The fact that it is the laborious product of institutions of government and that a large and complex machinery is devoted to its daily administration has been subordinated to other considerations. While this feature of taxation has attracted less notice than the more glittering generalities relating to taxation policy, it is of extreme importance in the process of gathering funds for governmental operation. Moreover, it also has its interesting sides. The following chapters are given over therefore to what might be called the birth and care of taxes.

THE BUDGETARY SYSTEM

Like most other phases of modern living the business of imposing taxes has grown more and more complicated with the passage of time. The democratic countries have come a long way from the days when the Persian satrap announced his tax edicts by armed horsemen and enforced them by lash and fire. Taxes today are the end product of a democratic procedure that is designed to give the elected representatives of the people full opportunity to examine, debate, consider, and, if necessary, refuse to sanction the government's tax proposals.

The general procedure which makes possible this free and full consideration is known as the "Budgetary System." It is followed in greater or lesser degree by all levels of government in Canada, and might be said to represent in governmental affairs a parallel to the housewife's practice of budgeting the family resources—taking into account all reasonable contingencies and making provision for them as far as possible. In its practical application to governmental housekeeping the budgetary system calls for the submission to the elected representatives of a carefully estimated forecast of both income and outgo for the coming year, and the introduction of appropriate measures to keep income and outgo in balance during the same year or in some circumstances deliberately to produce a surplus or deficit. The operations of the system range from the vast and immensely complicated process by which expenditures and taxes are authorized in the federal Parliament to their simplest form in the smallest local unit of government. At the federal level expenditures in billions of dollars are involved and the taxes run to dozens. At the local government level the expenditures may be only for a policeman and a school teacher, and the only tax the property tax. Both extremes, however, represent an application of the same fundamental principles.

The essentials of the budgetary system of financial administration were described by the Deputy Minister of Finance of the federal government in a paper delivered before the Canadian Economic and Political Science Association in 1938.[1] Although his words were used mainly in relation to the fully developed parliamentary system they apply in some degree to all forms of government where there are elected representatives of the people. His description, based on a similar study of the British system of budgeting, enumerated the following characteristics:

(1) The adoption of the principle of a budget. This means the definite acceptance of the principle that all the financial needs of the Government for the period to be financed shall be considered at one time, according to a well defined plan, to the end that the executive, the Parliament, and the people shall all have clearly before them the full purport of the problem as it affects the condition of the Treasury, present and prospective. (2) The adoption of the principle that the

[1] W. C. Clark, "Financial Administration of the Government of Canada."

preparation and submission of this definite financial plan with supporting details of information devolves upon the executive. (3) The adoption of the principle of control over the executive by the grant to Parliament of an opportunity to subject the executive's report of past operations and proposals for the future to critical examination. (4) The adoption of the principle that, while Parliament is thus to be given full and detailed information regarding financial transactions and to be afforded adequate opportunity to criticize, the responsibility not only for the proposal as initially submitted but for every change made in it as the result of discussion, shall formally rest with the executive. (5) The adoption of the principle that, although the determining voice in respect to the preparation of a plan for raising and expending all revenues lies with the executive, the latter must await approval by Parliament, and after approval must render a rigid accounting to Parliament in respect of the manner in which authorizations granted are carried out. This is secured by the establishment of a system of accounting and reporting which gives to Parliament and the people full information regarding all financial transactions in a clear and detailed manner. (6) The adoption of the principle of a *parliamentary* audit of receipts and expenditures as a means of exercising rigid scrutiny over the manner in which authorizations are carried out. (7) The adoption of the principle that the reports of the auditor-general, who is appointed by Parliament, shall be available for examination and scrutiny by members of Parliament. (8) The adoption of the principle that the work of exercising an immediate and direct control over the preparation of estimates and the expenditure of funds shall be performed by specialized agencies. (9) The adoption of the principle that in making appropriations a clear distinction shall be made between appropriation items and supporting details in order that the purposes for which funds shall be granted shall be specified in such detail as is consistent with adequate control and reasonable flexibility in the actual expenditure of funds. (10) The adoption of the principle that the expenditure of appropriations is not mandatory but rather that appropriations are mere grants to the executive who is held responsible for the manner in which his discretion to make use of the funds is exercised.

This budgetary system has found its most thorough application in Canada at the federal level. The mainspring in the process in the Dominion government is the Minister of Finance, since to him falls the task of directing and formulating financial

BUDGETARY SYSTEM, ESTIMATES 281

policy. By the Department of Finance and Treasury Board Act, the department of which he is the head is given "supervision, control and direction of all matters relating to the financial affairs and public accounts, revenue and expenditure of Canada, which are not, or insofar as they are not, . . . assigned to any other department of the Government." In the exercise of these broad executive powers, however, the Minister is entirely dependent on the approval by Parliament of the Government's "Estimates" and the annual "Budget Speech," both of which are keystones in the financial structure of government. The Estimates contain the Government's request for appropriations to meet expenditures in the coming fiscal year, and the Budget Speech contains the proposals for changes in tax rates necessary to finance these expenditures. By refusing to approve the Estimates, Parliament can bring the whole machinery of government to a standstill, and defeat of the Government's main proposals either for expenditure or revenue would mean the fall of the executive and probably the calling of an election.

Preparation of Estimates

The Estimates, contained in a volume of about three hundred pages, are usually presented to Parliament early in the session and always before the commencement of the fiscal year (April 1). Several months of intense activity will have preceded their submission to Parliament. The first step in this preparatory work is taken by the Minister of Finance in the fall of the preceding year. At that time he writes to his colleagues who head the operating departments of government and requests them to submit to him their proposals for expenditures during the next fiscal year, which in the case of the Dominion commences on the succeeding April 1. Following this request, the deputy minister and divisional or branch heads of each department prepare a detailed statement, in a form established by the Department of Finance, of their requirements for carrying out departmental activities. These Estimates are prepared in frequent consultation with the ministerial head of the department, and after receiving his approval are sent on to the Minister of Finance. In the Department of Finance the large permanent staff of the Treasury Board assembles all such reports and prepares them for submission to the Minister of Finance and the Treasury Board. A good deal of analysis and scrutiny of the expenditure proposals is carried out by the officials at this stage, and the maximum area of agreement is found through consultation and negotiation with the operating departments prior to the submission of the proposals to the Minister of Finance and Treasury Board.

THE TREASURY BOARD

The Treasury Board is a sub-committee of the Cabinet designated to act as its watch-dog in financial matters. It is composed of the Minister of Finance and any five other members of the Privy Council. Sitting almost weekly, it deals with the multitude of governmental financial transactions which by law require its approval. The Minister of Finance is Chairman of the Board. Its year-round administrative work is carried on under the direction of one of the assistant deputy ministers of the Department, who supervises the departmental staff attached directly to the Board and acts also as Secretary.

The Minister of Finance and his colleagues of the Treasury Board must first approve the Estimates before they are submitted to the Cabinet for consideration. In their scrutiny they are, of course, alleged to evince those harsh and gloomy characteristics typical of the treasury the world over. Discussions are protracted. The ministerial head and high officials of each department are given an opportunity to defend their proposals. This process is described succinctly and with authority by the Rt. Hon. J. L. Ilsley, the wartime Minister of Finance, in the following apt words: "The Staff of the Treasury Board, without reference to the Minister in the first place, go at those estimates and try to have them reduced. They are successful to a considerable extent in having them reduced. But various departments demur, and some go even further than that and vigorously and violently protest against the proposed cuts. The matter is then taken up by myself with the various Ministers and by the Treasury Board with the various Ministers, and after a considerable amount of argument the Estimates are still further reduced. . . ."[2]

When the Treasury Board has gone as far as it can go in the attempt at finality it recommends a programme to the Cabinet as a whole. In Cabinet there is likely to be further extensive discussion, particularly where matters of national importance, such as the amount of expenditure on defence or on social welfare, are involved. It is also possible that any minister who has suffered at the hands of Treasury Board may make a further plea for reconsideration of his rejected proposal. Eventually the struggle is terminated and on Cabinet approval the Estimates are submitted to the Governor-General, as a matter of form, following which they are ready for presentation to Parliament.

THE MAIN ESTIMATES

The volume, previously referred to, that is presented to Parliament is generally known as the Main Estimates, since later in the session the Government also presents Supplementary Estimates for additional appropriations. The Main Estimates represent the greater part of the Government's expenditure proposals for the year. They are presented to Parliament by message of the Governor-General, since by the British North America Act money measures can only be originated by the Governor-General-in-Council (in effect only a member of the Government may move an expenditure or a tax). At this time the Minister of Finance usually outlines briefly the general magnitude and some of the significant aspects of the Estimates.

To ensure an intelligent appreciation by the members of the House of the Government's proposals it is essential that they be given in sufficient detail. On the other hand, too much detail would submerge the main outlines of the programme. A method of presentation is therefore followed which combines generality with exactitude. In the first part of the Estimates are set forth only fairly general amounts covering the main activities of the branches and divisions of each department. The latter part of the volume, however, contains very detailed information in support of each of the foregoing amounts. Since it is the general

[2]*Canada, House of Commons, Debates*, Dec. 18, 1945, pp. 3734-5.

amounts in the first part of the volume that are voted by Parliament this method has the advantage of reducing the number of items to be voted to five or six hundred and, at the same time, provides the members of Parliament with access to more information than could otherwise be given.[3]

The Procedure in Parliament

The procedure followed in Parliament in considering and adopting the Estimates is lengthy and involved. Indeed, if it appears to the reader from the following description that it is better designed to obstruct than to facilitate progress he will not be far from the truth. Such has been the past experience of democratic peoples with their sovereigns that every precaution is taken to prevent arbitrary and precipitate action by the executive. Furthermore, as the following quotation testifies, democratic assemblies require protection, not only from their governments, but also from themselves, and the carefully hedged procedure for voting money serves as a wholesome restraint. The following words are Lord Durham's and appear in his report on conditions in British North America in 1839:

It is necessary that I should also recommend what appears to me an essential limitation on the present powers of the representative bodies in these colonies. I consider good government not to be attainable while the present unrestricted powers of voting public money and of managing the local expenditure of the community are lodged in the hands of an Assembly. As long as revenue is raised, which leaves a large surplus after the payment of the necessary expenses of the civil government, and as long as any member of the Assembly may, without restriction, propose a vote of public money, so long will the Assembly retain in its hands the powers which it everywhere abuses, of misapplying that money. . . . If the rule of the Imperial Parliament, that no money vote should be proposed without the previous consent of the Crown were introduced into these colonies, it might be wisely employed in protecting the public interests, now frequently sacrificed in that scramble for local appropriations, which chiefly serves to give an undue influence to particular individuals or parties.[4]

[3]For further discussion see *Canada, House of Commons, Committee on Public Accounts, Proceedings*, Sessions of 1950 and 1951.
[4]Lord Durham's *Report* (British Parliamentary ed.), p. 117.

Another writer, G. Fenety, speaking from even more intimate knowledge of Canadian affairs, described conditions as they existed prior to the introduction of responsible government and the budgetary system in the province of New Brunswick:

The business of the legislature was conducted with a loose hand. There was no restriction by the Government upon the expenditures; but every member had access to the public chest, in his own way, for the benefit of his constituents, without regard to system, calculation or economy. The Budget was formed not as now by the Provincial Secretary, with the whole Government answerable for it; but in a haphazard way, every member, no matter how outré his ideas of trade, having an equal voice in its preparation. There was no Board of Works at this time. The public moneys were expended on roads, bridges, etc., in accordance with the wants or wishes of the inhabitants of particular districts, affording large jobs sometimes to favorites and active supporters of candidates for the Assembly. The most influential members, whether in the House or with their constituents, generally managed to get the lion's share in the supply distribution.

There seemed to be a great deal of groping in the dark. The Initiation of the Money Votes resting with the House, there was no estimate made by anyone for the respective public services for which moneys were required. There was no individual responsibility in the matter. Members were like vessels at sea without a rudder or compass—subject to the fluctuations of the winds—sums were proposed by any member and carried, for all sorts of purposes, without due consideration as to whether the treasury contained money enough upon call to satisfy the demands. There could have been no better system in the world for running the Province into bankruptcy.[5]

Committee of Supply and Committee of Ways and Means

The procedure followed in Parliament today commences with consideration of the Estimates vote by vote in Committee of Supply, on adoption of the Government's motion to go into Committee. An explanatory word might be appropriate here in connection with the "Committee of Supply" and the "Committee of Ways and Means." There are many small committees of members which sit apart from the House to consider proposed legislation, such as the Banking and Commerce Committee, the Veterans Affairs Committee, and so on; a part of the

[5] G. Fenety, *Political Notes and Observations* (Fredericton, 1867), pp. 30, 203.

membership only constitutes these committees. So vital to parliamentary control are all financial measures, however, that they are not entrusted to small committees but are dealt with only by committees of the whole House. These are the Committee of Supply and the Committee of Ways and Means. In Committee, debate is also more informal than in full session, and the House takes on less of the atmosphere of a forum and more that of a business meeting. The Speaker leaves the Chair, which is taken by the Deputy Speaker who acts in a general way to maintain orderly procedure. The rule that forbids a member from speaking more than once on the same item is relaxed, although he may not speak for more than forty minutes, the general rule in all debates.

Before the Estimates are considered in Committee of Supply the House must first approve the Government's motion that it resolve itself into this Committee. The making of this motion is the occasion for a general debate which provides the members with an opportunity for exercising their historical right to the redress of grievances before granting funds to the Crown. In recent years this motion, along with the motion to go into Committee of Ways and Means and the debate on the Speech from the Throne, has been the occasion for a very broad debate on Government financial and economic policy. The Opposition may move amendments to the motion and if any of these amendments were to be adopted the Government would be defeated. Depending on the intervention of other business the motion may not be passed for some days or weeks after being moved by the Minister, although the total debate may not exceed eight days.

When the House is in Committee of Supply each individual vote is submitted by the Chairman to the Committee for approval as a resolution. It is a rule of parliamentary procedure that no private member may move an increase in any vote, but he may urge that any particular vote be decreased or he may argue in a general way for some policy which would, in the long run, require an amendment to an appropriation. In examining the Estimates ample opportunity is given for discussion of every item in which the members may be interested. The minister of each department is responsible for answering

BUDGETARY SYSTEM, ESTIMATES 287

questions regarding his own department and he is allowed in Committee to have with him on the floor of the House his deputy minister and other departmental officials to assist him. The authoritative words of Mr. Ilsley suggest that the opportunity given to members is not always used for urging that expenditures be reduced, however. On the contrary, Mr. Ilsley said:

We talk about putting a watch on expenditures but how much assistance do we get in this House in watching expenditures? Nine-tenths of the speeches in this House are asking for bigger and better expenditures. That was the case all through the last Parliament. While this session did not start out in that way, it finally got that way. If the Government is making large expenditures it is not because the ministers are trying to make those expenditures; it is because of public and parliamentary demands for those expenditures. That is why the expenditures are being made. At times I feel as though I am against the whole world when I try to keep a lot of these expenditures down. We just do the best we can, that is all, and keep them down.[6]

Consideration of the Estimates in Parliament usually extends over several months, since the discussion of them is adapted to the contingencies of other parliamentary business. In recent years there has been a tendency to leave much of it to the dying days of the session and on many occasions the pressure of other legislation has left time for only a cursory review. This practice has been made less subject to criticism in recent years with establishment of small committees to review the Estimates of a select group of departments each year. In this review most of the information that would ordinarily be presented by the Minister in the House is made available and appears in the printed records of the Committee.

When all the votes in the Estimates have been finally adopted, the Committee of Supply reports to the House. On receipt of this report the Estimates are referred in the aggregate to the Committee of Ways and Means, a formality for the purpose of granting the payment of funds out of the Consolidated Revenue Fund (the repository of all Dominion government revenues) to meet the supply so voted. This is done auto-

[6]*Canada, House of Commons, Debates,* Dec. 18, 1945, pp. 3734-5.

matically and the resolutions are again referred to the House in formal session.

Supply Bill

Up to this point Parliament has approved only resolutions submitted by a minister of the Crown. A resolution has no statutory force. The next step, therefore, is to introduce a bill which embodies in the form of law the same votes as those in the Estimates already adopted by the Committee of Supply. A proposal for an enactment before it is passed by Parliament is known as a bill, and in this case the proposal is called the Appropriation Bill. It must be read by Parliament three times; on second reading there is again an opportunity for debate on the Estimates although in practice this is unusual. Normally, passage of the bill through three readings is a formal procedure, and on completion of the third reading in the House of Commons the bill is sent to the Senate. After three readings there it is ready for the Royal Assent.

Interim Supply

One of the inevitable results of this involved procedure is a delay of many months between the beginning of the fiscal year and the time when authority to make expenditures has been granted by Parliament. While the Estimates are introduced early in the session they are normally almost the last piece of business to be completed; in the meantime the government of the country has been going on. To bridge this gap it has become the practice to pass a bill granting the government "interim supply," that is, some fraction, usually one-twelfth or one-sixth, of the aggregate amount requested in the Estimates. Passage of this bill does not restrict the right of the members to examine any vote in the Estimates at a later time.

SUPPLEMENTARY ESTIMATES

As mentioned above, in addition to the Main Estimates there are other requests for appropriations. These arise out of the difficulty of anticipating for as long a period as fifteen months every contingency that may arise in an organization as

BUDGETARY SYSTEM, ESTIMATES 289

vast as Canada's national government. They are known as the Supplementary Estimates; they are introduced in the same session as the Main Estimates but normally some months later, and cover items omitted from the Main Estimates. Early in the following session Further Supplementary Estimates are usually also introduced to provide for additional expenditures to be made in respect of the fiscal year just closing. The resort to these Estimates in addition to the Main Estimates is, in a sense, inconsistent with the principle of the budgetary system, since by breaking the over-all expenditures into two or three parts the total amounts appropriated are not presented at one time for review. These Estimates do, however, give a necessary element of flexibility to the financial administration of government, and in practice every effort is made to hold the further appropriations to a minimum.

Governor-General's Warrants

It is a basic tenet of responsible government that no expenditures should be made by the executive without parliamentary approval. In theory at least the authority of the federal executive to appropriate funds through Governor-General's Warrants runs counter to this principle. This power is given the executive by statute, in the following terms:

Where an accident happens to any public work or building when Parliament is not in session and an expenditure for the repair or renewal thereof is urgently required, or where any other matter arises when Parliament is not in session in respect of which an expenditure not foreseen or provided for by Parliament is urgently required for the public good, the Governor in Council, upon the report of the Minister that there is no appropriation for the expenditure, and the report of the appropriate Minister that the expenditure is urgently required, may order a special warrant to be prepared to be signed by the Governor General authorizing the payment of the amount estimated to be required for such expenditure.[7]

In actual practice this authority is used very rarely and seldom in recent years have funds been expended by the Dominion government under a Governor-General's Warrant.

[7]Financial Administration Act, Revised Statutes, Canada, 1952, c. 116.

CHAPTER 16

ENACTMENT OF THE TAX LAWS OF THE DOMINION
THE BUDGET SPEECH

DURING THE PERIOD when Parliament has been considering the Estimates it has also heard and debated the annual Budget Speech of the Minister of Finance. In Canada, as in most other countries, this event usually attracts far greater attention than the Estimates debate. The secrecy surrounding the preparation of the speech itself and the very natural interest shown by the public in matters affecting it as closely as changes in the tax rates undoubtedly account for this attraction.

The main purpose of the Budget Speech is to enable the Minister of Finance to present the financial position of the government in a well-rounded statement and to propose any changes in the tax rates deemed to be appropriate to sustain this financial position. In recent years this annual statement has had an increasingly broader horizon. It now includes a comprehensive survey of the financial and economic state of the nation and is used frequently as the vehicle for making announcements affecting government financial or economic policy whose importance is equal to or exceeds that of changes in the tax rates. In the narrower field of governmental financial accounts it sums up the position for the last fiscal year and provides a forecast of the probable position in the year ahead. In making this forecast the Minister takes into account the Main Estimates already presented to the House and makes allowance for Supplementary Estimates likely to come later. He then strikes a balance based on the estimates of revenue from existing taxes and, on the basis of this reckoning, proposes increases or reductions in taxes, as the case may be. If no tax proposals are made, all the existing tax rates remain in effect unchanged, since it is not necessary to re-enact the tax laws in Canada every year. In this important respect the Canadian system differs from that in United Kingdom where the major tax laws must be re-enacted annually.

Preparation of the Budget Speech

The delivery of the Budget Speech, like the presentation of the Estimates, is the final act of a sequence of events on the administrative side of government and the commencement of another series in Parliament. For some weeks prior to the evening when he rises at his desk in the House of Commons to give his budget address, the Minister of Finance is engaged in secret conclaves which have few parallels in the ordinary operations of government. This period of virtual confinement is devoted to an intensive study of an immense variety of problems relating to taxes. Some of these are worrisome technical problems which have accumulated since the last budget; others are major questions of tax policy, often involving entirely new departures into unexplored fields. During this unhappy time the Minister has the comfort and guidance of his colleague, the Minister of National Revenue, whose duty it is to administer the tax laws; his own parliamentary assistants are also present at most of the discussions. He is assisted too by the expert advice of his Deputy Minister and of his departmental officials, who are specialists in tax policy. Also present are the top officials of the Department of National Revenue to advise him on the administrative apects of the great variety of questions considered, and draftsmen from the Department of Justice who must prepare the resolutions and the statutes embodying the tax proposals for Parliament.

Not unnaturally, the arrangement of these meetings takes a pattern very similar to the form of the Minister's Budget Speech. The logical order of procedure is first to receive the best advice available on the economic and financial outlook for the year ahead. The Minister's own Deputy and officials study information obtained from various official sources in arriving at views for presentation to the Minister. The Minister also studies latest reports of the government accounts for the year just closed (or just closing) and is furnished with the best estimate his officials can make at that time of the probable revenues and expenditures of the year ahead. He also considers the government's requirements for cash for purposes outside of the ordinary accounts, such as loans to government enterprises and redemption of debt. These do not affect the budget position in the strictest sense but must be taken into account in considering the over-all financial outlook.

With this information in hand the Minister is in a position to indicate the tax policy that he will follow in his budget announcement. So manifold and complex is the present-day tax structure, however, that if all preparatory work were left to this late stage the budget would be delayed many weeks. On the basis of preliminary indications given by the Minister, the Taxation Division of his department, headed by an Assistant Deputy Minister (not to be confused with the Taxation Division of the Department of National Revenue), has commenced work on proposals many months before this time. Its studies may range from the analysis of the economic effects of some minor commodity tax to the development of a completely revised structure for the personal or corporation income tax. Proposals for revisions of the tax rates and technical amendments to the tax laws are studied and analysed by this division for the Minister. New developments in other countries are kept constantly under review. This work goes on almost the year round and is paralleled by similar studies of trade and tariff conducted in another branch of the Department.

As a result of these preparations, by the time a final indication is given by the Minister of the nature of the tax programme he wishes to present to Parliament, his officials are able almost at once to come forward with specific proposals, which before presentation to him will have been thoroughly reviewed by the Deputy Minister and a small group of advisers in the Department of Finance and in the Department of National Revenue. After the major policy proposals have been studied by the Minister and modified to suit his wishes, a further considerable period is devoted by the Minister to studying, with his officials, the countless "technical" problems which arise under the tax laws. At any time during these discussions the Minister may think it advisable to obtain further expert advice on these problems, and so varied is the subject-matter that on the same day an actuary from the Department of Insurance and a geologist from the Department of Mines and Technical Surveys may be called into consultation. Throughout all of these discussions the lawyers who are to draft the law giving effect to the decisions are constantly present or kept informed of developments, as are also representatives of the Department of National Revenue, whose job it is to administer the law after it has been enacted by Parliament.

While only a handful of the official family confer directly with the Minister during the actual preparation of the Budget Speech, it would be most misleading to suggest that this group alone influences the nature of its contents. Many of the proposals submitted to the Minister have arisen from the steady stream of suggestions and complaints received by him from taxpayers, great and small, the whole year round. To his door, and to the door of his tax specialists, comes a constant parade of members of Parliament, lawyers, accountants, business men, and representatives of trade and other associations, to discuss with him a multitude of proposals for changes in the tax laws. The Minister also hears daily by mail from taxpayers all over Canada, a correspondence which provides a very accurate and sensitive indication of the attitude of the public towards the government's tax policy and often reveals unintentional inequities or anomalies in the tax system. All such letters and briefs are summarized by his officials and presented for his consideration at budget time, for during this period practically all aspects of the tax laws come under review.

When, after the most painstaking study, the Minister's plans have finally reached maturity and have been approved by his colleagues in the Cabinet, and, in accordance with the constitutional requirement, by the Governor-General, they are embodied in the message which has come to be known as the

Budget Speech. So comprehensive is the scope of the speech now that its drafting is the joint work of a group of officials, each an expert in his own field. Some aspects of the presentation, particularly the estimation of the effect on revenues of major tax changes, involve economic and statistical problems of the first order. The preparation of the Economic and Accounting Appendix to the budget, now a printed booklet of many pages, which gives detailed information on economic conditions and the government accounts, is in itself a considerable job. The lawyers must be consulted frequently to be assured that their drafting carries out the intent of the Minister's decisions. Frequently also the Department of National Revenue must carry forward as far as possible the preparations by which a tax change is made known to departmental offices throughout the country on the morrow of the budget. All these activities are carried on in the greatest secrecy.

Budget Night

Finally all is made as ready as it can be and on the day announced by the Minister the elaborate arrangements developed in recent years to give the widest possible publicity to the event are put into operation. It is now the practice to furnish the members of the Parliamentary Press Gallery, of whom there are about a hundred, representing the press associations and individual newspapers throughout Canada, with copies of the speech prior to its delivery. During the afternoon these correspondents are confined under guard to a locked room in the Parliament Buildings where they are allowed to prepare their releases. They are not given their freedom, however, until the Minister has risen in the House at about 8 o'clock in the evening and may only send out their releases from Ottawa with the permission of an official of the Department. During the twenty-four hours prior to the speech sealed parcels will also have been delivered by air mail to cities throughout Canada to be released to a select list of persons on instructions by wire from Ottawa.

Of the nature of the speech itself, little need be added here to what has already been said. Most readers undoubtedly have some familiarity with it as a result of the wide publicity it receives. One feature of its effect on the tax laws is worthy of mention. In Canada, as in England, any tax changes proposed by the Budget Speech are brought into effect immediately. Changes in commodity taxes and the tariff are usually effective from midnight, despite the fact that many weeks will elapse before legislation therefor is enacted. This practice is followed to prevent any avoidance of the new rates, particularly when these are higher. Delay would allow taxpayers to forestall the effect of the proposed increases by heavy buying during the period between the speech and the enactment of the law. The statutory vacuum thus created is filled eventually by having the legislation, when enacted, apply retroactively to the date of the Budget Speech.

The Committee of Ways and Means

In keeping with the custom that all money bills must be considered in Committee before being enacted into law, the Minister introduces his speech by moving that "Mr. Speaker do now leave the Chair for the House to go into Committee of Ways and Means." His speech therefore is delivered in support of this motion and Parliament will not act on his proposals until the motion has been adopted. In concluding his speech the Minister anticipates the adoption of his motion by giving the House explicit notice of the tax changes which the Committee will be asked to approve. These changes are contained in the resolutions, which simply outline in plain language the major tax proposals made in the speech. There is a resolution for each taxing act to be amended, and the individual paragraphs of the resolution detail the proposed changes. They do not necessarily contain every change in the tax law that the Minister will submit but as a general rule any increase in taxes or any major change, whether upwards or downwards, will be set forth in a resolution. Many items of lesser importance are left to be dealt with in the amending bill introduced after the resolutions are adopted.

Normally a week elapses between the delivery of the Budget Speech and commencement of the general debate on the motion to go into Committee of Ways and Means. The debate on the motion provides the members with another field day for a discussion of the financial and economic conditions of the country and the policies of the Government. The speeches on the motion also reflect in a general way the attitude of the country towards the budget proposals. Generally the members of the Opposition conduct almost the entire debate and to an observer unfamiliar with this fact it would appear from its tenor that the budget had been pretty much of a dismal failure. (There have been, of course, such budgets.) The Opposition also moves amendments to the Minister's motion which express lack of confidence in the Government's financial policies; these amendments must be defeated before consideration of the detailed tax proposals can proceed. A period of several days or weeks is often occupied in intermittent debate on the motion, although the total time spent on it may not exceed eight days under the present rules of the House.

Budget Resolutions

With the passage of the Minister's motion (if it were not passed, the Government would fall), the way is clear for the consideration of the budget resolutions. During this consideration the Minister offers a detailed explanation of each paragraph and, in return, hears from the members, particularly those of the Opposition, the complaints and suggestions they have received from their constituents. He will himself have had an opportunity to learn the reaction of the country to his tax proposals during the period following his speech. If he is satisfied that there has been some oversight in any proposal and is willing to have it amended he will move this amendment during the discussion of the resolutions.

Each paragraph of the resolutions is proposed by the Chairman and debate is restricted by the rules of the House to the item being voted although, in practice, this rule appears to be broken as often as it is enforced. The occasion provides the members with a useful opportunity to bring to the Minister's attention any grievances of their constituents and to obtain information from him. As in the case of the consideration of the Estimates the whole system is designed to discourage precipitate action and to allow the fullest possible debate on the Government's proposals. The Minister is allowed to have two or three officials with him to assist him in answering questions when the House is in Committee of Ways and Means.

It should be said here that the debate on the resolutions has both its advantages and disadvantages. Undoubtedly the simple language in which they are expressed enables the members and the public to understand the nature of the proposed tax changes more easily than if they were couched in technical legal phraseology. On the other hand, the exact wording of the statutes giving effect to the general principles stated in the resolutions is of crucial importance. Few of the conditions surrounding the amendment can be expressed in the resolution and to attempt to do so would destroy the value of the resolution as a simple, clear, statement. Unfortunately most of the debate in the House is devoted to the resolutions and the time for considering the amending bills is often quite limited. These can only be introduced after the resolutions are adopted—often late in the session. While this is exactly the same procedure as is followed in the case of the Estimates there is the significant difference that the Appropriation Bill embodying the Estimates votes is in exactly the same form as the votes approved by Parliament in the resolution stage. As will be seen later, in many of the provincial legislatures the resolutions stage, as described here, has been abolished and amending bills are moved for introduction without being preceded by resolutions.

Amending Bills

When all resolutions have been approved by the Committee of Ways and Means a report to this effect is made to the House. Introduction of the amending bills then follows. A separate bill is introduced for each tax law requiring amendment and each separate bill contains all the amendments which are to be made to that act. Here again the procedure in Parliament is designed to give ample opportunity for consideration of the Government's proposals. Each bill must be read three times. As in the case of other bills a full discussion may take place on second reading but because of the extensive debate on the resolutions discussion of the bills is usually limited. A notable departure from the customary procedure was made in 1948 in the case of the new Income Tax Act, which was principally a technical revision of the old Income War Tax Act. The new act, which had been given first reading in the 1947 session, was reintroduced and after second reading was referred to the Banking and Commerce Committee for consideration. The Committee, composed only of a small fraction of the total membership, heard an explanation of the new bill by the Minister of Finance and officials for three days, and then reported the bill back to the House for final approval. The same procedure was followed again in 1957 with the new Estate Tax Act.

The Senate must also act on tax measures but, as in the case of appropriation bills, it makes no major changes although minor proposals have been adopted on occasion when they were acceptable to the Government. The amending bills become acts of the Parliament of Canada when Royal Assent has been given by the Governor-General.

Contrast with Procedure in the United States

The nature of the system of financial administration in Canada may be illustrated by contrasting it with that of the American federal government. In Canada the executive is fully responsible for its expenditure and tax proposals and, with a majority of members in the House of Commons, its measures, although fully considered by Parliament, normally become the law almost unchanged. By contrast, under the system in the United States the Executive, i.e., the President, can only propose to the Congress certain expenditures, or certain changes in the tax laws, which in his view would be desirable. The Congress, and particularly the Congressional Committees, have the real power in formulating the country's expenditure and tax programmes. In some years certain of the tax measures passed by the Congress have been so unsatisfactory to the President that he has exercised his veto.

On the matter of taxes, the President's budget message outlines in very general terms the type of programme he believes the Congress should enact. Having heard the President's budget message the Committee of Ways and Means of the House of Representatives holds public hearings on the President's proposals. Usually the first witness to appear before this Committee is the Secretary of the Treasury who explains in greater detail the nature of the tax programme which the executive believes to be appropriate. But there also appear before the Committee, in the weeks following the submissions of the Secretary, many other witnesses representing individuals, businesses, social and other organizations, who urge alternative proposals on the members of the Committee. Eventually, by combining their own views with all the suggestions so received, including those of the President, the Committee formulates a policy. The extent of variation in this policy from the President's proposals depends largely upon the degree of control exercised by the particular chief executive over the Congress. The Committee submits its proposals to the House of Representatives in the form of a bill ready for enactment. This bill is normally passed by the House of Representatives as presented although occasionally there are amendments.

After passage by the House the measure goes to the Senate, where it is referred to the Senate Finance Committee. Again public hearings are held and very often this Committee will make substantial amendments to the bill as passed by the House of Representatives and recommend quite a different measure for passage by the Senate. Eventually, following a joint meeting of the two Committees, a compromise bill is agreed upon which is then passed by both the House and the Senate.

In keeping with this system of congressional independence it is not surprising that the Committees of Congress have their own staff of tax experts to assist and advise them in developing their tax programmes. This group of experts is known as the Joint Technical Staff of the Congressional Committees. It is a further characteristic of this scheme that the President himself in formulating his tax proposals receives advice from economists and tax experts in addition to the recommendations made to him by the staff of tax experts in the Treasury.

The essential difference between the two methods of enacting tax legislation is that in Canada the executive stakes its life on the passage of its major proposals, whereas this is not at all the case in the United States. Another difference is the opportunity in the United States for full public discussion of all of the executive's proposals and for the submission of counter-proposals. It is questionable whether in Canada this procedure would be consistent with the responsibility of the executive for its financial measures. Arguments have been made, however, by groups in Canada, including the Canadian Tax Foundation, that there may be room for a compromise adaptation of the American system here, in particular to the extent of holding a public hearing on the aspects of the Government's proposals which do not touch Government policy.

No discussion of the budgetary system of the Dominion government would be complete without mention of the important role of the accounting, auditing, and reporting procedures. The actual disbursement of and accounting for funds during the year are under the control of the Comptroller of the Treasury who has a staff in each department which maintains the departmental accounts. At the same time the Auditor-General, who, although he is appointed by the government, may only be removed by Parliament, audits all records on behalf of Parliament and reports annually on the results of his examination. His report, and the Public Accounts, a detailed statement of the revenue, expenditure, and debt transactions for the past year, give Parliament full information on the state of the government's finances. These aspects of the budgetary system are as vital to its proper functioning as are those described above. Unfortunately space does not permit a full discussion of them here.

Chapter 17

ENACTMENT OF THE PROVINCIAL AND MUNICIPAL TAX LAWS

Most of the elements of the budgetary system of financial control just described are present in greater or lesser degree in provincial and municipal governments. The methods of the former resemble very closely the system of the Dominion government, but municipal arrangements present some interesting variations in the underlying principles.

Provincial Budgetary Systems

It need hardly be said that the structure of provincial government in Canada is basically the same as that of the Dominion, the notable difference being that only one province, Quebec, has retained a second chamber of the legislature comparable to the Senate. As in the federal House the sole power to introduce money legislation lies with the executive. The conduct of financial matters is in the hands of the Provincial Treasurer, or, in Quebec, British Columbia, and Newfoundland, of the Minister of Finance, and he must annually render an accounting to the legislature for the past year and seek approval of his expenditure and revenue proposals for the coming year. As in the Dominion Parliament the annual Estimates play a key role in this procedure, but the Budget Speech has a somewhat less important part.

Preparation of the Estimates

The procedure for preparation of the annual Estimates is very similar in all provinces. In most of them the authority responsible for their assembly and analysis is one of the executive or administrative branches of government. These include the Treasury Board in Prince Edward Island, the Executive Council in Nova Scotia, and the Provincial Treasurer or his counterpart in New Brunswick, Quebec, Manitoba, Alberta, and British Columbia.

In Ontario and Saskatchewan special agencies have been established for this purpose. In Ontario by authority of an Order in Council a Budget Committee, consisting of the Provincial Treasurer, his deputy, and three or four other officials of the financial administration, is responsible for, among other matters, the preparation of the Estimates. In Saskatchewan a more formal organization has been set up under the Economic and Advisory Planning Board and given broad powers to assist and direct the operating departments in this phase of their work. The Budget Bureau, as this office is known, has authority to designate an officer in each department to maintain budget supervision, to control the preparation of the budget programme through this officer, and, in consultation with ministers and deputy ministers, to prepare this programme for submission to the Cabinet and eventually to the legislature.[1]

Estimates of both revenue and expenditure, prepared on a uniform basis, are requested of the operating departments in the late fall or early winter. All of the provinces (including Newfoundland) are now on a fiscal year April 1 to March 31, and the general practice, therefore, is to do this preparation well in advance of the new year. Ordinarily several weeks are devoted to this work, and when the forms are completed they are returned to the responsible budgetary authority supported by detailed information and comparisons on the expenditure side of the amount granted or spent in previous years.

When the expenditure estimates have been compiled and analysed, along with the estimates of revenue provided concurrently by the tax collecting departments, the over-all programme is presented by the responsible authority to the Cabinet for final approval. In most provinces there is a financial sub-

[1] For a description of the Budget Bureau see paper delivered by T. H. McLeod at 1953 Annual Conference of the Institute of Public Administration of Canada.

committee of Cabinet known, as in the case of the Dominion government, as the Treasury Board, and the Estimates will have been carefully reviewed by the Board before reaching Cabinet. After a week or two of discussion with his colleagues the Treasurer is prepared to submit the Estimates of expenditure to the legislature for approval. These are printed in a separate volume, the form of which varies from province to province. The general vote by department or branch, with supporting information on the objects of expenditure under the vote, is the most usual pattern.

Legislative Procedure for the Estimates

As in the federal legislature, consideration of the Estimates in the provincial houses is preceded by a motion to go into Committee of Supply. The Budget Speech of the Provincial Treasurer or Minister of Finance is delivered on this motion, and usually accompanies or precedes by a day or two the presentation of the Estimates, which in the provinces replaces the Budget Speech as the legislative surprise package of the year. It would probably be more accurate to say that in the provincial assemblies the Budget Speech and the Estimates are unified in a single presentation, since the marked division between the two phases of financial legislation in the Dominion legislature is not found in the provinces.

Following the Budget Speech there is a general debate on the financial policy of the Government and, on its conclusion (signalled by the adoption of the motion), the Estimates are considered in Committee of Supply. The Committee of Ways and Means performs in the provincial houses only the limited and formal function of voting funds to meet the Estimates after they have been approved by the Committee of Supply. Appropriation bills which receive three readings give final legal effect to the expenditure votes.

The passage of legislation to implement tax changes proposed by the Provincial Treasurer or Minister of Finance in his Budget Speech does not differ greatly from that of any other legislation, except that it is preceded by a message from or resolution of the Lieutenant-Governor. There are no detailed resolutions setting forth each major tax change as there are in the Dominion House. Each bill is introduced and given first reading at once, and full discussion takes place on second reading, when the legislature has before it the full text of the amending bill. By this device the debate on the resolutions as such is omitted. In theory the amendments to the taxing statutes could be introduced at any time during the session; in practice they are proposed in the Budget Speech and introduced shortly after.

The Budget Speech

Brief mention has been made of the role of the Budget Speech in the provincial assembly. While less ambitious in scope than the efforts of the Dominion Minister of Finance the provincial Budget Speech usually contains a survey of economic and financial conditions in the province and, of course, a review of past and projected government finances. The Provincial Treasurer devotes a great deal more time in his Budget Speech than does the Dominion Minister of Finance to a review of the activities, past, present, and future, of most of the major departments of government and in some provinces also discusses the Estimates in detail. As a result of his general financial review the Provincial Treasurer may have some tax changes to announce, the legislative sequel to which has been described above. Although only two or three of the provinces publish any record of the legislative debates, the annual Budget Speech is usually made available in printed or mimeographed form. It can be obtained from the office of the Provincial Treasurer (or Minister of Finance in Quebec, Newfoundland and British Columbia).

Special Warrants

In most provinces in addition to the authority obtained through the Estimates (and Supplementary Estimates) there is also authority to expend moneys without legislative sanction under certain circumstances. It has been indicated earlier that in an emergency the executive of the federal government has authority to spend funds without parliamentary grant through Governor-General's Warrants. Similar authority has been given the executive in most provinces to expend money under Special Warrants in cases of emergency.

While it is not entirely germane to this study, one significant difference between Dominion and provincial accounting practice might well be mentioned here. In the Dominion accounts no real distinction is made between current and capital revenues or expenditures, and when a figure of surplus or deficit is given it represents the balance between the total income and total outlay of the Dominion government. On the other hand the provinces do distinguish between current and capital accounts, and a surplus or deficit figure is usually only the balance between current revenue and current expenditure. To compare surpluses or deficits at the Dominion and the provincial level of government, therefore, the provincial figures must be adjusted to include capital account revenues and expenditures. Quebec and Saskatchewan are exceptions, since in recent years they have struck an "over-all" balance.

Municipal Budgetary Systems

In Canadian local governments the principles of budgetary control are applied with varying degrees of success. While the underlying principles have been intensively studied by municipal authorities both here and in the United States and are by now well understood they have not as yet been as thoroughly applied as at the other levels of government.[1]

In regard to expenditure, of course, the municipalities are as in all other matters subject to the jurisdiction of the provincial governments, and their financial responsibilities are governed by provincial legislation. In most of the provinces there is legislation requiring the preparation of a general budget, and in Manitoba local governments are required by law to submit their budgets to the Department of Municipal Affairs for approval before adoption if the tax rate for general purposes exceeds the statutory limits set out in The Municipal Act. Severe limitations are also imposed on capital expenditures and borrowings

---

[1]They are discussed, for example, in a paper by L. G. Macpherson, Kingston, Ont., presented at the 1950 annual conference of the Institute of Public Administration of Canada, entitled "The Municipal Budget as an Instrument of Administration." Standard works are A. E. Buck, *Public Budgeting* (New York, 1929) and *The Budget in Governments of Today* (New York, 1936). See also various papers and studies presented at the annual conferences of the Municipal Finance Officers' Association, and articles in the periodicals devoted to municipal administration.

of local governments in most provinces. These controls are exercised by the provincial Department of Municipal Affairs or by a separate municipal board. The ratepayers also have the right in most municipalities to vote on any substantial capital expenditures before they can be made.

General Form of Municipal Government

A brief sketch of the general character of municipal and local government in Canada will perhaps assist in understanding municipal budgeting practices. There are several forms of local government designed to meet the needs at one extreme of the densely populated metropolitan area and at the other, of the smallest village or hamlet. Yet, despite this great variety, a fairly common pattern is found. The basic structure of all municipal government is the simple combination of an elected head or chief executive (the mayor or his counterpart) and an elected council.

While the elected mayor (warden, reeve, overseer, etc.) in most cases does not have any greater legal powers than the members of the elected council, as head of the local government his duties and responsibilities are quite extensive. In the larger centres his office is the focal point of most municipal activities. His principal duty in most Canadian municipalities is to exercise general management of and control over the day-to-day operation of the municipal services, which in the great metropolitan areas are very large undertakings. He must sign numerous documents, see many callers, and attend, usually as chairman, meetings of several committees and boards which often deal with important and vexatious problems. By and large the mayor is the work horse of the local government system.

The members of the council are also elected, usually for the same term as the mayor. Their exact duties and powers are set forth in the Municipal Act, Village Act, Town Act, City Act, or the special municipal charter, as the case may be. They include the authorization of expenditures on municipal services and the raising of money through taxes to finance such services, the letting of tenders for municipal projects, and the approval of disbursement of funds for municipal purposes. Meetings of the council are held weekly, bi-weekly, or in the very smallest centres only once or twice a year. Along with the mayor the council performs the duties of the Treasury Board, the Cabinet, the House of Commons, and the Senate of the Dominion government.

Most municipal councils are divided into committees which specialize in the conduct of some particular aspect of municipal affairs. These usually include standing committees on Finance, Social Services or Public Welfare, Fire Protection, Police and Traffic, Tourists, and Parks and Property. There are often also temporary committees set up to deal with municipal undertakings of limited duration. The chairman and members of each committee often take a lively interest in the affairs of the department of civic government falling within their jurisdiction. While a committee does not attempt to govern the day-to-day administration of any civic department and does not normally act on its own initiative without the approval of the council, it is usually looked to for general supervision over the municipal activity assigned to it. In financial matters the authority of the committee often extends to the approval of all estimates and disbursements of funds before they are submitted to the council for approval.

This is the pattern that obtains very generally throughout Canada, making appropriate allowances for differences in the size of the unit of government. In some of the larger cities, particularly in Ontario (those with over 100,000 population),[1] there is a board of control in addition to the head and the council. The controllers, four in number, are elected by all the voters of the municipality, as compared with the aldermen of the council who usually represent only the voters of one district or "ward". The powers of the board of control are extremely broad and their relationship to the council is almost a parallel to the relationship of the executive to the legislature in the higher levels of government. The duties of the controllers in Toronto are described in the City of Toronto *Handbook* for 1960 as follows:

The Board of Control is the executive body of Council and, as such, is responsible for the preparation of the annual estimates, the regulation and supervision of all matters relating to finances and expenditures, the consideration and revision of all by-laws and agreements that may

[1] Ontario cities of over 45,000 population may adopt a board of control with the assent of the municipal electors.

be authorized by the Council; the supervision and control of all books, documents, vouchers and securities belonging to the Corporation; the renting or leasing of any property belonging to the Corporation; the preparation of specifications, calling for tenders and the awarding of all contracts for works, materials and supplies required by the corporation; . . . the carrying on of public works authorized by council and the general administration of the affairs of the city.

It is apparent, as indicated earlier, that the controllers carry part of the burden usually shared by the mayor and council in most municipalities. Under such circumstances the duties and powers of the council are correspondingly circumscribed.

Civic Financial Officials

The above thumb-nail description of the elected portion of the municipal government must be supplemented by mention of certain paid employees. The key administrative officers on the financial side of municipal government are the treasurer, the assessor, and the tax collector. It appears to be one of the problems of municipal financial administration that by definition these officials are all responsible individually to the council, and there is neither co-ordination of their functions nor general supervision of finances at the administrative level. While this arrangement may operate well enough in small units of government, in the larger metropolitan organizations where expenditures run to millions it places an impossible burden on the council. An effort has been made, therefore, to localize responsibility for financial and often for general administration by appointing paid officials such as the city commissioner found in the western cities, the city manager found in many Quebec municipalities and to a lesser degree in other parts of Canada, and the commissioner of finance or clerk-comptroller found in some Ontario municipalities. While the council must assume final responsibility for financial policy these officials are looked to for assistance and guidance. The trend in the smaller municipalities towards consolidation of several positions under one official, such as the clerk-treasurer, the clerk-treasurer-collector, or even the clerk-treasurer-collector-assessor, is further evidence of the movement towards centralized control of municipal administration and of financial administration in particular.

Other Financial Agencies

Agencies outside of the municipal government also play an important role in the budget. These are the provincial Department of Municipal Affairs, municipal boards, and other agencies established by the provincial government. In most provinces provincial supervision is exercised over municipalities in default on debenture debt or otherwise in financial difficulty. Various provincial boards and bureaux must give approval to new debenture issues and in some provinces must approve all capital expenditures, whether or not there is to be a debenture issue. Most municipalities are also required to submit any capital expenditure or debenture issues to the electorate for approval before proceeding with them.

In addition to these authorities superimposed from above the municipal council must make its peace with other boards and bureaux having in some cases a position almost parallel with its own. The most common is the Board of Education, the members of which are elected by the voters independently of the council. These boards have considerable autonomy. They have almost complete power to budget their own requirements for the year and to call on the local municipal council to raise a tax to cover these estimated needs. As a rule the council must meet these indents, and usually is required to pay to the school authority the whole amount requested, whether or not the taxes are collected in that year. There are other boards, however, over which the council exercises a greater degree of control. Typical instances would be Library, Parks, and Health Boards, where the budget is commonly subject to the approval of the council.

Preparation of the Budget

This is the background of the budget at the municipal level. Its actual preparation and execution follow a pattern by now familiar. The chief financial officer of the municipality, usually the city treasurer, assembles the preliminary figures of revenue and expenditure, based on submissions from the operating branches of the local government prepared in November or December preceding the year concerned. Such departmental estimates sometimes come from the departmental heads and less often from the committees of council. The chief financial officer and the committees of council usually work together closely in preparing the estimates, and they are likely to be approved by the Finance Committee before being submitted to the whole council. As a permanent employee, usually of long experience, the chief financial officer can make his greatest contribution by advising against the adoption of plans which in the light of his experience appear to be over-ambitious, and indeed where his position is more than a routine administrative one, he is expected to give such advice. As a routine matter he must analyse the requests for appropriations and prepare them in sufficient detail, with adequate comparisons of expenditures in previous years, to enable the council, some of whose members may not have had any previous experience in this field, to make a judgment of the general character and magnitude of the expenditures proposed. At the same time he will obtain from the Board of Education, and the other boards mentioned above, an estimate of their requirements for submission to the council.

Certain municipal expenditures are fixed and must be met each year. These are mainly the interest charges on the debt and the moneys required to retire the principal of the debt. At the same time there are certain non-tax revenues such as fees which provide a fairly constant revenue that can be determined reasonably accurately in advance. The municipal financial programme as submitted to the council will take account of all these factors, and will include: (a) an estimate of the amount of money required to provide the municipal services during the coming years; (b) the amount of money required to meet the debt charges, both interest and principal; and (c) the amount of revenue to be expected from sources other than taxation.

Adoption by the Council

With this information before it, the council is in a position to approve the financial plans for the coming year—these as a whole are referred to as the "budget" at the municipal level. Almost any newspaper report of council proceedings during the spring months bears evidence of the anguish the councillors undergo in this process, which at best is a thankless and unhappy task, carried on under the watchful eye of critical property owners. By a series of compromises they eventually arrive among themselves at an agreed figure of the total expenditures of the municipality and related boards and bureaux and other activities, undoubtedly guided by their own rough projection of the rate of property tax required to meet the anticipated outlay.

"Striking" the Tax Rate

With the expenditure programme settled the necessary revenue to be obtained by taxation of assessed valuations is calculated by deducting from the proposed expenditures the revenue from other taxes and from non-tax sources. This leaves the council with an amount which will be the basis for "striking" the precise tax rate. This rate is established by dividing the amount of funds to be raised by taxation by the total of the taxable assessment as shown by the assessment rolls. The resulting rate is in most municipalities stated as a certain number of mills on the dollar.

Following the depression period when many municipalities went into default and others found themselves in serious financial difficulties, the practice of operating on a pay-as-you-go basis has become quite common, particularly in the larger centres. Under this plan provision is made in the budget for the non-collection of a certain proportion of the tax levy. This is accomplished by reducing the estimated yield by some fraction representing the expected delinquencies and increasing the tax rate in proportion. When municipalities are reaping the benefits of a generally high level of income this practice, combined with the payment of arrears of tax, has the effect of creating a reserve against bad times. In short the municipal tax rate on property is levied on the assumption that only a part of the taxes will be collected whereas in the long run a substantial part of the tax arrears are made good. Cyclical budgeting, therefore, is not limited entirely to the Dominion and provincial governments.

The estimates of any municipality are usually available for public distribution and a study of their contents gives a bird's eye view of the functions performed by the local governments of Canada.

Chapter 18

DOMINION TAX ADMINISTRATION
DIRECT TAXES

THE INSTITUTIONS and processes of government that create tax laws in Canada have been examined in preceding chapters. It is proposed now to examine the complicated machinery that is used in the day-to-day operation of tax collection under these laws. Attention will be devoted to the national administration, where one may find writ large almost all the problems encountered in tax collection, with the notable exception of those peculiar to property tax. These have been touched on briefly in the chapter on municipal taxation.

The Department of National Revenue

In the national government there are two separate departments that deal with taxes, each headed by its own minister and each performing a separate function. These are the Department of Finance and the Department of National Revenue. The part played by the Minister of Finance and his department in the formulation of tax policy has been described in the preceding chapters. His department collects no taxes. This job is carried out under another minister of the Crown, the Minister of National Revenue, who is head of a separate organization devoted exclusively to the administration of the tax laws. While there is the closest co-operation and liaison between the two departments their spheres of activity are quite distinct. The difference in their functions is best illustrated by the relative size of the staffs engaged in this work. In the Department of Finance there are at most half a dozen employees constantly engaged in tax work, all of them in Ottawa, while the Department of National Revenue has about 15,300 employees, mainly in its tax offices throughout the Dominion. These employees administer all the major federal taxes, including the income taxes, the death duties, the customs tariff, the sales and other indirect taxes.

The Department was established in 1927 under the Department of National Revenue Act[1] and represents a consolidation of what had at one time been three departments or branches of departments. In 1921 the Departments of Customs and Inland Revenue had been joined under one minister as the Department of Customs and Excise. In 1924 the income tax administration of the Department of Finance was added and in 1927 the whole became the Department of National Revenue. For many years the permanent heads were the Commissioners of Customs, Excise, and Income Tax respectively. However, in 1943 the last was reclassified as the Deputy Minister of National Revenue for Taxation and the work of the first two was consolidated under the Deputy Minister of National Revenue for Customs and Excise. These deputy ministers are today the permanent operating heads of the "Taxation" and "Customs and Excise" Divisions respectively of the Department. The work of these two divisions is divided roughly between the collection of the direct taxes on one hand and the indirect on the other, and for that reason their functions are dissimilar in many respects.

The Taxation Division

The Taxation Division at the present time administers the following statutes:

1. The Income Tax Act (including the withholding tax on non-residents and the gift tax) and its predecessor, the Income War Tax Act.

2. The Succession Duty Act, and its successor, The Estate Tax Act, 1958.

The Taxation Division is today the larger of the two main units of the Departments, a fact attributable to the prominent

[1]Revised Statutes, Canada, 1952, c. 75.

role played by direct taxation during the war and post-war years. Prior to the war total collections only in rare years reached the $100 million mark, and more frequently were half that amount. By the fiscal year 1943–4 they had soared to $1,635 million, and in 1959–60 had risen to nearly $3,150 million. Immediately prior to the war the returns of 200,000 individuals and 15,000 corporations were being processed, and today there are over 4 million individual and 80,000 corporate taxpayers. In addition over 1½ million returns are received from non-taxable individuals and 22,000 from co-operatives and inactive corporations, as compared with 200,000 non-taxable returns prior to the war. With this increase in the volume of work associated with normal tax collection procedure the Division has also assumed new functions, including the deduction of tax at the source, the administration of death taxes, and the compilation of statistics essential for national income computation and other purposes.

The handling of this increased volume of work has required an expansion in the staff of the Division. Between 1939 and 1949 the number of employees rose from about 1,300 to nearly 12,000. The latter figure undoubtedly represented a peak attributable to the drive to liquidate the backlog of assessment accumulated during the war, when heavy new burdens were being placed on the Division at a time when there was a serious shortage of trained accountants and other help. Despite the continuing heavy load, by improving its methods and employing mechanized equipment the Division has been able to reduce its staff substantially. At March 31, 1960, total staff was 7,794.

An historical summary of the total collections, the number of employees, and the cost of collections for the period 1937 to 1960 is given in Table XIV.

Figures of this magnitude attest to the fact that the Taxation Division represents an administrative organism having few peers in either private or public business in Canada. It would be foolhardy, therefore, to attempt to describe in anything but the most general terms the functions of an organization so vast and complex. The minutiae of its administrative techniques lend

TABLE XIV

TAXATION DIVISION, DEPARTMENT OF NATIONAL REVENUE, 1937–1960

Fiscal years	Total revenue collections[1] ($000)	Number of employees[2]			Total cost of collection[1] ($000)
		At head-quarters	In local offices	Total	
1937	102,365	196	1,018	1,214	2,132
1938	120,366	200	1,061	1,261	2,255
1939	142,026	204	1,087	1,291	2,426
1940	134,449	205	1,110	1,315	2,488
1941	272,138	246	1,509	1,755	2,891
1942	652,368	281	2,127	2,408	3,840
1943	1,378,043	328	3,404	3,732	5,443
1944	1,635,495	382	4,743	5,125	7,960
1945	1,555,814	467	5,954	6,421	9,926
1946	1,453,373	514	6,595	7,109	11,796
1947	1,435,732	587	6,843	7,430	13,735
1948	1,317,707	842	9,636	10,478	19,628
1949	1,368,341	853	10,848	11,701	28,062
1950	1,300,782	731	9,886	10,617	28,104
1951	1,556,876	550	6,448	6,998	25,174
1952	2,204,046	480	5,772	6,243	21,874
1953	2,593,961	n/a	n/a	6,772	21,810
1954	2,618,041	,,	,,	7,253	22,931
1955	2,456,965	,,	,,	7,492	25,676
1956	2,501,938	,,	,,	7,407	26,095
1957	3,017,244	,,	,,	7,277	28,431
1958	3,066,202	,,	,,	7,528	31,199
1959	2,709,476	,,	,,	7,237	31,800
1960[3]	3,147,580	,,	,,	7,794	31,600

[1]From Department of National Revenue, *Taxation Statistics*. Includes Old Age Security income taxes from 1952 on.
[2]Number of employees on payroll in March of fiscal year. In 1952 and 1958 small categories of employees not previously included were added so the later figures are not strictly comparable with the earlier ones. The breakdown between headquarters and local office staffs was also discontinued after 1952. Post-1952 figures from Dominion Bureau of Statistics monthly bulletin *Federal Government Employment*; earlier ones from annual bulletins *Federal Civil Service Employment and Payrolls* and *Summary Statistics of the Civil Service of Canada*.
[3]Preliminary.

themselves to generalization about as readily as a railway timetable. At the cost, however, of some blurring of details an attempt will be made to give a general perspective of its operation.

In a bird's-eye view the functions of the Division fall under three main headings:

1. Taxpayer Compliance: to assure as far as possible that a return has been filed by or for every individual, corporation, or estate subject to tax.

2. Tax Assessment: to determine as far as possible that the return filed is an accurate statement of the income (or estate, etc.) and a correct calculation of the tax.

3. Tax Collection: to collect the actual amount of tax payable (or refund any over-payment).

Taxpayer Compliance

In the administration of the income tax, possibly to an extent greater than for any other tax, all taxpayer compliance begins with the Tax Roll. By its nature an income tax must rest so heavily on the responsibility of each individual taxpayer that the Tax Roll becomes an essential arm of effective collection.

The Tax Roll is an index maintained in each district office showing the names, addresses, and other relevant information for the taxpayers in that district. It is compiled and kept up to date by a staff which devotes its full time to this work. Information for building up and maintaining the individual Tax Roll listings is obtained from many sources, including returns filed in previous years and names reported by employers making payroll deductions. Industrial and trade association directories are also constantly combed for the names of new business firms which are not on the Tax Rolls. At the present time the Tax Rolls list approximately 7 million names of persons or organizations who either are, have been, or may become taxpayers. One of the major problems encountered, and at the same time one of the principal reasons for the vital importance of the Tax Roll, is the constant migration of taxpayers from one income tax district to another. A taxpayer may work in as many as three or four districts during a year and file his return in the office of the district where he resides, on April 30 of the following year.

DIRECT TAXES 317

To keep track of such taxpayers requires constant cross-checking of the Tax Rolls and a steady exchange of information and documents between district offices. Recently substantial economies and increased efficiency have been achieved by consolidating the Files service with the Tax Roll work. The Division has over 6 million active files, and there is a natural and close relationship between the two phases of activity.

The Tax Roll plays a prominent part each year when the annual returns are being filed. By a process of eliminating or earmarking the names of taxpayers whose returns have been received the Tax Roll is reduced to a record of those who are late or delinquent. Of course no return may have been filed because there was no taxable income (a privilege allowed individuals but not corporations) but not even on this account would the taxpayer's listing be removed from the Tax Roll. It will remain there for future reference.

Tax Assessment

As used in the Division the word "assessment" may cover any operation from a simple arithmetical check of a taxpayer's return completed in a few minutes to an investigation into the financial affairs of a large corporation extending over many months or years. A considerable amount of assessment is desk work performed by the assessor in the office, only rarely requiring visits to or conferences with the taxpayer. Particularly is this true of the returns of individual taxpayers not in business, of whom only a minority have incomes of a character that cannot be reasonably verified from information returns received from employers, banks, dividend-paying companies, and other sources. Outside assessment work involving an audit of the taxpayer's own records is carried out at more or less regular intervals not only with the large corporations but also with the medium and smaller businesses and professions, such as retailers, farmers, doctors, lawyers, and so on. Because of their wholesome effect on taxpayer compliance, periodic assessments are made as frequently as staff and other conditions will permit.

Each return is assessed in the first instance in the district office. In the case of both corporations and individuals all but certain classes of returns are now dealt with finally in the field, without any further audit in the head office at Ottawa. The former division of assessment work into separate and distinct compartments for corporations, individuals, successions, and special investigation, has been abolished in favour of one combined operation in which all returns in a given class of business are under joint assessment. In discussing these changes the Deputy Minister of the Division explained: "One purpose is to obtain better co-ordination between the various functions of the Division. Another purpose is to encourage decentralization and a greater measure of District Office autonomy."[2]

It has been said by accountants that the income tax laws have given rise to most of the present-day accounting problems. No one is more aware of this than the income tax assessor. In his work he must be prepared to deal with an endless variety of accounts. He must instinctively detect any weakness in a balance sheet or profit and loss statement and be able to adapt his training and experience to the variations of bookkeeping practice employed by individual firms. A high degree of skill and experience is necessary for this work, and the Taxation Division employs more professional accountants than any other organization in Canada.

The investigation work of the Special Investigation Branch of the Division might appropriately be mentioned here. The Branch is a post-war innovation. If evidence of doubtful practices is uncovered by an assessor it may be able to conduct an investigation leading to the revelation of fraud or tax evasion. Its activities must necessarily be of a secret character. Investigations stem usually from information uncovered by the assessors but may be received also from other sources, including informers. The members of the Branch do not make use of the sensational methods of their fellow sleuths, the T-Men of the United States Treasury, but some good work for sound tax administration has been done quietly on several occasions.

[2]Address of Mr. Charles Gavsie, Deputy Minister of the Taxation Division, Department of National Revenue, before the annual conference of the National Tax Association at Toronto, September 1952, as reported in the *Tax Bulletin* of the Canadian Tax Foundation, Sept.-Oct., 1952.

Tax Collection

Finally, there is the important business of collecting the tax. Nowadays a considerable proportion of the amount due from individuals is withheld at the source through wage and salary deductions, or is paid in quarterly or monthly instalments by individuals and corporations, as required by law. This facilitates tax collection immensely in many ways although the introduction of pay-as-you-go in itself brought a new function to the Division requiring the establishment of a Tax Deduction Section in each local office. Its job is to check all employers constantly to make sure that they are complying with the requirements of the law regarding the deduction of tax from employees, to receive the cash actually deducted by employers, and to audit their tax deduction records. This unit assures both employer and employee that the moneys withheld from the employee's payroll are accounted for properly to the government.

The balance of the tax is payable with the annual returns, and the great flood of cash payments prior to April 30, when the annual tax returns are filed by individuals, begins a period of intense activity on the part of the cashiers and accounting units of the local offices reminiscent of Christmas time in a department store. The cheques or other payments which accompany the tax returns must be removed with dispatch from the hundreds of thousands of envelopes and deposited in the government's bank accounts. At the same time a record of the payment must be made, and as soon as possible the taxpayer and the appropriate branches of the local office must be notified of its receipt. As returns are assessed the assessors provide information as to the amount of the final tax liability determined by them, and the taxpayer is notified of the deficiency, if any. If he does not pay up in due course his file is turned over to the collection section for appropriate action.

As in any other large organization a great deal of bookkeeping and paper work can readily creep into and stultify an operation of this character, and studies are constantly in progress to speed up the processes wherever this is possible without prejudice to the revenue. The consolidation of the former Accounting, Collections, and Cashiers units into one unit is typical of the changes made as a result of these studies. In recent years also taxpayers have reaped the benefit of new and faster methods of assessing and accounting, with the result that most returns are currently being settled up within a fortnight of their receipt.

In brief outline these are the main duties of the district income tax office. In detail the exact procedures undoubtedly vary from office to office and quite different techniques may be employed under certain circumstances. An administrative set-up appropriate to a highly industrialized area may not be at all suitable for an agricultural district. All operations of the district office are under the charge of a Director, who is responsible to headquarters in Ottawa. In this work he is usually assisted by a deputy, and the Personnel Branch of the local office also is of particular importance, charged as it is with the recruiting and promotion of staff under the supervision of head office and of the Civil Service Commission. A statistical unit in each local office extracts from the taxpayers' returns filed there the information required for tabulation and analysis by the Statistics section at head office. The statistical by-products of income tax administration are now of immeasurable value in many economic studies, particularly in the compilation of statistics of national income.

Each district office also contains a separate unit to administer the death duties acts, a function closely integrated with the general income tax administration. This aspect of the work could in itself provide material for an extensive study, for it involves almost as wide a range of legal and accounting problems as does the income tax. The unit bears the responsibility for obtaining complete and proper reports on the assets, liabilities and bequests of estates, the checking of values of assets, liabilities, debts, etc., the issuing of notices of assessment and the collection of the duties, the releasing of assets, and so on. Study of income tax returns of deceased persons is closely correlated with gift tax and death duty work, both to expedite the settlement of income tax and death duty claims and also to disclose any inconsistencies between the taxpayer's financial position at death and the

DIRECT TAXES 321

amount of income he has reported during his lifetime. A final accounting of a taxpayer's worth at death sometimes gives the lie to his income tax returns of earlier years.

Head Office

For most taxpayers acquaintance with the Taxation Division begins and ends at the district office. The head office in Ottawa, however, provides many essential advisory and supervisory services for the national organization. One of the major concerns in an organization as large and as far flung as the Taxation Division is to maintain uniformity of practice in all its parts. This can only be accomplished through a strong chain of direction and co-ordination, in which the head office is the vital link.

In some respects the internal organization of the head office is similar to that of the district offices. As indicated above certain returns are audited again at head office after assessment by the district office and there is therefore, at the present time, an Assessment Branch at Ottawa. This branch is divided into Sections "A" and "B," each with units dealing with specialized areas of assessment. Other sections of the Branch include Special Investigations and Estate Tax, Succession Duties and Gift Tax.

Some of the head office units have no parallel in the district offices and of these by far the most important is the Legal Branch. This branch is responsible for giving all interpretations on questions of law that arise throughout the national administration and rulings on legal aspects of assessments or appeals, for the consideration of the adequacy of legal evidence for prosecutions in Court, for the preparation of cases for trial and the prosecution of such cases for the Department, for interviewing taxpayers and their solicitors, and in general for providing an essential over-all guidance to the whole Department on legal matters. Since the work of the Taxation Division is comprised entirely of the administration of statutes the Legal Branch, which is charged with the interpretation of these statutes, plays a most important role.

A separate division of the Legal Branch deals only with appeals from assessments, which, with the establishment of the Tax Appeal Board, now run to many hundreds every year.

The increased attention to administrative organization in recent years is reflected in the variety of functions now included in the Administrative Services Branch and also in the establishment of a new entity, the Planning and Development Branch. Under the former are included the numerous activities related to recruiting, training, and housing the staff, printing, accounting, mechanical equipment, public information, and other similar functions. The latter carries out studies in methods, computer application, and the compilation of statistics.

A final Branch—Inspection Services Branch—is responsible for the maintenance of efficiency in the local offices by periodic visits and studies.

CHAPTER 19

DOMINION TAX ADMINISTRATION
INDIRECT TAXES

THE INDIRECT TAXES imposed by the Dominion are administered by the Customs and Excise Division of the Department of National Revenue, under the following statutes: (1) the Customs Act; (2) the Customs Tariff Act; (3) the Excise Tax Act; (4) the Excise Act.

Until the last decade the Customs and Excise Division had been considerably the larger of the two divisions of the Department because of the historic reliance of the Dominion on indirect taxes. As a result it did not experience the spectacular wartime growth of the Taxation Division either in revenue collections or in staff. Nevertheless, revenue collections today are at roughly six times the pre-war level, and this growth has been accompanied by an increase in the total staff of this Division from about 4,400 to about 7,500, a rise of approximately 40 per cent. The great majority of these employees are situated in the local "ports," "outports," and "vessel clearing stations" throughout Canada, of which at December 31, 1960, there were 281, 119, and 55 respectively. Of the total staff of 7,541 at the same date only about 10 per cent were at headquarters in Ottawa. The largest staffs outside Ottawa are located in the importing and manufacturing centres of Montreal and Toronto.

Table XV presents for each year from 1937 to 1960 the total collections, the number of employees, and the cost of the collections of the Customs and Excise Division.

CUSTOMS ADMINISTRATION

Of all branches of tax administration the Customs is one of the oldest in almost every country. For nearly two-thirds of

TABLE XV

THE CUSTOMS AND EXCISE DIVISION, DEPARTMENT OF NATIONAL REVENUE

TOTAL REVENUE COLLECTIONS, NUMBER OF EMPLOYEES, AND TOTAL COST OF COLLECTION, FISCAL YEARS 1937 TO 1960

Fiscal years	Total revenue collections[1] ($000)	Number of employees[2]			Total cost of collection[3] ($000)
		At head-quarters	In local offices	Total	
1937	295,228	578	3,729	4,307	9,087
1938	341,663	598	3,925	4,523	9,324
1939	307,420	524	3,891	4,415	9,474
1940	346,004	536	3,849	4,385	9,576
1941	527,419	555	3,594	4,149	9,337
1942	738,274	552	3,697	4,249	9,588
1943	795,088	495	3,722	4,217	9,728
1944	1,007,391	480	3,680	4,160	9,737
1945	1,067,524	482	3,803	4,285	10,165
1946	975,357	527	4,135	4,662	10,805
1947	1,066,595	552	4,441	4,993	12,611
1948	1,163,743	616	4,936	5,552	14,246
1949	1,102,397	640	5,136	5,776	17,304
1950	1,054,213	650	5,436	6,086	19,696
1951	1,256,520	664	5,530	6,194	20,855
1952	1,514,255	669	5,606	6,275	23,854
1953	1,664,837	n/a	n/a	6,654	25,467
1954	1,726,652	,,	,,	6,790	26,972
1955	1,650,871	,,	,,	7,201	29,296
1956	1,849,564	,,	,,	7,235	29,995
1957	2,051,491	,,	,,	7,386	33,375
1958	2,001,159	,,	,,	7,717	36,493
1959	1,984,909	,,	,,	7,710	36,944
1960	2,189,529[4]	,,	,,	7,541	36,900[4]

[1]From annual *Report of the Department of National Revenue*. Includes Old Age Security Sales Tax from 1952 on.

[2]Number of employees on payroll in March of fiscal year. In 1952 and 1958 small categories of employees not previously included were added so the later figures are not strictly comparable with the earlier ones. The breakdown between headquarters and local office staffs was also discontinued after 1952. Post-1952 figures from Dominion Bureau of Statistics monthly bulletin *Federal Government Employ-*

INDIRECT TAXES 325

the period since Confederation the tariff was relied on for almost the entire national revenue and it is not surprising therefore that the procedures of this branch of tax administration have reached a greater maturity than has yet been attained in the newer and more recent forms of taxation.

The essence of tariff administration can be reduced to two principal problems: (a) to ensure that all imports into Canada enter through and under the inspection of the customs port; and (b) to ensure that the proper amount of duty, if any, is collected on the imports so admitted.

Under the first heading obviously falls the unrelenting battle against smuggling, an occupation as old as customs tariffs themselves. Every collector and examiner is constantly on guard against smuggling through the Customs ports, but the big task of patrolling isolated points on the thousands of miles of Canada's border is carried on by the Royal Canadian Mounted Police. By motor car, plane, and boat this vigil is maintained in all weathers, and a glance at the map of Canada is enough to demonstrate the magnitude of the problem. Nowhere else in the world is there a border as long and accessible as that between Canada and United States, where some towns are even found located partly in one country and partly in the other. Drastic powers are given and used in this battle, and to protect the revenues the preventive services have almost unparalleled rights of search and seizure under the Customs Act.

This aspect of customs administration undoubtedly presents fascinating possibilities worthy of further exploration but they must be foregone for the more prosaic and positive functions of revenue collection. In the main these are directed to getting control over goods being imported into Canada and holding them until the duty, if any, has been paid. At the base of this procedure is the system of "manifesting." Under this system the master (or purser) of a ship arriving in a Canadian port must proceed at once to the Customs office and give in the greatest detail, under oath, a written report known as a "Ship's Report

---

ment; earlier ones from annual bulletins *Federal Civil Service Empolyment and Payrolls* and *Summary Statistics of the Civil Service of Canada*.

³From Dominion *Public Accounts*.

⁴Preliminary.

Inward" regarding his voyage, his officers, passengers, crew, and cargo. He will incur severe penalties for unloading or even breaking open his cargo before he has so reported and obtained the necessary clearances (to be described later). Similarly, every carrier of freight by land, whether it be a motor transport, railway, or any other transport, must immediately on importation of goods into Canada file a "Report Inward" giving a description of the goods being imported.

Travellers in charge of a vehicle such as a motor car, boat, aeroplane, etc., and every person arriving on foot must also declare the goods in their possession, whether dutiable or not, and every person is enjoined by law to "truly answer all questions respecting such goods" and the vehicle in which they are being imported. The average traveller arriving at a Canadian port is hardly aware of the immense and complicated organization which supervises the importation of the vast quantities of merchandise which annually come into Canada through commercial channels. He is dealt with politely but firmly by a Customs officer, pays what duty, if any, is required of him, and goes on his way.

For commercial importation on a large scale, the process is more complex. Having filed a report inwards, the bonded carrier or his agents discharge the cargo into a sufferance warehouse, which is under Customs control, and possession of the goods can only be obtained by the importer or his broker by making "due entry" on a form prescribed by the Department and paying whatever duties and taxes are owing. Goods proceeding beyond the original port of entry travel "under manifest" to the ultimate port of destination, where they are placed in sufferance warehouse, and may be obtained by the importer on completion of the formal entry. This must be done within a specified time and the entry form, which shows the nature of the goods imported, their value for duty, the rate of duty, and sales tax applicable and the amount payable, must be accompanied by invoices describing the goods in detail, along with a certificate subscribed to by the exporter as to the country of origin of the goods imported and the accuracy of the value given for them.

At this point the second principal problem of tariff administration begins to emerge, namely, the determination of the proper amount of duty.

The first step is taken in this process by clerks who, under the direction of the collector of the port, check the correctness of the entry as far as possible from the invoices submitted with it, verify the computation of the duty, and so on. The computing clerk must also designate from the information given in the entry the packages of goods to be sent to the appraisers for examination. Before these goods are examined, on the certification of his entry by the clerk the importer either pays his duty or posts bond for it, and obtains possession of his goods, with the exception of the portions retained for examination. It would, of course, be too expensive and quite impracticable to retain all goods in the Customs warehouse until the appraisers have completed their work, and arrangements are usually made for the immediate release of perishable goods on the posting of a bond for the duties. But the importer does not obtain absolute control over his goods until his samples have been examined, and by law he may not open the goods within three days after the samples have been delivered for examination, although this rule is not followed in practice. By law the goods are also subject to recall at any time within ten days if the appraiser so requires.

The appraiser is an important figure in customs administration, since he must determine as reasonably as possible the value of the goods for duty purposes and the tariff item under which they belong. This task is undoubtedly facilitated by the fact that he has in his possession a representative sample of the goods to be appraised and he also has the importer's entry and invoices. Nevertheless, his task is difficult enough for he must determine the value for duty of imported goods as "the fair market value, at the time when and place from which the goods were shipped to Canada, of like goods when sold in like quantities for home consumption in the ordinary course of trade under fully competitive conditions and under comparable conditions of sale,"[1] and where these conditions do not exist rules are provided for other circumstances (s. 35, ss. (3) to (11)). His target, therefore, is not value at Canadian prices but value at

[1]Customs Act, s. 35 (2).

prices abroad. When the attendant complications of exchange adjustments, trade discounts, shipping charges, packaging allowances, rentals, royalties, and so on, are taken into account the calculations involved are seen in their full complexity. To perform his job efficiently he must be an expert in many aspects of industry, a requirement not diminished by the practice in recent years of having an appraiser deal only with one general class of imports such as hardware, textiles, machinery, or a similar general category.

Given an appraiser endowed with ability and probity the over-all degree of efficiency in valuation of imports and classification for duty purposes will undoubtedly depend on the extent to which examination is carried. The Customs Act requires that every package of goods imported bear marks or numbers and under the Act the collector has authority to order that up to one package in ten and such further packages as he may deem advisable may be sent to the examining warehouse for appraisal. When he is satisfied that all packages in the shipment contain similar goods he has power to require the examination of a smaller number. When it is realized that in the fiscal year 1960 the number of import entries at Customs ports in Canada exceeded 4,000,000, each entry often including many individual items, the magnitude of the problem of appraisal and selection becomes apparent. No hard and fast rule can be devised that is satisfactory under every circumstance.

The appraiser at the local port is not left entirely to his own resources, however. At headquarters in Ottawa control is exercised over the port administration by the entry checking section of the Dominion Customs Appraisers Branch. The former receives from the port a copy of each entry and the supporting invoices. These are checked not only to verify the calculations of the duty (and sales tax) but also to ensure that the proper rate of duty has been determined by the appraiser according to the description of the goods. If this verification cannot be made from the information available on the entry or the invoices frequently the checking section will call for samples or further data to be submitted to the Appraisers Branch for proper classification. The checking section also informs the local collector of any additional duty to be collected or refund to be paid on completion of the investigations.

The Director of the Appraisers Branch and his staff at Ottawa act as an internal board of referees on appraisals referred to them. Matters of doubtful appraisal may come to them both from within the departmental headquarters and from the appraisers at the local Customs port. This branch deals with questions of rates and classifications of imports and with valuations. There is also a laboratory attached to the branch at Ottawa for making chemical and other analyses of imported goods.

When a decision has been given by the Customs appraisers an importer has several means of appeal if he feels that he has a case relating either to classification or valuation which deserves further review. The Deputy Minister (Customs and Excise) may first review the decision of any appraiser. If the importer is not satisfied with the Deputy Minister's decision he may then lodge an appeal with the Tariff Board within sixty days. The Board, established in 1931 to succeed the former Board of Customs, has full power to give a decision on the rate of duty, on the value for duty, on exemption from duty, or on any other matter subject to appeal. Further, on a question of law either the importer or the Deputy Minister may carry the case to the Exchequer Court and a still further appeal may then be taken to the Supreme Court.

In this description of the process of importing goods into Canada through Customs it has been assumed that the customs transaction has been fully completed by the importer. In some cases this has not been done, and if due entry is not made or the duties are not paid within one month the goods are placed on the unclaimed list and removed from the sufferance warehouse to the Queen's Warehouse, where they are held pending sale by auction in due course or are claimed by the importer after paying duty and taxes and warehouse charges. The proceeds of the sale apply to the payment of duties and any other charges and the balance is turned over to the owner of the goods.

The one exception to the general rule that duties must be paid immediately upon entry is where the goods are entered "for warehouse." Under the warehousing system goods may be removed to approved and secure premises under the custody of the Customs authorities. The goods so stored may be later entered "ex-warehouse for export," or "for consumption" and in the latter case duties and taxes are then payable at the values as entered for warehouse, and at the tariff rates in effect when ex-warehoused.

This bare outline of the customs side of the Division gives a picture of the main functions; these are supported by other related and subsidiary offices. The latter include the Inspection Service, which has the task of maintaining efficiency by periodic visits to the local ports; the Investigation Service, which investigates false entries, importation or entry of goods at lower than proper duties and values, etc.; the Drawbacks Branch, which investigates claims for refunds of duties when goods are processed and re-exported from Canada or are entitled to lower duties by use; the Law Branch, serving both the Customs and Excise organizations, whose duty it is to give initial interpretations on questions of law, to prosecute in the courts delinquents in sales and excise tax payment where legal process is resorted to, and offenders on smuggling or other charges; the Seizures Branch, which is charged with the disposition of the goods seized by Customs officers under the various circumstances which give rise to this penalty; the Port Administration Branch and the Accommodation Branch, the Equipment and Supplies and Stamps Branch, the Records Branch, and the Personnel Branch, all dealing largely with the internal housekeeping of the Division. It should also be mentioned, of course, that the figures of foreign trade now compiled from a duplicate copy of the entry by the External Trade Branch of the Dominion Bureau of Statistics are also a direct by-product of the administration of the customs tariff. Traditionally the Division has also acted for other departments of government in the administration of many statutes requiring border controls and inspections.

Excise Administration

Having drawn a distinction between the main functions of customs collection and excise administration it will now be convenient to make a secondary division of activities between the administration of excise duties and that of excise taxes. The nature of the distinction between excise duties, levied under the Excise Act, and excise taxes, levied under the Excise Tax Act has already been explained. It will be recalled that the former apply only on tobacco and alcoholic products, while the latter are imposed on a variety of commodities and services, the principal excise tax being the general sales tax. The procedures followed in collecting these two forms of impost are markedly different and they will be dealt with separately.

Excise Duties Administration

The administration of excise duties has one feature in common with that of customs duties, i.e., the almost complete absence of a collection risk. Whereas the major problem in nearly every other form of tax administration is actually to collect the revenue, it has almost no relevance for customs duties because of the system of rigid control outlined in the previous pages. Similarly the collection of the excise duties is almost never at risk because of the method of licensing and bonding of manufacturers of exciseable goods.

The habitat of the exciseman is the brewery, the distillery, and the cigar, tobacco, and cigarette factory. Not only are these his native surroundings but in many instances they provide his abode during his working hours, since in some of the larger establishments, particularly in tobacco factories and distilleries, a staff of half a dozen or more employees of the Department is almost constantly on the premises. In smaller centres it is only necessary to have the staff available in the local departmental office for periodic visits.

The exciseman is less a tax collector than a combination of policeman, accountant, and chemist. He rules this field of manufacturing with almost undisputed sovereignty. No person may enter on any of the activities subject to excise without first obtaining a licence, renewable annually, from the Department of National Revenue, the granting of which is by no means automatic. A licence is issued only after the location of the buildings, the plan of construction, the nature, dimensions, capacity, and arrangement of the equipment, and many other details, have been submitted to and approved by the Department. It is provided by law, for example, that the Department may not issue a licence for a building or premises which appear "to be so situated with reference to surrounding buildings or places of business, or to be so constructed or arranged, as to embarrass or endanger the full collection of the revenue."[2] The fees for licences are not high but the requirements for obtaining them are very rigid.

Not only must a licence be obtained under the above circumstances but the brewer, distiller, cigar or cigarette manufacturer, must also provide a bond to guarantee the payment of the duties on his product; and the giving of this bond is a condition to the granting of the licence. The Excise Act sets forth the amount of bond that must be provided for each class of licensee. The bonding is usually graduated according to the capacity of the plant and must be increased for any extension of capacity or for any production beyond the amount covered by the bond.

In operating his plant every excised manufacturer must maintain detailed records on forms supplied by the Department and must make an annual inventory under the supervision of an excise collector of raw materials, semi-manufactured and manufactured goods on his premises. Further, he may not move any goods subject to excise from his premises until they have been entered for consumption on a prescribed form and the relevant duties have been paid. Goods may be stored in warehouse under prescribed conditions and provided an adequate bond is supplied to cover the duty on the average quantity of goods in the warehouse.

The Excise officers, including the preventive service of the R.C.M.P., are given the widest powers to enforce these regulations and the penalties for infractions are severe. This system

[2]Excise Act, s. 17 (2).

INDIRECT TAXES 333

of licensing and bonding, however, makes for almost fool-proof collection, subject always to the illegal evasions of the smuggler and the operator of the illicit still, against whom there is perpetual warfare.

Some particular features of the administration in the case of individual exciseable goods are outlined below.

1. *Distilleries.* Distillers must be bonded to cover a monthly amount of duty from a minimum of $100,000 to a maximum of $250,000, except for a chemical still where the bond is $1,000.

The actual duty on spirits may be computed on whichever of five bases yields the greatest amount of tax revenue. The first of these methods is based on the amount of grain entering into manufacturing and assumes an arbitrary ratio of spirits produced to grain entered; two other methods have bases involving calculations of alcoholic content during the course of manufacture; a fourth is calculated on the amount of spirits produced and drawn off into the spirit receivers; and the last is based on the quantity of spirits withdrawn for consumption after the necessary period of storage in warehouse. The duty on all these bases must be computed for each run and the highest duty is the duty payable. Duty is generally collected on the last computation but any of the other methods may be used at the discretion of the Excise officer. The accurate calculation of duty under such conditions requires the closest surveillance of production and the keeping of complete records as required in the Act and the regulations thereunder.

There are one or two other interesting aspects of the control over exciseable spirits. For example, all potable or beverage spirits must, with a few exceptions, by the provisions of the Excise Act be stored for at least two years before being entered for consumption. There is also a prohibition against labelling a bottle of spirits in any other manner or with any other design than that approved by the Deputy Minister.

2. *Breweries.* The duty on beer is relatively simple to collect compared with that on spirits. It applies simply to gallonage of beer brewed, the current rate of duty being 38 cents per gallon.

An unusual feature of the law is that none of the duties

related to brewing "are to be levied or collected upon beer brewed by any person for the sole use of himself and such members of his family as reside with him in the same dwelling house," an unexpected element of benevolence in an otherwise austere statute. No licence is required but the Collector of Customs and Excise must be notified of intention.

3. *Manufacturers of cigars, cigarettes, and tobacco products.* Every person carrying on a trade in the manufacture of tobacco products must be licensed and bonded. Duties on tobacco products are all paid through the purchase of an excise stamp which must appear on the package containing the product. Regulations also govern the conditions under which tobacco products may be packaged for sale and consumption. They may only be put up in a package prescribed by regulations and the package must not only bear a stamp but also such other information as the Department may require. According to the law both the stamp and the package must be destroyed upon being emptied. There are severe penalties for opening a package without breaking the stamp or for infractions of any of the other regulations.

The tobacco manufacturer is required to maintain records in a form prescribed by the Department and to render such reports as may be called for either regularly or from time to time. As in the case of other excised products tobacco and its products may be stored in warehouse provided proper records are kept and security is given. Generally the system resembles closely that already described for the other exciseable goods.

4. *Miscellaneous products.* Exemption from duty is granted under the statute for the manufacture and use of denatured and wood alcohol under regulations as to licensing, bonding for compliance with the law, and the labelling of bottles and other containers in which such alcohol is sold. Provision is also made for the use of spirits in certain processes such as the making of perfume, the manufacture of medicinal preparations, and the compounding of drugs by druggists under licence of the Department and at the lower rates of duty described in the earlier section on excise duties.

INDIRECT TAXES 335

Excise Taxes Administration

The collection of excise taxes is carried out under very different circumstances from those just described for customs and excise duties, where the taxable goods are completely under the control of the revenue authorities at every turn. The control is considerably less rigid, and as a result a correspondingly higher degree of voluntary co-operation is required of the taxpayer. It might be pointed out in this connection that this co-operation is elicited of the taxpayer without any compensation for his efforts. In this respect the Dominion differs from the provinces, where commissions ranging from one to five per cent of the tax collected are paid.

At the base of the excise tax administration is the system of departmental licensing, described earlier in dealing with the sales tax. Licences must be obtained by all persons required to pay or collect taxes under the Excise Tax Act. The fee for such licences is only $2, and they are granted automatically in the case of any eligible manufacturer or producer. The penalties for carrying on an unlicensed business in any of the lines subject to tax are fairly severe, and the administration relies on this penalty and the constant efforts of the audit and investigation services to assure compliance.

Another fundamental feature of the collection of excise taxes is the requirement that all licensees must make a monthly report to the local collector of their taxable sales or operations of the previous month. This report must be made not later than the end of the following month and must be accompanied by payment of the taxes due on the sales reported. The licensed taxpayer must make such a report whether or not he made any taxable sales in the previous month.

A third essential feature of this administration is the periodical inspection of the taxpayer's records carried out by the local staff of excise tax auditors attached to the Customs-Excise port. Because of the responsibility left with the individual taxpayer to assess and report his tax liability a full verification of his accounts is of the greatest importance, given the normal human tendency to minimize tax liability whenever possible. In this respect the excise tax auditor and the income tax auditor work in very similar circumstances. Accounts must be kept by every licensee at his place of business in such form as will enable the amount of tax duly payable to be determined. Licensees are also required by law to place their records at the disposal of the auditor and to give all assistance to him in his examination. Penalties are stipulated for non-compliance with this requirement since the keeping of proper books is essential to the collection of most of the excise taxes. In addition to the civil penalties imposed for several specific enumerated causes there is also a general criminal penalty involving a term of imprisonment not exceeding twelve months or less than two months for "everyone who wilfully attempts in any manner to evade or defeat any tax imposed by this Act" (Section 60).

Regulations are issued by the Department to clarify the application of each tax. Differences as to questions of liability are frequently settled by the taxpayer and the Department, although the taxpayer has the right to appeal to the Tariff Board for a ruling on the amount of tax payable and also on any claim for exemption under the statute. Prior to the establishment of the Tariff Board the Board of Customs acted in this appeal capacity almost from the inception of the sales tax.

Since most of the excise taxes are of the *ad valorem* type, problems of valuation arise in the case of both internally manufactured and imported goods. The tax is levied on the duty-paid value in the case of imports and any valuation given for the purposes of the tariff also applies automatically for sales tax purposes. For internal manufacturers the law and regulations for many products provide for the methods of determining the value subject to duty, but where disputes do arise presumably these are settled by the Deputy Minister or the Minister with a right of appeal to the Tariff Board. The Department will also often take legal action to enforce payment in a court of competent jurisdiction. Where it appears that the tax has been paid in error a taxpayer has two years in which to make application for a refund of the over-payment.

INDIRECT TAXES 337

The general sales tax has been left for separate discussion, since it occupies a place of distinction both as a producer of revenue and as an administrative mechanism. As explained earlier, the sales tax applies to all sales of goods produced or manufactured in Canada or imported into Canada unless specifically exempt by law. It is payable by the licensed vendor, whether producer, manufacturer, or wholesaler, at the time of sale or delivery, and by the licensed importer at the time of entry for consumption. In the case of unlicensed businesses it is payable at the time of purchase of taxable goods. The very breadth of coverage of the tax gives it rather special administrative aspects.

The licensing requirement under the sales tax is addressed to all manufacturers and producers of taxable goods in Canada and to the importers of taxable goods into Canada. Since there are very few lines in which at least one product is not taxable it is likely that substantially all the manufacturers of any size in Canada are licensed. The principal exceptions would be manufacturers of foods, which are almost all exempt, and also small producers whom the Department has power to exempt from the licensing requirement. In the case of wholesalers and jobbers, for reasons that will appear in a moment, the right to be licensed is restricted to firms where in the three months prior to the date of applying for the licence at least 50 per cent of their sales were of goods exempt from tax by the statute. This restriction has applied on applications for licences since September 1, 1938, but apparently did not apply prior to that time. Any wholesaler or jobber so licensed must give security for compliance with the Act and for payment of taxes, one of the rare cases in which security is mandatory under the Excise Tax Act.

In addition to giving the Department a means of keeping tab on manufacturers, as explained earlier the licence also performs another and unique function. It has permitted the adoption of a system whereby manufacturers pass materials and semi-manufactured goods from one owner to another without the necessity of collecting a tax on the sale as long as the purchaser can produce a sales tax licence and certificate. This has the advantage of allowing free movement of materials and goods still in process without the complications involved in a tax accounting and also has the merit that it provides an automatic warning at the time the tax becomes collectible, namely, when the purchaser cannot produce a sales tax licence and appropriate certificate.

As explained earlier, one of the incidental complications of the licensing system is the determination of status as a manufacturer or producer. This is not clear in every case, particularly where the process is largely one of assembling a few simple parts. The practical distinction between the holder of a licence and the person who does not hold a licence is that when not licensed as a manufacturer a taxpayer is taxed on his materials and supplies, but he may sell his completed product free of tax. When licensed as a manufacturer his parts and components may be purchased free of tax but his finished article is taxable unless sold to another manufacturer or wholesaler holding a licence.

It is because a sales tax licence grants the right to purchase free of tax that wholesalers and dealers are granted this privilege only sparingly. Their purchases are normally made for resale to the public and this is the last chance to collect the tax if it is to be collected at all. The granting of a licence where at least 50 per cent of the dealer's sales are exempted articles is a compromise solution between the alternative of taxing all his purchases and giving him a rebate on his sales that are not subject to tax.

The sales tax is payable at the local Customs-Excise port although under a recently inaugurated programme payments in the future will be made at regional centres established for this purpose. Like most of the excise taxes it is due by the end of the month following the month in which the taxable transaction occurred. Payment of the tax must be accompanied by a report of the taxable transactions in a form that can be verified by the Department. The actual collection of the tax therefore probably involves the employment of very little more staff than would be needed for the collection of customs and excise duties. The greatest part of the Excise staff is engaged in the investigation and auditing of taxpayers' records, a process which is carried on continuously. One of the difficult administrative problems that eternally defies satisfactory solution is the optimum size of staff to employ in this work. Recent improvement in the *over-all average* frequency of audit as indicated by a reduction from about $18\frac{1}{2}$ months in 1949 to under 12 months in 1959 suggests a closer approach to the optimum. Few accounts are now left unaudited for more than three years, and the advantages in reducing the possibilities of misapplication of the law, with attendant fines and penalties for the taxpayer, are self-evident.

APPENDIX

RATES AND CLASSES OF ASSETS SUBJECT TO CAPITAL COST ALLOWANCES
UNDER SCHEDULE B OF INCOME TAX REGULATION 1100
(as amended to September 1, 1961)

CLASS 1
(4 per cent)

Property not included in any other class that is
- (a) a bridge,
- (b) a canal,
- (c) a culvert,
- (d) a dam,
- (e) a jetty,
- (f) a mole,
- (g) a road, sidewalk, aeroplane runway, parking area or similar surface construction,
- (h) railway track and grading that is not part of a railway system, or
- (i) tile drainage.

CLASS 2
(6 per cent)

Property that is
- (a) electrical generating equipment (except as specified elsewhere in this Schedule),
- (b) a pipeline for oil, gas or water unless, in the case of a pipeline for oil or natural gas, the Minister, in collaboration with the Minister of Mines and Technical Surveys, is satisfied that the main source of supply for the business for which the pipeline was acquired is likely to be exhausted within fifteen years from January 1, 1949, or the date of commencement of the business, whichever is the later,
- (c) the generating and distributing equipment and plant (including structures) of a producer or distributor of electrical energy, except a property included in class 10, 13 or 14,
- (d) manufacturing and distributing equipment and plant (including structures) acquired primarily for the production or distribution of gas, except
  - (i) a property included in class 10, 13 or 14, or
  - (ii) a property acquired for the purpose of producing or distributing gas that is normally distributed in portable containers, or
  - (iii) a property acquired for the purpose of processing natural gas before delivery to a distribution system,
- (e) the distributing equipment and general plant (including structures) of a distributor of water, except a property included in class 10, 13 or 14, or
- (f) the production and distributing equipment and general plant (including structures) of a distributor of heat, except a property included in class 10, 13 and 14.

Class 3
(5 per cent)

Property not included in any other class that is
- (a) a building or other structure, including component parts such as electric wiring, plumbing, sprinkler systems, air-conditioning equipment, heating equipment, lighting fixtures, elevators and escalators,
- (b) a breakwater (other than a wooden breakwater),
- (c) a dock,
- (d) a trestle,
- (e) a windmill, or
- (f) a wharf.

Class 4
(6 per cent)

Property that would otherwise be included in another class in this Schedule, that is
- (a) a railway system or a part thereof except automotive equipment not designed to run on rails or tracks, that was acquired after the end of the taxpayer's 1958 taxation year, or
- (b) a tramway or trolley bus system or a part thereof, except property included in Class 10, 13, or 14.

Class 5
(10 per cent)

Property that is
- (a) a chemical pulp mill or ground wood pulp mill, including buildings, machinery and equipment but not including hydro-electric power plants and their equipment, or
- (b) an integrated mill producing chemical pulp or ground wood pulp and manufacturing therefrom paper, paper board or pulp board, including buildings, machinery and equipment but not including hydro-electric power plants and their equipment.

Class 6
(10 per cent)

Property not included in any other class that is
- (a) a building of
  - (i) frame,
  - (ii) log,
  - (iii) stucco on frame,
  - (iv) galvanized iron, or
  - (v) corrugated iron,

  construction including component parts such as electric wiring, plumbing, sprinkler systems, air-conditioning equipment, heating equipment, lighting fixtures, elevators and escalators,
- (b) a wooden breakwater,
- (c) a fence,
- (d) a greenhouse,
- (e) an oil or water storage tank,

APPENDIX

    (f)   a railway tank car,
    (g)   a wooden wharf, or
    (h)   an aeroplane hangar acquired after the end of the taxpayer's 1958 taxation year.

Class 7
(15 per cent)

Property that is
    (a)   a canoe or rowboat,
    (b)   a scow,
    (c)   a ship as defined in the Canada Shipping Act,
    (d)   furniture, fitting or equipment attached to a property included in this class (except radar equipment and radio equipment),
    (e)   a spare engine for a property included in this class, or
    (f)   a marine railway, or
    (g)   a ship under construction.

Class 8
(20 per cent)

Property that is a tangible capital asset that is not included in another class in this Schedule except land, or any part thereof or any interest therein, and also excepting
    (a)   an animal,
    (b)   a tree, shrub, herb, or similar growing thing,
    (c)   a gas well (other than a gas well that is part of the equipment of a farm and from which the gas produced is not sold),
    (d)   a mine,
    (e)   an oil well,
    (f)   radium,
    (g)   revoked,
    (h)   revoked,
    (i)   revoked,
    (j)   revoked,
    (k)   a right of way,
    (l)   a timber limit, and
    (m)   tramway track.

Class 9
(25 per cent)

Property that is
    (a)   electrical generating equipment, if
        (i) the taxpayer is not a person whose business is the production for the use of or distribution to others of electrical energy,
        (ii) the equipment is auxiliary to the taxpayer's main power supply, and
        (iii) the equipment is not used regularly as a source of supply,
    (b)   radar equipment,
    (c)   radio transmission equipment,
    (d)   radio receiving equipment that is used in conjunction with radio transmission equipment, or
    (e)   electrical generating equipment that has a maximum load capacity of not more than 15 kilowatts.

Class 10
(30 per cent)

Property not included in any other class that is
- (a) automotive equipment (including a trolley bus but not including a tramcar or railway locomotive),
- (b) repealed,
- (c) harness or stable equipment,
- (d) a sleigh,
- (e) a trailer, or
- (f) a wagon,

and property that would otherwise be included in another class that is
- (g) a building acquired for the purpose of gaining or producing income from a mine (except an office building that is not situated on the mine property and a refinery),
- (h) contractor's moveable equipment (including portable camp buildings),
- (i) a floor of a roller skating rink,
- (j) gas or oil well equipment (including a structure) that is normally used above ground,
- (k) mining machinery and equipment acquired for the purpose of gaining or producing income from a mine,
- (l) property that was acquired for the purpose of cutting and removing merchantable timber from a timber limit and will be of no further use to the taxpayer after all merchantable timber has been removed from the limit, unless the taxpayer has elected to include another property of this kind in another class,
- (m) mechanical equipment acquired for logging operations, but not including a property described in class 7,
- (n) access roads and trails for the protection of standing timber against fire, insects and disease,
- (o) property that was acquired for a motion picture drive-in theatre, or
- (p) property included in this class by virtue of subsection (8) or (9) of section 1102.

Class 11
(35 per cent)

Property not included in any other class that is an electrical advertising sign owned by the manufacturer thereof and used to earn rental income.

Class 12
(100 per cent)

Property not included in any other class that is
- (a) a book that is part of a lending library,
- (b) chinaware, cutlery or other tableware,
- (c) a kitchen utensil costing less than $100.00,
- (d) a die, jig, pattern, mould or last,
- (e) a medical or dental instrument costing less than $100.00,
- (f) a mine shaft, main haulage way or similar underground work designed for continuing use, or any extension thereof, sunk or constructed after the mine came into production,

APPENDIX 345

  (g) linen,
  (h) a tool costing less than $100.00,
  (i) a uniform,
  (j) the cutting or shaping part of a machine, or
  (k) apparel or costume, including accessories used therewith, used for the purpose of earning rental income therefrom,
  (l) video tape.

Class 13

Property that is a leasehold interest except
  (a) an interest in minerals, petroleum, natural gas, other related hydrocarbons or timber and property relating thereto or in respect of a right to explore for, drill for, take or remove minerals, petroleum, natural gas, other related hydrocarbons or timber, and
  (b) that part of the leasehold interest that is included in another class by reason of subsection (5) of section 1102 of these Regulations.

Class 14

Property that is a patent, franchise, concession or licence for a limited period in respect of property but not including
  (a) a franchise, concession or licence in respect of minerals, petroleum, natural gas, other related hydrocarbons or timber and property relating thereto (except a franchise for distributing gas to consumers) or in respect of a right to explore for, drill for, take or remove minerals, petroleum, natural gas, other related hydrocarbons, or timber, or
  (b) a leasehold interest.

Class 15

Property that would otherwise be included in another class of this Schedule but for the fact that
  (a) it was acquired for the purpose of cutting and removing merchantable timber from a timber limit, and
  (b) it will be of no further use to the taxpayer after all merchantable timber has been removed from the limit,
except property that the taxpayer has, in the taxation year or a previous taxation year, elected not to include in this class.

Class 16
(40 per cent)

Property that is
  (a) an aircraft,
  (b) furniture, fittings or equipment attached to an aircraft, or
  (c) a spare part for a property included in this class.

Class 17
(8 per cent)

Property, that would otherwise be included in another class in this Schedule, that is a telephone or telegraph system or a part thereof, except radio receiving and transmission equipment and property included in class 10, 13 or 14.

Class 18
(60 per cent)

Property that is a motion picture film.

TABLE XVI

Quebec Succession Duty Rates

1. Initial Rates on Transmission in Direct Line
(Aggregate value of estate)

Exceeds	And does not exceed	Rate of duty
	$ 10,000	No duty
$ 10,000	50,000	1% + 1/25 of 1% for each full $1,000
50,000	100,000	1% + 1/20 of 1% for each full $1,000
100,000		5% + 1/100 of 1% for each full $1,000 in such way that the rate so obtained shall not exceed 15%

1A. Additional Rates of Duty on Transmissions in Direct Line
(Aggregate value passing to one and the same person)

Exceeds	And does not exceed	Additional rates
$ 10,000	$ 50,000	1%
50,000	300,000	1% + 1/100 of 1% for each full $1,000
300,000		3% + 1/200 of 1% for each full $1,000 in such way that the rate so obtained shall not exceed 10%

2. Initial Rates on Transmissions in Collateral Line
(Aggregate value of estate)

Exceeds	And does not exceed	Rate of duty
	$ 1,000	No duty
$ 1,000	10,000	4%
10,000	60,000	4% + 1/10 of 1% for each full $1,000
60,000		10% + 1/100 of 1% for each full $1,000 in such way that the rate so obtained shall not exceed 20%

TABLE XVI (*Continued*)

2A. Additional Rates of Duty on Transmissions in Collateral Line
(Aggregate value passing to one and the same person)

Exceeds	And does not exceed	Additional rates
$ 1,000 100,000	$100,000	1% + 1/25 of 1% for each full $1,000 5% + 1/300 of 1% for each full $1,000 in such way that the rate so obtained shall not exceed 10%

3. Initial Rates on Transmission in Collateral Line of Degrees Other Than Those Included in the Preceding Table or to any Stranger
(Aggregate value of estate)

Exceeds	And does not exceed	Rate of duty
$100,000	$100,000	10% + 1/10 of 1% for each full $1,000 20% + 1/100 of 1% for each full $1,000 in such way that the rate so obtained shall not exceed 30%

3A. Additional Rates of Duty on such Transmissions
(Aggregate value passing to one and the same person)

Exceeds	And does not exceed	Additional rates
$100,000	$100,000	2% 2% + 1/400 of 1% for each full $1,000 in such way that the rate so obtained shall not exceed 5%

TABLE XVII

Ontario Succession Duty Rates

1. Initial Rates on Transmission in Direct Line
(Aggregate value of estate)

Exceeds	And does not exceed	Rate of duty		
$ 50,000	$ 75,000	2½% + 4/100 of 1%	for each full $1,000 by which the aggregate value exceeds	$ 50,000
75,000	100,000	3½% + 6/100 of 1%	" "	75,000
100,000	150,000	5% + 1/100 of 1%	" "	100,000
150,000	200,000	5½% + 1/100 of 1%	" "	150,000
200,000	300,000	6% + 1/100 of 1%	for each full $2,000 by which the aggregate value exceeds	200,000
300,000	400,000	6½% + 1/100 of 1%	" "	300,000
400,000	500,000	7% + 1/100 of 1%	" "	400,000
500,000	600,000	7½% + 1/100 of 1%	" "	500,000
600,000	700,000	8% + 1/100 of 1%	" "	600,000
700,000	800,000	8½% + 1/100 of 1%	" "	700,000
800,000	900,000	9% + 1/100 of 1%	" "	800,000
900,000	1,000,000	9½% + 1/100 of 1%	" "	900,000
1,000,000	5,000,000	10% + 1/100 of 1%	for each full $10,000 by which the aggregate value exceeds	1,000,000
5,000,000		14%		

In addition a surtax of 15 per cent on duty so calculated.

1A. Additional Rates of Duty on Transmissions in Direct Line
(Aggregate value passing to one person)

Exceeds	And does not exceed	Additional rate		
$ 50,000	$ 75,000	1½% + 2/100 of 1%	for each full $1,000 by which the amount so passing exceeds	$ 50,000
75,000	100,000	2% + 2/100 of 1%	" "	75,000
100,000	150,000	2½% + 1/100 of 1%	" "	100,000
150,000	300,000	3% + 1/100 of 1%	for each full $3,000 by which the amount so passing exceeds	150,000
300,000	400,000	3½% + 1/100 of 1%	for each full $1,000 by which the amount so passing exceeds	300,000
400,000	500,000	4½% + 1/100 of 1%	for each full $2,000 by which the amount so passing exceeds	400,000
500,000	600,000	5% + 1/100 of 1%	" "	500,000
600,000	700,000	5½% + 1/100 of 1%	" "	600,000

TABLE XVII (*Continued*)

1A. Additional Rates of Duty on Transmissions in Direct Line
(Aggregate value passing to one person)

Exceeds	And does not exceed	Additional rate		
700,000	750,000	6% + 1/100 of 1%	for each full $1,000 by which the amount so passing exceeds	700,000
750,000	800,000	6½% + 1/100 of 1%	" "	750,000
800,000	900,000	7% + 1/100 of 1%	for each full $2,000 by which the amount so passing exceeds	800,000
900,000	1,000,000	7½% + 1/100 of 1%	" "	900,000
1,000,000	1,200,000	8% + 1/100 of 1%	for each full $4,000 by which the amount so passing exceeds	1,000,000
1,200,000	1,400,000	8½% + 1/100 of 1%	" "	1,200,000
1,400,000	1,600,000	9% + 1/100 of 1%	" "	1,400,000
1,600,000	1,800,000	9½% + 1/100 of 1%	" "	1,600,000
1,800,000	2,000,000	10% + 1/100 of 1%	" "	1,800,000
2,000,000	2,200,000	10½% + 1/100 of 1%	" "	2,000,000
2,200,000	2,400,000	11% + 1/100 of 1%	for each full $2,000 by which the amount so passing exceeds	2,200,000
2,400,000	2,600,000	12% + 1/100 of 1%	" "	2,400,000
2,600,000	2,800,000	13% + 1/100 of 1%	" "	2,600,000
2,800,000	3,000,000	14% + 1/100 of 1%	" "	2,800,000
3,000,000		15%		

In addition a surtax of 15 per cent on duty so calculated.

2. Initial Rates on Transmissions to Near Collaterals
(Aggregate value of estate)

Exceeds	And does not exceed	Rate of duty		
$ 20,000	$ 30,000	6% + 10/100 of 1%	for each full $1,000 by which the aggregate value exceeds	$ 20,000
30,000	60,000	7% + 10/100 of 1%	" "	30,000
60,000	100,000	10% + 5/100 of 1%	" "	60,000
100,000	200,000	12% + 1/100 of 1%	" "	100,000
200,000	400,000	13% + 1/100 of 1%	for each full $2,000 by which the aggregate value exceeds	200,000
400,000	600,000	14% + 1/100 of 1%	" "	400,000
600,000	800,000	15% + 1/100 of 1%	" "	600,000
800,000	1,000,000	16% + 1/100 of 1%	" "	800,000
1,000,000		17%		

In addition a surtax of 20 per cent on duty so calculated.

TABLE XVII (*Continued*)

2A. Additional Rates of Duty on Transmissions to Near Collaterals
(Aggregate value passing to one person)

Exceeds	And does not exceed	Additional rate	
10,000	$ 60,000	2½% + 1/100 of 1%	for each full $1,000 by which the amount so passing exceeds $ 10,000
60,000	160,000	3% + 1/100 of 1%	for each full $2,000 by which the amount so passing exceeds 60,000
160,000	200,000	3½% + 5/100 of 1%	for each full $4,000 by which the amount so passing exceeds 160,000
200,000	300,000	4% + 1/100 of 1%	for each full $2,000 by which the amount so passing exceeds 200,000
300,000	350,000	4½% + 1/100 of 1%	for each full $1,000 by which the amount so passing exceeds 300,000
350,000	450,000	5% + 1/100 of 1%	for each full $2,000 by which the amount so passing exceeds 350,000
450,000	500,000	5½% + 1/100 of 1%	for each full $1,000 by which the amount so passing exceeds 450,000
500,000	600,000	6% + 1/100 of 1%	for each full $2,000 by which the amount so passing exceeds 500,000
600,000	700,000	6½% + 1/100 of 1%	" " 600,000
700,000	800,000	7% + 1/100 of 1%	" " 700,000
800,000	900,000	7½% + 1/100 of 1%	" " 800,000
900,000	1,000,000	8% + 1/100 of 1%	for each full $1,000 by which the amount so passing exceeds 900,000
1,000,000	1,500,000	9% + 1/100 of 1%	for each full $5,000 by which the amount so passing exceeds 1,000,000
1,500,000	2,000,000	10% + 1/100 of 1%	" " 1,500,000
2,000,000	2,500,000	11% + 1/100 of 1%	" " 2,000,000
2,500,000	3,000,000	12% + 1/100 of 1%	" " 2,500,000
3,000,000		13%	

In addition a surtax of 20 per cent on duty so calculated.

TABLE XVII (*Continued*)

Rates on Transmission in Collateral Line of Degrees Other Than Those Included in the Preceding Table or to Any Stranger
(Aggregate value of estate)

Exceeds	And does not exceed	Rate of duty		
$ 5,000	$ 10,000	7½% + 1%	for each full $1,000 by which the aggregate value exceeds	$ 5,000
10,000	50,000	12½% + 5/100 of 1%	for each full $800 by which the aggregate value exceeds	10,000
50,000	100,000	15% + 5/100 of 1%	for each full $1,000 by which the aggregate value exceeds	50,000
100,000	200,000	17½% + 5/100 of 1%	for each full $2,000 by which the aggregate value exceeds	100,000
200,000	300,000	20% + 5/100 of 1%	" "	200,000
300,000	400,000	22½% + 5/100 of 1%	" "	300,000
400,000	500,000	25% + 5/100 of 1%	" "	400,000
500,000	600,000	27½% + 5/100 of 1%	" "	500,000
600,000	700,000	30% + 5/100 of 1%	" "	600,000
700,000	800,000	32½% + 5/100 of 1%	" "	700,000
800,000		35%		

In addition a surtax of 25 per cent on duty so calculated.
No additional rates are payable by this class of beneficiaries.

TABLE XVIII
COMBINED DOMINION ESTATE TAX AND ONTARIO SUCCESSION DUTIES

Aggregate net value	Whole estate to widow	Estate to widow and two children under 21	Estate to two children over 25
$	$	$	$
50,000	0	0	0
75,000	5,644	0	5,669
100,000	11,725	9,925	10,850
150,000	23,062	20,862	23,637
200,000	35,368	32,968	36,350
250,000	48,242	45,642	49,275
300,000	62,100	59,300	63,175
350,000	78,019	75,069	77,316
400,000	95,150	92,150	92,086
500,000	130,025	126,825	123,722
600,000	168,200	164,800	157,900
700,000	209,675	206,075	197,275
800,000	259,050	255,250	239,950
900,000	307,700	303,700	283,337
1,000,000	359,650	355,450	329,450
1,500,000	608,037	603,237	565,400
2,000,000	887,150	881,950	834,850

TABLE XIX

Combined Dominion Estate Tax and Quebec Succession Duties

Aggregate net value	Whole estate to widow	Estate to widow and two children under 21	Estate to two children over 25
$	$	$	$
25,000	450	360	450
50,000	1,600	1,480	1,600
75,000	5,775	4,875	6,963
100,000	11,100	9,300	12,100
150,000	21,900	19,700	23,075
200,000	34,300	31,900	34,800
250,000	48,200	45,600	47,775
300,000	63,600	60,800	61,900
350,000	81,125	78,175	77,125
400,000	98,250	95,250	93,350
500,000	135,650	132,450	128,950
600,000	177,050	173,650	168,550
700,000	222,450	218,850	213,900
800,000	271,850	268,050	259,750
900,000	325,250	321,250	309,100
1,000,000	382,650	378,450	361,950
1,500,000	642,350	637,550	598,400
2,000,000	892,650	887,450	857,850

TABLE XX

Selected Taxes and Licences Levied by Provincial Governments in Canada in 1961 (September 1)

	Nfld.	P.E.I.	N.S.	N.B.	Que.	Ont.	Man.	Sask.	Alta.	B.C.
Corporation tax On capital	—	—	—	—	approximately 1/10 of 1% varying slightly according to types of corporation	approximately 1/20 of 1% varying slightly according to types of corporation	—	—	—	—
On net profits	—	—	—	—	12%	11%	—	—	—	—
Amusement tax	5¢ per ticket	approximately 10%	approximately 10%	approximately 11%	12½% (split between province and municipality)	10%	approximately 10%	—	—	10%
Pari-Mutuel Bets Tax	—	5%	approximately 10%	5%	5.5% and up	6%	10%	5%	5%	12%

TABLE XX—Continued

	Nfld.	P.E.I.	N.S.	N.B.	Que.	Ont.	Man.	Sask.	Alta.	B.C.
Motor Fuel Sales Tax	19¢ per gallon	16¢ per gallon	19¢ per gallon	18¢ per gallon	13¢ per gallon	13¢ per gallon	14¢ per gallon	14¢ per gallon	12¢ per gallon	13¢ per gallon
Diesel Fuel	—	—	27¢ per gallon	23¢ per gallon	13	18½¢ per gallon	17¢ per gallon	17¢ per gallon	14¢ per gallon	15¢ per gallon
Tobacco Sales Tax	—	4¢ per 20 cigarettes	4¢ per 20 cigarettes	4¢ per 20 cigarettes	4¢ per 20 cigarettes	—	—	—	—	—
General Retail Sales Tax	5%	4%	5%	3%	2%	3%	—	3%	—	5%
Meals Tax	—	—	—	—	5% on meals over 59¢	—	—	—	—	—
Succession Duties	(Various; see chapters on Dominion and Provincial Death Duties, and Appendix)									
Motor Vehicle Licences (1960)										
Passenger Car	$18.00	$19.60	$22.68	$23.00	$25.50	$25.00	$19.00	$15.00	$15.00	$22.50
Pick-up Truck	25.00	20.80	21.60	29.00	39.75	20.00	30.00	25.00	45.00	30.00
Van	245.00	168.50	194.25	155.00	136.00	179.00	225.00	200.00	150.00	180.00
Motor Vehicle Operators' Licences	$3.00	$1.00	$1.00	$1.00	$2.50	$1.00	$1.00	$1.00	$1.00	$5.00[1]

[1]Five-year licence.

TABLE XX—*Continued*

	Nfld.	P.E.I.	N.S.	N.B.	Que.	Ont.	Man.	Sask.	Alta.	B.C.
Land Transfer Tax	information not available	—	—	—	2½% of Sale Price (limited in application)	1/5 of 1% of purchase price	—	—	—	—
Mining Tax	5%	—	6c per ton	7% to 9%	4 to 7%	6 to 12%	8%	12½%	—	10%
Logging Tax	—	—	—	—	—	9%	—	—	—	10%
Security Transfer Tax	—	—	—	—	Applies to Quebec and Ontario only, where rates are similar. Shares under $1, 1/10c per share; from $1-5, ½c per share; $5-25, 1c per share; $25-50, 2c per share; $50-75, 3c per share; $75-150, 4c per share; over $150, 4c plus 1/10 of 1% of value over $150		—	—	—	—

TABLE XXI

Rates of Taxation for Various Selected Municipalities in Canada

Rate in mills (or percentage if specified)
(1959)

Cities	Real property	Personal property	Supplementary business	Sales	Amusement	Other	Basis of assessed valuations and percentage taxed
St. John's, Nfld.[1]	20%	—	20%	1¢ per gallon on fuel oil sales	10% on admission price	Water tax—various rates	Real property—100% of assessed rental value Business—Varies from 50% to 150% of assessed rental value
Charlottetown, P.E.I.	27.5	27.5	27.5	—	—	Poll—$25 on males; $12 on females	Real and personal property—66⅔% of real value Business—varies from 25% to 100% of assessed property value
Halifax, N.S.	Property of a residential character—19.5 Property of a business character—47.5	—	47.5	—	—	Poll—$20 male and female	Real property—100% of real value Business—50% of assessed value

[1]St. John's has a 2% tax on fire insurance premiums and a tax of $1.00 per main line telephone.

TABLE XXI—Continued

Cities	Real property	Personal property	Supplementary business	Sales	Amusement	Other	Basis of assessed valuations and percentage taxed
Sydney, N.S.	106	106	—	—	—	Poll—Males $4-20 Females $4-15	Real property—100% of real value Personal property—100% of real value
Fredericton, N.B.	52.8	Motor vehicles only at various rates	52.8	—	—	Occupancy—52.8 Poll—male, $10-$15; female, $10	Real property—$100% of real value Personal property—vehicles at fixed rates Business—various percentages of assessed value for different businesses Occupancy—10% of assessed value (owners) or 120% of rental value (tenants)
Saint John, N.B.	67	67	67	—	—	Poll—$20, male and female	Real property—100% of real value Personal property—motor cars 60% of real value Business—different percentages which vary between 60% and 150% of real value for different businesses Turnover—different percentages which vary between 10% and 25% of gross receipts

TABLE XXI—Continued

Cities	Real property	Personal property	Supplementary business	Sales	Amusement	Other	Basis of assessed valuations and percentage taxed
Montreal, Que.	Catholic, 23.197 Protestant and Jewish, 26.197 Neutral, 31.697	—	11⅜% of assessed rental value; special rates on retail and liquor stores, banks and bank branches; +8% surtax	2% on sales for municipality; 2% for schools	a	Water tax: 6.625 of rental value + 8% surtax Telephone: 25¢ for each line; 10¢ on each extension	Real property—100% of real value Business—100% of assessed rental value
Quebec, Que.	Catholic, 20.4 Protestant, 20.4 Neutral 22.9	—	18% of assessed rental value	2% on sales for municipality; 2% for schools	a	Snow: 19.5 mills on land valuation only Water: properties—7.2 mills; vacant lots—6.25 mills on assessed value Garbage: $9 per household with various rates for commercial properties	Real property—100% of real value Business—100% of assessed rental value

[a] An amusement tax levied by the province is shared between city and province.
[b] Water tax is comparable to water charges billed directly to consumers in other municipalities. Special rates are charged in certain cases.

TABLE XXI—Continued

Cities	Real property	Personal property	Supplementary business	Sales	Amusement	Other	Basis of assessed valuations and percentage taxed
Verdun, Que.	Catholic 20.5 Protestant 22.5 Neutral 27.0	—	11% of rental value	2% on sales for municipality; 2% for schools	a	Water:[b] 8% of rental value Garbage: 2% of rental value	Real property—100% of real value Business—100% of assessed rental value
Sherbrooke, Que.	Catholic 23 Protestant 23 Neutral 23	—	7% of rental value	2% on sales for municipality; 1% for schools		Rental: 5% of rental paid Garbage: $10 per dwelling	Real property—70% of real value Business—100% of assessed rental value
Trois Rivieres, Que.	Catholic 24.7 Protestant 28.7 Neutral 24.7	—	6% of rental value	2% on sales for municipalities; 2% for schools		Water:[b] 5.4 mills on assessed value	Real property—100% of real value Business—100% of assessed rental value
Toronto, Ont.	Residential: Separate schools 56 Public schools 56 Industrial and commercial: 59.7	—	59.7	—	—	—	Real property—100% of real value Business—different percentages of assessed value for different businesses

[a] An amusement tax levied by the province is shared between city and province.
[b] Water tax is comparable to water charges billed directly to consumers in other municipalities. Special rates are charged in certain cases.

TABLE XXI—Continued

Cities	Real property	Personal property	Supplementary business	Sales	Amusement	Other	Basis of assessed valuations and percentage taxed
London, Ont.	Residential: Separate schools 61.84 Public schools 56.84 Industrial and Commercial: Separate — 66 Public — 61	—	Separate 66 Public 61	—	—	—	Real property—100% of real value Business—different percentages of assessed value for different businesses
Ottawa, Ont.	Residential: Separate schools 51.45 Public schools 42.7 Industrial and Commercial: Separate 55.35 Public 46.6	—	Separate 55.35 Public 46.6	—	—	—	Real property—100% of real value Business—Different percentages of assessed value for different businesses
Niagara Falls, Ont.	Residential: Separate and Public schools 50.3 Industrial and Commercial: 54.5	—	54.5	—	—	Poll—$5, males only	Real property—100% of real value Business—Different percentages of assessed value for different businesses

TABLE XXI—*Continued*

Cities	Real property	Personal property	Supplementary business	Sales	Amusement	Other	Basis of assessed valuations and percentage taxed
Hamilton, Ont.	Residential: Separate schools 54.7 Public schools 53.7 Industrial and Commercial: Separate 59.1 Public 58.1	—	56	—	—	—	Real property—100% of real value Business—Different percentages of assessed value for different businesses
Winnipeg, Man.	43	—	6–20% of assessed rental value	Electricity and gas sales tax: 5% of commercial 2½% of domestic bills	—	Greater Winnipeg Water District 4 mills on land values only	Land—100% of real value Buildings, etc.—66⅔% of real value Business—100% of assessed rental value
St. Boniface, Man.	St. Boniface school 54.8 Northwood school 54.08	—	5½–15% of rental value	—	—	Greater Winnipeg Water District 3.5 mills on land values only	Land—100% of real value Buildings, etc.—66⅔% of real value Business—100% of assessed rental value
Brandon, Man.	79	—	12–14⅓% of rental value	—	—	—	Land—100% of real value Buildings, etc.—66⅔% of real value Business—100% of assessed rental value

TABLE XXI—*Continued*

Cities	Real property	Personal property	Supplementary business	Sales	Amusement	Other	Basis of assessed valuations and percentage taxes
Moose Jaw, Sask.	95	—	95	—	10% of admission price over 25¢	—	Land—100% of real value Buildings, etc.—60% of real value Business—Area of premises occupied, at varying rates for different businesses
Prince Albert, Sask.	Public schools 90.4 Separate schools 89.4	—	Licences	—	5% of admission price	Poll—$5 male and female	Land—100% of real value Buildings, etc.—60% of real value
Saskatoon, Sask.	74.5	—	74.5	—	Graduated rates on admission price	Poll—$5 male and female	Land—100% of real value Buildings, etc.—45% of real value Business—Area of premises occupied at varying rates for different businesses
Regina, Sask.	72	—	72	—	6-10% of admission price	—	Land—100% of real value Buildings, etc.—45% of real value Business—Area of premises occupied, at varying rates for different businesses
Medicine Hat, Alta.	49	—	13% of rental value	—	—	—	Land—100% of real value Buildings, etc.—60% of real value Business—100% of assessed rental value

TABLE XXI—*Continued*

Cities	Real property	Personal property	Supplementary business	Sales	Amusement	Other	Basis of assessed valuations and percentage taxed
Lethbridge, Alta.	71	—	10% of rental value	—	—	—	Land—100% of real value Buildings, etc.—60% of real value Business—100% of assessed rental vlaue
Edmonton, Alta.	61	—	6% to 20% of rental value	—	—	—	Land—100% of real value Buildings, etc.—residential—50% of real value, and others—60% of real value Business—100% of assessed rental value
Calgary, Alta.	51	—	10% of rental value	—	—	—	Land—100% of real value Buildings, etc.—60% of real value Business—100% of assessed rental value
Vancouver, B.C.	57.19	—	7% of assessed rental value	—	—	—	Land—100% of real value Buildings, etc.—50% of real value for municipal purposes, 75% for school purposes Business—100% of assessed rental value

TABLE XXI—*Continued*

Cities	Real property	Personal property	Supplementary business	Sales	Amusement	Other	Basis of assessed valuations and percentage taxed
Victoria, B.C.	49.75	—	6¼% of assessed rental value	—	—	—	Land—100% of real value Buildings—75% of real value Business—100% of assessed rental value
New Westminster, B.C.	54.06	—	9% of assessed rental value	—	—	—	Land—100% of real value Buildings, etc.—40% of real value for municipal purposes, 75% for school purposes Business—100% of assessed rental value
Trail, B.C.	69.09	—	—	—	—	—	Land—100% of real value Buildings, etc.—50% of real value for municipal purposes, 75% for school purposes.

NOTE: In making comparisons of tax rates as between cities and particularly as between cities in different provinces, it should be borne in mind that there is little uniformity in assessment practice. While it is almost a universal rule that real property shall be assessed at 100% of "real value," the methods of determining real value vary greatly and in all cases assessment as determined by the assessor is at a lower level of value than 100% of real value. Where assessment is at annual rental value in some provinces, the actual rent need not be taken; that is, the assessor may and invariably does determine a reasonable annual rent.

SOURCE: *Principles Taxes and Rates*, 1959, D.B.S.; *Local Finance*, nos. 4 and 5, Canadian Tax Foundation.

TABLE

COMBINED REVENUES—ALL GOVERNMENTS
Fiscal Years Ended
(millions

	Total		
	1939	1949	1960
Taxes:			
Income:			
1. Corporations	89	707	1,722
2. Individuals	61	622	2,041
3. Interest, dividends, and other income going abroad	11	48	80
4. General sales	145	481	1,365
5. Motor fuel and fuel oil sales	53	139	400
6. Other sales	3	35	59
7. Excise duties and special excise taxes	87	378	669
8. Customs import duties	107	226	580
9. Real and personal property	249	375	1,272
10. Succession duties	28	59	137
11. Other	49	104	180
12. Total taxes	882	3,174	8,505
Privileges, licences, and permits:			
13. Liquor control and regulation	—[2]	26	—[1]
14. Motor vehicles	28	58	—[1]
15. Natural resources	25	83	—[1]
16. Other	18	39	—[1]
17. Total privileges, licences, and permits	—	206	555
18. Receipts from government enterprises	—[2]	163	—[2]
19. Other revenue	124	247	876
20. Sub-total net general revenue after elimination of inter-government transfers	1,077	3,790	9,936
21. Transfers from other governments	—	—	—
22. TOTAL	—	—	—

[1]Detail not available.
[2]Included in other revenue.

XXII

IN CANADA FOR 1939, 1949, AND 1960
Nearest December 31
of dollars)

Federal			Provincial			Municipal		
1939	1949	1960	1939	1949	1960	1939	1949	1960
78	601	1,445	11	106	276	1	—	—
46	622	1,980	12	—	61	3	—	—
11	48	80	—	—	—	—	—	—
137	403	1,090	3	62	213	5	16	63
—	—	—	53	139	400	—	—	—
—	—	—	3	35	56	—	—	4
87	378	669	—	—	—	—	—	—
107	226	580	—	—	—	—	—	—
—	—	—	6	6	8	243	369	1,264
—	30	85	28	29	52	—	—	—
2	15	1	23	41	170	23	48	9
468	2,323	5,930	139	418	1,236	275	433	1,340
—	—	—[1]	—[2]	26	—[1]	—	—	—
—	—	—[1]	28	58	—[1]	—	—	—
1	1	—[2]	24	82	290	—	—	—
2	14	—[2]	9	12	25	7	13	24
3	15	—[2]		178	531	7	13	24
1	28	—[2]	—[2]	111	—[2]	10	24	44
52	179	487	36	26	249	25	42	96
2,545	2,545	6,417	236	733	2,016	317	512	1,504
—	—	—	22	108	535	5	9	91
—	—	—	258	841	2,551	322	521	1,595

TABLE XXIII

Dominion Government Revenues
Five fiscal years 1955–6 to 1959–60
(millions of dollars)

	1955–56	1956–57	1957–58	1958–59	1959–60
Tax Revenues—					
Income tax—					
Personal[1]	1,185.6	1,400.5	1,499.8	1,353.5	1,566.6
Corporation[1]	1,027.7	1,268.3	1,234.8	1,020.6	1,142.9
On dividends, interest, etc., going abroad	66.2	76.4	64.3	61.2	73.4
	2,279.5	*2,745.2*	*2,798.9*	*2,435.3*	*2,782.9*
Excise taxes—					
Sales tax[1] [2]	641.5	717.1	703.2	694.5	732.7
Other excise taxes—					
Automobiles	76.2	79.7	72.3	59.3	64.3
Beverages (soft drinks)	8.7	9.0	0.6	....	....
Candy and chewing gum	9.2	9.8	0.7	....	....
Cigarettes, cigars and tobacco	126.9	132.3	142.4	148.0	185.5
Jewellery, watches, ornaments, etc.	5.0	6.1	5.3	5.6	5.6
Matches and lighters	0.9	0.8	0.9	0.9	0.9
Television sets, radios, tubes, and phonographs	22.8	19.0	16.9	17.8	17.8
Tires and tubes	0.8	....	....	....	....
Toilet preparations	5.6	6.1	6.3	6.8	7.7
Wines	2.5	2.6	2.7	3.1	3.0
Sundry commodities	2.1	2.3	1.4	1.2	1.2
Licences, interest and miscellaneous	0.4	0.5	0.6	0.5	1.1
Less refunds	−0.4	−1.1	−0.7	−2.6	−0.4
	260.7	*267.1*	*249.4*	*240.6*	*286.7*
Customs import duties	481.2	549.1	498.1	486.5	525.7
Excise duties—					
Spirits and beer	141.9	153.4	171.9	179.6	193.1
Cigarettes, cigars and tobacco	110.4	121.1	131.7	141.2	146.2
Licences	(3)	(3)	(3)	(3)	(3)
Less refunds	−2.9	−3.1	−3.5	−4.1	−4.1
	249.4	*271.4*	*300.1*	*316.7*	*335.2*
Estate tax	66.6	79.7	71.6	72.6	88.4
Tax on insurance premiums	15.5	16.7	....	....	....
Miscellaneous tax revenue	1.3	1.6	1.5	1.2	0.9
Total tax revenues	3,995.7	4,647.9	4,622.8	4,247.4	4,752.3
Non-Tax Revenues—					
Post-office—net postal revenue	137.4	145.8	152.9	157.5	167.6
Return on investments	149.3	206.6	169.4	221.2	239.7
Other	117.6	106.2	103.7	128.6	130.1
Total non-tax revenues	404.3	458.6	426.0	507.3	537.4
Total Revenues	4,400.0	5,106.5	5,048.8	4,754.7	5,289.8

[1] Excluding tax credited to the old age security fund—

	1955–56	1956–57	1957–58	1958–59	1959–60
Personal income tax	102.5	125.0	135.0	146.4	185.6
Corporation income tax	53.3	67.3	60.7	55.3	91.3
Sales tax	160.4	179.3	175.8	173.6	270.0

[2] Net after deduction of refunds and drawbacks as well as transfers to the old age security fund.
[3] Less than $50,000.

BIBLIOGRAPHY

WHEREVER POSSIBLE in the preparation of the present work a Canadian reference has been used if one was available. The following list therefore contains most of the Canadian writings that pertain to the field covered. With a few exceptions, no attempt has been made to include foreign writings on the specific subject of taxation, since these are generally well catalogued already. Nor have the standard English and American academic works on public finance, which usually include chapters on the general principles of taxation, been listed. It is assumed that these are well known and easily available to most readers.

A detailed list of references has not been compiled for chapter 1. The many excellent historical sources that would ordinarily be listed for chapter 1 have been used for the preparation of the companion study, *Taxes, Tariffs, and Subsidies*, and appear in the bibliography of that volume.

GENERAL SOURCES

A. GOVERNMENT OF CANADA

Budget Speech of the Minister of Finance. Ottawa, Queen's Printer.
Canada, House of Commons. *Debates.* Ottawa, Queen's Printer.
Canada, House of Commons, Standing Committee on Public Accounts. *Minutes of Proceedings and Evidence.* Ottawa, Queen's Printer.

Canada, Senate, Standing Committee on Finance. *Proceedings.* Ottawa, Queen's Printer.
Statutes of Canada. Ottawa, Queen's Printer.
Statutory Orders and Regulations. Canada Gazette, Part II. Ottawa, Queen's Printer.

B. PROVINCIAL GOVERNMENTS

See the Budget Speeches of the Provincial Treasurers or Ministers of Finance, the Statutes of the various provinces, and the provincial Gazettes. All are publications of the provincial Queen's Printers.

C. TAX SERVICES (manuals, revised periodically)

Canada Tax Manual (loose-leaf). Toronto, Richard De Boo.
Canadian Master Tax Guide. 16th ed., Toronto, CCH Canadian Ltd. 1961.
Ontario and Quebec Corporation and Income Tax. Toronto, CCH Canadian, 1960.
NOTE: Manuals dealing with individual taxes or groups of taxes are listed with references for the relevant chapters.

D. TAX SERVICES (loose-leaf)

Canada Tax Appeal Board Cases. Toronto, Richard De Boo.
Canada Tax Cases. Toronto, Richard De Boo.
Canada Tax Service. Toronto, Richard De Boo.
Canadian Tax Reporter. Toronto, CCH Canadian Ltd.
Dominion Tax Cases. Toronto, CCH Canadian Ltd.
Provincial Taxation Service. Toronto, Richard De Boo.
British Columbia Tax Reporter. Toronto, CCH Canadian Ltd.
Maritimes Tax Reporter. Toronto, CCH Canadian Ltd.
Prairies Tax Reporter. Toronto, CCH Canadian Ltd.
Ontario Tax Reporter. Toronto, CCH Canadian Ltd.
Quebec Tax Reporter. Toronto, CCH Canadian Ltd.

E. TAXATION STATISTICS

1. *Dominion*

DEPARTMENT OF FINANCE. *Budget Speech of the Minister of Finance.* Ottawa, Queen's Printer. Annual. (Statistical appendix.)
───── *Public Accounts of the Dominion of Canada.* Ottawa, Queen's Printer.
DEPARTMENT OF NATIONAL REVENUE. *Report of the Department of National Revenue Containing Statements Relative to Customs-Excise Revenue and Other Services by Ports and Outports: Excise and Income of the Dominion of Canada.* Ottawa, Queen's Printer. Annual.
DEPARTMENT OF NATIONAL REVENUE, TAXATION DIVISION. *Taxation Statistics.* Ottawa, Queen's Printer. Annual. (Income tax and succession duty statistics.)
DOMINION BUREAU OF STATISTICS. *Trade of Canada.* Vol. III: *Imports.* Ottawa, Queen's Printer. Annual. (Customs revenue.)

2. *Provincial*

Public Accounts and Budget Speeches of the Provincial Treasurers or Ministers of Finance.

3. *Municipal*

BANK OF CANADA. *Statistical Summary* (monthly). Ottawa.
───── *Statistical Summary, Supplement* (annual). Ottawa.
See also annual reports of the provincial departments administering municipal affairs.

F. REPORTS OF ROYAL COMMISSIONS AND OTHER OFFICIALLY APPOINTED BODIES IN THE FIELD OF OR TOUCHING ON TAXATION

1. *Canada*

ROYAL COMMISSION ON CANADA'S ECONOMIC PROSPECTS. *Final Report and Studies* (W. L. GORDON, Chairman). Ottawa, Queen's Printer, 1958.
ROYAL COMMISSION ON CANADA'S ECONOMIC PROSPECTS. *Preliminary Report* (W. L. GORDON, Chairman). Ottawa, Queen's Printer, 1956.
ROYAL COMMISSION ON ENERGY. *First Report* (H. BORDEN, Chairman). Ottawa, Queen's Printer, 1959.
ROYAL COMMISSION ON ENERGY. *Second Report* (H. BORDEN, Chairman). Ottawa, Queen's Printer, 1959.

BIBLIOGRAPHY 371

ROYAL COMMISSION ON NEWFOUNDLAND FINANCES. *Report* (J. B. MCNAIR, Chairman). Ottawa, Queen's Printer, 1958.

2. *Alberta*

METROPOLITAN PLANNING COMMISSION ON SCHOOL AND MUNICIPAL SERVICES IN THE CITIES OF EDMONTON, CALGARY AND SURROUNDING AREAS. (G. F. MCNALLY, Chairman.) Edmonton, Queen's Printer, 1954.

THE METROPOLITAN COMMISSION ON SCHOOL AND MUNICIPAL SERVICES IN THE CITIES OF EDMONTON AND CALGARY AND SURROUNDING AREAS. (H. J. MACDONALD, succeeded by J. C. MAHAFFY, Chairman.) Edmonton, Queen's Printer, 1955.

3. *British Columbia*

COMMISSION OF INQUIRY INTO EDUCATIONAL FINANCE. *Report* (M. A. CAMERON, Commissioner). Victoria, King's Printer, 1945.

COMMISSION ON THE FOREST RESOURCES OF BRITISH COLUMBIA, 1956. *Report* (G. McG. SLOAN, Commissioner). Victoria, Queen's Printer, 1957.

ROYAL COMMISSION ON PROVINCIAL-MUNICIPAL RELATIONS IN BRITISH COLUMBIA. *Report* (H. C. GOLDENBERG, Commissioner). Victoria, King's Printer, 1947.

4. *Manitoba*

MANITOBA, PROVINCIAL-MUNICIPAL COMMITTEE. *Report and Memorandum of Recommendations.* Winnipeg, Queen's Printer, 1953.

ROYAL COMMISSION ON MUNICIPAL FINANCES AND ADMINISTRATION OF THE CITY OF WINNIPEG. *Report* (H. C. GOLDENBERG, Chairman). Winnipeg, King's Printer, 1939.

WINNIPEG. *Brief on Provincial-Municipal Relations Submitted to the Government of the Province of Manitoba* (H. CARL GOLDENBERG, Special Counsel of the City of Winnipeg). May 15, 1948.

5. *New Brunswick*

ROYAL COMMISSION ON GOVERNMENT GRANTS FOR SCHOOL ADMINISTRATOR UNITS IN THE PROVINCE. *Report* (W. H. MACKENZIE, Chairman). Fredericton, Queen's Printer, 1900.

ROYAL COMMISSION ON THE FINANCING OF SCHOOLS IN NEW BRUNSWICK. *Report* (W. H. MACKENZIE, Chairman). Fredericton, Queen's Printer, 1955.

6. *Newfoundland*

ROYAL COMMISSION TO REVIEW THE FINANCIAL POSITION OF THE PROVINCE. *Report* (P. J. LEWIS, Chairman). St. John's, Queen's Printer, 1954.

SOUTH COAST COMMISSION. *Report* (J. T. CHEESEMAN, Chairman). St. John's, Queen's Printer, 1957.

7. *Nova Scotia*

ROYAL COMMISSION ON PUBLIC SCHOOL FINANCE IN NOVA SCOTIA. *Report* (V. J. POTTIER, Chairman). Halifax, Queen's Printer, 1954.

8. *Ontario*

COMMITTEE ON THE ORGANIZATION OF GOVERNMENT IN ONTARIO. *Report* (W. L. GORDON, Chairman). Toronto, Queen's Printer, 1959.

PROVINCIAL-MUNICIPAL RELATIONS COMMITTEE. *Progress Report.* Toronto, Queen's Printer, 1953.
ROYAL COMMISSION ON EDUCATION IN ONTARIO. *Report* (J. A. HOPE, Chairman). Toronto, King's Printer, 1950.

9. *Prince Edward Island*
LATTIMER, J. E. *Taxation in Prince Edward Island.* Charlottetown, Dept. of Reconstruction, 1945.

10. *Quebec*
ROYAL COMMISSION OF INQUIRY ON CONSTITUTIONAL PROBLEMS. *Report* (T. TREMBLAY, Chairman). Quebec, Queen's Printer, 1956.

11. *Saskatchewan*
ROYAL COMMISSION ON AGRICULTURE AND RURAL LIFE. *Report* (W. B. BAKER, Chairman). 14 parts. Regina, Queen's Printer, 1955-7.

G. PERIODICALS

British Tax Review (6 issues yearly). London, Sweet & Maxwell.
Canadian Bar Review (10 issues yearly). Ottawa, Canadian Bar Association.
Canadian Chartered Accountant (monthly). Toronto, Canadian Institute of Chartered Accountants.
Canadian Tax Journal (bi-monthly). Toronto, Canadian Tax Foundation.
European Taxation (fortnightly). Amsterdam, I.B.R.D.
Journal of Taxation (monthly). New York, Journal of Taxation Inc.
Municipal Finance (quarterly). Chicago, Ill., Municipal Finance Officers Association of the United States and Canada.
National Tax Journal (quarterly). Sacramento, Calif., National Tax Association.
Taxation (weekly). London, Taxation Publishing Co.
Tax Policy (monthly). New York, Tax Institute.
Taxes—The Tax Magazine (monthly). Chicago, Commerce Clearing House.
Western Municipal News (official organ of municipal organizations of Manitoba, Saskatchewan, and Alberta). Winnipeg, Willson Stationery Co.

H. RESEARCH ORGANIZATIONS

Canadian Tax Foundation. Toronto. (Reports of annual tax conferences and special studies.)
Citizens' Research Institute of Canada. Toronto. (Annual report and yearbook; bulletin *Effective Government; Financial Statistics—Canadian Municipalities.*)
Institute of Public Administration of Canada. (Proceedings of the annual conference.)

CHAPTER 2

DOMINION INCOME TAX: RESIDENT INDIVIDUALS

Government Documents
CANADA, HOUSE OF COMMONS, STANDING COMMITTEE ON BANKING AND COMMERCE. *Minutes of Proceedings and Evidence.* Session 1947-1948.

BIBLIOGRAPHY 373

Ottawa, King's Printer, 1948. (Consideration of bill no. 338, an act respecting income taxes, pp. 547-728.)
CANADA, SENATE, SPECIAL COMMITTEE ON THE INCOME WAR TAX ACT AND THE EXCESS PROFITS TAX ACT, 1940. *Proceedings and Reports.* Sessions 1945 and 1946. Ottawa, King's Printer, 1945-6.
DOMINION-PROVINCIAL CONFERENCE ON RECONSTRUCTION, 1945. *Personal Income Taxes.* [Ottawa], 1945. (Reference book.)
GREAT BRITAIN, INCOME TAX CODIFICATION COMMITTEE. *Report* (Lord MACMILLAN, Chairman). London, H.M. Stationery Office, 1936. Cmd. 5131-2.
GREAT BRITAIN, ROYAL COMMISSION ON THE INCOME TAX. *Report.* London, H.M. Stationery Office, 1920. Cmd. 615.
GREAT BRITAIN, ROYAL COMMISSION ON THE TAXATION OF PROFITS AND INCOME. *First Report* (Lord RADCLIFFE, Chairman). London, H.M. Stationery Office, 1953. Cmd. 8761.
GREAT BRITAIN, ROYAL COMMISSION ON THE TAXATION OF PROFITS AND INCOME. *Second Report* (Lord RADCLIFFE, Chairman). London, H.M. Stationery Office, 1954. Cmd. 9105.
GREAT BRITAIN, ROYAL COMMISSION ON THE TAXATION OF PROFITS AND INCOME. *Final Report* (Lord RADCLIFFE, Chairman). London, H.M. Stationery Office, 1955. Cmd. 9474.
GREAT BRITAIN, COMMITTEE ON THE WORKING OF THE MONETARY COMMITTEE. *Report* (Lord RADCLIFFE, Chairman). London, H.M. Stationery Office, 1959. Cmd. 827.
UNITED STATES, BUREAU OF INTERNAL REVENUE. *Your Federal Income Tax.* Washington, U.S. Government Printing Office (annual).
UNITED STATES, CONGRESS, JOINT COMMITTEE ON INTERNAL REVENUE TAXATION. *The Taxation of Pensions and Annuities.* Washington, U.S. Government Printing Office, 1946. (A report on H.R. 2948 of the 79th Congress, 2nd session.)
UNITED STATES, TREASURY DEPARTMENT, DIVISION OF TAX RESEARCH. *The Income Tax Treatment of Pensions and Annuities.* [Washington], 1947.
―――― *Individual Income Tax Exemptions.* [Washington], 1947.
―――― *The Taxation of Farmers' Cooperative Associations.* [Washington], 1947.
―――― *The Tax Treatment of Earned Income.* [Washington], 1947.
―――― *The Tax Treatment of Family Income.* [Washington], 1947.
See also General Sources, sec. F (1), item 4.

Books and Pamphlets

Canadian Income Tax Act. 30th ed., Toronto, CCH Canadian Ltd., 1961.
Canadian Income Tax Regulations. 21st ed., Toronto, CCH Canadian Ltd., 1961.
CANADIAN INSTITUTE OF CHARTERED ACCOUNTANTS. *Recommendations in Respect of Bill 454: Proposed Income Tax Act.* Toronto, n.d.
Canadian Master Tax Guide. 16th ed., Toronto, CCH Canadian Ltd., 1961.
CANADIAN TAX FOUNDATION. *Conference on the Income Tax Bill, Ottawa, December 8th and 9th, 1947: Report of Proceedings.* Toronto, n.d.
―――― *Fourth Tax Conference, December 11 and 12, 1950: Preparatory Reports for Round Table.* Toronto, 1950.

────── *Can Capital Gains Confusion be Removed by Legislation?* 10th Tax Conference, 1956.
────── *Family Relationships Under Income and Death Taxes.* 13th Tax Conference, 1959.
────── *Identifying Income, General Sales Tax, Arms Length Concept.* Data Papers, Sixth Tax Conference. Toronto, 1952.
────── *Income Splitting between Husband and Wife.* Data Papers, Sixth Tax Conference. Toronto, 1952.
────── *The Income Tax Bill, a Review and Analysis.* Toronto (1947).
GORDON, M. L. *Digest of Income Tax Cases of the British Commonwealth of Nations and Principal Subdivisions thereof* (Ottawa, King's Printer, 1939). *1937 to 1939* (Toronto, Age Publications, 1940). *1939 to 1942* (Toronto, the author, 1943). *1942 to 1945* (Toronto, Mundy-Goodfellow Printing Co., 1947). *1945 to 1947* (Toronto, Goodfellow Printing Co., 1949). *1947 to 1949* (Toronto, Goodfellow Printing Co., 1950).
FORDHAM, R. S. W. *Canadian Income Tax Appeal Board Practice.* 2nd ed., Toronto, CCH Canadian, 1958
FREARS, R. I. *Annotated Income War Tax Act and Excess Profits Tax Act, 1947.* Toronto, Canadian Law List Publishing Co., 1947.
GILMOUR, A. W. *Income Tax Handbook 1960–61.* Toronto, Richard De Boo, 1960.
GOFFMAN, I. J. *Erosion of the Personal Income Tax Base in Canada and the United States.* Canadian Fiscal Theses no. 2. Toronto, Canadian Tax Foundation, 1959.
HALJAN, P. *A History of the Federal Income Tax in Canada.* Thesis. Edmonton, University of Alberta, 1954.
HANNAN, J. P. and FARNSWORTH, A. *The Principles of Income Taxation Deduced from the Cases.* London, Stevens and Sons, 1952.
KONSTAM, E. M. *The Law of Income Tax.* 12th ed., based on the Income Tax Act, 1952. London, Sweet and Maxwell, 1952, with 1955 supplement.
LABRIE, F. E. *Introduction to Income Tax Law—Canada.* Toronto, CCH Canadian, 1958.
────── *The Meaning of Income in the Law of Income Tax.* Toronto, University of Toronto Press, 1953.
LAW SOCIETY OF UPPER CANADA. Special Lectures on Taxation, 1944. Delivered by H. HEWARD STIKEMAN, MOLYNEUX L. GORDON, A. L. RICHARD. Toronto, Richard De Boo, 1944.
MCDONALD, J. G. *Capital Gains and Tax Minimization Devices.* Paper given at annual meeting of the Canadian Bar Association, 1952. (Mimeo.)
────── *Cases and Materials on Income Tax.* Toronto, Butterworth, 1957.
MCGREGOR, G. *Employees' Deductions Under the Income Tax.* Canadian Tax Papers no. 21. Toronto, Canadian Tax Foundation, 1960.
MAGILL, R. F. *Taxable Income.* Rev. ed., New York, Ronald Press, 1945.
MARCO, ANTONIO DE VITI DE. *First Principles of Public Finance.* London, Jonathan Cape, 1936.
NEEDHAM, R. W. *Income Tax Principles.* London, Gee, 1931.
PLAXTON, C. P. and VARCOE, F. P. *Dominion Income Tax.* Toronto, Carswell, 1921; 1929.
PLAXTON, H. A. W. *Canadian Income Tax Law and Excess Profits Tax Law.* 2nd supplement, Toronto, Carswell, 1949.

BIBLIOGRAPHY

───── *The Law Relating to Income Tax and Excess Profits Tax of the Dominion of Canada.* 2nd ed., Toronto, Carswell, 1947.
SIMONS, H. C. *Federal Tax Reform.* Chicago, University of Chicago Press, 1950.
───── *Personal Income Taxation.* Chicago, University of Chicago Press, 1938.
STIKEMAN, H. H. "Computation of Taxable Income under the Income Tax Act." *Report of the 1948 Tax Conference Convened by the Canadian Tax Foundation, Ottawa,* pp. 47-69.
───── *Income Tax Act Annotated 1960-61.* Toronto, De Boo, 1960.
The Tax Treatment of Retirement Benefits. A report submitted to the Chairman of the Board of Inland Revenue by the Federation of British Industries, the Association of British Chambers of Commerce, the Life Officers Association, the Association of Superannuation Funds. London, Feb., 1948.
WILLIS, JOHN. *The Mitigation of the Tax Penalty on Fluctuating or Irregular Incomes.* Canadian Tax Papers, no. 2. Toronto, Canadian Tax Foundation, Sept. 1, 1951.

Periodical Articles

ALLEY, P. "Personal Exemptions." *Canadian Tax Journal* 8: 129 (1960).
"The Application of Profits and Income." *Taxation* 42: 254 (Dec. 25, 1948).
AUXIER, G. W. "Some Notes on the Income Taxation of Farmers." *Canadian Bar Review* 24: 889-903 (Dec., 1946).
CANADIAN BAR ASSOCIATION, TAXATION SECTION, and CANADIAN INSTITUTE OF CHARTERED ACCOUNTANTS. "Recommendations for Amendment of Income Tax Act." *Canadian Bar Review* 27: 443-59 (April, 1949).
CARROTHERS, B. "Executive Compensation." *Canadian Tax Journal* 8: 393 (1960).
COVERT, F. M. "Capital Gains." *Canadian Tax Journal* 6: 348 (1958).
DOUGLAS, MONTEATH. "Current Trends in the Federal Tax Field." *Canadian Chartered Accountant* 60: 16-23 (Jan., 1952).
───── "Income Tax Revision." *Canadian Bar Review* 26: 1212-27 (Oct., 1948).
GLASSCO, J. G. "Changes in Income Tax Law." *Canadian Chartered Accountant* 54: 50-8 (Feb., 1949).
HOOD, W. C. "Structural Changes in the Dominion Personal Income Tax, 1932-49." *Canadian Journal of Economics and Political Science* 15: 220-7 (May, 1949).
HUGHES, G. B. "Post-war Changes in Individual Income Taxes: United States, United Kingdom, and Canada." *National Tax Journal* 1: 175-83 (June, 1948).
"Illegal Profits and the Income Tax." *Canadian Bar Review* 11: 125-6 (Feb., 1933).
"Income Tax Profits." *Taxation* 42: 413 (Feb., 1949).
KING, C. L. "Basic Herds." *Canadian Chartered Accountant Tax Review* [1949]: 87-8 (June).
LEACH, C. W. "Taxation of Lump Sum and Other Receipts." *Canadian Chartered Accountant,* March, 1959.
MACKAY, R. DEW. "Corporation Gains—Are They Always Taxable?" *Canadian Tax Journal* 1: 13 (1953).

McDonald, J. G. "Capital Gains and Losses in Canada." *Canadian Bar Review* 29: 907–27 (Nov., 1951).

McEntyre, J. G. "The Development of Federal Income Tax in Canada." *Tax Executive*, October, 1957.

May, G. O. "The British Treatment of Capital Gains." *Journal of Accountancy* 73: 502–7 (June, 1942).

Moller, George. "Approach to Tax Problems; Examination of Available Sources of Reference in Income Tax Matters." *Canadian Chartered Accountant* 54: 19–26 (Jan., 1949).

Monet, F. "The Income Tax Appeal Board: An Outline of the Constitution and Procedure of the Board." *Canadian Chartered Accountant* 57: 23–8 (July, 1950).

Musgrave, R. A. and Tun Thin. "Income Tax Progression, 1929–48." *Journal of Political Economy* 56: 498–514 (Dec., 1948).

Parker, R. G. "Pension Plans for Self-Employed Persons—Section 79B Income Tax Act." *Canadian Bar Review* (Aug.–Sept., 1957).

Petrie, J. R. "Capital Gains." *Tax Bulletin* (C.T.F.) 2: 264 (1952).

Pierce, Melville. "Business Profits and Income: Individual." *Canadian Chartered Accountant Tax Review* [1949]: 69–77 (May).

―――― "Income from a Source vs. Income of a Person." *Tax Review*, June, 1952: 127–9.

―――― "Payments for Patent Rights and Trade Secrets: Income or Capital." *Ibid.* (1949): 83–7 (June).

"Residence in Canada" (for purposes of income tax). *Canadian Chartered Accountant* 46: 275–90 (May, 1945).

Schulman, W. H. "The Artist and His Tax Burden." *Taxes* 27: 101–8, 165 (Feb., 1949).

Seltzer, L. H. "Evolution of the Special Legal Status of Capital Gains under the Income Tax." *National Tax Journal* 3: 18–35 (March, 1950).

Stikeman, H. H. "Differences Between Business Income and Income for Tax Purposes." *Canadian Chartered Accountant* (Sept., 1957).

"Taxation of Pension Schemes in the United Kingdom, Canada and U.S.A." *Taxation* 45: 436–7 (Aug. 5, 1950); 452–4 (Aug. 12, 1950).

Thom, S. D. "Capital Gains." *Canadian Chartered Accountant* (Dec., 1956).

Tresilian, R. "The Capital Gains Scare." *Canadian Tax Journal* 3: 196 (1955).

Vineberg, P. F. "Taxable Income in Canada." *Canadian Chartered Accountant* 50: 19–31 (Jan., 1947).

Willis, John. "Tax Avoidance in Canada." *Public Affairs* 12: 27–30 (Spring, 1949).

Wueller, P. H. "Concepts of Taxable Income." *Political Science Quarterly* 53: 83–110 (March, 1938); 557–83 (Dec., 1938).

Chapter 3

DOMINION INCOME TAX: RESIDENT CORPORATIONS

Government Documents

Canada, Department of Mines and Technical Surveys. *Summary Review of Dominion Tax and Other Legislation Affecting Mining Enterprises in Canada.* Ottawa, April, 1957.

CANADA, HOUSE OF COMMONS, STANDING COMMITTEE ON BANKING AND COMMERCE. *Minutes of Proceedings and Evidence.* Session 1947-48. Ottawa, King's Printer, 1948. (Consideration of bill no. 338, an act respecting income taxes, pp. 547-728.)

DOMINION-PROVINCIAL CONFERENCE ON RECONSTRUCTION, 1945. *Corporation Taxes.* [Ottawa], 1945. (Reference book.)

GREAT BRITAIN, COMMITTEE ON THE TAXATION OF TRADING PROFITS. *Report.* London, H.M. Stationery Office, 1951. Cmd. 8189.

UNITED STATES, TREASURY DEPARTMENT, DIVISION OF TAX RESEARCH. *Business Loss Offsets.* [Washington], 1947.

——— *Consolidated Returns and Intercorporate Dividends.* [Washington], 1948.

——— *The Postwar Corporation Tax Structure.* By RICHARD B. GOODE. [Washington], 1946.

——— *Taxation of Small Business.* [Washington], 1947.

See also General Sources, sec. F (1), items 1, 4.

Books and Pamphlets

ASSOCIATION OF CERTIFIED AND CORPORATE ACCOUNTANTS. *Accounting for Inflation.* London, Gee, 1952.

BUTTERS, J. K. *Effects of Taxation: Inventory Accounting and Policies.* Boston, Harvard Business School, 1949.

BUTTERS, J. K., et al. *Taxation and Business Concentration.* Princeton, Tax Institute, 1952.

BUTTERS, J. K. and LINTER, J. *Effect of Federal Taxes on Growing Enterprises.* Boston, Harvard Business School, 1945.

BUTTERS, J. K., LINTER, J., and CARY, W. L. *Effects of Taxation: Corporate Mergers.* Boston, Harvard Business School, 1951.

BUTTERS, J. K. and SMITH, D. T. *Taxable and Business Income.* New York National Bureau of Economic Research, 1949.

CANADIAN TAX FOUNDATION. *Business Income and Taxable Income.* 7th Tax Conference 1953.

——— *Businessmen's Brush-up on Postwar Tax Developments.* 9th Tax Conference 1955.

——— *Company Amalgamations.* 12th Tax Conference 1958.

——— *Corporate Amalgamations under the Income Tax.* 10th Tax Conference 1956.

——— *Corporation Profits and Dividends under the Income Tax Act.* Memorandum prepared for Third Tax Conference, December 5–6, 1949. Toronto.

——— *Fourth Tax Conference, December 11 and 12, 1950: Preparatory Reports for Round Table.* Toronto, 1950.

——— *Identifying Income, General Sales Tax, Arms Length Concept.* Data Papers, Sixth Tax Conference. Toronto, 1952.

——— *The Income Tax Act Part IA and Sections 73, 73A and 27 Respecting Private Companies and Controlled Corporations.* Memorandum of recommendations submitted to Minister of Finance and Minister of National Revenue. Feb. 12, 1951.

——— *Inventory Valuation.* 10th Tax Conference 1956.

——— *Legal and Accounting Principles Governing Deductible Expenses.* 12th Tax Conference 1958.

―――― *Tax Problems on the Purchase and Sale of a Business.* 9th Tax Conference 1955.
―――― *Valuation of Closely Held Businesses.* 13th Tax Conference 1959.
CCH CANADIAN LTD. *Canadian Depreciation Guide.*
―――― *Ontario Tax Acts Consolidated.*
―――― *Quebec Tax Acts Consolidated.*
―――― *Special Tax on Private Companies Undistributed Income.* Editorial comment prepared by K. L. Carter and John L. Stewart. Toronto, 1950.
―――― *Undistributed Income Guide.* 2nd ed. revised to Dec. 1, 1951. Toronto.
Corporate Management Conference. Canadian Tax Papers no. 19. Toronto, Canadian Tax Foundation, 1960.
Corporate Management Conferences. Canadian Tax Papers no. 15. Toronto, Canadian Tax Foundation, 1959.
DOUGLAS, MONTEATH. *The Tax Treatment of Corporation Profits and Dividends in Canada.* Toronto, Canadian Tax Foundation, Oct. 15, 1949. (Mimeo.)
GAA, C. J. *The Taxation of Corporate Income.* Urbana, University of Illinois Press, 1944.
GOODE, R. *The Corporation Income Tax.* New York, Wiley, 1951.
HELLBORN, L. S. and MILLER, M. H. "Farmers' Marketing and Purchasing Cooperatives in the United States, Canada and Great Britain." *Proceedings of the 38th Annual Conference of the National Tax Association, 1945,* pp. 288–306.
INSTITUTE OF COST AND WORKS ACCOUNTANTS. *The Accountancy of Changing Price Levels.* London, Gee, 1952.
LABRIE, F. E. and WESTLAKE, J. R. *Deductions under the Income War Tax Act: A Return to Business Principles.* University of Toronto Studies, Legal Series, no. 3. Toronto, University of Toronto Press, 1948.
LAW SOCIETY OF UPPER CANADA. *Special Lectures, 1950: Company Law.* Toronto, Richard De Boo, 1950. See H. H. Stikeman, "Corporation Taxation," pp. 111–252.
―――― *Special Lectures on Taxation, 1944.* Delivered by H. HEWARD STIKEMAN, MOLYNEUX L. GORDON, and A. L. RICHARD. Toronto, Richard De Boo, 1950.
LEONARD, W. G. *Canadian Income Tax for Accountants.* 2nd ed. Toronto, CCH Canadian, 1959.
MAY, G. O. *Periodic Business Income and Changing Price Levels.* Toronto, Canadian Tax Foundation, 1951.
MCGREGOR, G. *Business Deductions under the Income Tax.* Canadian Tax Papers no. 13. Tronto, Canadian Tax Foundation, 1958.
―――― *Personal Corporations.* Canadian Tax Papers no. 18. Toronto, Canadian Tax Foundation, 1960.
MACKAY, R. DEW. *Definition of the Term Income.* Address to the Taxation Section of the Canadian Bar Association. Washington, D.C., Sept. 20, 1950. (Mimeo.)
MORRISEY, L. E. *The Many Sides of Depreciation.* (Tuck Bulletin 23). Hanover, Amos Tuck School of Business Administration, 1960.
NATIONAL TAX ASSOCIATION. *Final Report of the Committee on the Federal Corporate Net Income Tax.* Sacramento, Calif., 1950.

BIBLIOGRAPHY 379

―― *Proceedings of the 40th Annual Conference, 1947.* Sacramento, Calif., the Association, 1947. (A large part of this conference was devoted to corporation and other business taxes.)
―― *Proceedings of 41st Annual Conference, 1948; Proceedings of 42nd Annual Conference, 1949; Proceedings of 43rd Annual Conference, 1950; Proceedings of 44th Annual Conference, 1951; Proceedings of 45th Annual Conference, 1952.* Sacramento, Calif., the Association, 1948; 1950; 1951; 1952; 1953.
NEEDHAM, R. W. *Incidence of United Kingdom Income Tax and Sur-Tax on the Company's Profits and the Shareholders' Dividends.* London, Allen & Unwin, 1944.
The New Depreciation System, 1950. Toronto, CCH Canadian Ltd., 1950.
OWEN, C. F. *Business Financing and Taxation Policies.* Canadian Fiscal Theses no. 1. Toronto, Canadian Tax Foundation, 1960.
PETRIE, J. R. *Some Economic Aspects of the Taxation of Corporate Income and Dividends.* Address to 1949 Tax Conference of the Canadian Tax Foundation. Montreal, Dec. 5, 1949. (Mimeo.)
―― *The Taxation of Corporate Income in Canada.* Toronto, University of Toronto Press, 1952.
RIEHL, G. W. *Incorporation and Income Tax in Canada.* 2nd ed. Toronto, CCH Canadian, 1961.
SELTZER, L. R. *The Nature and Tax Treatment of Capital Gains and Losses.* New York, National Bureau of Economic Research, 1951.
SMITH, D. T. *Effects of Taxation: Corporate Financial Policy.* Boston, Harvard Business School, 1952.
SMITH, D. T. and BUTTERS, J. K. *Taxable and Business Income.* New York, National Bureau of Economic Research, 1949.
STIKEMAN, H. H. *Corporate Taxation, 1950.* Toronto, Richard De Boo, 1950.
STUDY GROUP ON BUSINESS INCOME. *Changing Concepts of Business Income.* New York, Macmillan, 1952.
TAX INSTITUTE. *Depreciation and Taxes.* Princeton, Tax Institute, 1959. 247 pp.
―― *Economic Effects of Section 102: The Penalty Tax on Unreasonable Accumulation of Profits.* Princeton, 1951.
―― *How Should Corporations be Taxed?* Symposium, 1946. New York, the Institute, 1947.
TAX POLICY LEAGUE. *How Shall Business be Taxed?* Symposium, 1936. New York, the League, 1937.
UNITED NATIONS. *Corporate Tax Problems.* New York, 1952.
NOTE: See manuals on the Income Tax Act and Income War Tax Act listed with references for chap. 2.

Periodical Articles

ABBOTT, D. "Corporation Tax Policy." *Canadian Tax Journal* 2: 20 (1954).
BAILEY, G. D. "Accelerated Depreciation: Criteria for Its Use." *Journal of Accountancy* 88: 372-7 (Nov., 1949).
BARRETT, O. H. "Double Taxation of Corporate Income." *Industrial Canada* 49: 280-1 (July, 1948).
BELANGER, M. "Transactions Not at Arms-Length." *Canadian Tax Journal* 7: 107 (1959).

BYRD, K. F. "A Long Step Backward: Diminishing Balance Depreciation." *Canadian Chartered Accountant* 56: 63–8 (Feb., 1950).
CAPON, F. S. "Inventory Valuation for Tax Purposes." *Industrial Canada* 49: 278–80 (July, 1948).
CARLYLE, W. "Associated Companies." *Canadian Tax Journal* 8: 369 (1960).
CARPENTER, J. L. "Partnership Buy-and-Sell Agreements." *Canadian Chartered Accountant*, December, 1958.
CARTER, K. L. "Double Taxation of Corporation Incomes." *Industrial Canada* 47: 218–20 (July, 1946).
—— "New Canadian Legislation Reduces Double Taxation of Corporate Income." *Journal of Accountancy* 92: 209–13 (Aug., 1951).
—— "Taxation of Corporate Income by the Dominion Government." *Canadian Chartered Accountant* 42: 354–60 (May, 1943).
CARSON, A. B. "The Terminal-Date-Group Method of Depreciation Accounting." *Journal of Accountancy*, April, 1955.
CHOMMIE, J. C. "Surtax Avoidance and Extra Taxation of Corporate Earnings in the U.S., U.K., and Canada." *Tax Law Review*, March, 1957.
"Computation of Taxable Profits—Australia." *Taxation* 42: 114–15 (Nov. 6, 1948); 129–30 (Nov. 13, 1948).
CLARK, P. T. "Depreciation of Capital Assets under Canadian Income Tax Law." *Canadian Journal of Accountancy* 2: 5 (Dec., 1952).
COURTOIS, R. "Capital Cost Allowance Provisions." *Tax Review* 1952: 165–6 (Sept., 1952).
COYNE, J. M. "Capitalization of Corporate Surpluses: The New 15 Per Cent Tax on Private Companies." *Canadian Chartered Accountant Tax Review* [1951]: 1–6 (Jan.).
CRATE, H. E. "Sale and Lease-Back Arrangements in Canada." *Tax Executive*, October, 1959.
DINKEL, R. S. "Tax Incentives for the Petroleum Industry." *Canadian Tax Journal* 5: 440 (1957).
"Dividends out of Capital." *Taxation* 42: 432–3 (Feb. 26, 1949).
EATON, A. K. "Canadian Federal Income Tax, with Particular Reference to Recent Significant Developments." *Tax Bulletin* 2: 253–63 (Sept.-Oct., 1952).
—— "Recent Developments in Corporation Taxation in Canada." *National Tax Journal* 3: 75–81 (March, 1950).
—— "Where Angels Fear to Tread." *Canadian Tax Journal* 7: 432 (1959).
EATON, K. E. "The Death of the 'Profit Earning Process Test.'" *Canadian Tax Journal* 5: 271 (1957).
EGAN, H. J. "Corporate Surpluses." *Canadian Tax Journal* 6: 401 (1958).
EDWARDS, S. E. "Company Law Problems Arising under Part 1A of the Income Tax Act." *Canadian Bar Review* 29: 937–49 (Nov., 1951).
—— "Problems Raised by the Undistributed Income Provisions of the Income Tax Act." *Canadian Chartered Accountant* 58: 116–24 (March, 1951).
ELLIOTT, R. F. "S. 95A Distributions—Tax and Accounting." *Tax Review*, May, 1952: 109–12.
FERGUSON, G. R. "Sale-Lease-Back Financing." *Canadian Chartered Accountant*, December, 1959.

BIBLIOGRAPHY

FLYNN, W. H. "Notes on the New Depreciation Regulations." *Canadian Chartered Accountant Tax Review* (1950): 177–81 (Nov.).
FREARS, R. I. "Charter Powers and Liability to Income Tax." *Canadian Bar Review* 23: 480–94 (June–July, 1945).
GAVSIE, M. C. "Some Aspects of Income Taxation in Canada." *Canadian Chartered Accountant* 55: 159–68 (Oct., 1949).
GIBSON, K. "Tax Implications of Incorporating Small Businesses." *Canadian Tax Journal* 7: 100.
GILMOUR, A. W. "Canada Should Re-Appraise its Taxation of Corporate Surplus." *Canadian Tax Journal* 8: 6 (1960).
——— "Diminishing Balance Depreciation under the Income Tax Act." *Canadian Chartered Accountant* 56: 273–83 (June, 1950).
GLASSCO, J. G. "Depreciation Accounting." *Canadian Chartered Accountant* 53: 172–80 (Oct., 1948).
——— "The New Corporation Income Tax Act." *Board of Trade Journal* (Toronto), 38: 24–30 (Feb., 1948).
——— "The Proposed Income Tax Act." *Canadian Chartered Accountant* 52: 133–42 (March, 1948).
——— "The Treatment of Depreciation under the Income Tax Bill." *Ibid.* 51: 324–35 (Dec., 1947).
GOFFMAN, I. J. "Taxation of Corporate Surplus in Canada—Further Comments." *Canadian Tax Journal* 8: 276 (1960).
GOODE, R. "Corporate Income Tax and Price Level." *American Economic Review* 35: 40–58 (March, 1945).
GOODMAN, W. D. "Taxation—Income Tax—Cash Basis and Accrual Basis—Income War Tax Act and Income Tax Act." *Canadian Bar Review* 30: 532–7 (May, 1952).
HIPP, C. E. "Depreciation under the New Income Tax Act." *Industrial Canada* 49: 275–7 (July, 1948).
"Industry's Tax Free Loan." *Economist* 156: 1197-9 (June 25, 1949). (New concepts of depreciation allowances for industry.)
INNES, J. S. "Aspects of Capital Cost Allowances." *Canadian Chartered Accountant Tax Review* (1951): 41–4 (March).
"Interest as a Deductible Expense." *Canadian Chartered Accountant Tax Review* (1949): 6–9 (Jan.).
KEEPING, G. P. "Tax on Undistributed Income of Closely-Held Companies." *Canadian Chartered Accountant Tax Review* (1950): 133–6 (Sept.).
KELSEY, D. J. "Some Taxation Aspects of Corporate Amalgamations." *Canadian Tax Journal* 8: 236 (1960).
KING, C. L. "The Accounting Treatment of Certain Income Tax Items." *Canadian Chartered Accountant* 51: 336–42 (Dec., 1947).
——— "Depreciation on Replacement Cost." *Canadian Chartered Accountant* 53: 77–84 (Aug., 1948).
LAING, S. B. "Deductions and Depreciation under the Income Tax Act." *Canadian Chartered Accountant Tax Review* (1950): 36–43 (March).
LEMON, K. W. "Canadian Taxation and the Businessman." *Business Quarterly* Spring 1960.
LEONARD, W. G. "Income Determination for Tax Purposes." *Canadian Tax Journal* 7: 240 (1959).

LINCOLN, ALEXANDER. "Stock Dividends and Stock Rights." *Taxes* 27: 109–12 (Feb., 1949).
LITTLE, A. J. "Corporate Amalgamations under the Income Tax." *Canadian Tax Journal* 5: 23 (1955).
LOUGHEED, W. F. "Some Observations on the Taxation of Capital Gains." *Canadian Chartered Accountant* 60: 43–55 (Feb., 1952).
MCALPINE, A. D. "Corporate Amalgamations under Income Tax." *Canadian Tax Journal* 5: 12 (1957).
MCCOLL, J. A. "To Incorporate or Not." *Canadian Chartered Accountant* 56: 121–6 (March, 1950). See also letter to the editor, pp. 120–2, issue of Sept., 1950.
MCGREGOR, D. A. "Mergers in the Mining and Oil Industries." *Canadian Chartered Accountant*, February, 1960.
MCGREGOR, G. "Deducted, Depreciated or Disallowed?" *Canadian Tax Journal* 5: 404 (1957).
—— "The 'Reasonable' Test for Business Expenditures." *Canadian Tax Journal* 7: 318 (1959).
MCGURRAN, H. D. "Deferred Depreciation." *National Tax Journal* 4: 299–303 (Dec., 1951).
MANNING, R. E. "Depreciation in the Tax Laws and Practice of the United States, Australia, Canada, Great Britain, New Zealand, and South Africa." *National Tax Journal* 1: 154–74 (June, 1948).
MOFFETT, H. S. "Capital Cost Allowance Problems." *Canadian Chartered Accountant Tax Review* (1950): 181–4 (Nov.).
MOLLER, GEORGE. "The Application of Straight Line Depreciation under the New Capital Cost Allowance System." *Canadian Chartered Accountant Tax Review* (1951): 81–8 (May).
—— "Historic Costs—the Lesser Evil." *Canadian Chartered Accountant* 55: 21–9 (July, 1949).
—— "The New Income Tax Regulations on Allowance of Capital Cost (Depreciation)." *Cost and Management* 24 (Jan., 1950).
"Mutual Transactions." *Taxation* 44: 48–50 (Oct. 15, 1949). (Taxation aspects of mutual organization in British experience.)
PATTERSON, C. A. "Application of the Income War Tax Act to Corporations." *Canadian Chartered Accountant* 45: 270–8 (Nov., 1944).
PENTLAND, H. C. "The Royal Commission on Co-operatives." *Commerce Journal* 2: 60–4 (March, 1947).
PERRY, J. H. "The Canadian Tax Structure, Federal, Provincial and Local." *Tax Bulletin* 2: 230–43 (Sept.-Oct., 1952).
—— "Depreciation Allowances under the Canadian Income Tax." *Canadian Chartered Accountant*, February, 1954.
—— "Development of the Canadian Corporation Income Tax." *Canadian Chartered Accountant* 58: 3–14 (Jan., 1951).
—— "Double Tax Burden of Limited Companies." *Canadian Tax Journal* 3: 342 (1955).
PETRIE, J. R. "How Should Corporations Be Taxed?" *Canadian Business* 23: 25–6, 80–4 (Jan., 1950).
—— "Small Business and Its Tax Problems." *Canadian Chartered Accountant* 57: 249–59 (Dec., 1950).

——— "Some Aspects of Recent Corporation Income Tax Legislation in Canada." *Tax Policy* 17: 3–16 (Sept.-Oct., 1950).
PIERCE, M. "Business Profits: Year of Charge." *Tax Review*, Nov., 1951: 187–96.
——— "Prepayment for Goods and Services." *Tax Review*, Dec., 1952: 219–28 and Jan., 1953: 1–12.
——— "The Taxation of 'Capital Gains' in Canada." *Tax Review*, Feb., 1952: 27–33.
"Plant and Machinery, a Summary of Options Available on Sale." *Taxation* 42: 510–512 (March 10, 1949).
RICHARDSON, G. G. "The Impact of Income Taxes on Depreciation Accounting in Canada." *Canadian Chartered Accountant*, November, 1953.
——— "Taxes—Accumulation of Undistributed Income, Consolidation and Mergers." *Canadian Chartered Accountant*, January, 1957.
SCOTT, D. G. "Holding Company Methods." *Canadian Chartered Accountant*, February, 1960.
SHAKESPEARE, W. C. "Statutory Mergers." *Canadian Chartered Accountant*, February, 1960.
SHARP, M. W. "Deferred Depreciation—a Canadian Anti-Inflationary Measure." *Journal of Finance*, May, 1952.
SINCLAIR, L. R. "Some Effects of Income Taxes and Succession Duties on Privately Owned Companies and Their Shareholders." *Canadian Chartered Accountant* 45: 290–5 (Nov., 1944).
SOMERS, H. M. "The Place of the Corporation Income Tax in the Tax Structure." *National Tax Journal* 5: 279–85 (Sept., 1952).
SOPHIAN, T. J. "Bonus Shares and Debentures." *Accountant* 3960: 474–6 (Nov. 11, 1950).
——— "Capitalization of Profits." *Taxation* 46: 119–21 (Nov. 11, 1950).
STAPLES, RONALD. "Computation of Taxable Profits." Paper read before the International Fiscal Congress, Rome, 1948. *Taxation* 42: 27–9 (Oct. 9, 1948); 48–9 (Oct. 16, 1948).
"Taxable Profits." *Taxation* 43: 467–9 (Aug. 27, 1949).
THOM, S. "Defining Taxable Income Held Not an Easy Matter." *Financial Post*, Nov. 18, 1950.
——— "Depreciation and Income Tax." *Canadian Banker*, Winter, 1951.
THOM, S. and McDONALD, J. G. "Capital Gains and Losses in Canada." *Canadian Bar Review* 30: 98–101 (Jan., 1952).
"The Use of the Term 'Reserve' for Accounting for Reserves." *Canadian Chartered Accountant* 62: 126–8 (March, 1953).
WELLINGTON, C. O. "Accounting Income vs. Economic Income." *Canadian Chartered Accountant* 54: 27–34 (Jan., 1949).
WIGHT, J. B. "Ascertainment of Profit in Business." *Canadian Chartered Accountant*, February, 1958.
WYNNE, W. H. "The Burden of Obsolescence: Depreciation Relief under the Income War Tax Act of Canada." *Canadian Chartered Accountant* 31: 312–26 (April, 1937).
YOUNG, A. B. "Depreciation and Depletion—An Inter-American Comparison." *Taxes* 30: 278–98 (April, 1952).

CHAPTER 4

DOMINION INCOME TAX: NON-RESIDENTS AND FOREIGN INCOME OF RESIDENTS

Government Documents
CANADA. Advisory Committee on Overseas Investment, *Report* (G. R. BALL, Chairman). Ottawa, King's Printer, 1950.
Agreements for the avoidance of double taxation of incomes—Treaty Series
Canada—United States
>Signed at Washington, March 4, 1942. Treaty Series, 1942, no. 2. Ottawa, King's Printer, 1942.
>Signed at Ottawa, June 12, 1950. Ratified Nov. 21, 1951. Treaty Series, 1951, no. 22. Ottawa, Queen's Printer, 1951.
>Signed at Ottawa, Aug. 8, 1956. Ratified Sept. 26, 1957. Treaty Series, 1957, no. 22. Ottawa, Queen's Printer, 1958.

Canada—United Kingdom
>Signed at London, June 5, 1946. Treaty Series, 1946, no. 17. Ottawa, King's Printer, 1946.
>Signed at Ottawa, July 27 and Aug. 14, 1951. Treaty Series, 1951, no. 19. Ottawa, Queen's Printer, 1951.
>Signed at Ottawa, May 9 and 22, 1952. In force July 8, 1952. Treaty Series, 1952, no. 11. Ottawa, Queen's Printer, 1954.
>Signed at Ottawa, June 30 and July 21, 1953. In force Aug. 29, 1953. Treaty Series, 1953, no. 10. Ottawa, Queen's Printer, 1954.
>Signed at Ottawa, Feb. 27 and April 9, 1953. In force May 1, 1953. Treaty Series, 1953, no. 6. Ottawa, Queen's Printer, 1954.
>Signed at Ottawa, May 1 and July 16, 1957. In force July 16, 1957. Treaty Series, 1957, no. 15. Ottawa, Queen's Printer, 1959.
>Signed at Ottawa, May 1, 1957 and Feb. 13, 1958. In force Feb. 13, 1958. Treaty Series, 1958, no. 7. Ottawa, Queen's Printer, 1959.

Canada—South Africa
>Signed at Pretoria, Nov. 26, 1951. In force Feb. 29, 1952. Treaty Series, 1952, no. 1. Ottawa, Queen's Printer, 1952.
>Signed at Ottawa, Sept. 28, 1956. Ratified Oct. 11, 1957. In force Jan. 1, 1958. Treaty Series, 1957, no. 23. Ottawa, Queen's Printer, 1958.

Canada—France
>Signed at Paris, Mar. 16, 1951. In force Jan. 1, 1952. Treaty Series, 1953, no. 7. Ottawa, Queen's Printer, 1954.

Canada—Ireland
>Signed at Ottawa, Oct. 28, 1954. Ratified Dec. 20, 1955. Treaty Series, 1955, no. 22. Ottawa, Queen's Printer, 1957.

Canada—Denmark
>Signed at Ottawa, Sept. 20, 1955. Ratified Sept. 5, 1956. Treaty Series, 1956, no. 7. Ottawa, Queen's Printer, 1958.

Canada—Germany
>Signed at Ottawa, June 4, 1956. Ratified July 5, 1957. Treaty Series, 1957, no. 12. Ottawa, Queen's Printer, 1958.

Canada—Netherlands
> Signed at Ottawa, April 2, 1957. Ratified Dec. 17, 1957. Treaty Series, 1957, no. 30. Ottawa, Queen's Printer, 1959.

Canada—Australia
> Signed at Mont Tremblant, Oct. 1, 1957. In force May 21, 1958. Treaty Series, 1958, no. 16. Ottawa, Queen's Printer, 1959.

Canada—Finland
> Signed at Ottawa, March 28, 1959. Ratified Dec. 27, 1959. Treaty Series, 1959, no. 23. Ottawa, Queen's Printer, 1960.

Books and Pamphlets

AMERICAN MANAGEMENT ASSOCIATION. *The Taxation of Business Income from Foreign Operations.* New York, American Management Association, 1958.

BIANCHI, S. and WALTER, O. L. *Swiss Tax Shelter Opportunities for U.S. Business.* Zurich, Schulthers & Co., 1960.

BLOUGH, R. "Treatise to Eliminate International Double Taxation and Fiscal Evasion." *Proceedings of the Fifth Annual Institute on Federal Taxation.* New York University, 1946.

CANADIAN TAX FOUNDATION. *Canada's Income Tax Treaties.* 12th Tax Conference, 1958.

—— *Corporate Residence as a Tax Factor.* Corporate Management Conference, 1961 (Tax Paper no. 24, May 1961).

—— *Foreign Business Corporations.* 13th Tax Conference 1959.

—— *Foreign Tax Havens for Canadian Business.* 11th Tax Conference 1957.

—— *Income from Multiple Sources.* 14th Tax Conference, 1960.

—— *Recent Foreign Tax Developments.* 8th Tax Conference 1954.

—— *Taxation and Foreign Investment.* 10th Tax Conference 1956.

CARROLL, M. B. *Prevention of International Double Taxation and Fiscal Evasion: Two Decades of Progress under the League of Nations.* Geneva, League of Nations, 1939.

DE LA GIRODAY, J. B. *Canadian Taxation and Foreign Investment.* Canadian Tax Papers, no. 9. Toronto, Canadian Tax Foundation, 1955.

DEPERON, PAUL. *International Double Taxation.* New York, Committee on International Economic Policy in cooperation with the Carnegie Endowment for International Peace, 1945.

ECKER-RACZ, L. L. "Tax Stimulants to Foreign Investment." *Proceedings of the 42nd Annual Conference of the National Tax Association. 1949,* pp. 142–52.

EHRENZWEIG, A. A. and KOCH, F. E. *Income Tax Treaties.* New York, Commerce Clearing House, 1949.

FEDERATION OF BRITISH INDUSTRIES. *Taxation in Western Europe.* 3rd (revised) ed., London, F.B.I., 1961.

GARLAND, C. E. and HUGHES, P. F. *Double Taxation.* London, Taxation Publishing Co., 1960.

GIBBONS, W. J. *Tax Factors in Basing International Business Abroad.* Cambridge. Harvard University Law School, 1957.

INTERNATIONAL BUREAU OF FISCAL DOCUMENTATION. *Company Taxation in Western Europe.* Amsterdam, R. Mees & Zoonen, 1959.

—— *Foreign Securities and Taxation.* Amsterdam, R. Mees & Zoonen, 1960.

KING, E. P. "Income Tax Reciprocity with Canada." *Proceedings of the 31st Annual Conference of the National Tax Association, 1938*, pp. 551–7.

KOCH, F. E. *The Double Taxation Conventions*. London, Stevens, 1950. Supplement to the author's *Taxation of Income* (London, Stevens, 1947), vol. I.

KOCH, F. E. and Moss, R. *Double Taxation Relief in the U.K.* Amsterdam, International Bureau of Fiscal Documentation, 1957.

LEAGUE OF NATIONS. *Memorandum on Double Taxation*. By B. P. BLACKETT. Geneva, 1921.

—— *Report on Double Taxation Submitted to the Financial Committee*. By W. G. J. BRUINS, LUIGI EINAUDI, E. R. A. SELIGMAN, and Sir JOSIAH STAMP. Geneva, 1923.

—— *Double Taxation and Tax Evasion*. Report and resolutions submitted by the technical experts to the Financial Committee. Geneva, 1925.

—— *Draft Conventions on Double Taxation*. Geneva, 1927.

—— *Report on Double Taxation and Tax Evasion: Model Conventions for the Prevention of Double Taxation*. Geneva, 1928.

—— *Taxation of Foreign and National Enterprises*. Edited by M. B. CARROLL. Geneva, 1932-3. 5 vols. (A study of the tax systems and the methods of allocation of the profits of enterprises operating in more than one country.)

—— *Double Taxation and Fiscal Evasion: Collection of International Agreements and Internal Legal Provisions for the Prevention of Double Taxation and Fiscal Evasion*. Geneva, 1928-36. 6 vols.

—— *London and Mexico Model Tax Conventions, Commentary and Text*. Geneva, 1946.

ORGANIZATION FOR EUROPEAN ECONOMIC CO-OPERATION. *The Elimination of Double Taxation*. 1st, 2nd, & 3rd Reports of the Fiscal Committee. Paris, 1958–60.

PHILLIPS, N. F. *United States Taxation of Nonresident Aliens and Foreign Corporations*. Toronto, Carswell, 1952.

SELIGMAN, E. R. A. *Double Taxation and International Fiscal Cooperation*. New York, Macmillan, 1928.

SHERE, L. "Taxation of American Business Abroad." *Proceedings of the Seventh Annual Institute on Federal Taxation*. New York University, 1948. P. 812.

UNITED NATIONS. *Resolution on Double Taxation* (Council of the International Chamber of Commerce). E/C. 2/126, June 8, 1946.

—— *Questionnaire on the Tax Treatment of Foreign Nationals, Assets and Transactions*. E/CN.8/W19, Aug. 5, 1948.

—— *Taxation of Foreign Taxpayers and Foreign Income in Canada*. New York, 1952. (Also in other countries.)

—— *Tax Treatment of Foreign Nationals, Resources and Transactions*. E/CN. 8/45, Dec. 20, 1948; E/CN.8/45 Add. 1, Dec. 31, 1948.

—— *Replies of Member Governments to Questionnaire on Tax Treatment of Foreign Nationals, Assets and Transactions*. E/CN.8/46 Add. 1-18, Dec., 1948–Dec., 1952. See especially Reply of the Government of Canada, E/CN.8/46 Add. 18.

—— *Statements of Views of Member Governments on Mexico and London Model Tax Conventions*. E/CN.8/W22, Nov. 15, 1948.

——— *Report of the Second Session of the Fiscal Commission, Economic and Social Council.* Resolution 226 (IX), July 22, 1949.
UNITED NATIONS, DEPARTMENT OF ECONOMIC AFFAIRS. *International Tax Agreements.* Lake Success, N.Y., 1948. 9 vols.
——— *The Effects of Taxation on Foreign Trade and Investment.* Lake Success, N.Y., 1950.

Periodical Articles
BARKMEIER, J. H. "Avoidance of Double Taxation: New Convention with Canada." *Foreign Commerce Weekly* 8: 10-11, 36 (Aug. 22, 1942).
BLOCH, H. S. and HEILEMANN, C. E. "International Tax Relations." *Yale Law Journal* 55: 1158-73 (1946).
CAMERON, A. "Taxes in organizing a business abroad." *Journal of Accountancy* (July, 1958).
CARROLL, M. B. "International Tax Conventions." *Taxes* 30: 269-73 (April, 1952).
——— "The New Tax Convention between the United States and Canada." *Taxes* 20: 459-64, 512 (Aug., 1942).
———"How tax treaties benefit U.S. companies doing business abroad." *Journal of Taxation* (April, 1958).
EATON, A. K. "Canada's international income tax agreements." *Canadian Chartered Accountant* (May, 1957).
GIBSON, J. K. Choosing between branch and subsidiary." *Canadian Chartered Accountant* (July, 1960).
GILPIN, E. R. and WELLS, H. G. "International Double Taxation of Income, Its Problems and Remedies." *Taxes* 28: 9-32 (Jan., 1950).
KING, E. P. "Fiscal Cooperation in Tax Treaties." *Taxes* 26: 889-95 (Oct., 1948).
——— "Modifications of United States Tax Law by Treaty." *Ibid.* 26: 1001-8 (Nov., 1948).
KOCH, F. E. "Liability of Americans to Tax on Income from Employment and Profession in the United Kingdom." *Taxes* 27: 461-3 (May, 1949).
——— "Taxation of Foreign Subsidiaries: The Doctrine of Control by Parent Companies." *Ibid.* 28: 955-8 (Oct., 1950).
LAIRD, J. K. M. "U.S.A.–Canada Border Problems of Taxation." *Tax Review*, March, 1952: 53-8.
MACKAY, R. DEWOLFE. "Some aspects of accounting and legal problems confronting foreign companies carrying on business in Canada." (Paper presented at the 1958 Conference of the Canadian Institute of Chartered Accountants.)
MCALPINE, A. D. "Income from multiple sources." (Paper presented at the 1960 Conference of the Canadian Tax Foundation.) Toronto, C.T.F., 1961.
MCENTYRE, J. G. "Canada—United States Tax Convention." *Tax Bulletin* 2: 318-25 (Nov.-Dec., 1952).
NORTCLIFFE, E. B. "Tax Exemption of Foreign Income: Outline of the Practice in Seven Countries." *Accountant* 128: 7-10 (Jan. 3, 1953).
SHAKESPEARE, W. C. "Foreign tax problems affecting Canadian Corporations." *Tax Executive* (July, 1957).
SHARP, G. A. "Canadian Taxation of Non-Residents." *Tax Review*, Sept., 1952: 167-8.

SHELBOURNE, PHILIP. "Double Taxation and its improvement." *British Tax Review* (March, 1957).
SMITH, DAN THROOP. "The functions of tax treaties." *National Tax Journal* (December, 1959).
SMITH, L. J. "Taxation of U.S. citizens resident in Canada." *Canadian Chartered Accountant* (March, 1958).
SOPHIAN, T. J. "Taxation of Foreign Income." *Taxation* 49: 164-5 (May 31, 1952).
SURREY, S. S. "The Pakistan tax treaty and 'tax sparing.'" *National Tax Journal* (June, 1958).
STIKEMAN, H. H. "'Carrying on Business in Canada' in Dominion Income Tax Law." *Canadian Bar Review* 20: 77-108 (Feb., 1942).
"Trading by Non-Residents." *Taxation* 43: 71-2 (April 23, 1949).
WANG, KE-CHIN. "International Double Taxation of Income: Relief through International Agreement, 1941-1945." *Harvard Law Review*, 59: 73-116 (1945).
WARD, DAVID A. "Corporate residence as a tax factor." Canadian Tax Papers no. 24. Corporate Management Conference, 1961. Toronto, C.T.F., 1961.

CHAPTER 5

DOMINION ESTATE TAX AND GIFT TAX

Government Documents

Agreements for the avoidance of double taxation of estates—Treaty Series
Canada—United States
  Signed June 8, 1944. Treaty Series, 1944, no. 17. Ottawa, Queen's Printer, 1951.
  Signed at Ottawa, June 12, 1950. Ratified November 12, 1951. Treaty Series, 1951, no. 23. Ottawa, Queen's Printer, 1951.
  Signed at Washington, February 17, 1961 [not yet ratified].
Canada—United Kingdom
  Signed at London, June 5, 1946. Treaty Series, 1946, no. 18. Ottawa, King's Printer, 1946.
Canada—South Africa
  Signed at Ottawa, September 28, 1956. Ratified October 11, 1957. In force, January 1, 1958. Treaty Series, 1957, no. 24. Ottawa, Queen's Printer, 1958.
Canada—France
  Signed at Paris, March 16, 1951. In force, May 28, 1953. Treaty Series, 1953, no. 8. Ottawa, Queen's Printer, 1955.
Canada—Ireland
  Signed at Ottawa, October 28, 1954. Ratified December 20, 1955. Treaty Series, 1955, no. 23. Ottawa, Queen's Printer, 1957.
Canada—Switzerland
  Signed at Ottawa, March 28 and June 23, 1958. In force, September 8, 1958. Treaty Series, 1958, no. 30. Ottawa, Queen's Printer, 1960.
CANADA, DEPARTMENT OF NATIONAL REVENUE, SUCCESSION DUTIES DIVISION. *Dominion Succession Duty Act, Explanatory Brochure*. Rev. March, 1947. Ottawa, King's Printer, 1947.

BIBLIOGRAPHY 389

DOMINION-PROVINCIAL CONFERENCE ON RECONSTRUCTION, 1945. *Succession Duties.* [Ottawa], 1945. (Reference book.)

The Dominion Succession Duty Act (including the Canada-United States of America Tax Convention Act, 1944, and the Canada-United Kingdom Succession Duty Agreement Act, 1946). Office consolidation, Sept., 1949. Ottawa, King's Printer, 1950.

The Estate Tax Act. Assented to September 6, 1958. Ch. 29, *Statutes of Canada, 1958,* vol. I. Ottawa, Queen's Printer, 1958.

Act to Amend the Estate Tax Act. Assented to July 7, 1960. Ch. 29, *Statutes of Canada, 1960,* vol. I. Ottawa, Queen's Printer, 1958.

UNITED STATES, TREASURY DEPARTMENT. *Federal Estate and Gift Taxes. A Proposal for Integration and for Correlation with the Income Tax.* Washington, Government Printing Office, 1948.

Books and Pamphlets

CCH CANADIAN. *Estate Tax Act.* 2nd ed. Toronto, CCH Canadian, 1960.

CANADIAN TAX FOUNDATION. *Fourth Tax Conference December 11 and 12, 1950: Preparatory Reports for Round Table.* Toronto, 1950.

——— *Death Duties.* 8th Tax Conference 1954.

——— *Death Tax Revision.* 9th Tax Conference 1955.

——— *Family Relationships Under Income and Death Taxes.* 13th Tax Conference 1959.

——— *Federal Estate Tax Act 1958.* 12th Tax Conference 1958.

——— *Gift Tax—Its Purpose and Effects.* 13th Tax Conference 1959.

Canadian Succession Duties Reporter. Toronto, CCH Canadian Ltd. (Looseleaf.)

COURTICE, A. R. "Succession Duties." *Report of the 1948 Tax Conference Convened by the Canadian Tax Foundation, Ottawa,* pp. 61-72.

Dominion Succession Duties Service (loose-leaf). Toronto, Richard De Boo.

Green's Death Duties. 4th ed., ed. by C. D. HARDING. London, Butterworth, 1958.

JAMESON, M. B. *Canadian Estate Tax.* Toronto, Butterworth, 1960.

LEAGUE OF NATIONS. *London and Mexico Model Tax Conventions, Commentary and Text.* Geneva, 1946.

LINTON, W. I. *A Review of the Estate Tax Act.* Canadian Tax Papers, no. 14. Toronto, Canadian Tax Foundation, 1960.

LOFFMARK, R. R. *Estate Taxes.* Toronto, Carswell, 1960.

NATIONAL TAX ASSOCIATION, COMMITTEE ON INTERNATIONAL TAX RELATIONSHIPS. "Report." *Proceedings of the 36th Annual Conference of the National Tax Association, 1943,* pp. 13-20. (Problems of taxation between the United States and Canada.)

——— "Report." *Proceedings of the 37th Annual Conference of the National Tax Association, 1944,* pp. 220-3. (Further consideration of "domicile" vs. "situs" in determining superior right to tax intangible personal property in death duties.)

OVENS, GEORGE. *The Valuation of Private Companies and Other Properties for Succession Duties and Similar Purposes.* Paper read to the Canadian Bar Association, Sept. 13, 1951.

SHULTZ, W. J. *The Taxation of Inheritance.* Boston, Houghton Mifflin, 1926.

Periodical Articles

BARNA, TIBOR. "Death Duties in Britain." *Taxes* 26: 1062-3 (Nov., 1948).

BISSONETTE, A. L. "Canadian Death Duty Legislation 1892–1958." *Canadian Bar Review*, May, 1958.
BURGER, J. T. "The Dominion Succession Duty Act." *Alberta Law Quarterly* 4: 220-4 (1940-2).
CRAWFORD, H. "Retention of a Benefit in Estate Planning." *Canadian Tax Journal* 8: 31 (1960).
ELLIOTT, C. F. "The Dominion Succession Duty Act: A Reply" (to P. B. Mignault; see below). *Canadian Bar Review* 20: 141-5 (Feb., 1942).
FAIRBANKS, E. B. "Shares of a Non-Resident Decedent—A Canadian View." *Taxes* 22: 103, 135 (March, 1944).
GRAHAM, J. W. "The Estate Tax Act—Some Shortcomings." *Canadian Tax Journal* 7: 32 (1959).
HAWKES, G. R. "Death Duties and Double Taxation: Canada and the United States Compared." *National Tax Journal* 5: 145-54 (June, 1952).
HOCKLEY, V. S. "Estate Duty." *Accountant* 127: 538-41, 570-2 (Nov. 8, 15, 1952).
KNIGHTON, R. A. "Canada's New Estate Tax Act." *Trusts and Estates*, November, 1958.
LABRIE, F. E. "Canadian Estate Tax Act." *University of Toronto Law Journal* vol. XIII, no. 1 (1959).
LOWNDES, C. L. B. "Tax Avoidance and the Federal Estate Tax." *Law and Contemporary Problems* 7: 309-30 (Spring, 1940).
MIGNAULT, P. B. "The Dominion Succession Duty Act: Its Effect on the Succession Law of Quebec." *Canadian Bar Review* 19: 719-32 (Dec., 1941).
NASH, T. B. "The Provisions of the Dominion Succession Duty Act." *Canadian Chartered Accountant* 59: 241-8 (Dec., 1951).
PAXTON, C. D. "Death Duties Around the World." *Trusts and Estates*, June, 1957.
STEEN, D. G. "Estate Duty" (Great Britain). *Accountants' Magazine* 53: 201-10 (July, 1949).
"Succession Duties under Canada–United States Convention." *Canadian Chartered Accountant* 47: 223-30 (Oct., 1945). (Memorandum of instructions and forms issued by Succession Duties Division, Dept. of National Revenue.)
VINEBERG, P. F. "Succession Duty Valuations." *Canadian Chartered Accountant* 55: 49-58 (Aug., 1949).

CHAPTER 6

DOMINION COMMODITY TAXES
THE CUSTOMS TARIFF; THE GENERAL SALES TAX

CUSTOMS TARIFF

Government Documents

CANADA, DEPARTMENT OF NATIONAL REVENUE, CUSTOMS DIVISION. *The Customs Tariff and Amendments, with Index to June 1, 1960*. Office consolidation. [Ottawa, 1960.]

BIBLIOGRAPHY 391

────── *Memoranda to Collectors of Customs and Excise* (loose-leaf). Supplement to *Customs Tariff and Amendments*. (Regulations, rulings, tax changes, trade agreements, etc.)
CANADA, ROYAL COMMISSION ON THE TEXTILE INDUSTRY. *Report* (W. F. A. TURGEON, Commissioner). Ottawa, King's Printer, 1938. See chap. 4, "The Canadian Customs Tariff and Its Administration in Recent Years," pp. 64-92.
See also General Sources. sec. E (1), item 3.

Books

ANNETT, D. R. *British Preference in Canadian Commercial Policy*. Toronto, Ryerson, 1948.
ANNIS, C. A. "A Study of Canadian Tariffs and Trade Agreements." Ph.D. thesis, Cornell University, 1936.
MCDIARMID, O. J. *Commercial Policy in the Canadian Economy*. Cambridge. Mass., Harvard University Press, 1946.

GENERAL SALES TAX

Government Documents

CANADA, DEPARTMENT OF FINANCE. *Sales Tax Committee Report*. Ottawa, Q.P., 1956.
GREAT BRITAIN, PURCHASE TAX/UTILITY COMMITTEE. *Report*. London, H.M. Stationery Office, 1952. Cmd. 8452.
GREAT BRITAIN, PURCHASE TAX (VALUATION) COMMITTEE. *Report*. London, H.M. Stationery Office, 1953. Cmd. 8830.
UNITED STATES, CONGRESS, HOUSE OF REPRESENTATIVES, COMMITTEE ON WAYS AND MEANS. *Revenue Revision, 1943: Hearings*. . . . Washington, U.S. Government Printing Office, 1943. See Treasury Dept., "Considerations Respecting a Federal Retail Sales Tax," pp. 1095-1272.
UNITED STATES, CONGRESS, JOINT COMMITTEE ON INTERNAL REVENUE TAXATION. *Sales Tax Data*. Washington, U.S. Government Printing Office, 1942. Canadian manufacturers' sales tax, pp. 105-7.

Books and Periodical Articles

BUEHLER, A. G. *General Sales Taxation, Its History and Development*. New York, Business Bourse, 1932.
CANADIAN MANUFACTURERS ASSOCIATION. *Sales Tax Canada*. Toronto, Canadian Manufacturers Association, 1956.
CANADIAN METAL MINING ASSOCIATION. *Federal Sales Tax and the Mining Industry*. Toronto, C.M.M.A., 1959.
Canadian Sales and Excise Tax Guide. Toronto, CCH Canadian Ltd., October, 1960.
CANADIAN TAX FOUNDATION. *Review of the Report of the Sales Tax Committee*. 10th Tax Conference 1956.
────── *Sales Tax*. 8th Tax Conference 1954.
────── *Sales Tax*. 9th Tax Conference 1955.
────── *The Tariff*. 11th Tax Conference 1957.
DUE, J. F. "American and Canadian Experience with the Sales Tax." *Journal of Finance*, September, 1952.

———— *The General Manufacturers Sales Tax in Canada.* Canadian Tax Papers, no. 3. Toronto, Canadian Tax Foundation, Oct. 15, 1951.
———— "The Incidence of a General Sales Tax." *Public Finance* 5: 222-39 (no. 3, 1950).
———— "Lessons from Canada's Experience with the Manufacturers' Sales Tax." *Annual Conference Proceedings.* National Tax Association, 1952.
———— "The Sales Tax as an Anti-Inflationary Measure." *Public Finance* 1951.
———— *Sales Taxation.* London, Routledge & Kegan Paul, 1957.
———— "Toward a General Theory of Sales Tax Incidence." *Quarterly Journal of Economics*, May, 1953.
HODGINS, J. E. "The Canadian Sales Tax" (history and development). *Bulletin for International Fiscal Documentation* 4: 5-12 (1950).
———— "The Sales Taxes of Canada and New Zealand, a Comparative Study." *Bulletin for International Fiscal Documentation* 5: 281-90, 1951.
MCCORMICK, R. N., ed. *Sales tax—Canada. The Excise Tax, as Amended, with Regulations Issued by the Department of National Revenue and with Rulings and Regulations re Sales Tax and Other Excise Taxes.* Toronto, Canadian Manufacturers' Association, 1950.
MCLAUGHLIN, C. "Federal Sales Tax." *Cost and Management*, January, 1960.
NATIONAL INDUSTRIAL CONFERENCE BOARD. *Sales Taxes: General, Selective and Retail.* New York, the Board, 1932.
NELSON, C. L., BLAKEY, G. C., and BLAKEY, R. G. *Sales Taxes.* Minneapolis, League of Minnesota Municipalities, 1935.

CHAPTER 7

DOMINION COMMODITY TAXES
EXCISE TAXES, EXCISE DUTIES, AND MISCELLANEOUS TAXES

Government Documents

CANADA, DEPARTMENT OF NATIONAL REVENUE, EXCISE DIVISION. *The Excise Tax Act and Amendments to Date.* Office consolidation, August, 1960. Ottawa, Queen's Printer, 1960.
———— *Regulations under the Excise Act.* Ottawa, Queen's Printer, July, 1959.
CANADA, DOMINION BUREAU OF STATISTICS. *The Control and Sale of Alcoholic Beverages in Canada.* Ottawa. Annual report.
UNITED STATES, CONGRESS, JOINT COMMITTEE ON INTERNAL REVENUE TAXATION. *The Provisions of the Internal Revenue Code Relating to Excise Taxes.* 2nd ed., Washington, U.S. Government Printing Office, March 31, 1949.
UNITED STATES, LIBRARY OF CONGRESS, LEGISLATIVE REFERENCE SERVICE. *Federal Excise Taxes*, by R. E. MANNING. Public Affairs Bulletin, no. 72. Washington, 1949.
UNITED STATES, TREASURY DEPARTMENT, BUREAU OF INTERNAL REVENUE. *Regulation 132 Relating to Excise and Special Tax on Wagering under Chapter 27A of the Internal Revenue Code.* Washington, U.S. Government Printing Office, 1951.

BIBLIOGRAPHY 393

UNITED STATES, TREASURY DEPARTMENT, DIVISION OF TAX RESEARCH. *Excise Taxes: United States, Canada and the United Kingdom*. [Washington, 1944.]
——— *Federal Excise Taxes on Alcoholic Beverages, 1948*. [Washington, 1948.] (See especially Part 5, a comparison of taxes on alcoholic beverages in the United States, Canada, and the United Kingdom.)
——— *Federal Excise Taxes on Tobacco*. [Washington, 1948.] (See especially Part 5, a comparison of tobacco taxes in the United States, Canada, and the United Kingdom.)
——— *Federal Excise Taxes on Transportation*. [Washington, 1947.]
——— *Federal Retail Excise Taxes*. [Washington, 1947.]
See also General Sources, sec. E (1), item 2.

Books and Periodical Articles

Canadian Sales and Excise Tax Guide. Toronto, CCH Canadian Ltd. (annual).
CARTER, K. "Federal Sales Tax in Canada," *Canadian Chartered Accountant*, November, 1959.
DUE, J. F. *The General Manufacturers Sales Tax in Canada*. Canadian Tax Papers, no. 3. Toronto, Canadian Tax Foundation, 1951.
——— "The Manufacturers' Sales Tax." *Tax Bulletin* 2: 311–17 (Nov.-Dec., 1952).
MARKS, BENJAMIN. *Proof Spirit*. Mimico, Ont., L. J. McGuinness, 1943.
THOM, S. D. "Identifying the Manufacturer under the Excise Tax Act." *Canadian Tax Journal* 7: 219 (1959).

CHAPTER 8

CONSTITUTIONAL LIMITATIONS ON PROVINCIAL TAXATION

Government Documents

CANADA, *Minutes of the Proceedings in Conference of the Representatives of the Provinces in the Years 1887, 1902, 1906, 1910, 1913, 1918, 1926*. [Ottawa, King's Printer], 1926.
CANADA, ROYAL COMMISSION ON DOMINION-PROVINCIAL RELATIONS. *Report*. See General Sources, sec. F (1). Book I: *Canada: 1867-1939*. See also studies prepared for the Commission: D. G. CREIGHTON, *British North America at Confederation* (Ottawa, 1939); L. M. GOUIN and BROOKE CLAXTON, *Legislative Expedients and Devices Adopted by the Dominion and the Provinces* (Ottawa, 1939).
CONSTITUTIONAL CONFERENCE OF FEDERAL AND PROVINCIAL GOVERNMENTS (Second Session). *Proceedings*. Quebec, Sept. 25-8, 1950. Ottawa, King's Printer, 1950.
Dominion-Provincial and Interprovincial Conferences from 1887 to 1926. Ottawa King's Printer, 1951.
Dominion-Provincial Conferences, 1927, 1935, 1941. Ottawa, King's Printer, 1951 (reprint).
DOMINION-PROVINCIAL CONFERENCE ON RECONSTRUCTION, 1945. *Dominion and Provincial Submissions and Plenary Conference Discussions*. Ottawa, King's Printer, 1946.

FEDERAL-PROVINCIAL CONFERENCE, 1955. *Report of preliminary meeting.* Ottawa, Queen's Printer, 1955.
FEDERAL-PROVINCIAL CONFERENCE, 1955. *Report of Fiscal Meeting.* Ottawa, Queen's Printer, 1955.
FEDERAL-PROVINCIAL CONFERENCE, 1957. *Report.* Ottawa, Queen's Printer, 1958.
DOMINION GOVERNMENT AND CANADIAN MUNICIPALITIES INFORMAL CONFERENCE, 1958. *Proceedings.* Ottawa, Queen's Printer, 1958.
FEDERAL-PROVINCIAL CONFERENCE, July 1960. *Report.* Ottawa, Queen's Printer, 1960.

Books and Pamphlets

CANADIAN TAX FOUNDATION. *Federal Provincial Tax Arrangements.* 10th Tax Conference, 1956.
DAWSON, R. M., ed. *Constitutional Issues in Canada, 1900-1931.* London, Oxford University Press, 1933.
DAWSON, R. M. *The Government of Canada.* 3rd ed., revised. Toronto, University of Toronto Press, 1957.
GÉRIN-LAJOIE, PAUL. *Constitutional Amendment in Canada.* Toronto, University of Toronto Press, 1950.
GETTYS, LUELLA. *The Administration of Canadian Conditional Grants.* Chicago, Public Administration Service, 1938.
HELLERSTEIN, J. R. *State and Local Taxation, Cases and Materials.* New York, Prentice-Hall, 1952.
KENNEDY, W. P. M. *The Constitution of Canada, 1534-1937: An Introduction to Its Development, Law and Custom.* 2nd ed., London, Oxford University Press, 1938.
KENNEDY, W. P. M. and WELLS, D. C. *The Law of the Taxing Power in Canada.* Toronto, University of Toronto Press, 1931.
LEFROY, A. H. F. *Canada's Federal System, being a Treatise on Canadian Constitutional Law under the British North America Act.* Toronto, Carswell, 1913. See pp. 388-424.
────── *A Short Treatise on Canadian Constitutional Law.* Toronto, Carswell, 1918.
MOORE, A. M. and PERRY, J. H. *Financing Canadian Federation.* Tax Paper no. 6. Toronto, Canadian Tax Foundation, March, 1953.
PLAXTON, C. P., ed. *Canadian Constitutional Decisions of the Judicial Committee of the Privy Council, 1930 to 1939.* Ottawa, King's Printer, 1939.
QUEBEC. *Royal Commission of Inquiry on Constitutional Problems. Report.* Quebec, Q.P., 1956.
WOLFE, J. N. *Taxation and Development in the Maritimes.* Canadian Tax Papers, no. 16. Toronto, Canadian Tax Foundation, 1960.

Periodical Articles

CHATER, H. J. "Distribution of Functions and Revenue Sources between Province and Municipalities." *Canadian Journal of Accountancy* 1: 57-64 (Sept., 1952).
COTTON, C. M. "Is the Tax on Stock Transfers in the Province of Quebec Constitutional?" *Journal of the Canadian Bankers' Association* 13: 331-

BIBLIOGRAPHY 395

41 (July, 1906). (An interesting and useful discussion of the division of taxing powers at Confederation.)
GAGNON, J. O. "The Viewpoint of Quebec's Government." *Canadian Chartered Accountant* 62: 17-24 (Jan., 1953).
GRAHAM, J. F. "Fiscal Equity Principle in Provincial-Municipal Relations." *Canadian Public Relations*, March, 1960.
JOHNSON, A. W. "Problems of Provincial Finance." *Canadian Tax Journal* 8: 76 (1960).
LASKIN, B. "Provincial Marketing Levies: Indirect Taxation and Federal Power." *University of Toronto Law Journal* vol. XIII, no. 1 (1959).
MACDONALD, V. C. "The Licensing Power of the Provinces." *Canadian Bar Review* 17: 240-7 (April, 1939).
—— "Taxation Powers in Canada." *Ibid.* 19: 75-95 (Feb., 1941).

CHAPTER 9

PROVINCIAL INCOME AND CORPORATION TAXES

Government Documents

CANADA, DEPARTMENT OF FINANCE. *Provincial Corporation Taxes: A Tabulation of Revenues with Rates and Methods of Assessment.* Prepared for the National Finance Committee. [Ottawa, 1936].
—— ROYAL COMMISSION ON DOMINION-PROVINCIAL RELATIONS. *Report.* See General Sources, sec. F (1). Book III, pp. 134-41: taxes on corporations (provinces).
DOMINION-PROVINCIAL CONFERENCE ON RECONSTRUCTION, 1945. *Corporation Taxes.* [Ottawa], 1945. (Reference book.)

Books and Pamphlets

CANADIAN TAX FOUNDATION. *Overlapping Federal-Quebec Rules for Allocation of Corporate Profits.* 9th Tax Conference 1955.
—— *Provincial Corporate Profits Taxes.* 13th Tax Conference 1959.
CLARK, P. T. "The Tax Structure of Ontario in Relation to the Tax Structure of Other Provinces in Canada." *Revenue Administration, 1948: Proceedings of the 16th Annual Conference of the National Association of Tax Administrators*, pp. 33-7.
DOMINION ASSOCIATION OF CHARTERED ACCOUNTANTS. *Provincial Taxation Respecting Corporations and Individuals.* [Toronto], 1936. (Amendments to 1942 inserted.)
Ontario and Quebec Corporation and Income Tax. Toronto, CCH Canadian, 1960.

Periodical Articles

CLARK, P. T. "Ontario Corporations Tax." *Canadian Chartered Accountant* 37: 246-59 (Oct., 1940); 306-14 (Nov., 1940).
COFFEY, F. A. "Corporation Profits Taxation in Ontario and Quebec." *Tax Executive*, January, 1960.
GUNN, D. D. "Provincial Taxation of Paid Up Capital of Foreign Corporations." *Canadian Bar Review* 19: 31-6 (Jan., 1941).

KILGOUR, D. G. "Income Tax Allocation: a Problem of Law and Accounting." *University of Toronto Law Journal* vol. XIII, no. 1 (1959).
MOLLER, GEORGE. "Certain Accounting Aspects of Provincial Corporations Taxation." *Canadian Chartered Accountant* 51: 343-9 (Dec., 1947).
TOUSAW, A. A. "Taxation Problems of Life Insurance." *Canadian Journal of Economics and Political Science* 6: 440-7 (Aug., 1940).
TURCOT, WILFRID. "The Quebec Corporation Tax Act." *Canadian Chartered Accountant* 58: 241-8 (May, 1951).
WYNNE, W. H. "The Taxation of Corporations in Canada." *Bulletin of the National Tax Association* 27: 66-79 (Dec., 1941); 98-111 (Jan., 1942).

CHAPTER 10

PROVINCIAL SUCCESSION DUTIES

Government Documents
DOMINION-PROVINCIAL CONFERENCE ON RECONSTRUCTION, 1945. *Succession Duties*. [Ottawa], 1945. (Reference book.)
Minutes of the Proceedings in Conference of the Representatives of the Provinces in the Years 1887, 1902, 1906, 1910, 1913, 1918, 1926. [Ottawa, King's Printer], 1926. See especially proceedings of 1926.

Books and Pamphlets
BAYLY, R. A. *Succession Duty in Canada*. Toronto, Carswell, 1902.
Canadian Succession Duties Manual. 2nd ed., Toronto, CCH Canadian Ltd., 1949.
Canadian Succession Duties Reporter. Toronto, CCH Canadian Ltd. (Looseleaf.)
CANADIAN TAX FOUNDATION. *Ontario and Quebec Succession Duties*. 13th Tax Conference 1959.
DOMINION MORTGAGE AND INVESTMENTS ASSOCIATION. *Submission to the Royal Commission on Dominion-Provincial Relations*. Part I. *Taxation and Jurisdiction Respecting Trust and Loan Companies*. Toronto, the Association, Jan., 1938.
FARWELL, C. F. *The Law of Succession Duties in Ontario*. Toronto, Canadian Law List Publishing Co., 1942.
FISHER, R. M. "Succession Duties." Citizens' Research Institute of Canada, *Convention Proceedings, Canadian Tax Conference, 1925*, pp. 10-33.
JAMESON, M. B. *Ontario Succession Duties*. Toronto, Butterworth, 1959.
LAW SOCIETY OF UPPER CANADA. *Special Lectures on Taxation, 1944*. Toronto, Richard De Boo, 1944. Pp. 217-75.
QUIGG, SAMUEL. *The Law Relating to Succession Duties in Canada*. 2nd ed., Toronto, Carswell, 1937. See also *Supplement*, 1940.
RIVARD, E. *Les Droits Sur les Successions dans la Province de Québec*. Quebec, Les Presses Universitaires Laval, 1956.
SHULTZ, W. J. *The Taxation of Inheritance*. Boston, Houghton Mifflin, 1926.

Periodical Articles
ANDERSON, J. R. "Succession Duties—Double Taxation." *Canadian Bar Review* 15: 620-32 (Oct., 1937).
ARCHER, E. L. "Ontario Succession Duty Charges Analyzed." *Canadian Tax Journal* 7: 283 (1959).

FALCONBRIDGE, J. D. "Administration and Succession in the Conflict of Laws." *Canadian Bar Review* 12: 67-79 (Feb., 1934); 125-41 (March, 1934).
GOOD, J. M. "Notes for Students Regarding the Taxation of Succession Duties." *Alberta Law Quarterly* 4: 65-73 (1940-2). (Examples of mathematical computations of the amount of duty payable.)
HENRY, W. A. "Double Payment of Succession Duties." *Journal of the Canadian Bankers' Association* 24: 337-9 (July, 1917).
——— "Succession Duty and the Bank Act." *Ibid.* 26: 374-9 (July, 1919).
HOLT, C. M. "The Quebec Succession Duties Act as Applied to Bank Stocks." *Journal of the Canadian Bankers' Association* 10: 37-40 (July, 1903).
JAMESON, M. B. "Ontario and Quebec Succession Duties." *Canadian Tax Journal* 8: 110 (1960).
KEIRSTEAD, W. C. "Succession Duties in Canadian Provinces." *Journal of Political Economy* 30: 137-54 (April, 1922).
LASKIN, BORA. "Taxation and Situs: Company Shares." *Canadian Bar Review* 19: 617-37 (Nov., 1941).
QUIGG, SAMUEL. "Constitutionality of Succession Duties." *Canadian Bar Review* 16: 344-64 (May, 1938).
——— "Succession Duties in Canada." *Ibid.* 2: 40-9 (Jan., 1924).
WYNNE, W. H. "Double Taxation of Inheritances in Canada." *Canadian Chartered Accountant* 39: 148-72 (Sept., 1941).
See also articles by C. F. Elliott and P. B. Mignault, listed under chap. 5.

CHAPTER 11

PROVINCIAL CONSUMPTION AND EXPENDITURE TAXES

Government Documents

CANADA, DOMINION BUREAU OF STATISTICS. *The Motor Vehicle in Canada.* Ottawa. Annual report. (Gasoline taxes and revenues.)

Books and Periodical Articles

BURNS, R. M. "Problems in the Introduction of a Consumer Purchase Tax." *Proceedings of the 41st Annual Conference of the National Tax Association, 1948*, pp. 324-30. (Introduction of consumer purchase tax in British Columbia.)
DETWILLER, L. F. "Provincial Sales Tax." *Proceedings of the 1st Annual Conference of the Institute of Public Administration of Canada, 1949*, pp. 60-81.
DUE, J. F. *Provincial Sales Taxes.* Canadian Tax Papers, no. 7. Toronto, Canadian Tax Foundation, July, 1953.
——— *The Indirect Sales Tax Illusion.* Tax Memo, no. 23. Toronto, Canadian Tax Foundation, September, 1960.
——— "The Nova Scotia Hospital (Sales) Tax." *Canadian Tax Journal* 7: 388, 487 (1959); 8: 52, 135 (1960).
——— *Ontario Sales Tax 1. Structure.* Tax Memo, no. 27. Toronto, Canadian Tax Foundation, April, 1961.
——— *Ontario Sales Tax 2. Regulations and Rulings.* Tax Memo, no. 28. Toronto, Canadian Tax Foundation, July, 1961.
GIMAIEL, PHILIPPE. "Evolution in the Administration of the Gasoline Tax."

Proceedings of the 2nd Annual Conference of the Institute of Public Administration of Canada, 1950.

JACOBY, N. H. *Retail Sales Taxation.* Chicago, Commerce Clearing House, 1938.

SHAUGHNESSY, E. C. "Provincial Sales Tax." *Canadian Chartered Accountant* 33: 179-91 (Sept., 1938).

SHINK, G. H. "The Sales and Use Tax Laws of the Province of Quebec." *Proceedings of the 42nd Annual Conference of the National Tax Association, 1949*, pp. 336-46.

STANTON, R. H. "Sales Taxation in the Provincial and Municipal Fields." *Canadian Chartered Accountant* 60: 219-27 (June, 1952).

WATTS, E. W. "The Gasoline Tax." Citizens' Research Institute of Canada, *Convention Proceedings, Canadian Tax Conference, 1929*, pp. 27-34.

CHAPTER 12

PROVINCIAL LIQUOR AND MOTOR VEHICLE REVENUES AND MISCELLANEOUS TAXES

Government Documents

CANADA, DOMINION BUREAU OF STATISTICS. *The Motor Vehicle in Canada* Ottawa. Annual report.

———— *The Control and Sale of Alcoholic Beverages in Canada.* Ottawa. Annual report.

Books and Pamphlets

CANADIAN AUTOMOBILE CHAMBER OF COMMERCE. *Facts and Figures of the Automobile Industry.* Toronto. Annual.

DISTILLED SPIRITS INSTITUTE. *Public Revenues from Alcoholic Beverages.* Washington, D.C., the Institute. Annual.

CHAPTER 13

PROVINCIAL REVENUES FROM THE PUBLIC DOMAIN

Government Documents

CANADA, DEPARTMENT OF MINES AND TECHNICAL SURVEYS. *Summary Review of Federal Taxation and Certain Other Legislation Affecting Mining, Oil, and Natural Gas Enterprises in Canada.* Ottawa, Jan., 1959. (Mimeo.)

CANADA, DEPARTMENT OF MINES AND TECHNICAL SURVEYS, MINES BRANCH. *Digest of the Mining Laws of Canada.* 5th ed. Prepared by H. A. GRAVES and G. R. L. POTTER. Ottawa, Queen's Printer, 1957.

CANADA, DEPARTMENT OF RESOURCES AND DEVELOPMENT. *Canada's Forests 1946-1950.* Report to Sixth British Commonwealth Forestry Conference, held in Canada, 1952. Ottawa, Queen's Printer, 1952.

———— *Focus on Forestry.* Address by ROBERT H. WINTERS, at joint annual meeting of the Canadian Institute of Forestry and the Society of American Foresters, Montreal, Nov. 18, 1952. Ottawa, Queen's Printer, 1952.

DRUMMOND, G. F. *The Taxation of Forest Resources.* [Victoria,] Commission of Inquiry into Forest Resources of British Columbia. *Ca.* 1945. (Mimeo.)

ONTARIO, ROYAL MINING COMMISSION. *Report* (N. C. URQUHART, Chairman). Toronto, King's Printer, 1944. See Part 3: "Mining Taxation."
SASKATCHEWAN, DEPARTMENT OF NATURAL RESOURCES AND INDUSTRIAL DEVELOPMENT. *Report for the Year Ending March 31, 1948*. Regina, King's Printer, 1949. (Contains brief review of the administration of the Mineral Taxation Act.)
See also General Sources, sec. F (3), item 1; (7), item 3.
NOTE: For revenue statistics and other information regarding taxes in this field the reader should consult the provincial public accounts and the annual reports of the provincial departments administering lands, forests, mines, natural resources, etc.

For Tax Sharing Agreements between the Government of Canada and each of the provinces of Newfoundland, Prince Edward Island, Nova Scotia, New Brunswick, Manitoba, Saskatchewan, Alberta, and British Columbia, see provincial statutes.

Books and Periodical Articles

CROCKETT, E. C. "Some Policy Questions Relating to the Taxation of Mineral Resources." *Proceedings of the 41st Annual Conference of the National Tax Association, 1948*, pp. 223-30.
GEORGE, H. W. "Some Thoughts on Taxation of Mining Companies." *Canadian Chartered Accountant* 34: 92-101 (Feb., 1939).
IMPERIAL OIL LTD. *Facts and Figures about Canadian Oil*. Toronto, Oct., 1952.
MARQUIS, R. W. *Forest Yield Taxes*. Washington, Department of Agriculture, April, 1952.
—— "Severence Taxes on Forest Products and Their Relation to Forestry." *Land Economics* 25: 315-19 (Aug., 1949).
MCDONALD, J. G. "Preferential Taxation of the Natural Resources Industries in Canada." *Canadian Bar Review* 30: 119-36 (Feb., 1952).
MICKLE, G. R. "Mine Taxation in Ontario." Citizens' Research Institute of Canada, *Convention Proceedings, Canadian Tax Conference, 1927*, pp. 10-19.
MID-WEST METAL MINING ASSOCIATION. *Review of Taxation: Manitoba Metal Mining Corporation 1883-1942*. [Winnipeg, n.d.]
MOORE, A. M. *Forestry Taxes and Tenures*. Canadian Tax Papers, no. 11. Toronto, Canadian Tax Foundation, 1957.
MUTCH, D. A. *Brief on Taxation of the Metal and Asbestos Mining Industries, Province of Quebec, 1916-1941*. Prepared for the Western Quebec Mining Association and the Quebec Asbestos Producers Association. Quebec, July, 1943. (Processed.)
MUTCH, D. A. and NEILLY, BALMER. *Brief on Taxation of the Ontario Metal Mining Industry 1907-1941*. Prepared for the Ontario Mining Association. Toronto, March, 1943. (Processed.)
ONTARIO MINING ASSOCIATION. *Report of the Directors*. Toronto. Annual.

CHAPTER 14

MUNICIPAL TAXATION IN CANADA

Government Documents

CANADA, DEPARTMENT OF AGRICULTURE. *Taxation in Rural Ontario*. By S. C. HUDSON. Publication 489; Technical Bulletin 4. Ottawa, 1936.

CANADA, DOMINION BUREAU OF STATISTICS. *Canada Year Book.* Ottawa, Queen's Printer (annual).
────── *Financial Statistics of Municipal Governments.* Ottawa. Annual.
────── *The Tax Systems of Canada: Dominion, Provincial and Municipal Governments.* Ottawa, 1940.
ONTARIO, DEPARTMENT OF MUNICIPAL AFFAIRS. *Basis of Grants and Subsidies Payable to Municipalities.* Toronto, Q. P., 1957.
SASKATCHEWAN, ASSESSMENT COMMISSION. *The Saskatchewan System of Rural Land Assessment.* By T. H. FREEMAN. 2nd ed., Regina, 1950.
SASKATCHEWAN, DEPARTMENT OF MUNICIPAL AFFAIRS. *The Municipal System of Saskatchewan.* Regina, 1947.
See also General Sources, sec. F (2); (3), items 2, 3; (4); (5); (6); (7), items 1-3; (8); (9).
NOTE: It has not been feasible to list Assessment Manuals individually. However, almost every city and provincial department of municipal affairs has published handbooks on assessing principles and practice.

Books and Pamphlets

CAMERON, M. A. *Property Taxation and School Finance in Canada.* Canada and Newfoundland Education Association, 1945.
CANADIAN TAX FOUNDATION. *Municipal Business Taxes.* 13th Tax Conference 1959.
────── *Municipal Finance and Taxation.* 11th Tax Conference 1957.
────── *Uniform Assessment.* 12th Tax Conference 1958.
CLARK, R. M. *A Brief on the Proposed Business Tax By-Law for Vancouver* Jan. 9, 1948.
────── *The Municipal Business Tax in Canada.* Canadian Tax Papers, no. 5. Toronto, Canadian Tax Foundation, Feb. 29, 1952.
COLTER, E. R. "New Brunswick's Solution of a Difficult Problem." *Assessment Administration, 1946: Papers Presented at the 12th National Conference on Assessment Administration, Chicago, 1947,* pp. 98-100.
CRAWFORD, K. G. *Canadian Municipal Government.* Toronto, University of Toronto Press, 1954.
CURTIS, C. A. "The Functions of Municipalities in Ontario and Their Financial Problems." *Revenue Administration, 1948: Proceedings of the 16th Annual Conference of the National Association of Tax Administrators,* pp. 5-11.
DAWSON, G. F. *The Municipal System of Saskatchewan.* Rev. ed., Regina, Department of Municipal Affairs, April, 1952.
GOLDENBERG, H. C. *Municipal Finance in Canada.* Study prepared for the Royal Commission on Dominion-Provincial Relations. Ottawa, 1939.
────── *Statistical Report on Taxable Valuation and Exemptions in Canadian Municipalities.* Prepared by H. Carl Goldenberg, Economist of the Canadian Federation of Mayors and Municipalities. Montreal, 1937.
HOBBS, W. E. *Brief Setting Forth the Need for Considering Municipal Affairs and Finances at the Forthcoming Federal-Provincial Conference in September 1950.* Montreal, Canadian Federation of Mayors and Municipalities, 1950.
────── *Report of Enquiry into Municipal and School District Finances, November 1951 to January 1952.* Made at the request of the Union of British Columbia Municipalities. 1952. (Mimeo.)

BIBLIOGRAPHY 401

Local Finance. Reports issued periodically. Toronto, Canadian Tax Foundation, 1959—.

MACKAY, D. H. *A Review of the Past and Recommendations for Better Provincial-Municipal Relations.* Aug., 1952. (By the Mayor of Calgary.)

MACKINTOSH, W. A. *Economic Problems of the Prairie Provinces.* Toronto, Macmillan, 1935.

MANNING, H. E. *Assessment and Rating, being the Law of Municipal Taxation in Canada.* 3rd ed., Toronto, Canadian Law List Publishing Co., 1951.

MOONEY, G. S. *Public Finance, Federal, Provincial, Municipal, with Special Reference to Municipal Revenues and Expenditures for the Years 1930, 1939 and 1948.* Montreal, Canadian Federation of Mayors and Municipalities, Feb., 1951.

QUINTO, L. J. *Municipal Income Taxation in the United States.* New York, Mayor's Committee on Management Survey of the City of New York, May, 1952.

Periodical Articles

BARCLAY, J. A. "Municipal Tax Collections and Delinquency Trends in Canada." *Municipal Finance* 19: 5-8 (Feb., 1947).

CARTER, J. W. P. "The Property Tax in Ontario, Its Significance in Local Finance." *Tax Bulletin* 2: 353-60 (Nov.-Dec., 1952).

CLARK, D. H. "Real Property and Personal Income Taxes—Some Comparisons." *Canadian Tax Journal* 6: 186 (1958).

CLARK, R. M. "The Municipal Business Tax in Canada." *Canadian Journal of Economics and Political Science* 14: 491-501 (Nov., 1948).

―――― "Municipal Business Tax." *Canadian Tax Journal* 8: 339 (1960).

CRAWFORD, K. G. "Prepayment Discounts and Penalties in Tax Delinquents." *Municipal Finance* 19: 12-16 (Feb., 1947).

―――― "Some Aspects of Provincial-Municipal Relations." *Canadian Journal of Economics and Political Science* 16: 394-407 (Aug., 1950).

CURTIS, C. A. "Municipal Government in Ontario." *Canadian Journal of Economics and Political Science* 8: 416-26 (Aug., 1942).

FINNIS, F. H. "Property, Progress and Poverty." *Canadian Tax Journal* 8: 210, 283 (1960).

―――― "Prospects of Equity in Property Assessment." *Civic Affairs*, January, 1959.

GROVES, H. M. "The Property Tax in Canada and the United States." *Land Economics* 24: 23-30 (Feb., 1948); 120-8 (May, 1948).

HARDY, E. "Provincial-Municipal Financial Relations." *Canadian Public Administration*, March, 1960.

HILL, R. "Industrial Tax Sharing Essential." *Civic Administration*, January, 1960.

LOWTHER, J. H. "Uniformity in Municipal Accounting and Reporting." *Canadian Chartered Accountant* 57: 191-205 (Nov., 1950).

MANNING, H. E. "The Problem of Land Taxation." *Canadian Bar Review* 21:290-303 (April, 1943).

MOONEY, G. S. "Can the Property Tax Stand the Burden of Local School Costs?" *Listening Post*, November, 1959.

PERRY, J. H. "The Alberta Unearned Increment Tax." *University of Toronto Law Journal* no. 1, 1957.

——— "Municipal Finance Needs and Federal Fiscal Policy—A Canadian View." *Canadian Tax Journal* 7: 308 (1959).
ROBERGE, LACTANCE. "Montreal's Revenues." *Municipal Finance* 15: 12-14 (Feb., 1943).
STEWART, ANDREW and HANSON, E. J. "Some Aspects of Rural Municipal Finance." *Canadian Journal of Economics and Political Science* 14: 481-90 (Nov., 1948).
TAYLOR, W. G. "Determining the Basis and Enforcement of Business Licences and Taxes." *Municipal Finance*, November, 1957.
TINGLEY, L. T. "Moncton's Tenancy (Rental) Tax." *Municipal Finance* 15: 14-16 (Feb., 1943).

CHAPTERS 15, 16

ENACTMENT OF THE TAX LAWS OF THE DOMINION

CANADA, DEPARTMENT OF FINANCE. *Budget Speech of the Minister of Finance.* Ottawa, Queen's Printer (annual).
——— *Estimates.* Ottawa, Queen's Printer (annual).
CANADA, HOUSE OF COMMONS, COMMITTEE ON PUBLIC ACCOUNTS. *Minutes of Proceedings and Evidence.* Session 1950. Ottawa, King's Printer, 1950. (See especially evidence of R. B. Bryce and Watson Sellar.)

Books and Periodical Articles
BALLS, H. R. "Budgetary and Fiscal Accounting in the Government of Canada." *Canadian Tax Journal* 4: 14, 132 (1956).
BRYCE, R. B. "Expenditure Control in Canadian Federal Financing." *Tax Bulletin* 2: 279-86 (Sept.-Oct., 1952).
BUCK, A. E. *The Budget in Governments of Today.* New York, Macmillan, 1936.
——— *Financing Canadian Government.* Chicago, Public Administration Service, 1949. (Bibliography, pp. 349-57.)
CLARK, W. C. "Financial Administration of the Government of Canada." *Canadian Journal of Economics and Political Science* 4: 391-419 (Aug., 1938).
DAWSON, R. M. *The Government of Canada.* Toronto, University of Toronto Press, 1947.
DURELL, A. J. W. *The Principles and Practices of the System of Control over Parliamentary Grants.* Portsmouth, Gieves, 1917.
Budgeting in Public Authorities: Royal Institute of Public Administration, Study Group Report (R. S. EDWARDS, Chairman). London, Allen & Unwin, 1959.
FRASER, T. M. "The Budget System in Canada." *Political Science Quarterly* 35: 621-36 (Dec., 1920).
SELLAR, W. "Auditing for Parliament." *Canadian Chartered Accountant* 60: 176-80 (May, 1952).
THORSON, D. S. "Some Problems of Tax Drafting." *Canadian Tax Journal* 7: 462 (1959).
VILLARD, H. G. and WILLOUGHBY, W. W. *The Canadian Budgetary System.* New York and London, Appleton, 1918.

WILLOUGHBY, W. F. *The National Budget System.* Baltimore, Johns Hopkins Press, 1927.

CHAPTER 17

ENACTMENT OF THE PROVINCIAL AND MUNICIPAL TAX LAWS

PROVINCIAL

BUCK, A. E. *Financing Canadian Government.* Chicago, Public Administration Service, 1949. See chap. 11, "Canadian Provincial Finance."
DAWSON, R. M. *Democratic Government in Canada.* Toronto, University of Toronto Press, 1949. See chap. 8, "Provincial Government."
MACQUARRIE, J. H. "Provincial Government in Canada." *Municipal Finance* 17: 10-13 (Aug., 1944).

MUNICIPAL

Government Documents

CANADA, DOMINION BUREAU OF STATISTICS. *Manual of Instructions.* Part 1. *Financial Statements of Municipal Corporations;* Part 2. *Municipal Accounting Terminology;* Part 3. *Assessments, Area, Population and Road and Street Statistics;* Part 4. *Financial Statements of Municipal Superannuation or Pension Funds.* 3rd ed. Ottawa, Queen's Printer, 1960.
See also General Sources, sec. F (4), item 1; (6); (9).

Books and Pamphlets

BRITTAIN, H. L. *Local Government in Canada.* Toronto, Ryerson, 1951.
BUCK, A. E. *Financing Canadian Government.* Chicago, Public Administration Service, 1949. See chap. 12, "Canadian Municipal Finance."
CHESTER, D. N. *Central and Local Government, Financial and Administrative Relations.* London, Macmillan, 1951.
CLOKIE, H. *Canadian Government and Politics.* 2nd ed., Toronto, Longmans Green, 1945. See chap. 8, "Local Government in Canada."
CORBETT, D. C. *Urban Growth and Municipal Finance.* An analysis and study prepared for the Canadian Federation of Mayors and Municipalities. Montreal, the Federation, 1952.
DAWSON, R. M. *Democratic Government in Canada.* Toronto, University of Toronto Press, 1949. See chap. 14, "Municipal Government."
MACPHERSON, L. G. "The Municipal Budget as an Instrument of Administration." *Proceedings of the 2nd Annual Conference of the Institute of Public Administration of Canada, 1950.*
QUEEN'S UNIVERSITY, INSTITUTE OF LOCAL GOVERNMENT. *The Municipal Council and Councillor in Ontario.* Publication no. 1. Kingston, Ont., 1945.
Ross, R. K. *Local Government in Ontario.* Toronto, Canadian Law List Publishing Co., 1949.
UNIVERSITY OF WESTERN ONTARIO, EXTENSION DEPARTMENT. *Papers and Addresses, School for Municipal Officers, October 14-22, 1937.* See A. J. B. Gray, "Levying and Collection of Taxes"; J. H. Lowther, "Municipal Budgeting." London, Ont.

Periodical Articles

BELANGER, CYRILLE. "The City Treasurers as Finance Officers in the Province of Quebec." *Municipal Finance* 18: 20-2 (Nov., 1945).

BRITTAIN, H. L. "The Municipal Budget as an Administrative Instrument." *Municipal Review of Canada*, 33: 9-11 (July-Aug., 1937).

CRAWFORD, K. G. "The Independence of Municipal Councils in Ontario." *Canadian Journal of Economics and Political Science* 6: 543-54 (Nov., 1940).

DANBY, E. A. "The City Treasurer as Finance Officer in Brantford, Ontario." *Municipal Finance* 18: 17-19 (Nov., 1945).

CHAPTER 18

DOMINION TAX ADMINISTRATION: DIRECT TAXES

Government Documents

CANADA, SENATE, SPECIAL COMMITTEE ON THE INCOME WAR TAX ACT AND THE EXCESS PROFITS TAX ACT, 1940. *Proceedings and Reports.* Sessions 1945 and 1946. Ottawa, King's Printer, 1945-6. (See especially testimony of C. Fraser Elliott.)

Books and Pamphlets

BUCK, A. E. *Financing Canadian Government.* Chicago, Public Administration Service, 1949. Pp. 45-8.

CANADIAN INSTITUTE OF CHARTERED ACCOUNTANTS. *Brief to Senate Committee* (on the Income Tax Act and the Excess Profits Tax Act, 1940). Submitted April, 1946. Toronto, the Institute.

CANADIAN TAX FOUNDATION. *Advance Rulings.* 13th Tax Conference 1959.
——— *The Government's Problems in Tax Administration.* 10th Tax Conference 1956.
——— *Is Judgment Lacking at the Local Level?* 12th Tax Conference 1958.
——— *Methods of Enforcing the Personal Income Tax.* 12th Tax Conference 1958.
——— *Tax Traps and Penalties.* 13th Tax Conference 1959.

LAW SOCIETY OF UPPER CANADA. *Special Lectures, 1950: Company Law.* Toronto, Richard De Boo, 1950. See H. H. Stikeman, "The Sources of the Law and the Philosophy of Administration," pp. 113-38.

MCGREGOR, G. *Tax Appeals.* Canadian Tax Papers, no. 22. Toronto, Canadian Tax Foundation, 1960.

ROWLAND, A. H. "Canadian Experience in Decentralization." *Income Tax Administration: Symposium Conducted by the Tax Institute, 1948*, pp. 102-12. New York, 1948.

Periodical Articles

BARBEAU, J. "Advance Tax Rulings." *Canadian Bar Journal*, February, 1960.

FERGUSON, T. M. "New Role for Computers: Assessing Your Income Tax Return." *Canadian Business*, January, 1960.

GAVSIE, CHARLES. "Tax Administrative Organization at the Federal Level." *Tax Bulletin* 2: 271-8 (Sept.-Oct., 1952).

BIBLIOGRAPHY 405

HARRISON, W. H. "Work of the Board of Referees under the Excess Profits Tax Act, 1940." *Canadian Bar Review* 20: 242-52 (March, 1942).
HERBERT, H. F. "How the Federal Tax Department Operates." *Canadian Chartered Accountant*, April, 1957.
MACGIBBON, D. A. "The Administration of the Income War Tax Act." *Canadian Journal of Economics and Political Science* 12: 75-8 (Feb., 1946).
MCENTYRE, J. G. "What to do When the Tax Assessor Comes." *Industrial Canada*, April, 1958.
MCTAGUE, C. P. "The War Contracts Depreciation Board." *Canadian Bar Review* 20: 575-83 (Aug.-Sept., 1942).
MONET, FABIO. "The Income Tax Appeal Board." *Canadian Chartered Accountant* 57: 23-8 (July, 1950).
SCULLY, V. W. T. "The Accountant and the Tax Collector." *Canadian Chartered Accountant* 58: 27-35 (Jan., 1951).
STIKEMAN, H. H. "Descriptive Outline of Income Tax Law and Administration in the Dominion of Canada." *Bulletin for International Fiscal Documentation* 4: 170-5; 5: 199-210; 6: 247-58 (1946-7).
———— "The Income Tax Appeal Board and Its Place in the Profession of Accountancy." *Canadian Chartered Accountant* 50: 246-57 (May, 1947).
———— "Taxation Law: 1923-1947." *Canadian Bar Review* 26: 308-33 (Jan., 1948).
THOM, S. D. "Appeal Procedure under the Income Tax Act." *Canadian Chartered Accountant Tax Review* [1951]: 15-20 (Feb.).
THORSTEINSSON, P. N. "The Department of National Revenue." *Canadian Tax Journal* 5: 367 (1957).
TOLMIE, J. R. "Excess Profits Taxation: The Canadian Act and Its Administration." *Canadian Journal of Economics and Political Science* 7: 350-63 (Aug., 1941).

CHAPTER 19

DOMINION TAX ADMINISTRATION: INDIRECT TAXES

Government Documents

CANADA, ROYAL COMMISSION ON CUSTOMS AND EXCISE. *Interim Reports* (nos. 1-10). *Final Report*. Ottawa, King's Printer, 1928.
CANADA, ROYAL COMMISSION ON THE TEXTILE INDUSTRY. *Report* (W. F. A. TURGEON, Commissioner). Ottawa, King's Printer, 1938. Pp. 64-84.
CLARKSON, GORDON and DILWORTH. *Report Respecting Re-organization of the Department of National Revenue*. Ottawa, King's Printer, 1928.

Books and Periodical Articles

AUDETTE, L. C. "How the Tariff Board Works." *Industrial Canada*, April, 1960.
BLAKE, G. *Customs Administration in Canada*. Toronto, University of Toronto Press, 1957.
———— "The Customs Administration in Canadian Historical Development." *Canadian Journal of Economics and Political Science*, November, 1956.

BUCK, A. E. *Financing Canadian Government.* Chicago, Public Administration Service, 1948. Pp. 45-8.

ELLIOTT, G. A. *Tariff Procedures and Trade Barriers.* Toronto, University of Toronto Press, 1955.

FLAHERTY, F. "How Canada's Tariff Board Operates." *Canadian Business,* May, 1958.

GOODMAN, WOLFE D. "Problems of Litigation Under the Excise Tax Act." *Canadian Bar Review,* February, 1954.

MACPHERSON, R. B. *Tariffs, Markets and Economic Progress.* Toronto, Copp Clark, 1958.

MAYNARD, L. E. "The Canadian Customs Labyrinth" (series of five articles). *Monetary Times* (April to Aug., 1950).

SMITH, R. E. *Customs Valuation in the United States.* Chicago, University of Chicago Press, 1948. See chap. 10, "Methods of Valuation in Foreign Countries: Canada," pp. 305-11.

INDEX

ACCELERATED DEPRECIATION; *see* Capital cost allowances
Admission and Amusement taxes (municipal), 207, 271; (provincial), 23, 206-9; *see also* Pari-mutuel bets taxes
Alcohol, industrial, excise duties, 334
Alcoholic beverages
  Customs duty, 125
  Excise duties, 13, 141, 142-4; administration, 331-4; international comparison, 142-4; rates, 144; revenue, 144
  Excise taxes on wines, 139-40
  Manufacturers' sales tax, 129
  Provincial licences, 213-15; monopoly, 22, 211-13; retail sales taxes, 205, 206; revenue, 216
Amusement taxes; *see* Admission and amusement taxes
Annuities, contributions of employers and employees, 49; and estate tax, 107, 112; succession duties (provincial), 194; taxation, 55-9; *see also* Pensions
Appraisers, customs administration, 327-9
Appropriation bills, 288, 297
Artists, income tax, 59-60
Assessment, real property (municipalities), 260-4, 311; roll, 311; uniform, 264
Auditor-General, 300
Authors, income tax, 59-60
Automobiles, taxes, 19, 140; *see also* Gasoline taxes; Motor vehicles, Licences and fees

BAYLY, R. A., 184 n.
Beer, excise duties, 141, 144, 331-4; provincial licences and taxes, 151,
205, 213-15; *see also* Alcoholic beverages
Betting taxes, 208-9; *see also* Admission and amusement taxes; Pari-mutuel taxes
Board of Customs; *see* Tariff Board
Board of Referees, 329
British North America Act, 146, 148; allocation of tax powers, 283; Crown property, tax exemption, 265-6; natural resources, provincial rights, 230-1; proposed amendment, 157-61; provincial licensing powers, 5, 156-63; *see also* Privy Council, Judicial Committee
British preference, 9, 14-15, 117-19, 121
Britnell, G. E., 273 n.
Buck, A. E., 305 n.
Budget (Dominion), authorization, 279-81; Cabinet approval, 293; Estimates, 283-4; parliamentary procedure, 284-8; resolutions and bills, 296-8; Speech, 290-300; tax changes, 294-5; U.S. procedure, 298-9
Budgetary system, 278-81, 290-300
Budgets (municipal), 301, 305-6, 309, 311; *see also* municipalities
Budgets (provincial), 285, 301-5; speech, 304; special warrants, 304-5
Buisson, Arthur, 236 n.
Burns, R. M., 201 n.
Business profits war tax, 18-19, 20
Business tax (municipal), 16, 255, 266-7; (provincial), 175

CABINET, Dominion, approval of budget, 293; review of Estimates, 283

407

INDEX

Cameron, M. A., 258 n., 265 n.
Campbell, D. L., 273 n.
Canada-U.K. tax agreements; *see* Tax treaties
Canada-U.S. tax conventions; *see* Tax treaties
Capital, taxes on paid-up, 16, 23, 174-5
Capital cost allowances, 9, 33, 68-72; accelerated depreciation, 70-1; initial allowance, 70-1; rates, 341-6; recapture, 70
Capital gains, 39, 43, 45, 69
"Carrying-on business," 88-9
Charitable donations, corporate, 75, 77
Chater, H. J., 273 n.
Cigarettes and cigars; *see* Tobacco products
City managers, 308
Clark, W. C., 267 n., 279 n.
Commissioners on Uniformity of Legislation in Canada, Conference (1922), 189
Committee of Supply, House of Commons, 285-7; provincial legislatures, 303
Committee of Ways and Means, House of Commons, 285-7, 295-6; Provincial, 304
Committee on Banking and Commerce, 285
Commodity taxes; *see* Alcoholic beverages, Excise duties, Excise taxes, Gasoline taxes, Manufacturers' sales tax, Retail sales taxes, Tobacco products
Comptroller of the Treasury, 300
Constitution; *see* British North America Act; Privy Council, Judicial Committee
Consumption taxes; *see* Alcoholic beverages, Excise duties, Excise taxes, Gasoline taxes, Manufacturers' sales tax, Retail sales taxes, Tobacco products
Co-operatives, and income tax (Dominion), 77, 78-80
Corporation fees, 181

Corporation income tax (Dominion), administration, 316; appeals, 322; assessment of returns, 317-21; associated companies, 76; bad debts, 73; capital cost allowances, 68-72; charitable donations, 75; compliance and collection, 316-17, 319-20; co-operatives, 77, 78-80; deductions allowed, 68-75; diallowed, 65-8; depletion allowances, 71-2; designated surplus, 75, 87; double taxation of dividends, 81-2, 84; exempt corporations, 77; history, 19, 25-6, 35; inter-company dividends, 84; inventory valuation, 73; investment companies, 78; liability, 62; losses, carry-forward, 75; "non-arm's length" concept, 73-4, 76; payment, 77; personal corporations, 78; rates, 75; revenue, 87; tax credit, companies carrying on business in Ontario and Quebec, 76; taxable income, 74; undistributed profits, 81-2, *see also* Capital cost allowances; Dividends; Double taxation; Undistributed income
Corporation income tax acts (provinces parties to Tax Rental Agreements), repealed, 166; reinstatement for 1962-6, 166-7
Corporation income taxes (provincial), 166-72; abatement, 167; allocation, 169; federal collection, 167; history, 166-7; liability, 167; permanent establishment, 167-8; rates, 166; regulations, 167; revenue, 166 *see also* Corporation Tax Act (Ontario), Corporation Tax Act (Quebec), Corporation taxes
Corporation Tax Act (Ontario), 166-80
Corporation Tax Act (Quebec), 166-72; allocation of income among tax jurisdictions, 167-72; exempt permanent establishment, 169-71; rates, 172; revenue, 172; taxable

INDEX 409

income, 167-9; *see also* Corporation taxes
Corporation taxes, definition Tax Rental Agreements, 172-5; history, 5, 10, 16, 29, 31, 35-6, 173; Ontario, 172-3, 175, 177-9; Quebec, 172, 175, 177-9; rates, 177-9; revenue, 180; suspension under Tax Rental Agreements, 172-3; *see also* Business tax (municipal); Corporation income tax (Dominion); Corporation income tax acts
Credit unions, 77
Crown corporations (Dominion), 77
Crown lands, exemptions of government property from tax, 265-6; *see also* Natural Resources
Cumming, L. R., 273 n.
Customs Act, 323, 328
Customs duties, 116-21; administration, 323-30; British preference, 117, 119, 121; drawbacks, 330; GATT, 117; general tariff, 117, 119; history, 7-9, 12, 13, 14-15, 18; most favoured nation, 117, 118; payment, 327-30; rates, 120, 121; revenue, 119, 121, 122-3; valuation for duty, 327-9
Customs Tariff Act, 323

DEATH DUTIES; *see* Estate taxes; Succession duties (provincial)
Deductions; *see* each tax
Depletion allowances, extractive industries, 49, 71-2; forestry, 49
Depreciation; *see* Capital cost allowances
Detwiller, L. F., 201 n.
Direct taxation; *see* Taxation
Dividends, deemed paid, 85-6; depletion allowances, 49; double taxation, 81-2, 84; from foreign subsidiaries, 99-100; inter-company, 84; non-residents, 95-6; patronage, 79-80; tax credit, 84, 165; tax-paid, 85-6; withholding tax, 88, 95-6, 101; *see also* Investment income; Undistributed income
Domicile, test for liability to succession duties, 106-12; *see also* Situs vs. domicile
Dominion payments to provinces, 27-30, 34-5, 164-5, 166, 183
Dominion-provincial conferences, 161
Tax Rental Agreements, *see* Tax Rental Agreements, Wartime Tax Agreements
Double taxation, corporation dividends, 81-2, 84; estates and successions, 188-91; foreign income, 96-100; *see also* Tax treaties
Due, J. F., 201 n.
Durham, Lord, 284 n.
Duties; *see* Customs duties, Excise duties

EATON, A. K., 66
Education taxes, municipal, 264, 268-9; provincial, 176, 200, 221
Entertainment taxes; *see* Admission and amusement taxes
Estate Tax Act (Dominion), 105, 193, 313
Estate tax agreements with U.K. and U.S.; *see* Tax treaties
Estate taxes, 35-6; administration, 320-1; aggregate net value, 106-8; aggregate taxable value, 109; credits, 111-12; definition, 102-5; domicile, 106-112; exemptions, 109; history, 102; liability, 105; non-domiciled persons, 112-13; property subject, 106-8; rates, 109-111, 352-3; revenue, 115; situs, 113; treaties, 112-13; valuation, 105-9; *see also* Gift tax; Succession duties (provincial)
Estates and trusts, taxation, 60, 95
Estimates (Dominion), 281-9; appropriation bills, 288-97; Cabinet review, 283; Main, 283-8; preparation, 281-2; procedure in Commons, 283-8; supplementary, 283, 288-9; Treasury Board approval, 282-3

(provincial), legislative procedure, 303–4; preparation, 301–4; Special warrants, 304–5
Excess profits tax, 31 f., 62
Excise Act, 323, 332, 334
  Excise duties, administration, 331–4; distinguished from excise taxes, 124–5; exemptions, 333–4; history, 13, 15, 141; licences, 331–4; provincial duties, 141; rates, 141–4; revenue, 144; *see also* Alcohol, industrial, Alcoholic beverages, Manufacturers' sales tax; Tobacco products
Excise Tax Act, 323, 335–9
  Excise taxes, administration, 335–9; distinguished from estate duties, 124–5; history, 13, 15, 137; licences, 137, 335–9; rates, 138–40; revenue, 140; valuation for tax base, 137; *see also* Alcoholic beverages, Manufacturers' sales tax; Tobacco products
Export taxes, electricity, 145

FAMILY ALLOWANCES, 10, 54, 59
Farmers, averaging of income, 50, 60
Federalism, financial problems, 3–7, 13 f.
Fees; *see* Licences and fees
Fenety, G., 283 n.
Finance, Dept., 281, 312–13; preparation of Budget Speech, 291–300; Taxation Division, 292, and Treasury Board, 281, 282–3
Finance, Deputy Minister, 291; Secretary of Treasury Board, 282; *see also* Finance, Dept.
Finance, Minister of, Budget Speech, 290–300; chairman of Treasury Board, 282–3
Fishermen, averaging of income, 50, 60
Foreign business corporations, 100–1
Foreign taxes, allowances, 96–100
Forestry operations, taxes; *see* Logging taxes
Foster, G. E., 8–9
Franchise taxes; *see* Corporation taxes

Fuel taxes, exemptions, 198; heating, 199; motive, 197–9; special fuels, 198
Furs, export taxes, 18

GARBAGE COLLECTION TAX, 271
Gasoline taxes (Dominion), 22, 23 (provincial), 153–4, 197–9; history, 5, 10, 20, 23; rates, 197, 199; revenue, 199
GATT, 117
Gavsie, Charles, 318 n.
General agreement on tariffs and trade, 117
General sales tax; *see* Manufacturers' sales tax
George, Henry, 17, 221–2; *see also* Single tax
Gift tax, 102, 113–15, 313, 320–1
Goldenberg, H. C., 273 n.
Governor-General's warrants, 289
Grants to municipalities, by the Dominion, 256, 266; by provinces, 255, 266
Grants to provinces, by Dominion, 4 f., 27 f.
Groves, H. M., 259

HAIG, R. M., 38
Health, Insurance, 224–5
Horse tax, 220
Hospital insurance, charges, 224–5
Hospital taxes, 200, 205–6
House of Commons, Committee of Supply, 285–7; Committee of Ways and Means, 285–7, 295–6; procedure on Budget, 284–8, on Estimates, 283–4

ILSLEY, J. L., 27 f., 282–3, 287
Imports; *see* Customs duties, Manufacturers' sales tax
Improvements, taxation, 256–60; *see also* Single tax
Income, concept of, 37–46
Income tax (Dominion); *see* Corporation income tax (Dominion), Personal income tax (Dominion)

INDEX 411

Income tax (provinces); *see* Corporation Tax Act (Quebec); Personal income taxes (provincial)
Income tax (Municipalities), 13, 14, 253-5
Income Tax Act, 313
Income tax agreements; *see* Tax treaties
Income Tax Appeal Board; *see* Tax Appeal Board
Income War Tax Acts, 10, 45, 313
Indirect sales tax, 157-61
Indirect taxation; *see* Taxation
Inheritance taxes; *see* Estate tax (Dominion); Succession duties (provincial)
Insurance, health, 224-5
Insurance, life, proceeds taxed, 59
Insurance companies, life, taxable income, 75; mutual, 72, 80, 83
Insurance premiums, tax, 145; provincial, 177, 180; Dominion, 145
Interim supply, bills, 288
Ives Commission, 55

JACOBY COMMISSION, 24
Judicial Committee Privy Council; *see* Privy Council, Judicial Committee

KENNEDY, W. P. M., 150 n.

LABRIE, F. E., 46 n.
Land taxes; *see* Real property taxes; Single tax
Land transfer fees, 222-3
League of Nations Fiscal Committee, model treaty, 89, 97
Licences and fees, admission and amusements, 23, 207, 208, 271-2; alcoholic beverages and beer, 211, 213-15, 331-4; distinguished from corporation fees, 174; excise duties, 331-4; excise taxes, 137, 335-9; hunting and fishing, 249; incorporation fees, 181; land transfer, 222; logging, 247-8; manufacturers and wholesalers, 125, 130-1, 331-4, 337-9; manufacturers' sales tax, 125, 130-1, 331, 337-9; mining, 244-5; motor vehicle, 22, 216-19; municipal, 207, 271-2, 276; petroleum and natural gas, 244-5; prospectors', 244; provincial powers, 151, 156-7, 173-5, 181; retail sales tax, 203; tobacco products, 331-4
Liquor; *see* Alcoholic beverages
Lobley, O., 262 n.
Logging taxes, 227-36, 245-8; credit for other taxes, 73, 235-6; licences, 247-8; profits, 233-6; rates, 249; revenue, 249; royalties, 227-33, 245-8; stumpage, 248
Love, R. J., 273 n.

MACDONALD, V. C., 157 n.
McGregor, G., 78 n.
McLeod, T. H., 302 n.
Macpherson, L. G., 305 n.
Magill, R. F., 43 n.
Manning, H. E., 262 n.
Manufacturers' sales tax, 36, 124, 125-35, 337-9; administration, 128-31, 328; comparison, 135; exemption, 131, 132-5, 338; export refunds, 135; history, 11, 20; imports, 125, 132, 135; liability, 125 f.; licensing of manufacturers and wholesalers, 125, 130-1, 331-4, 337-9; payment, 132; rates, 135; revenue, 136; rules, 128-9; sale price definition, 126-7; valuation for tax base, 126-9; wholesale price definition, 127-8
Meals taxes, 205-6, 207
Mill, J. S., 148, 149
Mining profits, definition in Tax Rental Agreements, 234-5
Mining Tax Act (Ontario), 233-4, 238-40; (Quebec), 237-8
Mining taxes, 16 f., 227-49; credit for municipal and provincial taxes, 73, 235-6; depletion allowances, 49, 71-2; exemption, new mines, 77; exploration expenses deductible, 72; income tax, provincial,

233–5; leases, 244; licences and fees, 244–5; pre-production expenses, 72–3; rates, 249; revenue, 249; royalties, 232–44; *see also* Mining Tax Act (Ontario), Mining Tax Act (Quebec)
Mining taxes, provincial, 236–44
Montreal, miscellaneous taxes, 25; retail sales tax, 255, 269–70, 271
Moore, A. M., 245 n.
Most-favoured nation, 117, 118
Motion picture films, tax on payment to non-residents for, 96
Motor vehicles, licences and fees, 22, 216–19; passenger vehicles, 217–18; rates, 218; revenue, 219
Municipal Affairs departments, Provincial, 305–6, 309
Municipal Finance Officers' Association, 305 n.
Municipal taxation, administration, 305–11; admission and amusement, 207, 271; assessment of property, 256–8; business taxes, 255, 266–7; history, 13 f., 251 f.; income taxes, 13, 14, 253–5; licensing powers, 156–7; poll taxes, 220, 253, 270–1; property tax, 256–68; rates, 356–65; retail sales tax, 206, 255, 269–70, 276; revenue, 256, 271, 276; school levies, 268–9; tax rate determination, 311; tax-exempt property, 265–6; *see also* Budgets, municipal; Municipalities
Municipalities, 251–3; autonomous boards, 309; budgets, 301, 305–11; Dominion grants, 256; financial organization, 308–9; government, 306–8; provincial grants, 255, 263; provincial supervision, 263-4, 305-6, 309; revenue, 272

NATIONAL REVENUE, Dept., 312–13; Budget preparation, 291
Customs and Excise Division, 323–39; customs administration, 323–30; excise duties administration, 331–4; excise taxes administration, 335–9; manufacturers' sales tax administration, 124–36
Taxation Division, 312–22; district offices, 317–21; head office, 321–2; Special Investigations Branch, 318, 321; *see also* each tax, administration
Natural gas, *see* Petroleum and natural gas
Natural resources, (provincial) definition in Tax Rental Agreements, 227–33; forest charges, 245–8; leases, 244; licences and fees, 244, 248, 249; profits taxes, 233-6; provincial rights, 230–1; rentals and royalties, 227–33; revenue, 249; *see also* Depletion; Logging taxes; Mining; Petroleum and natural gas.
Newfoundland, municipal taxation, 272–5
Non-profit organizations, tax exempt, 75, 77
Non-resident owned companies, 88 f., allocation of income, 92; branches, 96; "carrying on business," 88; liability, 88–9; permanent establishment, 90–2; shipping and transportation, companies, exemption, 93; taxable income, 88–93
Non-resident-owned investment corporations, 100–1
Non-residents, exemption, 94–5; liability, 88, 93–6; withholding tax, 23, 88, 96, 313

OCCUPANCY TAXES, 267
Oil and gas industries; *see* Petroleum and natural gas
Old Age Security Tax Act, 34
Old Age Security taxes, 133, 135

PAID-UP CAPITAL TAXES, 16, 23, 174–5
Pari-mutuel bets taxes, 208–9
Parliament, procedure on Budget, 284–8; on Estimates, 283–4
Partnerships, 60–1
Pay-as-you-go tax collection, 319

INDEX 413

Pension funds, 55-9; contributions of employees and employers to funds, 49; estate taxes, 107, 112; succession duties, 194; veterans, 49, 194-5; *see also* Annuities; Registered retirement savings plan deduction

Personal corporations, 78

Personal income tax (Dominion), 19, 37, 46-61; administration, 312-22; annuities, 55-9; appeals, 54, 322; assessment, 54, 317-21; averaging of income, 54; compliance and collection, 316-17, 319-20; deductions from income, 49; dividends, depletion allowance, 49; tax credit, 55, 84; estates and trusts, taxed as individuals, 60; exempt income, 49-52; history, 19 f.; investment income, 53; liability, 46; part-time residents, 60; payment, 54; rates, 52-3; revenue, 61; taxable income, 47-52; *see also* Double taxation

Personal income taxes (municipal), 13, 14, 253-5

Personal income tax (provincial), 164-5; abatement, 54-5, 165; Dominion collection, 54-5; history, 5, 15, 164-5; Quebec, 165

Personal property taxes, 10, 11, 13, 15, 220, 253, 259, 276

Petrie, J. R., 273 n.

Petroleum and natural gas, 71-3, 227-49; depletion allowances, 49, 71-2; exploration expenses, 72-3; licences and fees, 244-5; provincial taxation, 242; rents and royalties, 241-3; tax credits, 73

Place of business taxes, 175, 177-80

Poll taxes, 220, 253, 270-1

Power utilities, Quebec, 176, 180; rents and royalties, 231, 248

Private corporations, 80-2

Privy Council, Judicial Committee, corporation income allocation, 170-2; provincial succession duties, 185 f.; table of tax decisions by, 161-3; tax powers of Dominion and provinces, 148-54;

Profit-sharing plans, 57

Profits, taxable, corporations, 63, 169-73; logging, 233-6; mining, 233-5, 249; non-resident-owned corporations, 88 f.

Profits, undistributed; *see* Undistributed income

Proof spirit, definition, 142-4

Property taxes; *see* Personal property taxes, Real property taxes

Provinces, aid to municipalities, 255, 256; Dominion payments to, 4 f., 27 f.

Provincial taxation, constitutional limitation, 4, 5, 146-63, 227-8; corporation income taxes, 166-72; history, 146 ff. international comparison, 154-5; licences and fees, 156-7, 203; limitations, 149-54, 172-5, 181; mining, 236-44; personal income tax, 164-5; petroleum and natural gas, 242-3; rates, 345-55; sales taxes, 200-4; *see also* Alcoholic beverages; Budgets, provincial; Corporation income tax (provincial); Corporation taxes (provincial); Natural resources; Personal income tax (provincial); Real property

Public accounts (Dominion), 300; (provincial), 305

Public domain; *see* Natural resources

Public utilities, 255, 276

QUEBEC CITY, income tax, ; miscellaneous, 271; retail sales tax, 255, 269-70

RATES OF TAX; *see* each tax

Real estate; *see* Real property

Real property, assessment, 256-68; definition, 258-9, 261 f.; improvements, 221, 257-8; tax-exempt, 221, 265-6

Real property taxes (municipal), 13, 220, 253, 256; administration, 267-8; assessment, 260-4, 311; exemption of improvements, 257-8; revenue, 276; tax exempt property, 265-6;

(provincial), 10, 219–23, 248, 255, 263; *see also* Single tax

Registered retirement savings plan deduction, 49

Rentals and royalties, definition of, in Tax Rental Agreements, 227–33; logging, 233–6, 245–8; mining, 232–44; petroleum and natural gas, 241–3; power utilities, 231, 248; withholding tax on payments to non-residents, 95–6

Residence, as test for liability to income tax (individuals), 46, 88 f., 93–4; (corporations), 62, 88–93

Resources; *see* Natural resources

Retail sales taxes (Dominion), 20 (municipal), 206, 255, 269–70, 276 (provincial), 5, 10, 200–6; administration, 200, 203; alcoholic beverages, 213; constitutional limitations, 5, 157–61, 200–1; exemptions, 203; licensing, 203; rates, 204; revenue, 204; scope, 201–3; *see also* Admission and amusements taxes, Gasoline taxes (provincial), Meals taxes, Tobacco products

Rowat, D. C., 272 n.

Rowell-Sirois Commission, 6, 27–30

Royal Commission on Co-operatives, 78 f.

Royal Commission on Dominion-Provincial Relations, 6, 27–30, 147 n., 160

Royal Commission on the Income Tax (U.K.), 42

Royal Commission on the Taxation of Annuities and Family Corporations, 55

Royalties; *see* Rentals and royalties

St. John's, Nfld., 260, 270

Sale Price, definition for manufacturers' sales tax, 126–9

Sales tax, *see* Excise taxes, Manufacturers' sales tax, Retail sales taxes

School taxes, *see* Education Taxes

Security, transfer taxes, 223–4

Seltzer, L. H., 45 n.

Severance taxes, *see* Rentals and royalties, Logging taxes, Mining taxes

Shink, G. H., 201 n.

Simons, H. C., 38 n.

Single tax, 17, 221–2, 255, 257

Situs vs. domicile (Dominion), 113; (provincial), succession duties, 185, 188–9

Social services taxes, 200, 221

Sole proprietors, taxable income, 60

Special warrants in provinces, 304–5

Stamp taxes, 150–1

Students' fees, 50

Stumpage, 245–8, *see also* Logging taxes

Succession duties, 5, 16, 102–5; *see also* Estate Tax Act (Dominion), Estate taxes (Dominion)

Succession duties (provincial), 183 f.; constitutional limitations, 156, 185; Dominion credit, 111; double taxation agreements, 188–91; Federal abatement, 183; history, 10, 16, 24, 183; inter-provincial agreements, 189–90; property subject, 185–8; rates, 346–53; situs vs. domicile, 185, 188–9; *see also* Succession Duty Act (Ontario), Succession Duty Act (Quebec)

Succession Duty Act (Ontario), 183–4, 194–5; exemptions, 191–3; rates, 193–4, 348–52; revenue, 196; *see also* Succession duties (provincial)

Succession Duty Act (Quebec), 184, 185, 195; exemptions, 191–2; rates, 193–4, 346–8, 353; revenue, 196; *see also* Succession duties (provincial)

Succession duty agreements; *see* Tax treaties

Superannuation and retirement benefits; *see* Pensions

Supplementary estimates, 288–9

Supply bills, 288

Tariff; *see* Customs duties

Tariff Board, 329, 336

Tax administration; *see* each tax

Tax agreements, *see* Tax Treaties

INDEX

Tax Appeal Board, 322
Tax conventions; *see* Tax Treaties
Tax credits, dividends, 84, 165; foreign income taxes, 55, 96–100; municipal taxes, 238, 239; provincial income taxes, 172; successions, 183
Tax-exempt property in municipalities, 265–6; Dominion grants, 266
Tax exemptions; *see* each tax
Tax rates; *see* each tax
Tax Rental Agreements, 6, 27–30, 34, 36, 164, 166, 255; corporation taxes, definition, 173–5; Dominion payments to provinces, 4f., 27f.; mining profits, definition, 233–5; natural resources of the province, definition, 227–33; rentals and royalties, definition, 227–33; succession duties, 183, 196; *see also* Wartime Tax Agreements
Tax revenue; *see* each tax
Tax Roll, 316–17
Tax treaties, estates, 112–13; income tax, 89–90, 94–5, 98–9; succession duties, 189–91; *see also* Tax Rental agreements
Taxation, direct and indirect, definition, 147–8; history, 13f.; international comparisons, 154–5; limitation of Dominion power, 148–9; limitation of provincial powers, 149–54, 172–5, 181; powers under B.N.A. Act, 146–63; U.S. government, 154–5; *see also* Budgets, and each tax
Telephone tax (Nova Scotia), 226
Three Rivers, water tax, 271
Timber limits, charges, 245–8; *see also* Logging taxes
Tobacco products
 Excise duty, 13, 141–2; administration, 331–4; international comparison, 142–4; manufacturers' sales tax, 129; rates, 141–2, 144; revenue, 144
 Excise taxes, 139; rates, 140; revenue, 144
 Retail sales tax (provincial), 205; rates, 206; revenue, 206

Treasury Board, 282–3; review of Estimates, 281
Treasury boards, provinces, 301–3
Trusts and estates; *see* Estates and trusts

ULTIMATE PURCHASERS TAX (Alberta), 24, 200
Undistributed income, 81–7; capitalization, 83; distribution on winding-up, 82, 84–5; dividends exempt, 85; excessive accumulation, 82; private corporations, 82; redemption, 83–4
Uniform assessment, 264
Uniformity of Legislation in Canada, Conference of Commissioners on, 189
United Kingdom-Canada tax agreements; *see* Tax Treaties
United States, budget and fiscal procedures, 298–9; taxing powers, constitutional limitations, 154–5
United States-Canada tax conventions; *see* Tax treaties
Unorganized provincial territory, 251; taxation, 220

VALUATION, customs duty, 327–9; estate taxes, 320–1; excise duties, 333–4; excise taxes, 336; manufacturers' sales tax, 126–9
Verdun, Que., water tax, 271

WAR FINANCE, Dominion, 18–19, 20, 25, 27–8, 30–1
War veterans' pensions, 49, 194–5
Wartime Tax Agreements, 27–8, 164, 166, 173, 255; *see also* Tax Rental Agreements
Water tax, 271
Wells, D. C., 150n.
Wholesale price, definition for manufacturers' sales tax, 127–8
Willis, J., 60n.
Wines, *see* Alcoholic beverages
Winnipeg, 16, 25, 255, 270
Withholding tax, non-residents, 23, 88, 95–6, 313; rates, 101; revenue, 101

www.ingramcontent.com/pod-product-compliance
Lightning Source LLC
Chambersburg PA
CBHW020238030426
42336CB00010B/530